ALSO BY PATRICK K. O'DONNELL

Into the Rising Sun

Beyond Valor

OPERATIVES, SPIES, and SABOTEURS

The Unknown Story of the Men and Women of World War II's OSS

Patrick K. O'Donnell

FREE PRESS

NEW YORK LONDON TORONTO SYDNEY

_f_**P**

FREE PRESS

A Division of Simon & Schuster, Inc.
1230 Avenue of the Americas
New York, NY 10020

Copyright © 2004 by Patrick K. O'Donnell

FREE PRESS and colophon are
trademarks of Simon & Schuster, Inc.

For information about special discounts for bulk purchases,
please contact Simon & Schuster Special Sales:
1-800-456-6798 or business@simonandschuster.com

Designed by Joseph Rutt

Manufactured in the United States of America

1   3   5   7   9   10   8   6   4   2

Library of Congress Cataloging-in-Publication Data is available

ISBN 0-7432-3572-X

This book is dedicated to the men and women of OSS,
especially OSS's foreign and German prisoner-of-war agents,
many of whom gave their lives for a higher cause.

Contents

Prologue   ix

ONE: Spy School   1

TWO: R&D and "The Campus"   16

THREE: Intrigue in North Africa and Iberia   26

FOUR: Up the Boot   49

FIVE: On Hitler's Doorstep
         The OSS in Switzerland   67

SIX: Into the Balkans
         Yugoslavia and Albania   79

SEVEN: "SMASHEM"
         Greece   102

EIGHT: From Frogmen to SEALs
         The OSS Maritime Unit (MU)   124

NINE: Infiltrating France   143

TEN: Paving the Way for Overlord   160

ELEVEN: Dragoon   181

TWELVE: X-2
              Counterespionage   194

THIRTEEN: Approaching the Reich   206

FOURTEEN: Catastrophe in Czechoslovakia   217

FIFTEEN: Psych Ops
              Morale Operations (MO) and
              Origins of Psychological Warfare   228

SIXTEEN: Penetrating the Reich   240

SEVENTEEN: Backroom Negotiations
              Sweden and Norway   263

EIGHTEEN: Northern Italy   278

NINETEEN: Final Missions and Conclusion   297

              Notes   315

              Glossary   331

              Selected Bibliography   339

              Acknowledgments   347

              Index   349

Prologue

A Gestapo dragnet was closing in on the abandoned farmhouse in northern France where agent René Joyeuse was busy on his radio. He was feverishly reporting the exact location of an underground V-1 rocket factory and a German oil refinery when his last sentence was cut short by the glare of a very powerful flashlight. "The house was surrounded. So I told the resistance fighters with me, 'We're surrounded, let's get out of here fast!' I was picking up my Colt .45 lying on the table when four German hand grenades were thrown into the room.

"The blasts from the grenades violently threw me on the ground twice. Miraculously, I wasn't wounded.

"We dashed into the alley and reached a small service staircase in the back of the house. We succeeded in leaving the house at the moment that the Germans entered through the garden gate.

"We were continuously attacked from 10 meters behind by grenades and submachine-gun fire, and blazing torches lit up the night. I attempted to cover our retreat with my Colt but it jammed on the fourth shot. With Colt in hand I arrived in front of a big wall separating the Secours National Park from a neighboring property next to the railroad tracks by a freight station. We all tried to scale this wall. I made two unsuccessful attempts and told the FFIs [Resistance fighters] that I wasn't going to make it and would try the wall further down. They kept trying and I never saw them again.

"I was able to scale the wall about 20 meters down. At this moment the Germans, who were posted on both sides of the block near the tracks, fired at me at a distance of 10 meters and missed me. I came upon a patrol. Seeing a running man passing them, they fired on me with their machine guns at point-blank range. They still missed me. I crossed all the tracks and came to another gate leading to a street on the side of the station. I climbed over. At this moment, two other Germans with machine guns woke up to what was going on and fired. Luckily, in climbing over the gate, I had fallen flat on my face behind a small cement parapet which caused all the bullets to ricochet. When their magazines were empty, I got up again and ran off in the direction of nearby houses. After about 200 or 300 meters of painful progress, since I was wounded in the right foot and hand, the left kneecap, and had suffered numerous contusions, I got into a house where the gate was half open and met a women who, seeing that I was going to bring her a lot of grief, told me, 'Don't come in here! Beat it! Get out of here!' I threatened her with my pistol, begging her to 'shut up!', and went up to the fourth floor by a back staircase. I dropped down to a door to another apartment, which seemed to belong to a woman who was an informer for the Gestapo! I stayed there, near the door, the whole time holding in one hand my Colt and in the other my potassium cyanide pill [L-pill, or lethal pill]. I decided to use one or the other on myself if I were surrounded. The dragnet continued for me all night, all the nearby houses were searched, with the exception of the one I was in."[1]

Joyeuse, leader of a two-man spy team, narrowly escaped with his life. The resistance men were captured and summarily executed. Despite the disaster, Joyeuse continued to gather valuable intelligence on German troop movements. Additionally, the oil refinery and German rocket plant were destroyed by Allied bombers.*

---

*After the war, Joyeuse returned to the United States, where he became a physician.

Joyeuse's mission was part of the "shadow war," one of the few remaining aspects of World War II that has not been fully appreciated. While the most visible part of World War II was fought by armies, navies, and air forces, a largely invisible and covert war was also raging around the globe. Saboteurs were demolishing railroad tunnels, spies were stealing secrets, and "operatives"—uniformed soldiers trained to fight behind enemy lines—were parachuting into occupied countries to organize and lead resistance fighters. Mathematicians were breaking codes. Radio propagandists were demoralizing German soldiers and civilians, while academics were analyzing the German economy to determine which were the crucial industries that should be targeted by Allied strategic bombers in order to cripple the German war effort.

Before World War II, America's use of covert, or shadow, warfare was limited. There had been spies in the Revolutionary and Civil Wars, among others, but American intelligence services were so much inferior to those of the world's other great powers that one senior Foreign Service officer observed: "Our Intelligence organization in 1940 was primitive and inadequate . . . operating strictly in the tradition of the Spanish-American War."[2]

Perhaps this was to be expected in a nation that seemed to have an innate aversion to spying. A navy intelligence officer complained that to Americans, "Espionage is by its very nature not to be considered as 'honorable' or 'clean' or 'fair' or 'decent.' . . . The United States has always prided itself on the fact that no spies were used and its intelligence officers accredited overseas have always kept their hands immaculately clean."[3] When deciphered Japanese messages landed on his desk in 1929, Hoover administration Secretary of State Henry Stimson infamously remarked, "Gentlemen do not read each other's mail."[4] Appalled by what he perceived to be underhanded techniques, Stimson shut down the "Black Chamber," a cryptographic service cracking Japanese codes. Fortunately, the military pressed on with code-breaking efforts.

In the prewar years, the vital task of gathering foreign intelligence fell on the shoulders of four departments within the federal government: the State Department; the Office of Naval Intelligence (ONI); the War Department's Military Intelligence Division (MID), better known as G-2; and the Federal Bureau of Investigation (FBI). While the FBI had no mandate to gather foreign intelligence until 1940, it indirectly gathered intelligence in conjunction with the investigation of crimes in the United States. In 1940, the bureau set up a Special Intelligence Service to conduct operations in Latin America.

State Department diplomats obtained intelligence through the course of official business or covertly in secret meetings with contacts they established. State's Division of Information was little more than a press office that distributed news releases to the press, governments, and universities.

The military intelligence departments of ONI and G-2 were understaffed and underfunded. Most of ONI's intelligence was gathered by attachés serving overseas who openly visited shipyards; in peacetime the attachés were instructed to refrain from cloak and dagger activity. By 1939, ONI had only 17 attaché posts, 9 in Europe and the remainder in South America. G-2 was equally diminutive: in 1940, G-2 numbered only 80 staffers.[5]

Analysis and dissemination of intelligence were also problems. The departments arbitrarily sent reports up the chain of command, hoping that the most critical information would find its way to the White House, but no clearinghouse existed to ensure that information was shared among the departments. While the departments were all focusing on countering sabotage and espionage within the United States, they seemed more concerned about jealously guarding their turf than about coordinating their efforts. In 1939, President Franklin Delano Roosevelt urged better cooperation between the groups, but little progress had been made by 1940. ONI candidly summed up the situation: "A real undercover foreign intelligence service, equipped and able to carry on espionage, counter-intelligence, etc. does not exist."[6]

Under pressure from the British to improve intelligence matters, Roosevelt took decisive action.[7] On July 11, 1941, the president ordered the establishment of a new White House agency, the Coordinator of Information (COI), effectively creating America's first peacetime national intelligence organization. The COI received a powerful mandate, the "authority to collect and analyze all information and data, which may bear upon the national security; to correlate such information and data, and to make such information and data available to the President and to such departments and officials of the Government as the President may determine. . . ."[8]

The president could not have chosen a more dynamic or better qualified man to lead COI: war hero, former assistant U.S. attorney general, Wall Street lawyer, and executive William J. Donovan. During WWI, Donovan commanded a battalion in the 165th Infantry Regiment, more commonly known as the "Fighting 69th" from its Civil War heritage. Donovan personally led his command in combat. During one battle, the battalion was pinned down when "Wild Bill," pistol in hand, leaped from the trenches, yelling, "They can't hit me, and they won't hit you." The men surged forward and "were dropping all over," as Donovan recalled. "Beside me three men were blown up, and I was showered with the remnants of their bodies."[9] Donovan took a machine-gun bullet to the knee. Bleeding profusely, he refused to be evacuated and continued to command his battalion, leading it to victory. His actions that day won him the Congressional Medal of Honor. By the end of the war he had earned the Distinguished Service Cross, Distinguished Service Medal, and two Purple Hearts. A number of foreign governments also recognized him for his valor, making him one of the most decorated veterans of the American Expeditionary Force.

After the war, Donovan traveled extensively and resumed his legal practice. He also served as assistant attorney general under Calvin Coolidge.

In 1940, Donovan traveled overseas as an official emissary for President Roosevelt to report on Britain's staying power in the war. Hoping to win American support, Prime Minster Winston Churchill granted him unprecedented access to Britain's greatest intelligence and defense secrets. The president, impressed by Donovan's reports, sent him on a second tour to the Mediterranean and the Balkans. The trips provided Donovan with ideas on how to improve America's intelligence operations and develop shadow-war capabilities.

In Washington, Donovan's fledgling COI came under assault by the government agencies responsible for gathering intelligence, who viewed him as an intruder in their territory. The very agencies the COI was attempting to coordinate, FBI, ONI, G-2, and State, formed a loose anti-COI alliance that would continue throughout the war. The four departments took steps to curb the new agency's scope and influence. For example, the military put code-breaking off limits, and ONI and FBI excluded COI from operating in the Western Hemisphere.

COI nevertheless expanded into research and analysis and propaganda, collaborating closely with the British intelligence services. Special operations and secret intelligence lagged behind other divisions, as spies and saboteurs took so long to train.

December 7th marked America's entry into WWII. COI, still in its infancy and mostly focused on the threat of Nazi Germany, did not play a role in one of America's worst intelligence failures of the war. Hawaii lay within the territory of ONI and G-2, and it was they who failed to detect the attack on Pearl Harbor.

The advent of war would transform COI's relationship with the newly formed Joint Chiefs of Staff, who largely sided with their own intelligence organizations and distrusted Donovan. In order to solve this perception problem and gain access to military support and greater resources, Donovan proposed bringing COI under the control of the Joint Chiefs.

On June 13, 1942, the president officially endorsed the idea. COI's name was changed to the Office of Strategic Services (OSS), and the organization was placed under the authority of the Joint Chiefs. Part of the change also included the loss of COI's Foreign Information Service (FIS). FIS conducted America's "white propaganda" campaign, which consisted of truthful information publicly acknowledged to be of American origin. Nearly half of COI's staff was placed into a separate, newly created organization, the Office of War Information (OWI).

The realignment and name change did not placate OSS's intelligence rivals at FBI, State, G-2, and ONI. When Donovan proposed creating a special code-breaking facility known as the COILs project, a presidential decree inspired by OSS's intelligence rivals effectively blocked the project.[10] The FBI continued to prevent OSS counterespionage operations in the Western Hemisphere.

While under the tutelage of the British, OSS developed many of its own independent concepts practically overnight, emphasizing an integrated "combined arms" of shadow-war techniques. Wild Bill Donovan's vision held that "persuasion, penetration and intimidation . . . are the modern counterparts of sapping and mining in the siege warfare of former days." Propaganda represented the "arrow of initial penetration," followed up by espionage. Sabotage and guerrilla operations would then soften up an area before conventional forces invaded.[11] The integration of all shadow-war techniques was a groundbreaking approach to covert warfare. The British secret services were not integrated, but operated in separate divisions.

A central element of the shadow war was special operations, a new concept that OSS would develop during the war. At the end of March 1941, Donovan urged the president to permit him to develop special operations forces, which would take the war to the Germans in an unexpected, irregular way. Teams of operatives would penetrate behind enemy lines to sow mayhem in rear areas. Donovan considered the Germans "big league professionals" of warfare, and America the "bush league club." He explained to the president that the only way to get America up to speed quickly against Germany was to "play a bush league game, stealing the ball and killing the umpire."[12] He would succeed remarkably well, as the stories in this book suggest.

Major departments of OSS under Donovan included:

Research & Analysis (R&A) for intelligence analysis.

Research and Development (R&D) for weapons and equipment development.

Morale Operations (MO) for subversive, disguised, "black" propaganda.

Maritime Units (MU) for transporting agents and supplies to resistance groups. MU frogmen also conducted naval sabotage and reconnaissance.

X-2 for Counterespionage.

Secret Intelligence (SI) covered agents in the field who covertly gathered intelligence.

Special Operations (SO) for sabotage, subversion, fifth-column movements, and guerrilla warfare.

Operational Groups (OG) also for sabotage and guerrilla warfare, made up of highly trained foreign-language-speaking commando teams.

Donovan used his vast array of personal contacts to recruit the best and the brightest. OSS tapped Ivy League schools, law firms, and major corporations for their talent. Innovativeness and youth were common denominators among the new recruits. OSS wanted "out-of-the-box" thinkers, and fostered an organizational culture of creativity. OSS was unorthodox, brilliant, and at times bizarre. One proposed mission would have dropped pornography on Hitler's HQ, in a farcical attempt to addict the Führer. Nevertheless, it was a dynamic and groundbreaking organization that, as OSS psychologists concluded after the war, "Undertook and carried out more different types of enterprises calling for more varied skills than any other single organization of its size in the history of our country."[13]

OSS's shadow war required a wide range of skills. Safecrackers were sprung from prison, and Ivy League professors were recruited to analyze what was stolen from the safes. U.S. Army paratroopers and other elite troops were recruited to serve as operatives. Communists who fought against Franco in the Spanish Civil War were recruited for operations in Spain or potentially to work with Communist resistance networks. Americans and foreigners alike were trained as citizen spies. Very few professional spies existed, and, because of language differences, most Americans were not ideally suited for certain aspects of secret intelligence work. Therefore, foreigners, including some Axis prisoners of war, were trained to collect information and sometimes fight in occupied countries, even in Germany herself. After Italy's surrender, for example, elite Italian maritime commandos joined up to work against the Germans. Tragically, countless foreign agents were killed in the line of duty with little recognition after the war by OSS or CIA.

This book focuses on the main operational arms of the OSS: Special Operations (SO), along with its Operational Groups (OG) offshoot, and Secret Intelligence (SI), particularly in the European theater. Due to the sheer number of missions, OSS operations in Asia require separate treatment. *Operatives, Spies, and Saboteurs,* just as its title suggests, is the first substantial "agent-level" history of OSS. It is not an analysis or traditional history, but the story of the main operational units in their own words. The book is arranged in rough chronological and campaign order. Branches that provided more of a supporting role, such as MU, X-2, MO, R&D, and R&A, are highlighted in separate chapters.*

---

*The MU chapter contains the previously untold story of OSS's frogmen. Several crucial operations in the Pacific theater were included in this volume since they were absolutely germane to the history.

Over the past several years I have felt like a detective tracking down the surviving men and women of OSS. Over 300 oral history interviews were conducted with these remarkable individuals around the country. Many told me their stories for the first time, breaking vows of silence and revealing secrets held for nearly 60 years. Both male and female agents were interviewed; however, only a tiny percentage of women actually operated behind the lines. The interviews provide the heart of this book. Their stories were carefully crosschecked with supporting documentation.

The oral histories were supplemented by over two years of research in the massive documentary OSS archival collection housed at the National Archives. Nearly all of the documents of this entire intelligence organization are on file (in comparison, most of the British and Soviet records still remain sealed). Tens of thousands of documents have only recently been declassified, having previously been held back as top secret "sources and methods" by the CIA.

This agent-level history touches on the heart of OSS's story. OSS had to overcome many obstacles. The new agency had to build an organization and develop techniques from the ground up in a short period of time. Then it had to "sell" its services to traditional military commanders who understood neither its role nor how it functioned. Despite resistance from American rivals and from British intelligence, which viewed OSS as a junior partner rather than an equal, OSS expanded and was engaged in nearly every theater of the war. Historians have tended to relegate OSS to a sideshow, suggesting that it made little difference in the war's outcome. Now that the records are open, and the veterans are telling their stories, however, it can be shown that OSS played a key role in the Allied victory.

ONE

Spy School

A few days after Pearl Harbor, General Donovan summoned two men to his office: Dr. J. R. Hayden, former vice-governor of the Philippines, and Kenneth Baker of the Psychology Division of COI's Research and Analysis department. Neither had any idea what the meeting was about. After the men were seated, Wild Bill quickly came to the point: "I want you to start the schools."

"What schools?"

"The SI training schools."

"But we don't know anything about espionage schools—"

"Who does?"[1]

Baker and Hayden had their hands full. The newly designated Co-ordinator of Information (COI), later redesignated OSS, had the un-precedented task of creating a world-class intelligence organization overnight, from scratch. It was hampered by America's traditional aversion to spycraft. Unlike most of the world's great powers, America had limited experience in espionage.

The same could not be said of America's British allies. Britain's SOE (Special Operations Executive) and SIS (Secret Intelligence Service), having been at war for over two years, had all the experience necessary to lay the foundation for COI's undercover training pro-gram. The British worked with a team of COI personnel, led by Hay-den and Baker, to develop a training curriculum designed to produce spies, saboteurs, and guerrillas.

While the curriculum was being written, OSS was also constructing training facilities in the Washington, D.C. area, but they wouldn't be up and running for several months. Therefore, the first COI/OSS agents trained in Canada, at "Camp X." Established by the British expressly to assist America with the shadow war, Camp X was the first secret agent training school in North America. Also referred to as Special Training School 103, Camp X was located in the countryside between the sleepy towns of Oshawa and Whitby, about thirty miles outside of Toronto. The camp was so secret that even the Canadian War Cabinet wasn't informed of its existence.

Camp X played such an important role in the war that the head of the British Security Coordination (BSC), Sir William Stephenson, described it as the "clenched fist" of all Allied secret operations in World War II.[2] A number of notable British and American agents passed through the school. Ian Fleming is said to have drawn from the underwater frogman exercises in Lake Ontario for his James Bond character.

One of the first Americans trained at Camp X was Frank Devlin. "I was given a set of orders that read like a spook book. 'Have civilian clothes. Take train such and such to Penn Station New York and get a train to Toronto, Canada. Go to Hotel and there you will find a message with a number. That number indicates the license on the vehicle you will take and it will be at the west entrance of the hotel.'

"After I got in the vehicle, we were taken to Camp X and were enrolled as the first class. We learned night work going out. On one of our missions they told us that we had to blow part of the Canadian-Pacific railroad. There were a set of rails right before a bridge. They said that this area was completely guarded and we haven't told the guards that you are coming and they have loaded weapons. We had to rehearse it, work it out in the woods so when we did it we didn't get shot. It worked like clockwork. We planted all the charges under the rails and didn't blow it up of course but we could have done it.

OSS Training Areas on the East Coast

CANADA

Camp X • Oshawa

Whitby
Toronto •

Lake Ontario

Lake Erie

UNITED STATES

New York City

Area B
(Camp David)   Area E   Philadelphia

Baltimore

Washington,
D.C.
(SEE INSET)

Atlantic

Ocean

0   100
Miles

"The Farm" _____ RTU-ll advanced or finishing
                    intelligence school
Area A _____ Primarily for basic or SO training
Area B _____ Paramilitary training. Now Camp David
Area C _____ Communications training
Area D _____ Maritime training
Area E _____ OSS basic training
Area F _____ OG training
Station S _____ Assessment
Station W _____ (area near Georgetown) Assessment
                    for clerical and service personnel

Inset:

0   10 Miles   RTU-11 ■
Miles   ("The Farm")

MARYLAND

Potomac R.

Area F
(Congressional
Country Club)

Washington,
D.C.
Georgetown
Arlington   Station W

Station S
(Fairfax)

Alexandria

VIRGINIA

Potomac R.

Area D
Area A, C
(Quantico)

"We had lots of classes on what to do if you were behind the lines. We learned all the things that could give you away. There was the use of weapons, close-up and hand-to-hand, all common today. It was all stuff that was dirty, not the kind of thing you learned in infantry school. You played dirty here. We learned how to dislocate someone's arm while you had a knife under their rib. I can still do it. If I try it I might take you and throw you over the back of that chair. Eifler [commanding officer in Detachment 101] did it to everybody. He would get their hand and do something with it, turn it in the right place. You just do a flip and you're helpless."[3]

One of Devlin's instructors was British Captain William Ewart Fairbairn, also known as "Fearless Dan" or the "Shanghai Buster." During the twenties and thirties, Fairbairn rose to the rank of assistant commissioner of the municipal police of one of the toughest cities on earth, Shanghai. He created one of the first SWAT teams, a counter-terrorist outfit known as the Reserve Unit (RU), to quell the Chinese gangs and the organized crime that ran rampant in the city. In the back alleys of Shanghai, Fairbairn developed his own revolutionary hand-to-hand fighting system, a deadly mix of jiu-jitsu and street fighting, known initially as "Gutter Fighting" and later renamed the "Fairbairn Technique." In his own words, Fairbairn described his black art. "When I organized and trained Riot Squads for the Shanghai Police I developed a system of fighting out of the methods that got results . . . but in modern warfare, the job is more drastic. You're interested only in disabling or killing your enemy. That's why I teach what I call 'Gutter Fighting.' There's no fair play; no rules except one: kill or be killed."

Fairbairn made a lasting impression on just about everyone he met, including OSS, who got him on more or less permanent loan from the British. OSS promoted Fearless Dan to the rank of major and transferred him to Area B, a 9,000-acre compound in the Catoctin Mountains outside Washington, D.C., the present-day site of Camp

David. At Area B, Fairbairn taught his lethal hand-to-hand fighting technique, and also how to handle the Fairbairn-Sykes fighting knife, a razor-sharp stiletto of his personal design.

"The knife is a silent, deadly weapon. It's great for sentries. Never mind the blood. Just take care of it quickly."

After completing a course in knife fighting, the new students took a course in unarmed "Gutter Fighting."

"In a sense, this is for fools, because you should never be without a pistol or knife. However in case you are caught unarmed, foolishly or otherwise, the tactics shown here will increase your chances of coming out alive."

A technique that Fairbairn demonstrated was the "Tiger's Claw," a clenched hand that is directed at an opponent's eyes. "Deceive your opponent. Make him think you're out on your feet. Now bring the Tiger's Claw up from the cellar and put force behind it. It will knock your opponent out. But you must attack with surprise."

The Shanghai Buster gave this advice on how to counter a bear hug: "To break a bear hug . . . go limp . . . grab his testicles. Ruin him. . . ."

When asked if the typical American trainee was reluctant to employ the "Fairbairn Technique," since it runs counter to the American sense of sportsmanship, Major Fairbairn responded: "He does have a natural repugnance to this kind of fighting. But when he realizes that the enemy will show him no mercy, and that the methods he is learning work, he soon overcomes it."[4]

Fairbairn was joined by several other legends in hand-to-hand combat such as Rex Applegate, a crack pistol shot and the pioneer of a technique known as "offensive shooting." Applegate taught recruits how to handle a pistol in combat. "When a man is faced by an assailant who has a gun in his hand and murder in his heart, he must be able to use his pistol instantly and effectively."[5]

COI and OSS recruited a broad variety of men and women. The common thread was creative, "out of the box" thinkers distinguished by boldness and decisiveness. One such man, Lieutenant Charles Parkin, Jr., was unceremoniously transferred to OSS from the U.S. Army Engineer School at Fort Belvoir after displaying some unwelcome initiative.

"On our way back from maneuvers I saw all of these National Guard units guarding bridges. Security was pathetic. Some units were guarding the railroad bridges with unloaded rifles or a single shotgun so I decided once I got back to Fort Belvoir to try to change things so the bridges would get proper security. I put together a plan to take my platoon to one of the bridges. First, I mentioned the plan to the officer in charge, a captain. I told him about the lack of security and that I wanted to do something about it. He said, 'Charlie, I wouldn't touch that with a ten-foot pole!' I went ahead with the plan since this was good training for my men. I wanted to show them we better get off our asses and start doing things right.

"Anyway, I called out half of my platoon that night and we rode on assault boats across the Occoquan River. These were the only railroad bridges that crossed the river into D.C. from the south. We landed and silently planted dummy explosives on the girders of the railroad bridges. It was raining that night, and to divert the guard's attention I went up and talked to him. The fake charges were set in all the right places; if they had been real explosives we could have blown the bridges sky high. When I got back to the base that morning I sat down and wrote a report of what we did and why we did it. The report went to my battalion commander and I don't know what he said but the next thing I knew I was being called to HQ with his boss. He said in essence, 'This thing is too hot to handle. The National Guard versus the Army? I'm transferring you to an outfit in Washington called the Coordinator of Information that can put your talents to use.'"[6] Parkin soon became COI's primary demolition instructor.

One of Parkin's first recruits was his fraternity brother from Penn State, a former national wrestling standout, Frank Gleason. After the war Gleason continued a career in demolitions and special operations, retiring as a colonel and professor at the U.S. Army Command and General Staff College in Fort Leavenworth, Kansas. "Charlie recruited me and one of the first things he did was send me to industrial sabotage school in England run by the SOE. What they teach you at sabotage school will blow your mind. Six or seven people that are properly trained can cripple a good-sized city. It is as easy as can be. These terrorists scare me. If they know this stuff, which I'm sure they do, it's really easy to cripple a medium-size city with trained demolitionists and arsonists. We learned how to operate and destroy locomotives and power plants, the turbines in power plants, communication systems, and telephones. We also learned how to make people sick by poisoning a city's water supply. Shitty stuff like that—we were taught how to fight dirty.

"Using a locomotive we learned how to take the controls and get the train moving at a high speed, and jump off—creating a runaway train that would plow into something—isn't that awful? We destroyed rolling stock by removing grease in the gearboxes and putting sugar in gasoline tanks to destroy the engines. We learned how to make explosives from sugar, from basic household supplies. How to start a fire that could take out a city.

"I knew Stanley Lovell, head of OSS R&D, quite well, and he introduced me to 'Aunt Jemima.' It was a plastic explosive that looked like baking flour. The concept of it was that you could easily transport it behind the lines. In China we made muffins from the stuff. I wanted to show Major Miles how you could bake Aunt Jemima into muffins, put a blasting cap into it and blow something up. It looks like regular flour but if you look carefully at a little piece you'd see it was gritty, unlike flour. It could make bread so I told this Chinese cook at Happy Valley to make some muffins out of the explosive flour. I said, 'Do not eat those muffins! They are poison. Do not eat them!' You should have seen them when they came out of the oven, they were gorgeous. The cook thought to himself, 'Well those damn Americans want those muffins for themselves.' He violated what I told him and he ate one. He almost died."[7]

One of Area B's early trainees was Milt Felsen, an ambulance driver and machine gunner who had fought in the Abraham Lincoln Brigade during the Spanish Civil War in the thirties. After the war Felsen went to Hollywood to produce movies, including the hit *Saturday Night Fever.* "Donovan came to the headquarters of the Veterans of the Abraham Lincoln Brigade. We had a little place in New York City. He came up and said he wanted a half dozen or so guys to help set up the OSS. He questioned folks and chose about ten of us. He told us to meet him in Washington, which we did.

"We went to D.C. and were sent to an abandoned boy's camp, called Area B, now Camp David.

"We went up to Area B. We helped set up the place as a training base for the OSS. There were cabins and a big hall and another building we later set up as a training building. One of the things we faced was Fairbairn's house of horrors. As you entered, pop-up targets that looked like Nazis would come at you from darkened rooms. This would be accompanied by simulated gun shots and strange lights. The goal was to get off two quick shots on the targets. You had to make your way through an obstacle course which also included pop-up targets that you had to hit and keep going.

"At Area B we met Jerry Sage, our commanding officer in North Africa. He saw that we were veterans and he stuck to us. We advised him on what we thought was needed to work behind German lines. One of the things we got was a little booklet that Mao put together on guerrilla warfare. There was nothing else in those days and we had to create it.

"We did five parachute jumps. We did everything on the basis that nothing existed and we had to create it. On our jump training we jumped in different places, i.e., mountain, river, etc. We got as many weapons as we could from the Axis and other European countries. In the event we were in Europe and came across weapons they were using, we'd know what to do with them.

"We went out on a submarine. After the sub surfaced we inflated a raft on the deck and paddled to shore. Once ashore we had to hide the raft and go someplace where the people guarding the area did not know we were coming and I'm sure would be very offended and take shots at us if they discovered us. It was as realistic as it could be . . . maybe too realistic."[8]

Realistic training was a hallmark for the OSS commandos, who worked in units called Operational Groups (OGs). The OGs received most of their training on the lavish 18-hole Congressional Country Club, known as Area F. "Aggressiveness of spirit and willingness to close with the enemy were stressed,"[9] so OG training was designed to be as close to reality as possible. Tragic mistakes were inevitable, as OG trainee Al Materazzi found out. "We moved to the Congressional Country Club and were trained by a Russian prince, Serge Obolensky, whose last wartime experience had been with the White Russian guerrillas. Major Fairbairn trained us in knife fighting and hand-to-hand combat. Tragically, a private accidentally killed another private during a simulation."[10]

The first independent Secret Intelligence training school set up by OSS was RTU-11. Known as "the Farm," since it was located on a sprawling country estate about 20 miles north of Washington, RTU-11 offered elementary and advanced intelligence training. Recruits were taught the importance of cover, intelligence-gathering methods, and the use of "cut-outs" (individuals who would work as intermediaries between the OSS agent and subagents).[11]

SI training culminated in a course requiring students to execute practice undercover assignments, or "schemes," in the nearby industrial centers of Baltimore, Richmond, and Philadelphia. The first scheme was relatively easy, generally involving brief intelligence work or sabotage, as Geoffrey Jones recalls. "We tested the FBI and plant security and were in teams of three. The first mission we had was to blow up a plant in Baltimore. What we did was put a note on the main boiler that said "This is a bomb" and called up the FBI. Luckily we never got caught. I understand some people got really roughed up before the FBI called OSS to see if they were OSS or not."[12]

The second scheme was more advanced. Students were allowed to carry forged documents that were produced at the training center, such as Social Security cards and draft cards. The recruits were often required to secure jobs and pass off the information they gathered to another person, in code. Jones's final mission was in Philadelphia. "My cover story was that I was an advance man from Twentieth Century Fox, I'd been out in California and I knew show business and so on. I had letterhead from the studio and used my middle names, Montgomery Talbot. I wrote a letter to the managing director of the steel mill and told him I was making a film about the plant's contribution to the war effort. I checked into a hotel in Philadelphia and invited him and his wife to dinner.

"He wined and dined me, I wined and dined him. The bonus to that was while I was waiting for him to go to lunch I noticed that his secretary in the outer office had a big long typewriter. I'd never seen anything like that. I said, 'What is that typewriter?' She said, 'I use it to type all of the procurements for the steel mill.' While she wasn't around I noticed she kept putting her carbon papers in a wastepaper basket. Over a couple of days I took all of the carbon papers. From the carbon papers we were able to project how much steel they were supposed to make.

"OSS told me I could do anything I could get away with so I just walked out on a $3,000 bill at the hotel. I paid for a fancy room, extravagant meals for him and his wife; ultimately, I had to pay half, something I've never been too happy about."[13]

X-2, or counterespionage, was sometimes described as an elite within an elite. X-2 training included many of the elements of SI training, along with double agent handling, investigative techniques, and chicanery such as lock picking, wiretaps, and burglary. Ed Weismiller remembers his training and final scheme. "I had been a Rhodes Scholar and therefore I'd been overseas just before the war and had a pretty good command of French. It turned out that X-2 heard about me and decided that they would interview me. When they did, they asked me to join. They had slots in all the branches of the armed services and I could pick the service I wanted. Because I was a poet and was publishing poetry, I picked the Marine Corps just out of levity! All I had to do was go through marine training, officers training. I went through two courses in the Maryland and Virginia countryside during the summer of 1943 before my marine training started. I passed with ease and even was a marksman with the .45 pistol thanks to the OSS training. What you learned in the OSS courses was mainly to keep your mouth shut. You were also trained in ciphers, decipherment, coding of messages. You were taught how to use a pistol; how to read compasses and make your way through in the dark, places you didn't know. Dan Fairbairn even taught us how to roll an ordinary newspaper into a lethal dagger.

"The graduation exercise was probably one of the most interesting. We were all shipped to Baltimore and let loose on the town and we were simply to come back with as much information as we could about what was going on that had to do with the war effort. If we got in trouble, they didn't know us; we were in trouble on our own. I picked the Baltimore-Ohio Railroad because I knew that it was probably in touch with just about everything that was going on. I went in and said that I was a writer. With any lie you learned to make it as close to the truth as possible. If you make up an elaborate lie then you have to be able to repeat all aspects of the elaborate lie over and over at any time, in any order. So I said I was a writer just down from Cambridge, about to go into the war myself but I wanted to write one big story before I went into the war. I picked Baltimore because so much was going on in terms of manufacturing supply for the armed services and the more I thought about it the more I thought the key to the whole thing would be the Baltimore-Ohio Railroad. They thought this was just swell. They asked me of course for ID. I said that I'd spilled a cup of coffee on my lap just before I came over and I had to change my clothes quickly and I didn't transfer all of my stuff, but I would bring my complete ID the next day. They said that was fine.

"They assigned me a car and a driver and a photographer and drove me around to the various railroad entities. When you got to a secure area, they would say politely, 'Well, we're not supposed to let you through here.' The driver had various errands of his own to do while he was taking me around and he would say, 'Well you're not supposed to come in here but surely there's no harm.' And I would go. I would go and I got notebooks full of information about what was being manufactured and where it was being shipped to and where it was being shipped out from. Just being a nice guy could get you into the most sensitive areas. I went back to the OSS training area with this appalling load of stuff, turned it in, and was later informed that I graduated."[14]

Another student posed as a purchasing agent for a friendly neutral country and was able to walk out the front door of a plant with the complete blueprints of the latest bomber.

But not all of the schemes had happy endings. Several students were arrested and incarcerated by the local authorities or FBI. One student who posed as an electrician was taken to a remote location, interrogated under a spotlight, and summarily beaten for hours. "I never broke," he later exclaimed. He was released 48 hours after he was hauled in.[15]

Beginning in late 1942, OSS dispatched instructors overseas to train foreign nationals for work in Europe. Over 2,500 male and dozens of female agents passed through OSS parachute training, although few women took part in the activities of the operational branches of OSS. Many OSS agents also were trained by the British, including members of the Jedburgh program (three-man Special Operations [SO] teams that jumped into France, Holland, and Belgium on or after D-Day).

"We were trained at an estate outside Peterborough, at Milton Hall, a huge mansion, several thousand acres," recalled former "Jed" Joseph de Francesco.

"One test involved a group of five or six of us. They said you have a mission in occupied territory and you are going to destroy a radar station. You land a few miles from there. On your way you come across a civilian going to work, then they asked, 'What are you going to do about it?' One of the men in my group was a Catholic priest and he said, 'I'd kill him.' I said to myself, 'Jesus, this guy is pretty bloodthirsty.' I said I'd try to avoid him. They also said, 'On landing one of the men on your team breaks a leg.' The priest said, 'I'd kill him.' I said to him, 'You are a bloodthirsty bastard aren't you!' This guy was later captured and beheaded by the Japs."[16]

As the war progressed OSS expanded. The rapid expansion taxed the training areas. This led to the development of a groundbreaking assessment program that included screening the qualifications of OSS candidates before they underwent expensive and time-consuming individual training. Today, a shopping center stands on the land once occupied by OSS's main assessment center—Station S, located in Fairfax, Virginia.

Candidates wore green army fatigues with no rank and were subjected to a battery of intelligence and aptitude tests designed to test ingenuity, creativity, leadership, personality, and even patience, as secret intelligence agent Gene Searchinger remembers. "There were some large Tinkertoy poles and blocks with holes that the poles could go into. They handed you a diagram and they said, 'Build this but you're not allowed to touch it. You're supposed to give orders to these two helpers and they'll build it.'[17] The diagram looked like a very complex rectangle.

"The 'helpers' greeted me, 'Hello, boss.'[18] I said something like 'Let's get started.' And one said, 'Who me?' Why don't you call us by name? We have names, you know. Don't you care who the people are you have working for you.' They shook my hand and said, 'I'm Kippy and this is Buster.' They tried to get me to reveal my real name. One of them did everything you told him to very slowly, the other one always had a better idea. 'Why don't you try it in that order . . . or try it in that order . . . or try it this way, put it in this hole.' It turned into a Three Stooges comedy routine since they were trying to sabotage the effort. They claimed only one person got it to work." That person was a massive Texan who reportedly flattened the two "helpers" with two well-timed blows.[19]

Searchinger remembers another test. "They would take you into a room and tell you to go to L-House. (By this time you were supposed to know where L-House was even though no one told you.) 'Go to L-House and go to the library and you'll find a book there called Lu-LaLuLa and memorize what it says and come back here. And by the way if anything should happen while you're coming back have a good excuse why you are there. Good-bye!' They'd click a stopwatch and you'd have to scramble over to L-House.

"You'd have to run to get there. You'd find the book which contained a piece of paper that was filled with phone numbers and addresses. It was an impossible thing to memorize. At the bottom of the paper it read, 'Further information will be found in a container behind the bookshelf.' I looked there and saw a box with a wire going inside it so I decided not to look into it. You didn't touch it if you were smart. You left the house in the dead of night and a guy steps forward with a bayonet and says, 'Stop!' You are taken to another house and a light is pouring on a bench and they are interrogating you as to why you were there and what was going on. (By this time you were supposed to have a clever story.) I think I played the nervous man and somehow came off as believable."[20]

Written tests were given to assess everything from propaganda skills to memory skills to personality. The most exotic test was the Murder Mystery, which was designed to test students' investigative and inference skills. At noon on the third day of the program students were given copies of the mythical *Fairfield Chronicle* announcing the discovery of a dead body of a woman several miles from the village. Additional clues were provided in the form of dozens of letters and testimonials. The group was told they were the sole party investigating the murder and to solve it. On the evening of the last day, a senior member of the assessment staff judged each team's results and declared a winner.

For those that made it through the program a party was thrown for "relaxation." Of course nothing was what it seemed, as Gene Searchinger discovered. "The final test was a relaxing party. They wanted to see if you'd relax and give up your cover."[21] A document describing the party describes its true purpose further: "The informality and conviviality were aided and abetted by the use of liquor, debates, the telling of off-color stories, horseplay between students and staff. Although social relations were the most important trait measured, data were frequently obtained on practical intelligence, emotional stability, and motivation and propaganda skills."[22]

OSS's greatest asset was its people. Remarkably, while the organization operated in every theater of the war, in neutral and occupied countries, and even in Berlin itself, only 143 Americans died in the line of duty.[23] This number, however, does not include the hundreds of foreigners who were killed while working for OSS. Nevertheless, character and training that emphasized leadership, creative thinking, self-confidence, and decisive action were deciding factors in their success. Most of all, OSS expected its men and women to win. They did both during the war and in life after it.

TWO

R&D and "The Campus"

"Professor Moriarty is the man I want for my staff here at OSS. I think you're it."

"Do I look to be as evil a character as Conan Doyle made him in his [Sherlock Holmes's] stories?"

"I don't give a damn how you look," Donovan replied sharply. "I need every subtle device and every underhanded trick to use against the Germans and Japanese—by our own people. . . . You will have to invent all of them, Lovell, because you're going to be my man."[1] Thus did Dr. Stanley Lovell become head of OSS's Research and Development branch. As the real-life counterpart to James Bond's legendary Q, Lovell had a hand in developing many of the gadgets and special weapons needed to conduct covert warfare.

The day after his meeting with Donovan, Lovell set about recruiting some of America's top scientists and young talent to work with him at the Maryland Research Laboratory. Scientists and other specialists were organized into four divisions: Technical, Camouflage, Documentation, and Special Assistants.

The Technical Division designed and built the specialized weapons used in the field, such as the flourlike "Aunt Jemima," an explosive substance that could be baked into muffins and bread. Then there was the "Casey Jones," an explosive device that could be attached to the underside of railroad cars. When Casey's electronic eye sensed a sharp reduction of light, such as when the train entered a tunnel, the device detonated, and blew off the car's wheels. By derailing long lines of train cars in tunnels, where they had to be removed by hand, Casey could block rail lines for days at a time. In the event the device was found, an official-looking warning sticker was attached to the device that read in German: "This is a Car Movement Control Device. Removal or tampering is strictly forbidden under heaviest penalties by the Third Reich Railroad Consortium. Heil Hitler."[2]

OSS scientists also developed the "Beano" grenade, a far more lethal alternative to the conventional hand grenade. Twenty-four-year-old Al Polson was a leading person behind the Beano.

"I did a lot of the testing on the Beano 'baseball' grenade. We had 12 or 15 man-sized paper silhouettes and we'd detonate a standard black powder grenade and count the holes. Then I would throw a Beano which had a butterfly on the top of the grenade. You throw it like a baseball and the wind would catch under the butterflies and pull a pin out and it would explode once it contacted something. Unlike a regular army grenade, you didn't have a second or two to throw it back. The way it killed people was that it stunned them first and then sent little pieces of steel into their internal organs such as the kidneys and heart and they would die. We loaded the Beano with TNT, which packed about twice the explosive force of a typical grenade. The Beano vaporized the steel frame on some of the silhouettes. I was horrified when one person died mishandling the grenade. An army engineer giving a lecture on the grenade said it could be handled like any normal baseball. During the lecture he threw it up in the air over his head. The grenade armed, and when he stepped under the grenade to catch it he was blown apart by the explosion."[3]

Silenced high-standard pistols, submachine guns, dart guns, and other weapons were developed for OSS field operations. Uniquely, Lovell's scientists created weapons such as the "Stinger," a seemingly innocent-looking three-inch pen that was actually a miniature .22 caliber gun. The labs also produced tobacco pipes that doubled as pistols, and an umbrella pistol. As Polson recalls, "We worked on a little assassin's pistol that was the same size as a pack of Chesterfield cigarettes. One secret agent had a mission where he was sent off to assassinate people and asked, 'So could you put the pistol in my umbrella handle?' So we took a couple of umbrellas and we figured out how to put the gun into the handle of the umbrella. You could have it under your arm and just turn it half a turn and it would go off. The way they would kill people was by putting it right up against a guy's kidney and bam it was gone. If you don't have a kidney—you're gone. If I was doing the stuff today that I did during the war, I would be in jail for 56 consecutive life sentences without a chance for parole."[4]

On the high-tech side, R&D teams worked on projects such as "Javaman." While a Javaman looked like an ordinary boat complete with a rusty sea-battered exterior, the craft was actually a high-powered speedboat that was packed with explosives, designed to infiltrate enemy harbors and sink ships or destroy installations. In one of the first proposed wartime uses of television, the unmanned boat was radio-controlled from a plane and aimed using a television camera mounted on the forward deck. During tests in the Gulf of Mexico, Javaman sent a 5,000-ton derelict ship to the bottom. Several of these craft were sent to the Pacific, but the war ended before they could be used.

Not all of the equipment developed by R&D was grim and deadly. "Who? Me?" was a chemical that smelled like a bowel movement crammed into a toothpaste-sized tube. Japanese soldiers took great pains to defecate in private since it was considered shameful to do it in public, even in combat situations. According to Lovell, 'Who? Me?' was distributed to children in Chinese cities like Peking, Shanghai, and Canton. When a Japanese officer, preferably of high rank, came walking down a crowded sidewalk, little Chinese boys and girls would slip up behind him and squirt a shot of 'Who? Me?' at his trouser seat . . . it cost the Japanese a world of face."[5] The substance could only be removed with dry cleaning chemicals.

Camouflage Division personnel provided everything an agent needed for undercover work in the field. Dental work, eyeglasses, and clothing were scrutinized on a microscopic level. The division created a variety of surreptitious accoutrements such as lipstick and buttons with hidden compartments. Shoes were crafted with heel and sole cavities, and women's corsets were equipped with razor-sharp stilettos.

Camouflage Division also developed weapons that looked like everyday objects. For example, they hid explosives in lumps of coal, which were to be thrown into a train's coal car. These "poison pills" looked just like coal, but they exploded when shoveled into the train's boiler. Then there were the candlesticks that exploded when the wick burned to a predetermined level.

The Documentation Division created work permits, chauffeur's licenses, and identity papers. Engraving shops were set up in the United States and overseas to produce the documents needed on missions. The division even produced nearly perfect duplicates of the metal Gestapo badge that conferred unlimited power on its bearer.

The final R&D unit was the Special Assistants Division. Among other things, the unit created "L," "K," and "TD" pills. "L" stood for "lethal" and could be administered in the event of capture for "self-termination" to "preclude the possibility of revealing information under the strain of interrogation and torture."[6] Biting down on the capsule and ingesting its contents caused instant death, otherwise the rubber-coated capsule could be swallowed and passed harmlessly through an agent's body. Tragically, a number of OSS agents were forced to use the deadly pill. "K" pills were liquid knockout drops, while "TD" (truth drug) tablets were an early form of truth serum derived from narcotics.

OSS assembled a committee of prestigious psychologists and neurologists to develop the truth drug. After reviewing half a dozen drugs, the committee selected tetrahydrocannabinol acetate, a derivative of India hemp. In trials, cigarettes laced with the drug successfully loosened the tongues of test subjects. The most extraordinary experiment was conducted by a former New York City detective, Captain George White: "On May 27, 1943, I conducted a field test with cigarettes containing Loewe's acetate upon a subject who did not know he was the subject of experimentation and who, because of his position, had numerous secrets he was most anxious to conceal, the revelation of which might well result in his imprisonment.

"This subject's alias is Augie Dallas, alias Dell, alias Little Augie. Subject is about 46 years of age, in good health, and is an occasional user of opium. He is known as a 'pleasure' smoker, which means that while he is not addicted to the use of opium he might smoke once or twice during a month.

"[Little Augie] is a notorious New York gangster, and in his youth has served prison sentences for felonious assault and murder. In 1936, he was imprisoned in a concentration camp in Germany for a two-year period on narcotic law charges. For the past 20 years he has been one of the outstanding international narcotic dealers and smugglers and at one time operated an opium alkaloid factory in Turkey. He is a leader of the Italian underworld in the Lower East Side of New York City, where he resides and owns considerable property.

"On several occasions I have arrested this subject but was never able to obtain sufficient evidence to warrant a conviction.

"In connection with a plan to utilize members of New York Italian underground in SO and SI operations in Italy, I have had frequent occasion to talk intimately with the subject during the past six weeks. During the course of these conversations, we have also frequently discussed the narcotics situation in New York in general terms. Upon no occasion did he show willingness to provide any concrete information whatsoever which might be of value to the government as evidence against narcotic law violators. [Augie] prides himself on the fact that he has never been an informer and that he has been instrumental in killing some persons who have been informants. He is intimately acquainted with all the major criminals in the New York area.

"On the day of the experiment, I requested [Augie] to visit me at my apartment in New York on the pretext that I wanted to talk further about plans to utilize his services in Italy. I had previously prepared cigarettes of the same brand I knew him to smoke loaded with both .04 grams of Loewe's acetate and .02 grams of Loewe's acetate. [Augie] entered the apartment at 2:00 p.m. and at that time stated that he could not remain long as he had a friend waiting for him in an automobile outside. After a short conversation regarding the pretext on which he had come to the apartment, I gave him a .04 cigarette at 2:10 p.m. At 2:30 p.m., having noticed no perceptible effects, I gave him a .02 cigarette. Shortly thereafter [Augie] became obviously 'high' and extremely garrulous. He monopolized the conversation and was exceedingly friendly. I turned the conversation into 'Enforcement' channels, whereupon with no further encouragement subject divulged the following information.

"A prominent enforcement official had been receiving a bribe over a period of years from [Augie] and his associates.

"The place formerly occupied by 'Lucky' Luciano in the American underworld has now been taken over by a 'combination' headed by: Meyer Lansky, Frank Costello, Longie Zwillman, Willie Moretti."[7]

OSS R&D was also involved in developing biological weapons of mass destruction. In a recently declassified top-secret memorandum, R&D scientist James Hamilton wrote: "Six months ago I collected data which indicated that a very rare bacterium (provisionally designated 'peach fuzz') would be particularly useful for bacterial warfare. Through Dr. Rogers, I was put in touch with the secret BW [Biological Warfare] Committee and transmitted the information to them. Later, Stanley Lovell was appraised of the organism's possibilities.

"After considerable pressure from Lovell and myself, [the BW Committee's chairman] finally assembled a group of experts to evaluate the organism. The unanimous opinion was that the organism had tremendous possibilities, and might prove to be a most lethal BW weapon.

"The most difficult problem which developed was that of producing large quantities of the material. At our suggestion the Committee set up an extensive research project to solve this problem, and a man selected by us was put in charge. Chemical Warfare is ready and anxious to go into mass production within the next two or three months, or as soon as production methods are worked out on a large scale."[8]

Perhaps the Special Assistants' most farcical plan involved lacing Hitler's food with estrogen. An OSS operative with access to Hitler was to inject the female sex hormone into the Führer's vegetarian diet of carrots and beets. Lovell provided a tongue-in-cheek recollection of the projected outcome: "His poor emotional control, his violent passions, his selection of companions like Röhm, all led me to feel that a push to the female side might do wonders. The hope was that his moustache would fall off and his voice become soprano."[9] It is unlikely that the scheme went much beyond high-level planning.

While R&D was making the weapons and gadgets OSS personnel used in the field, the Research and Analysis branch analyzed the information OSS gathered. OSS initiated the concept of a structured research and analysis division. At the time, independent strategic intelligence analysis was virtually nonexistent in most of the world's intelligence organizations.[10]

Known as "The Campus," this "chairborne" division was staffed by more than nine hundred scholars, practically a *Who's Who* of the leading academic minds in America. R&A was unlike the OSS's other branches. As historian Robin W. Winks put it, "SI [Secret Intelligence] and X-2 [counterespionage] were the coaches, the clever men, the quarterbacks, while SO housed the rest of the jocks. R&A gave refuge to the glassy-eyed students who came out to cheer the team on and who burrowed in the libraries, moles of a kind."[11]

Instead of guns or knives, the bespectacled economists, historians, political scientists, and anthropologists wielded 3x5 index cards against the Axis, gleaning crucial intelligence from the raw data obtained by

OSS's operational arms. New filing systems were created and micro-film was employed. Most importantly, R&A created a methodology for studying intelligence. Teams of scholars were assigned problems, something virtually unheard of on prewar college campuses. The teams produced reports on a wide variety of topics ranging from German economic war production to Hitler's state of mind.

Headed by William Langer, R&A stressed the importance of "objective and neutral" reports, and use of the team method checked by peer review and under supervisory control.[12] But in spite of Langer's best efforts to remain objective and neutral, some branches of the government and military viewed R&A as a hotbed of radicalism. R&A produced over 3,000 formal research studies and 3,000 maps.[13]

OSS economists, working in a group known as the Enemy Objectives Unit (EOU), played a key role in the Allies' precision bombing campaign against Germany. Using empirical data gathered from a variety of intelligence sources, the EOU determined which targets should be attacked to maximize damage on the Third Reich's industrial infrastructure.

The EOU, created in 1942, was housed in the American embassy in London. Fifteen professional economists, all but two from OSS, served in the group. One of the mainsprings of the organization was 26-year-old Rhodes Scholar Walter Rostow, who recalls the evolving methodology the group created: "We sought [to create] target systems where the destruction of the minimum number of targets would have the greatest, most prompt, and most long lasting direct military effect on the battlefield. . . . The EOU view was, then, a doctrine of warfare, not of economics or politics."[14]

Charles Kindleberger, another key player in the EOU, reveals the evolving nature of target selection within the Reich: "There was an industry called 'abrasives,' using carborundum to polish steel. [One camp] held that 'if you only attack grinding wheel plants, you will win the war.' We thought that was crazy because the smoothing of steel was way back in the process, and substitution could make up for the losses. So, you have a substantial cushion and repair time. Those were the two issues. We thought that attacking the airplane industry would do this. . . . I was wrong: we thought the ball bearings would be a good target, but German industry redesigned the process. They hand-carried ball bearings to the assembly line. We were wrong on that. On the other hand we were right on with oil."[15]

Oil was an essential limiting factor on the effectiveness of Second World War armies. The EOU helped create a strategy that enabled the Allied strategic bombing campaign to inflict significant damage on Germany's oil production.* Ultimately, the bombing idled thousands of tanks and planes.

Another puzzle that R&A solved was how to make an accurate estimate of German tank production, which the British estimated was as high as 2,000 per month in 1942. The Germans knew Allied spies were monitoring the tank factories, so they staggered the serial numbers on the tanks they produced, not using all the numbers in a given sequence of consecutive numbers. British troops in North Africa provided R&A analyst Sidney Alexander with the key to the puzzle: a register of all tanks in a specific German tank regiment. Alexander combined this report with other information to produce a revised tank production figure significantly lower than the British estimate. This thread of information, in turn, allowed R&A to produce accurate German order of battle numbers, providing the Allies with a clearer picture of German strength in the field. During the height of the Allied bombing offensive R&A was able to determine, contrary to other reports, that tank production was actually increasing rather then declining.[16]

---

*Oil was only part of the solution. Postwar studies reveal that 90 percent of Germany's energy needs were sustained by brown coal and 90 pecent of the coal was transported by Germany's railroads.[17] Allied bombing of Germany's transportation network, known as the Transportation Plan, had a crippling effect on Germany's military capacity. At the time no one, including the EOU, made the connection between the coal, synthetic oil, and the Reich's rail network.

Some of R&A's earliest reports focused on North Africa. Walter Rostow recalls: "We did Northwest Africa because the Germans were coming into North Africa. That was a turnaround. Then as the Germans were lining up to go into southern Russia, we said, 'How far will they go?' Well, to do that, we had to get very dirty with logistics. We studied the logistics of the Germans at land and sea. We knew exactly how many tons of ammunition you needed. If you came by truck, how many were needed. . . .

"But the point we established was that logistics was the heart of a military affair. You could figure out German logistics by extrapolation. These exercises taught us a lot about the German army and how it worked and the tonnages that were involved and so on."[18]

In the R&A department of OSS, some of America's brightest scholars put forth their best efforts for the war effort.

THREE

Intrigue in North Africa and Iberia

"4 Left 5

3 Right 20

2 Left 95

1 Right 2

Stop . . .

"I entered the naval room of the French Embassy at 1:00 a.m. with Mrs. Gordon and a specialist in safes who was brought from New York by the [OSS]. Under the most dangerous conditions, the combination was solved and the safe opened. . . . the naval cipher book was delivered to an agent, who came to the door of the chancery, had the pages photostatted and came back at 4:40 a.m."[1] So wrote Charles Brousse, a press attaché at the Vichy French embassy in Washington, D.C. and a spy working for OSS.

Some of the most important OSS operations affecting North Africa and Spain actually took place in Washington, D.C. In March 1942, Donovan began to send teams of men and women to break into Washington embassies. The teams were pulling off what were known as "black bag" jobs, pilfering cipher and code books and recruiting Vichy and Spanish diplomats like Brousse. Even with Americans dying overseas, the diplomatic and legal risks incurred by breaking into foreign embassies potentially outweighed the value of the information the penetrations might yield, so the break-ins had to be approved at the highest levels. The theft of the Vichy ciphers was authorized by the Joint Chiefs. Donovan presented all important materials—office memos and telegrams—directly to President Roosevelt.[2]

The British Security Coordination (BSC), the North American arm of British intelligence, initially conducted the break-ins, until a new law known as the McKellar Act placed limits on British activities in the United States. BSC chief William Stephenson wisely decided to turn the bulk of the work over to Donovan. Most of the embassy teams were managed by Donald Downs, a former prep school teacher whose only intelligence experience involved limited work with the Office of Naval Intelligence in Turkey. Described by his peers as more of an adventurer than a spy, Downs nevertheless was a rising star in the new agency.

By the summer of 1942, Donovan's organization, now called OSS, had several black bag jobs in play. Downs had people in the Argentine embassy. A young Spaniard, Ricardo Sicre, penetrated the Spanish embassy. According to Downs, Sicre was "the handsomest man I've ever seen." Equipped with wads of money, Sicre first seduced the embassy's unsuspecting secretaries, and then his team broke into the embassy at night. After cracking the safe, the men carried out four large suitcases of photographed documents.

The most spectacular black bag job was Brousse's and Mrs. Gordon's work in the Vichy French embassy. "Mrs. Gordon" was actually the super-agent "Cynthia," who worked jointly for the BSC and OSS. "Cynthia," whose real name was Elizabeth "Betty" Pack, seduced a number of men in the line of duty.

Pack was tall, slim, and beautiful. She had led a life of privilege, was educated in the United States and Europe, and summered with the elites in Newport, Rhode Island. Her charm and sophistication instantly attracted most of the men she met.

Cynthia made her grand espionage debut in Poland in 1938. As the wife of Arthur Pack, the British commercial secretary in Warsaw, Betty had access to men in power. Her relationship with her husband had soured and they were in the middle of a divorce. Adventurous and full of restless energy, Pack contacted the British secret service to see if she could use her contacts and position to gather information. The British at first were reticent but recognized her potential.

In Warsaw, Pack used her beauty and charm to seduce Michal Lubienski, a Pole with information on Polish cryptanalysis efforts. For a number of years Poland had been secretly trying to break the German cipher system known as Enigma. Pack was one of the agents responsible for discovering that the Poles had developed a high-speed calculating machine and vital keys needed for breaking Enigma. Pack's information on Poland's Enigma program would later prove helpful to British code-breaking efforts.

Over a year later, Pack returned to America and plied her powers of seduction again, this time in the service of the BSC. In New York she scored a major intelligence coup: her affair with an Italian admiral led to the capture of the Italian naval codes. The official BSC history states it succinctly: "He [the Italian admiral] put her in touch with his own cipher clerk, who produced the ciphers after a suitable financial agreement could be reached."[3] What the British did with the material Cynthia provided is harder to determine, but information gleaned from the ciphers may have been partially responsible for the British victory at Cape Matapan in March 1941, which crippled the Italian navy for the remainder of the war.

Her next assignment was the joint BSC/OSS effort to penetrate the Vichy embassy, which would prove invaluable to the upcoming invasion of Vichy French North Africa. Cynthia was to cultivate a relationship with an embassy official and secure information and cipher books. Posing as a pro-Vichy freelance writer, she met Ambassador Gaston Henry-Haye and his press attaché, Charles Brousse. Brousse, instantly smitten by Cynthia's charm and beauty, sent her a dozen roses the next day. She responded by making love to him in her Georgetown home.

Cynthia became Brousse's case officer and lover. Through Brousse, intelligence started flowing in the form of daily reports. The next step was more difficult: finding a way to photograph the ciphers without the embassy staff knowing about it.

A complex plan was devised that called for Brousse and Cynthia to befriend the embassy guard and convince him that they needed to use the embassy for a tryst. When he wasn't looking they would drug him and the embassy guard dog. Next, an OSS safecracker would pick the lock on the naval attaché's room and crack the safe that contained the cipher books. (When the need arose, safecrackers and other criminals with a specific expertise were plucked from prisons by the OSS and given the opportunity to reduce or eliminate their sentences in return for their services.) The codebooks would be given to a team waiting outside the embassy, photographed, and returned before dawn and the arrival of Vichy personnel.

Brousse beguiled the guard by pleading that using a hotel for meetings with Cynthia could arouse the suspicions of his wife, who might call him while he was supposedly "working" late at night. The watchman agreed to make the embassy available to the couple.

On June 19, 1942, Cynthia and Brousse made their first attempt to steal the ciphers. The couple swaggered into the embassy with several bottles of champagne. Telling the guard that it was their first anniversary, they offered him a glass of bubbly, which he gladly accepted. Cynthia slipped Nembutal, a sleep-inducing barbiturate, into his second glass. Another dose went into the guard dog's water bowl. Within minutes both canine and watchman were out cold. Next, Cynthia opened the front door, and gave a prearranged signal. The "Georgia Cracker," a safecracker working for the OSS, sauntered through the front door. The Cracker easily picked the lock on the naval attaché's office door and went to work on the safe containing the Bible-sized cipher books. At around 4:00 a.m., he solved the combination and pulled out the books. But it was too late to copy the books; within two hours embassy personnel would be arriving for work. Reluctantly, Betty placed the ciphers back into the safe, and the group left the embassy before guard or hound awoke.

A few nights later Cynthia and Brousse returned to the embassy and the unsuspecting watchman allowed them once again to enter. Drugging the guard again would have been too risky, so after waiting about an hour, Cynthia picked the lock on the naval attaché's door and opened a window for the safecracker to enter. Sensing that the guard would return to investigate their activities, she stripped completely naked except for her pearl necklace and high heels and hissed at Charles to undress as she started to kiss him. Suddenly the door swung open, and the guard's flashlight shone upon the naked lovers. Sheepishly, the watchman stammered, "I beg your pardon a thousand times, madame. I thought . . . ," and he closed the door.[4]

As the door closed, the Georgia Cracker scrambled up a wooden ladder and climbed through the open window. Deftly, his fingers turned the tumblers and opened the safe. The agents handed the cipher books to a confederate waiting in the alley below the window, who whisked them away to a waiting OSS team. Several hundred pages were photographed and the books safely returned before dawn.

All OSS embassy break-ins eventually ceased after Sicre's teams crossed wires with an FBI team that was also infiltrating the Spanish embassy. Neither team knew about the other's operation. Sicre's men were making their final foray into the embassy's safe room to photograph the last batch of documents when they accidentally blundered into the FBI team. Fortunately, Sicre's men were able to scurry out of the embassy before they could be apprehended by the D.C. police, who were responding to a report of a burglary attempt. The incident resulted in FBI control of all future black bag work.

The importance of the ciphers to the Allied invasion of North Africa will never be fully known. But after the landings took place, Cynthia was told by her case officer and subsequent commander of the OSS detachment in North Africa, "American and British troops landed in North Africa, and have met practically no resistance. The reason there has been no resistance is a military secret. But I think that you should know that it is due to your ciphers. They have changed the course of the whole war."[5]

America's covert activity in North Africa proper had begun over a year earlier with a trade agreement between the United States and Vichy France. Signed in March 1941, the Murphy-Weygand accord allowed the Vichy government to buy badly needed non-military goods and foodstuffs from the United States. To ensure that the trade goods were not diverted to Germany, 12 American vice-consuls, or monitors, were stationed in North Africa. By late 1941, all 12 monitors were working with COI. Eight would later become OSS agents.

Known as Murphy's "Twelve Apostles" (for Robert Murphy, the leading State Department official on the team), the group was a mixed bag of characters including an oil man, a Coca-Cola branch manager, a librarian, and a former member of the French Foreign Legion. German intelligence dismissed the group as "a perfect picture of the mixture of races and characters in that savage conglomeration called the United States"[6] However, the Apostles proved highly effective. They got into the spy game quickly, setting up radio stations in Tangiers, Algiers, Tunis, and Oran that reported Vichy French troop movements and other military intelligence. COI and later OSS personnel were also gradually added to the group.

The OSS contact with the Apostles was 53-year-old Marine Corps Colonel William Eddy, who arrived under the cover title of naval attaché at Tangiers. Eddy was an ideal candidate for the mission. Born in Syria of missionary parents, he spoke fluent Arabic and was a distinguished scholar and war hero who had lost a leg in the First World

War. Eddy was introduced to Major General George Patton at a dinner party in London. Patton could not help but notice Eddy's five rows of World War I ribbons and decorations and remarked: "I don't know who he is but that son-of-a-bitch's been shot at enough, hasn't he?"[7]

As Eddy was setting up shop, the British and Americans began to dispute operational control of intelligence and special operations in North Africa. As the senior intelligence partner, the British wanted to be in charge. Donovan, however, insisted that North Africa should be an OSS operation. He noted that America would spearhead the invasion, that British nationals were banned from operating in North Africa, and that through the Murphy-Weygand treaty America already possessed an existing intelligence network. Ultimately, North Africa was designated OSS turf in an agreement known as the Donovan-Hambro accords, which created a framework for conducting SOE and OSS special operations and defined British and U.S. operating areas. SOE remained physically separate but continued operating under the general direction of the OSS.

With the turf war in North Africa more or less settled, the OSS and the Apostles prepared for the invasion. A major concern was the possibility of a German-Spanish invasion of French North Africa from Tunisia and Spanish Morocco. Accordingly, Eddy formed chains of informants to gather intelligence, spread subversive propaganda, and organize a resistance movement. Among the collaborators were "Strings," the leader of a powerful Muslim brotherhood in northern Morocco, and "Tassels," a leader in the Rif (a coastal area between Spanish and French Morocco). Guided by OSS, the networks gathered important intelligence on ports, landing beaches, and key military targets.

The OSS agent most responsible for cultivating the embryonic resistance movement and intelligence network was Harvard anthropologist Carleton Coon. Coon was an expert on the region. Beginning in the 1920s, Coon had made several expeditions to North Africa, where

OSS Operations in North Africa

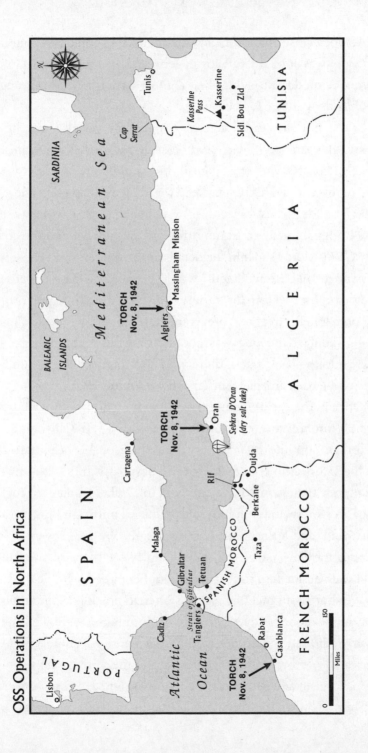

he developed close relationships with the native people and their leaders. Coon was joined by fellow agent and lifelong friend Gordon Browne. Coon describes their first contact with the Muslim leader in the Rif, code-named "Tassels."

"It was not easy to arrange meetings with Tassels, since he is a well-known man and if he should be seen with us by the Spanish or anyone in contact with the Spanish, he would be shot. He was well aware of this and did his best to keep these meetings secret. The usual system was for Gusus to see him by coincidence in the Tingis café, where both habitually sat at noontime, to eat lunch and drink coffee. There Gusus would slip him the details of the rendezvous. These were always nocturnal. Browne and I would get out the car, or if possible borrow some other car for variety. We would be at a prearranged place on a lonely street at a prearranged hour, and would see Tassels walking along. If no one was about, we would stop and get him quickly into the back seat; if there were too many people around, we would come back and pick him up a few minutes later.

"Once in the car we would transform him. Sometimes we would turn him into a *Fatma,* or Arab woman, with a veil. Other times we would turn him into a *shaush,* with a tall fez on his head garnished with the U.S. seal in gold metal, or the naval attaché's seal—thus we were merely taking one of our servants to a villa to wait on a cocktail party. Later we would shift him to a Spaniard, putting a European hat on his head, and a European coat over him. We never were able to eliminate the baggy trousers, but when we got out of the car we would walk beside him so that these would not be so visible.

"We shifted our meeting place as often as possible. Sometimes we saw him in Colonel Eddy's villa on the mountain, where we kept the Midway radio set; sometimes at el Farhar Pension, a hotel run by an American, Winthrop Buckingham; sometimes in the home of an obliging British lady, Mrs. Bertram Thomas. Once, when we were to meet him at Mrs. Thomas's, I was stationed to lie under the rose bushes near the entrance to her garden, to lead him in when he should appear at the gate. Colonel Eddy, Mrs. Thomas, and Browne were on the roof. I lay in the bushes next to a reed fence, and spiders and ants crawled over me and spun webs over me. Meanwhile a pair of Spanish lovers lay down on the other side of the fence; I was treated to all their physiological noises as well as their periodic inane conversation. Finally, after what seemed to me a distinguished effort (compared to the graph on sexual intercourse published by Boaz and Goldschmitt in 'The Heart Rate,' *American Journal of Physiology*), they left, and I was able to move and brush off a few cobwebs. I retired to the roof and Gordon made a sortie, finally picking up Tassels, who was wandering about lost several blocks away.

"During these meetings we laid our plans for the revolt of the Riffians if needed, and plotted the landing of troops, the dropping of parachutists, the delivery of guns, the cutting off of roads and garrisons, etc. We laid on a system of signals by which the Riffians were to assemble and seize various key positions, and to await our arrival. . . .

"Tassels gave us much combat intelligence, battle order, troop movements, etc., in great detail, and most of this we passed on to Colonel Johnson, the military attaché, who sent it on to G-2 in Washington. Most of it checked with other sources; it was seldom that Tassels was inaccurate. . . ."[8]

While OSS continued to nurture a North African resistance movement, a greater issue still remained: how to seize French North Africa without provoking armed resistance from the Vichy French. Weeks before the invasion, Murphy and Eddy secretly contacted the Vichy high command in North Africa, in an attempt to forestall French resistance to the landings. The Vichy commanders feared German retaliation and occupation of the rest of France (Vichy France at the time was not occupied by German troops). The final clandestine meeting with high-ranking French officers occurred when Ike's deputy, Major

General Mark Clark, and several other senior American officers were dropped off at an isolated beach house about 75 miles from Algiers by the former French submarine *Seraph*. After paddling ashore in flimsy canvas dinghies, Clark and company were greeted by Murphy and another vice-consul, Ridgeway Knight, and the chief of staff of the French XIX Corps, Major General Charles Mast. After a four and a half hour meeting, Mast agreed to cooperate, and provided Clark with "extremely valuable" intelligence.[9]

As the meeting was coming to a close, local police received a tip that something was afoot at the beach house. Clark's men frantically burned their papers and hid in a foul-smelling wine cellar. After a hasty search the police left, and Clark's group began the journey back to the sub.[10]

"Ecoute! Robert Arrive!" These code words transmitted by the BBC signaled the start of the Allied invasion of North Africa on the morning of November 8, 1942. Code-named Torch, the trident-shaped attack landed amphibious forces along the sprawling North African coast. The invasion achieved total surprise. On the ground, Mast and other French commanders with Allied leanings were informed shortly before Allied troops started landing, too late to seize control of key individuals and installations. Mast managed to slow the Vichy response to the invasion, but pandemonium reigned as officers with pro-Allied leanings attempted to take over the Vichy government. Their efforts were suppressed and Vichy France decided to fight back. Hundreds of French and American lives were needlessly sacrificed by the decision.

During the early hours of the invasion, OSS personnel severed Vichy communications, sabotaged military targets, and guided Allied troops to landing areas. Gordon Browne recalls his attempt to bring Edson Raff's 509th Parachute Infantry Battalion to key drop zones near airfields using a top secret radio beacon known as Rebecca.

"As evening approached, I rejoined the family and hung around the radio waiting for the BBC broadcast in French. Soon it came, about 8:50

p.m. and at the end was the crucial message I had been waiting so long to hear. 'Attention Yankee, Attention Franklin, Attention Lincoln, Robert Arrive.' Yankee was Algiers, Franklin was Oran and us, Lincoln was Casablanca, Robert was the Torch Operation—arriving as scheduled. One of my men looked at me as I jumped up. I told him that tonight was the big night. He said, 'Jesus, is it true?' He rushed out shouting for his wife, 'Marie! Marie!' He came back with a gun strapped to his belt, a French campaign hat on his head saying, 'My friend, Browne, I am with you, whatever it is. Thank God, Thank God.' Just then two French ambulances drove up, part of the plan laid on by Ridgeway Knight. . . .

"Rebecca balanced on my knee, Sten in my hands, we bounced over bumpy roads to the appointed place (x), and I was relieved to find that the good-looking French girl driving the ambulance had a map with (x) on the same place as mine. We were stopped a couple of times by French patrols, but passed safely, the second time after some argument with a French sergeant, handled by our girl driver. At these stops, and when passing lights, we all crowded down on the floor, ready to shoot it out if necessary. After what seemed a long, long time, we stopped, got out, found our direction by compass, and were left in the inky black night as the ambulances drove off.

"We walked our 1,000 paces, then our 1,500, and there we were at (x). I had been told by Radio in Tangier to start Rebecca going at 11:30, and that the planes were due at 1:00 a.m. GMT time. . . . Rebecca all set up—connections checked five times, hook-ups checked up, we waited for 11:30. It finally arrived, zero hour plus one and one-half hours and Rebecca was turned on; 12:00 arrived; 12:30, 1:00 a.m. Nothing stirred except the bicycle patrols and they didn't come near. It was very quiet, a few snipe or plover called, and there was a faint hum from Rebecca. Zero hour arrived—nothing happened—2:00 a.m., 2:30 a.m., 3:00 a.m., nothing happened. Then coastal guns opened up— heavy stuff—and big naval guns—colored lights shot up in the dis-

tance all around us. No planes—we got jittery. It was quite a feeling to
be the focal point of the spearhead attack—to know that for the moment I was of great importance. The heavy guns fluctuated in their
firing—moving further away. Marcel and I looked at each other with a
great and overwhelming despair. We found that we were all thinking
the same thing—that the great invasion had failed, that the fleet had
been intercepted by the Germans and French and driven off, that the
planes had been intercepted and knocked down, and we had no orders. False dawn was approaching; the sky was getting gray in the
East. Never again in my life time will I feel as low as I did then, I am
sure. Five o'clock, no buzzing in the skies, only Rebecca percolating
with a faint hum like a plane in the far distance. We shook hands with
our Spaniards, and told them to scatter, everyone for himself, and to
keep their mouths shut. They were brave men."[11]

Most of the paratroopers never arrived on Browne's drop zone.
Headwinds scattered the paratroopers' 39 C-47 Dakotas throughout
North Africa with some planes even landing in Franco's Spanish Morocco. Eventually several planes managed to land or drop paratroopers near the airdromes but American ground troops had already
secured the area.

Fortunately, Vichy military resistance to Torch effectively ended
on November 10, when a deal was struck with the ranking Vichy official in North Africa, Admiral Darlan.[12] A notorious collaborator, Darlan stalled for two days and only stopped the fighting in exchange for
joint administration of North Africa. The agreement did not sit well
with de Gaulle's Free French forces, and many Americans denounced
it as a sellout to Fascism. The issue was ultimately settled by a bullet.
On December 24, 1942, Darlan was assassinated by Fernand Bonnier
de la Chapelle, a de Gaulle supporter who had been trained by the
SOE and Carleton Coon. The SOE and Coon connection has been a
continuous source of controversy since the end of the war, but recently uncovered evidence suggests de la Chapelle was acting indepen-

dently. Nevertheless the anthropologist/agent was asked to disappear for a while and was relocated to the remote Tunisian SOE base camp at Cape Serrat.[13]

No one seemed to miss Darlan. Churchill summed up the assassination in his six-volume history of World War II: "Darlan's murder, however criminal, relieved the Allies of their embarrassment at working with him, and at the same time left them with all the advantages he had been able to bestow during the vital hours of the Allied landings."[14]

As 1942 came to a close, a patchwork of American, French, and British units spread across the North African desert was slowly pushing the Germans into Tunis, the main port in Tunisia, while General Montgomery's Eighth Army was squeezing the Germans from the east. The OSS office was moved to Algiers, where a special mission code-named Massingham was established by the SOE. The two organizations worked together with the British First Army and American divisions on missions to gather tactical intelligence and sabotage enemy communications and transportation.

Instead of withdrawing from Tunisia, Hitler became obsessed with holding it to buy time to build up defenses in Europe. Axis reinforcements streamed into Tunis. The desert war in Tunisia became fluid, with forces spread out over long distances. It became an outpost war. Each side conducted raids on enemy outposts in an effort to keep the other side off balance.

One of those remote outposts was Carleton Coon's Cap Serrat. Donning a British captain's uniform and the assumed name of Captain Retinitis, Coon commanded a mixed group of French, Arab, and American guerrillas. His band of 50 desperadoes raided and gathered intelligence on nearby German and Italian outposts. At Cap Serrat, Coon perfected his explosive "mule turds," specially sculpted explosives that could destroy truck tires or knock a track off a light tank.

"Mule turds were to be found in great abundance . . . we added a few samples of local mule dung, and this was carefully packed and sent to London. We took care to explain that the full, rich horse dung of the British countryside would not do in Morocco; it was the more watery, smaller mule type that would pass there without suspicion. Also, it was important to have it a deep sepia color, sometimes with greenish shades, the product of straw and grass, not of oats and hay. In due course of time the British London office made up explosive turds from these samples, and we used them to good effect later in Tunisia."[15]

Using an abandoned lighthouse as a base camp, Coon and his motley crew sowed the roads with turds, destroyed a bridge, and conducted raids on a nearby Italian outpost. The locals were put to work gathering intelligence. Coon used hostages to stiffen loyalty. "When we entered a distant village where loyalty was wavering we would take the eldest son of the most important man and hold him in the lighthouse pending his father's arrival. The old man inevitably came, with gifts, demanding his son. He was sent back to get good information on enemy positions, and when he came back the second time his son would be released if the information was satisfactory."[16]

In late January the Afrika Korps launched a counteroffensive, culminating in the 10th Panzer Division smashing green American troops at Sidi Bou Zid. Entire Allied units fled the battlefield, withdrawing toward Kasserine Pass.

In the chaos of the German offensive, OSS agents were thrust into the front lines and misused as infantry. A mixed group of French, Arab, and American guerrillas led by Carleton Coon linked up with the members of OSS's first Special Operations team, under the command of Captain Jerry Sage. Sage's SO team had been tasked by Donald Downs to recruit Spanish refugees in North Africa for covert work in Spain.

Sage, a former football player from Washington State University, was a youthful officer in command of a group of OSS agents who were actually slated for operations in Spain. Five of Sage's men were Americans who fought in the Abraham Lincoln Brigade during the Spanish Civil War in the 1930s and were members of the Communist

Party of the USA. The other half of the group were part of the Union Democratica Espanola (UDE), which acted as the Spanish Republican government in exile.

The Lincoln Brigade veterans had been handpicked by Donovan to form the core of a team tasked, under the overall leadership of Donald Downs, to recruit Spanish refugees in North Africa for covert work in Spain. Given the fluid situation in Tunisia, Downs's operation was put on hold.

The group also included OSS's first African-American operator, a Corporal Drake. Drake's membership in OSS was purely happenstance since OSS, and the rest of America's armed forces, had not been integrated. Shortly after arriving in North Africa, Sage tried to procure a 6x6 truck to carry the men but was told by the ordnance officer that "you can't get the truck without the driver."[17] Sage retained the enthusiastic corporal, training him in knife fighting and explosives.

Eddy needed special operators, so the Downs team moved to the front, joined Coon's men, and the OSS agents went about "helping the Army destroy anything destroyable." The men sowed explosive camel turds, blew up a bridge, and destroyed a German fuel dump.

Most line commanders had no idea how to utilize the OSS men. Coon recalls being called on to flip Molotov cocktails on the approaching Panzers. "Colonel Howze . . . said if we boys wanted to do something we could go down front and sit in foxholes and toss petard grenades and Molotov cocktails at the German heavy tanks as they rolled over us. . . . It was not OSS work."[18]

One proposed "suicide mission" required Sage's men to spike four 88 mm guns deep behind German lines and blow up German tanks. He was ordered to "just get behind them and slow them up a bit."

Milton Felsen recalls his last mission, to reconnoiter a pass swarming with German troops and tanks. "I got a bullet through my left ear, and the ear bleeds profusely. Irv Goff comes over and bandages me and fixes my ear. However, he put a white bandage around my head, it was dusk and that God damned white bandage was visible to the Germans. I was the target. So wherever I went I was shot at by the Germans. I vividly remember the bullets and shells from their tanks were flying by my head.

"As we were scrambling forward we saw tank tracks in the sand. In the distance I could hear the Arab call to prayer. The Arabs saw us coming and signaled the Germans. Shortly after that I got hit a couple times in the leg, and got hit in the hand. That's when I went down and started to dig. I tried to bury myself in the sand in the hope that the Germans would somehow not see me. Things happened rapidly, it was twilight.

"Sage and I were alone. The roar of tank engines got louder and then time seemed to stop. Things got quiet, several tanks appeared and German soldiers surrounded me. They stripped me. I had stuff on me that was ridiculous: a gun under each arm, a special dagger, a special belt, a vest with hidden pockets made by Abercrombie and Fitch, spy gadgets, all kinds of OSS shit. I knew this was dangerous stuff, [so] when the German soldiers started to strip us I handed them everything I could. I didn't want any of this stuff on me when the Gestapo got to me. I gave them anything that was a tip off that I was OSS.

"That's when the Gestapo started interrogating me. I acted stupid. I said, 'Where are we?' 'What country is this?' 'Do you mind telling me what country we are in?' The Gestapo [man] got bored and he let the doctors tend to me. They turned me over to the Italians."[19]

The German advance was halted after the battle at Kasserine Pass. The U.S. II Corps, now under the command of Lieutenant General George Patton, resumed the offensive, pushing the Germans into a pocket around Tunis. In May 1943, Axis forces in North Africa capitulated, and over 275,000 prisoners were taken in a Stalingrad-sized Allied victory.

North Africa proved to be a valuable proving ground for both the Allied military and OSS. Army investigators would criticize virtually every aspect of the invasion—except for intelligence.[20]

• • •

Throughout the war, Spain and Portugal served as a no-man's-land for the Axis and Allied intelligence services. OSS gained its first foothold in Iberia through a State Department program to monitor the importation of gasoline and fuel oil that was allocated to Spain by the Allies. Much as in North Africa, where vice-consuls doubled as secret intelligence agents, the State Department agreed to use the program in Iberia to insert OSS agents as oil attachés. The men spent half their time ensuring that the gasoline and fuel oil did not flow into Axis hands and the other half spying on Spain and Portugal.

Within both countries OSS expanded by forming substations and networks that gathered information about order of battle, economic aid to the Axis, whether Spain intended to join the Axis, and the possibility of a German invasion.

During the Allied advance on Tunis, Spain remained a constant worry. German troops moving through Spain to Spanish Morocco could derail Torch by cutting Allied supply lines. Fifth Army commander General Mark Clark, in charge of security in the region, described the threat in his memoirs. "We were like a deep-sea diver moving farther and farther from his ship and maintaining only a slim life-line connection with his air pumps, which might be severed by a single, sudden and fatal blow."[21]

To counter the threat of invasion through spain, Clark needed intelligence. Seeing the value of Carleton Coon's "Strings and Tassels" network, he recalled Coon from Tunisia. Donald Downs's team, minus Felsen and Sage, was reconstituted and brought back to Oujda, Algeria. On a remote mountaintop, Downs and his operations chief, Ricardo Sicre, set up a training school under the cover of "Fifth Army Meteorological Station." Downs's men, known as the "Banana" team, fanned out and combed Vichy concentration camps for Spanish Republicans. Thirty-five men were recruited and trained. Several crossed the border to observe what their Nazi intelligence counterparts were up to.

One of Banana's first missions was "Beetroot," a combined OSS-SOE operation to penetrate a Nazi spy camp in Spanish Morocco. Carleton Coon recalls Beetroot.

"Stripes [an agent] in Tangier sent a man through the Tetuan school [German spy school], and he was supposed to cross the border through the Gzennaya, and come to Taza to fire a gasoline dump and blow a bridge. The plan was for us to meet him in Taza, let him make a little fire and pull off a bang, pay him, and send him back. General Clark was not too inclined to let him set anything on fire, but we wanted only to get a few leaking tins and some old oil and rags, and to have the sentries on the bridge fire a few shots. The general said that he would defer his decision until the man had come through. We made plans for the Riffian to present himself to a Corsican garageman named Serrutti, in Taza, but he never came. Many messages passed between Tangier and Oujda on the subject before we gave up."[22]

Downs and Coon were after even bigger fish. The target was the German spymaster in charge of the camp. AKA Harry Wood, Emilio Darrio, or just Carlos, the German's real name was Karl Frick. During the Great War Frick was involved in the destruction of Black Tom, a munitions storage facility located near New York City. "We laid elaborate plans to capture or kill the Germans, and presented them to General Clark; he said that we could not set foot in Spanish territory nor shoot over it; we would have to get the Germans onto French territory before we could touch them. Colonel Parsons, Captain Bourgoin, Legrand, Captain Bachelot and I were to pull the job. But unfortunately, a few days before the meeting was to take place [an Axis sympathizer and double agent] collapsed in the street in Berkane, and had to be carried home where he lay in a coma. He is probably by now dead. It is my belief and that of Captain Bourgoin that [one of our men] had him poisoned, but we cannot prove this. At any rate [agent's] illness prevented our carrying out this very interesting operation. It also saved Frick some painful moments, for Captain Bourgoin had a technique to make him talk, which he practiced on the rest of us for illustration."[23]

OSS oil attachés also participated in setting up networks in Spanish Morocco and Tangiers to monitor Spain's intentions with North Africa. OSS "oil man" Waller Booth recruited a most unlikely agent, the elderly African-American leader of an orchestra called the Perkins Jazz Devils. Henry Perkins had moved to Paris during the Jazz Age. From Paris, Perkins moved to Italy, then Barcelona, and finally Tangiers, where he married a Jewish women half his size. On the Tangiers beachfront, Perkins and his bride built a ramshackle inn they called Uncle Tom's Cabin out of driftwood and began to serve southern-style food.

Perkins's major coup involved obtaining intelligence from a friend who was a janitor at the Tangeria Hotel, a disreputable establishment that served as informal general headquarters for the Spanish army in Morocco as well as a brothel. The janitor informed Perkins that Spain planned to invade French North Africa during the third week of November, but the plans were dropped after the Allied invasion. Perkins later watched shipping at the port of Tangiers. According to O. C. Doering, a high-level OSS agent in Spain, Perkins was relieved of his agent duties "for breaking rule number 1 of the agent code: he spent his new pay on an elegant super-zoot costume with whipcord riding breeches, a tweed jacket with stock, and a Panama hat set at a rakish angle over his graying curls."[24]

With the May 1943 capitulation of Axis forces in North Africa, the threat of a backdoor Axis invasion of North Africa through Spain subsided. However, a swift Spanish invasion could still sever the Allied supply line. With the approval of Fifth Army, OSS began to penetrate Spain from North Africa.

The first operation was launched from Oujda into Spain in June 1943. Downs's first agent was Ignacio Lopez Dominguez, code-named "Dick." Dick organized an intelligence network that was code-named Banana I.

OSS Operations in Iberia

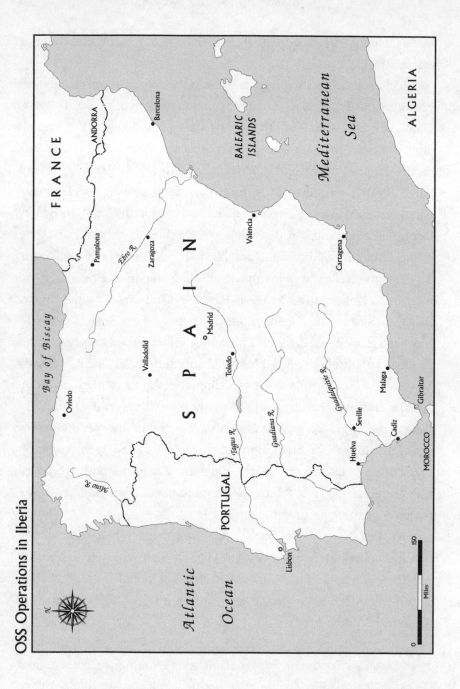

The network expanded and more Banana men were spirited into Spain in operation Banana II. Ricardo Sicre recalls bringing the men into Spain.

"We did not find a single Spanish patrol boat. We took to the sea and got about a mile from the landing point. There a small motorboat and rowboat were put in the water and the motorboat towed the other boat.

"I put the agents inside the rowboat and we headed straight inland. We found a cave familiar to the guide of the party just below the Miel tower."[25]

Sadly, all the "Banana Boys" were being sent to their deaths. Banana unraveled when Spanish police captured Dick. He blew the cover on Banana II, identifying their hideout in Malaga. Based on Dick's information, the Spanish secret police surrounded the hideaway and killed nine men in a shootout. Thirteen more Banana men were captured and put on trial. Arms and equipment stamped with U.S. markings and serial numbers were found in their hideout. When the men came to trial, they were disavowed out of political necessity, sealing their doom.

When Banana was launched it was not clear whether Spain would join the Axis or remain neutral. Ultra intercepts (something Downs didn't have access to) indicated that Franco would not allow German troops to enter Spanish territory as long as the Allies took no hostile military actions against Spain. Allied policy makers decided to try not to antagonize Franco, for fear of pushing him into the Axis alliance.

The exposure of Banana threatened to become a diplomatic disaster. The official Allied response was that the Banana Boys were a renegade group of agents that OSS lost control over. The families of the 13 captured men pleaded with the government to intervene during the trial, but the State Department and OSS stuck with the cover story and decided not to lift a finger. All the men were executed. Franco issued a mild protest and Banana seemed to have passed into history.

But Banana was not the last disaster to plague OSS in Iberia. OSS Portugal used an undercover informer to pilfer documents from the Japanese embassy's code room. The informer pulled documents from the Japanese naval attaché's office that contained ciphers for the special naval attaché's code (code-named JMA by British and U.S. codebreakers). The Allies had cracked JMA and were using it as a lever to help break the more complex naval code dubbed Magic by the Allies.

Further complicating the OSS operation, OSS Lisbon foolishly had no way of translating the purloined documents, so the material had to be sent back to Washington for translation. The code material was then forwarded to the army's cryptographic service.

From an unknown source, the Japanese caught wind that their embassy had been penetrated and codebooks had been compromised, and they launched an investigation.

Soon Washington learned that the Japanese were investigating the Lisbon embassy penetration and was alarmed at the possibility that the Japanese might change Magic and JMA.

JMA was changed, but, fortunately, the Japanese did not change Magic. OSS operations in Spain and Portugal went through a massive reorganization, and restrictions were placed on OSS operations in Iberia. OSS also issued a directive forbidding agents from obtaining code material without the approval of the director of OSS.

The changes improved the quality of OSS operations in Iberia. OSS intelligence networks there continued to gather valuable information, and Spain was used to feed agents into occupied France.

FOUR

Up the Boot

"Donovan got behind my light machine gun and had a field day. He shot up the Italians single-handed. He was happy as a clam when we got back," recalled Captain Paul Gale, a member of the 1st Infantry Division.[1] Wild Bill Donovan landed on Sicily's Gela Beach on the first day of the invasion, and advanced inland with the Big Red One. Always a hands-on leader, Donovan would take part in most of the Allied invasions in the European theater.

Operation Husky, the invasion of Sicily, jumped off on July 10, 1943. OSS could play only a minor role in the invasion since the new intelligence organization had been forbidden to conduct operations prior to the invasion by AFHQ (Allied Forces Headquarters), who feared that OSS operations would alert the Germans to the pending landings. Compounding the problem, OSS had a relatively small number of Italian–American personnel in the theater.

Nevertheless, OSS helped shape a mysterious espionage agreement before the battle. The Office of Naval Intelligence, backed unobtrusively by OSS, secured the help of "Murder Incorporated." The deal was negotiated by Murray Gurfein, assistant district attorney of New York (and later an OSS colonel in Europe), and New York mob boss Lucky Luciano, then behind bars. The arrangement called for the Mafia in Sicily to gather intelligence prior to the invasion and help police the New York waterfront against Nazi spies and saboteurs. Whether the Mafia actually gathered any worthwhile intelligence is

OSS Operations in Italy and the Mediterranean

still rather murky, and documentary evidence is limited. Nevertheless, a representative for ONI would declare, "[The deal] had helped shorten the war in Sicily." In return for Luciano's assistance, he was deported from the United States the day the war ended.[2]

In any event, OSS operations in Sicily evolved slowly. The main OSS unit consisted of two officers and several enlisted men who landed in Sicily on D-plus-four. The men had no experience gathering tactical intelligence and AFHQ loosely defined their role. Operations proceeded in a trial-and-error fashion.

With Allied forces engaging the Germans in the mountains of Sicily, a small detachment from OSS Special Operations (SO) attempted several abortive operations that were canceled due to the rapid Allied advance. Believing he needed to gain firsthand mission experience, the green SO chief, Lieutenant Colonel Guido Pantaleoni, unwisely decided to lead an SO mission in person. Pantaleoni had extensive knowledge of OSS operations at the highest levels. If captured, he could compromise the security of OSS. Tragically, it was Pantaleoni's first and last mission, as Private Anthony Ribarich, who played a key role in the doomed operation, reveals.

"We started crossing over enemy lines at Acquarossa and, in order not to be too conspicuous to the enemy patrols, we decided to split into three sections.

"We continued to move ahead until we decided to hide in a gully and wait for the third segment of the mission that we had left behind at Acquarossa.

"After almost two hours I saw a German patrol guided by a civilian (which was also seen by the third segment of the mission). I hardly had time to alert my teammates before the enemy saw us, shouted orders to surrender and then began firing at us. Considering our situation, we decided to get rid of our civilian clothing, which we had put on over our uniforms. I unloaded my pistol at the civilian whom I am certain I hit. The exchange of fire lasted about twenty minutes. We were only armed with .45s while the enemy was using hand grenades, rifles, and machine guns. [Sergeant Serafin] Buta was wounded in the spinal area and the colonel, I believe, was wounded in one leg. When it became obvious that any further resistance would be useless, the colonel decided to surrender.

"Disobeying the order, though wounded in several places, I rolled down the hillside, chewing part of the communication code that I was carrying. While running away I exploded another land mine. I heard for the last time the colonel's voice as he was saying to the enemy that his group included Sergeant Buta and Sergeant Ribarich, thus promoting me under battle conditions. I barely had time to hide our civilian clothing and money. After about an hour, surrounded by enemy troops, and without possibility of escape, I gave myself up.

"They took me to the Acquarossa farm where I found Buta on a stretcher. I did not see the colonel whom I believe they had immediately taken away after his capture. The two owners of the farm who had befriended us were also taken prisoner. They were summarily executed.

"The two civilians and I were escorted to the headquarters of the 7th Company, 15th Panzer Regiment whose [command post] was located at Passo dei Tre. Interrogated by the [commanding officer] of the 7th Company and by an Italian officer, I made out that I did not understand either German or Italian and spoke only English. They took all my personal belongings including my 'dog tags,' but neglected to take my pen knife. They had found the transmitting key and the earpieces of the radio in the gully.

"At approximately 9:00 p.m., Buta was brought in on a stretcher and the entire regiment began to retreat toward Randazzo. I heard the order to leave Buta on the road so he could be found by our troops. They ordered me to get into the car with the German lieutenant.

"When the driver had disappeared and the only thing I could hear was the slight snoring of the lieutenant, I slowly felt for my knife, and when I was certain, with a rapid movement I pressed the spring that released the blade and in a moment sliced his throat.

"I jumped out of the car and fled as fast as my legs could carry me, despite the pain from my wounds, as I knew what it would mean if they recaptured me." Ribarich eventually found an American headquarters unit. There he was debriefed and his wounds were treated.[3]

Even before Sicily fell in August, Italy's King Victor Emmanuel was trying to convince Mussolini to break with Berlin. Unable to convince Il Duce to sever the Axis, the king took action, arresting Mussolini on July 25, 1943. He then formed a new government under the former Italian Army Chief of Staff, Marshal Pietro Badoglio. Badoglio informed Hitler that Italy would fight the Allies, but secretly his emissaries were discussing surrender with the Allies.

The Germans were not fooled by Badoglio's overtures, and German forces seized control of Rome and most of Italy. The Italian military was effectively disarmed so it could not be used as an Allied fighting force, while a brilliant commando operation led by German special operations ace Otto Skorzeny freed Mussolini from a mountaintop prison. Il Duce was then installed as dictator.

On September 9 the American Fifth Army landed at Salerno, just south of Naples, a few days after the British Eighth Army crossed the Straits of Messina and landed near the toe of the Italian boot at Reggio di Calabria. The Allies failed to find the "soft underbelly" predicted by Churchill. The Germans fiercely defended southern Italy, and nearly drove the Fifth Army into the sea.

Two major OSS units landed at Salerno.* One was known as the McGregor Project, while the other was the OSS Fifth Army Detachment, a special 90-man intelligence unit led by Donald Downs and attached to the Fifth Army. Trained Italian-speaking operatives were in short supply, so Downs brought along many of his Communist operatives from North Africa. The men were thrust into the front lines to gather tactical intelligence for Darby's Rangers [America's comman-

---

*Before the invasion, OSS/MedTO was reorganized. Units in the Mediterranean were renamed the 2677th Headquarters Company (Provisional). The 2677th was then redesignated the 2677th Regiment OSS (Provisional) with separate companies such as A, B, C, and D. Several detachments were assigned to the advancing Allied armies: the OSS Fifth Army Detachment and OSS Eighth Army Detachment. The British Eighth Army preferred OSS's intelligence services to their own. Secret Intelligence also had a larger intelligence organization that spanned all of Italy. It was known as SI/Italy.

dos], who landed on Salerno's Amalfi coast. Captain André Bourgoin, a Frenchman and an officer in Downs's troop, recalls his short-ranged intelligence missions behind the German lines.[4]

"Colonel Darby, commanding the Rangers, requested a very capable agent for a dangerous mission. I supplied him an Italian air force officer of the SIM [Italian intelligence service] by the name of Gastone Famos. This agent crossed the lines, was captured by the Germans and he succeeded in getting their confidence and he was finally utilized as an interpreter. He returned four days afterwards and supplied to the organization the most useful information and reports.

"German heavy batteries were shelling front line troops and the Army requested an agent to discover [their] location. I presented an Italian artillery officer [by the name] of Roberto Correale who volunteered for that mission. . . . His very accurate information pinpointing the German heavy batteries at Belvedere and Agerola [led to their] complete destruction by the naval fire of the cruisers.

"As the army approached Naples, information was needed between this city and the Volturno River. A special mission was sent under the orders of an Italian infantry officer by the name of Visnara, who landed on the coast near Gaeta and crossed the lines on his way back and joined the detachment in Naples after the town fell into Allied hands. He supplied useful information to the Army."[5]

Frank Monteleone, initially part of the OSS Fifth Army Detachment that landed at Salerno, recalls his first truly face-to-face encounter with an Italian double agent.

"They caught another guy playing the double agent game and [one of our men] started to interrogate him. Headquarters told him to work on this guy, find out what we could. It seems that this guy had given us information and as a result we sent about eight infantrymen out on a patrol and they got wiped out. We nailed the guy. In fact we caught him in Naples and brought him back. [One of the men] tied him to a platform on a bed and beat the shit out of him. He physically abused him. The guy sort of cracked but it was too late. The information he gave us was bad but he didn't give us any new information about who he was working with. He was an Italian agent working for the Germans but we thought he was working for us. At that time I don't think it mattered, they just wanted revenge. They killed him. I'm always a little squeamish talking about it."[6]

Operation McGregor was a wildly ambitious mission intended to convince the Italian naval command to surrender their fleet to the Allies. McGregor was led by John Shaheen and Marcello Girosi, a New York journalist whose brother was an admiral in the Italian navy. The mission turned out to be a bit of a farce, since nobody bothered to inform the McGregor team that the Italian navy had already agreed in secret to surrender to the British at Malta.[7] Nevertheless, a few aspects of the mission were salvaged, including the capture of a key Italian scientist, as John Shaheen recalls: "The McGregor party of officers and agents went ashore with the invasion forces on the Salerno beaches on D-plus-two. The Salerno Italian naval commandant, . . . the Italian naval commandant, Vice Admirals Barone and Minisini on Capri, and various other Italian naval officers were successfully reached and aided and intelligence gathered from them. Through Vice Admiral Barone, contact was established with Vice Admiral Minisini and OSS was informed . . . of all new weapons and devices in production, models, plans, and results of experiments which have been salvaged by Lieutenant Henry Ringling North [famous circus celebrity] of the OSS from the naval torpedo factories and research laboratories in Naples, Baia, Fusaro, San Martino, and by divers from the bottom of the Bay of Naples where a barge holding some secret devices had been sunk, on orders from Badoglio, some days before we invaded Italy. This equipment is now aboard a U.S. Navy ship and is being transported to the United States."[8]

OSS brought Minisini and some Italian scientists to the United States where they shared their expertise with the U.S. Navy. According to the navy, the captured Italian equipment and scientists saved a year's worth of research.

As the Salerno beachhead was being secured, the Allies also had to contend with the nearby large islands of Sardinia and Corsica. Sardinia was garrisoned by 270,000 Italians and 19,000 Germans. Donovan chose a four-man OG team for the job, led by the intrepid Lieutenant Colonel Serge Obolensky.[9]

Obolensky was a Czarist prince and officer during the Russian revolution. He later emigrated to the United States, married an Astor, and became vice president of Hilton International. Obolensky had presence, making him just the man to deliver special letters from the Badoglio government and General Eisenhower that ordered Sardinia's Italian commander to surrender his forces. Obolensky's team parachuted into Sardinia on the night of September 13th: "We left Algiers in a Halifax bomber at 2100 on the 13th of September and landed by parachute in the foothills of Sardinia about 2330 [11:30 p.m.], about 15 miles from Cagliari. I was ordered to leave the two radio operators and their radios in the foothills and proceed with Lieutenant Formichelli to the nearest Italian military base, and demand to be taken immediately to the Italian Army Headquarters. In case we failed to do so and did not contact the radio operators within 48 hours they were to proceed and carry out the same mission.

"Having hidden our radio operators and their equipment in the foothills, Lieutenant Formichelli and myself set out on foot in the direction of Cagliari. . . .

"We arrived at Bordigali about 1700 [5:00 p.m.] the same day without incident and were received with great courtesy by the Chief of Staff, Colonel A. Bruno, who took me to General Basso to whom I presented General Castellano's letter and explained the purpose of my mission. I told the general that the Allied Headquarters expected him to press the Germans relentlessly and in every way try and destroy them during the process of their evacuation. I also told him that we had some special units that we could send to him for that purpose. The general answered that he was doing all he could to push the Germans out of Sardinia and that his troops had already been given orders to exert pressure wherever they could. He objected to American units being sent in. I gathered later that this was done because he was uncertain of some of his units and was afraid of a possible clash between Italian and Allied soldiers. Except for one or two small skirmishes with the Germans, the Italian troops never really fought them but just moved up when the Germans had evacuated a place.

"Colonel Bruno asked me to keep my men and myself indoors for two or three days until straggling German patrols were cleared of the region so as to avoid any possible incident. I insisted on permission to see him twice a day to gather information on the progress of the evacuation. This was granted.

"On the afternoon of the 14th, while I was on my way to Italian headquarters, Lieutenant Formichelli went back to the foothills and brought back the two radio operators, Second Lieutenant Russell and Sergeant W. Sherwood, to Bordigali. I spent a few very trying hours waiting for their arrival as the roads were not safe. I will never forget the happy moments of our reunion."[10]

A few days after the Sardinia operation, OSS was loosed on the Italian and German garrisons on Corsica. Once again OGs were chosen to spearhead the task, along with a French unit known as the Battalion de Choc. The first OG team was led by spy/anthropologist Carleton Coon. The Germans conducted a fighting withdrawal, engaging the OGs in several small-unit actions. However, it was not a battle so much as a withdrawal from territory that the Germans decided to abandon.

By November, OSS and the French controlled the island, allowing the OGs to use Corsica as a base for operations against the Italian mainland. The OGs and British commandos embarked on a series of missions designed to give the impression that the Allies were launching amphibious attacks on both the Tyrrhenian and Adriatic coasts—forcing the Germans to garrison troops away from the main battle south of Rome. The OGs also struck vulnerable German supply lines that ran through rail tunnels and along narrow roads in the Apennine Mountains.[11]

The OGs launched raids by boat or parachute. Each team was self-contained, consisting of between 15 and 30 men. All volunteers, the men were highly trained in a variety of special operations, such as planning and raising guerrilla forces, demolition, sabotage, gathering intelligence, and hit-and-run raids. The typical OG team was described as "a small self-sufficient band of men who might be required to live and fight in the manner of guerrillas."[12]

The OSS commandos were bilingual or multilingual, speaking the language and understanding the customs of the country they fought in. Many were first generation Americans, whose parents had come from those very countries. The men, many of whom were drawn from the ranks of U.S. Army paratroopers, numbered among the best-trained and equipped troops in the American military. In short, OSS's commandos were America's first Special Forces.

If captured, the OGs faced execution. Following a British commando raid on the Channel Islands, during which a German prisoner was tied up and stabbed in the heart by the commandos, Hitler issued his famous "Commando order" to all German forces in the daily Wehrmacht communiqué.

> In the future, all terror and sabotage troops of the British and their accomplices, who do not act like soldiers but rather bandits, will be treated as such by the German troops and will be ruthlessly eliminated in battle, wherever they appear.

Ten days later, after discussions among the Reich's military lawyers and headquarters staff, a secret order was issued to German units that all sabotage parties, whether in uniform or civilian clothes, armed or unarmed, were to be "slaughtered to the last man."[13]

Such was the fate of the Ginny team.

Ginny set out in early January to destroy a critical railroad tunnel at Stazione Framura. Weather and other factors delayed the mission until the night of March 21–22, 1944. Albert Materazzi, the operations officer who planned Ginny, recalls that fateful night.

"I came up with the plan after a thorough map reconnaissance and all the information I could possibly get. I enlisted the aid of a Spitfire pilot, an American that lived down the road from us. I borrowed a camera from [John] Ford's operation, a handheld aerial camera. Jim Bickford cut a hole in his fuselage and rigged the camera up to his bomb release and flew almost level. The pictures have disappeared; they were perfect and used in my planning. I felt we could damage both ends of the tunnel and booby-trap the rail. We could keep it out of operation for maybe a week and in the meantime our aviation would have a field day because there'd be a lot of traffic backed up in both directions.

"The team went ashore in three rubber boats. It was dark night. They landed there; they camouflaged their boats the best they could; at least from the land side but not from the sea side. They stayed overnight in a stable. The next morning a girl came out to feed a chicken or something and they asked her to sell them food. They had D rations but she brought them some stuff. Vinny Russo, the team leader, in the meantime found a farmer, and told him that he wanted to go to the 'little house,' a signaling station. Vinny, in Venetian dialect, which is all he knew, translated the signaling station into 'little house.' It was about a kilometer and half, overland, over the tunnel. The farmer took him there. By the time he got back, they were discovered.

"A fisherman saw the OG's rubber boats that were not hidden well in the rocks and reported them to the local Fascists. They got the Germans involved and they started searching for the team, found them, and started a brief firefight. Vinny might have been wounded slightly and they surrendered to the Germans.

"They questioned our guys pretty extensively. They sent a guy to interrogate them who worked as a German intelligence agent on Hamburg-America Line ships in the 1930s. As luck would have it, you couldn't write a story like this. Sessler, who was this interrogation officer, had been an officer on board a German freighter and when the ship docked in Brooklyn . . . one of our guys used to bring ice to the boat. During the interrogation they instantly recognized each other. I think Sessler really tried to help. He left his gun on a peg and told our guy, 'Don't shoot any Germans.' In other words inviting our guy to take it, for which Sessler was chastised royally. The gun was given to Paul Traficante who was the head of the security part of the mission. He never got a chance to use it; the guards were too alert and disarmed him before he could use it.

"The Germans had Italian employees from the Todt Organization. They were told to dig a large hole that was going to be used for a gun emplacement. Next the Ginny team was lined up and shot and buried in that hole.

"A day later the German army issued a communiqué saying a group of American commandos were executed while attempting to sabotage a tunnel. After that we got all kinds of information on the team, including from a priest coming through the lines. Some of the soldiers who participated in the execution played soccer with the townspeople and one of them bragged about killing a bunch of Americans. That information got to this priest and he came through the lines and came out where one of our officers was and he sent him to me. I noted the location of the grave and prepared for when we took over the area to send people up there to pick up everything they could. As we were going up there two of our men went up and found their grave."[14]

Had Ginny been successful it would have disrupted German supply lines. Initially, the mission would have coincided with the last great amphibious landing in Italy—Anzio.[15]

The landings were driven primarily by Winston Churchill, who pressed the Allied high command to launch an amphibious invasion just south of Rome to capture the city. Since the Fifth Army's breakout at Salerno, the Germans had turned the rugged, mountainous Italian landscape into elaborate defensive belts, grinding the Allied advance to a standstill outside Cassino. Churchill hoped that the amphibious landings at Anzio would break the deadlock.

Code-named Shingle, the invasion called for just 36,000 men to land behind German lines at the beach resort town of Anzio.[16] The force was inadequate for the task. Landing on January 22, 1944, the Allies consolidated the beachhead, rather than striking at Rome. Fears of another Salerno weighed heavily on the Allied commander, and rightly so. British 1st Division commander W.R.C. Penny later wrote, "We could have had one night in Rome and 18 months in P.W. Camps."[17]

The Germans quickly responded to the landings by implementing their contingency plans for a behind-the-lines invasion. Within a week tens of thousands of battle-hardened German troops ringed the beachhead.

At dusk on January 20, ahead of the invasion fleet, 23-year-old Peter Tompkins landed about 100 miles north of Rome in a small rubber boat. The OSS agent traveled to Rome, where he contacted Maurizio Giglio, a young anti-Fascist police officer and OSS agent who was operating a secret radio station code-named Vittoria. Giglio was joined by the leader of the socialist underground, Franco Malfatti, who placed 500 socialists at Tompkins's disposal. The intelligence network would prove to be crucial to the invasion.[18]

Tompkins, code-named "Pietro," organized his intelligence assets masterfully. Malfatti's "watchers" were placed along all the major highways that entered Rome.

Tompkins collected and organized their reports on troop movements, tanks, and supply and ammunition dumps, and sent the priceless intelligence to the Fifth Army and OSS. Secretly, Tompkins maintained a wartime diary recording his exploits: "Then I found I was getting too much varied info and that I'd have to organize a system for checking rapidly and eliminating duplications or I'd go nuts and serve the base no good at all. The greatest problem was trying to keep track of all the vehicles and tanks, men and guns that went in and out of Rome on more than a dozen roads. From all the political parties and from two or three other strange organizations I received small bits of paper with the numbers of cars and tanks, etc. that had passed on a certain road, but one source would count them from three in the afternoon to seven at night and give me a total of thirty-seven trucks, nineteen tanks, twenty-two guns, etc., while another watching from five in the evening till midnight gave a completely different set of figures and I had no idea at what point they overlapped. As checking on German movements was for the moment practically our main job, I decided it either had to be done properly or not at all."[19]

Malfatti's watchers were everywhere including, most remarkably, an operative directly in Field Marshal Albert Kesselring's headquarters. "One of our best sources, a trained intelligence officer who spoke fluent German, acted as liaison between the Fascist command of the open city of Rome and Kesselring's headquarters. Thus with a little ingenuity and a small amount of risk, he was able to get access to the German operational maps from which we obtained the complete German battle order at the beachhead, the disposition of their real and phony tanks and guns, their intended feint attacks, and the direction of the main attacks whose object was to split the beachhead and force it to evacuate."[20]

The informant next furnished Tompkins with a crucial piece of information: when the Germans were going to launch a massive counterattack to crush the fragile beachhead. Tompkins radioed on January 29 that a German attack was imminent from the Practica di Mare region near the beachhead. Thanks to the intelligence, Allied bombers struck Practica di Mare, destroying German assets and an entire German corps communications network.

On February 2, 1944, Tompkins again sent out a crucial message: "Force now facing beachhead called Fourteenth Army to consist of two army corps plus two divs [sic] reserve x actually in line fiftyfive thousand men in four divs x Göring x ninetieth x sixtyfifth and unknown corps also have strong units anti-tank guns x other four divs coming down include three five six at Civitacastellana X in spite of bombing Germans planning new attack from Practica di Mare X."[21]

Martin Blumenson, a U.S. Army official historian, credits Tompkins's network with providing the key intelligence that helped save the beachhead: "Intelligence from Rome seems to have played an important part in this belief [calling off an Allied attack in order to defend against the impending German attack], which was substantiated in Clark's personal war diary."[22] Tompkins's network illustrates effectively how human intelligence independently confirmed or even anticipated information developed by the British Ultra codebreaking efforts. Ultra provided the Allies with information on many of Germany's key strategic moves and battle plans. But Ultra had its shortcomings. OSS's human agents confirmed its findings but in some cases brought to light key intelligence several days before German codes could be broken and sent to the front.[23]

Tompkins barely avoided capture, but several of his net were captured and executed by the Gestapo, including Maurizio Giglio, the original OSS agent who had operated Radio Vittoria. Giglio was mercilessly tortured and practically beaten to death by the Gestapo, but never revealed Tompkins or the other operatives. Giglio was finally turned over to the SS and slaughtered with 320 Italians in a mass execution known as the Massacre of the Ardeatine Caves.

To avoid capture by the Germans and Fascist police, Tompkins enrolled in the PAI (Italian African Police), which, remarkably, consid-

ering Africa was in Allied hands, was still in existence, and more remarkably, even recruiting. After deftly dodging numerous questions
about his background during the application process, Tompkins went
through PAI training, including a run-in with a *brigadiere,* the Italian
equivalent to a drill instructor. "The minute he saw us the *brigadiere* let
out a yell and pounced upon us. For five minutes he swore incoher-
ently at us while we stood rigidly at attention. Catching sight of my
hair he asked me why I hadn't had it cut, repeating it two or three
times at the top of his voice. I pointed out to him, still rigidly at attention, that I had had it cut.

"'What do you mean you had it cut?'

"With my left hand I removed my cap. 'I had it cut,' I said again.

"'Oh you did, did you? You'll have it shaved to nothing after the
drill. You are all confined to barracks. Take their names.'"[24]

Within a matter of days Tompkins's unit was ordered to demobi-
lize and he was back on the run: "[We] walked out free as the wind.
The last thing we saw was the seven-foot *brigadiere* looking like a child
who lost a lollipop."[25]

Toward the end of May, the Allies mounted their final drive on the
Eternal City. As Allied troops entered the city, OSS infiltrated a mission into Rome led by a true Renaissance man, Moe Berg. Berg was
assigned the task of locating key Italian scientists and technical information on Germany's efforts to develop the atomic bomb.[26] Prior to
the war, Berg had been a Major League Baseball player. After graduat-
ing from Princeton, he joined the Brooklyn Dodgers, and then played
with the Chicago White Sox until 1942.

But Berg's real passion was books. He had a lust for knowledge and
he spent a semester in Paris learning French. Between baseball seasons
Berg earned a law degree at Columbia and briefly took a position with
the law firm of Satterlee and Canfield before resigning and returning to
baseball. Berg had the qualities of a perfect spy: athletic, worldly, schol-
arly, self-reliant, and secretive. Frank Monteleone recalls the mission.

"Moe Berg needed a radio operator and I was chosen. We infiltrated through the lines into Rome. At that time the Allies were
breaking out from Anzio. They sent Moe Berg to interview Italian
scientists on what they knew about Germany's efforts to develop the
atomic bomb and jet propulsion technology. Berg also visited a bookshop to pick up secret documents. On the surface, you'd think why
a bookshop? But the more you think about it, it's the perfect place
to hide documents that the Italians didn't want the Germans to find.
At the time some of these Italian scientists were trying to help us.
Berg was sent in to get this information before the Germans pulled
out of the city.

"A guy by the name of Peroni owned the leading newspaper in
Rome and had a huge villa. We lived in this magnificent mansion. I
was up in the attic; it was hot as hell. I would send back my messages
from there and that's where I was billeted and Moe Berg would send
up the information.

"Berg was the most mysterious man I ever met. He moved in and
out and I never saw him again."[27]

Rome finally fell to the Allies on June 3, and around that time
Tompkins was able to make his way to Allied lines: "The GIs, still
stony-eyed from action, dusty and tired, not altogether conscious of
the fact that they were the first Allied soldiers ever to occupy the heart
of Rome, lay in their blankets on the hoods of the half-tracks, or gazed
in a friendly way at the excited *paisanos*. I knew that they would not
understand it if I went up to any of them and addressed them in English, and told them who I was. They were combat troops fresh from
action, and would not understand. But I could not resist saying just
'Hello' to one of them. A young lieutenant jostled past me in the
crowd. I just caught the glimmer of his silver bar in the sticky dark-
ness. 'Hello Lieutenant,' I stammered, and he turned suddenly on his
heels. 'Could I . . . could I bum a cigarette? I haven't had an American
cigarette in almost five months. . . .'"

"Automatically the lieutenant reached for his shirt pocket and offered me a Lucky Strike, then, before he could get out his forty-five, I disappeared into the crowd.

"I dragged deeply on the cigarette and blew the smoke out into the warm Roman night. It was strong and perfumed and made me a little giddy. It was odd to think that after all those months, when the Fifth Army had finally arrived, I had to hide from them too [some of the agents OSS appointed to work with Tompkins were former fascists and were not above sacrificing a colleague to advance their own cause], but I knew it would only be for a little while. In a matter of hours my own people would arrive.

"The next day, just outside Rome, they found the mangled bodies of Sorrentino, Enzo the radio operator, the two who had come to get me my first day in Rome, and three other of our agents. Each had a small round bullet hole in the nape of his neck."[28]

FIVE

On Hitler's Doorstep

The OSS in Switzerland

Shortly after the invasion of North Africa began, a middle-aged man carrying a single suitcase and a million-dollar letter of credit arrived in Switzerland. Bearing the title "Special Representative of the President of the United States," Allen Dulles was no stranger to Switzerland or to the world of espionage.

During World War I, Dulles had been posted to Vienna and Bern, where he spied on Germany and Austria-Hungary. He returned to Europe to spy on Nazi Germany. Within two years his small organization—just five OSS officers and more than a dozen cipher clerks as of early 1944—would gather some of the most important pieces of intelligence of the war.

Surrounded on all sides by the Axis, Switzerland offered OSS unique access to the Reich. Geography dictated that Switzerland would be a primary listening post for Axis and Allies alike. Both sides sent their agents to Bern to watch one another.

It did not take long for Dulles to set up shop. Although Switzerland was officially neutral, Swiss intelligence allowed Dulles to operate covertly. As the war progressed and the Nazis threatened to invade, Dulles furnished Swiss intelligence with information about the German order of battle, as a forewarning to any Axis attack.

To gather information about Germany, Dulles had to rely on indirect rather than direct infiltration. Agents sent directly into a hostile po-lice state such as Germany had little chance of survival. Fortunately, Dulles was able to turn to his vast network of personal contacts, which included trade unionists, doctors, diplomats, and enemy intelligence agents. Dulles managed to weave a web of more than 100 agents, who in turn had hundreds of subagents working for them.[1]

One of Dulles's best contacts was a balding, middle-aged func-tionary in the German Foreign Office named Fritz Kolbe. Kolbe claimed he had important information to give to the United States. Since 1939, Kolbe had worked as a liaison between the Foreign Service and the German General Staff, and had access to some of the Reich's most closely guarded secrets.

Before being introduced to Dulles, Kolbe first approached the British, who thought he was too good to be true. Suspecting that Kolbe might be a German plant or agent provocateur, the British turned him away. Dulles saw the value in Kolbe and took the risk. OSS counterintelligence vetted Kolbe, and determined him to be legiti-mate. Kolbe received the code-name "George Wood."

Kolbe's intelligence reports, designated the "Boston Series," were given fairly wide distribution at the highest levels. Even the White House received the material on a frequent basis. Kolbe exposed Ger-man policy, plans, and the Reich's relations with neutral countries, and warned that the Germans had broken U.S. communications from Cairo. Following are excerpts from an intelligence report orally sub-mitted by George Wood to Allen Dulles.

KAPPA. . . .
    Hitler, Himmler, Göring, and all of the other bigwigs are
at the General Headquarters in East Prussia. . . .
    The entire Nazi idea of the British and American battle
order for invasion troops has been viewed by Wood. This bat-tle order states that there are 50 to 60 divisions stationed in

the south of England and prepared to leave. The Nazis think
that they know exactly where each division is located. . . .[2]

The intelligence reports furnished by Dulles's organization typically addressed military matters, such as German troop movements,
order of battle, bombing results, and even information on Germany's
secret weapons programs. Dulles's data consistently validated the information that the Allies were receiving from Ultra, the Allied effort
to break Germany's codes.

Another crucial piece of intelligence Kolbe furnished to Dulles
was the presence of a German agent working in the British ambassador's residence in Turkey. Code-named "Cicero," Elyesa Bazna was
Sir Hughe Knatchbull-Hugessen's butler and valet. The swarthy Albanian, a trained locksmith, copied the key to the ambassador's safe
and regularly photographed and sold important documents to the
Germans. In January 1944, Cicero photographed a "most secret" letter from General Eisenhower that stated, "Maintain a threat to the
Germans from the eastern end of the Mediterranean until Overlord
is launched."[3] The most secret code word in the Allied lexicon was
revealed to the Germans. Fortunately, Kolbe saw the information Cicero passed to German intelligence and traveled to Switzerland and
informed Dulles that an unidentified agent working out of the Turkish embassy was passing sensitive documents to German intelligence.
Dulles immediately informed his counterparts in British intelligence.
British counterespionage interviewed staff in the embassy but not the
employees of the residence. Cicero, sensing impending capture,
smashed his camera and threw it into a river and stopped spying. He
later resigned from the residence and was never caught. His exploits
were later depicted on the silver screen by James Mason in *Five
Fingers.*

Kolbe worked in the face of constant danger. The German Foreign Office was riddled with Gestapo informants. After the war,

Dulles asked Wood to record his experiences, and the account was translated into English in the third person. "George had a very narrow escape from being caught by the Gestapo nets. Once he sent a trunk with clothes through the courier to [Switzerland]. The pockets of the clothes contained films with photographs of a long letter giving valuable information on Nazi activities. In general the officials of the Berlin courier service handled George's activities without investigation, but this time the wrong man was at the desk and started to search every corner of George's trunk. Discovery seemed imminent. George saw himself lost and as he always carried a revolver since he started his activities—he already had his hand in his pocket in order to shoot some Nazis before his suicide—the only way to escape from death by torture. Suddenly, another official entered the room, with whom George started a conversation. The official turned to share in the conversation and stopped his search of the trunk, just before he reached the critical piece of clothing."[4]

One of the Bern operation's greatest challenges was relaying the information it gathered back to Allied headquarters. Many of Dulles's reports, dubbed "flashes," went back to the U.S. via a scramble-equipped radiotelephone. One of the more significant flashes, sent on June 24, 1943, involved German rockets.

"The rocket [V-1] is approximately sixty centimeters in diameter and three meters in length. It is said to weigh 2,000 kilos. The driving turbine and propelling material etc. occupy four fifths of the volume, and about one fifth is devoted to the projectile. . . . I understand that the explosions which drive the turbine are produced by a saltpeter solution [possibly meaning nitrate] and gas-oil under a pressure of fifty atmospheres. The assembly plant and the testing grounds are in Pomerania at Peenemuende. . . . Manufacture is now at a point where quantity production is expected for use in September, October. Our information understands that a much larger model is in the experimental stage."[5]

• • •

When Bern gathered information that could not be transmitted via radiotelephone, such as maps, drawings, and full-text reports, they delivered it to OSS headquarters by an ingenious courier system. First, the materials were microfilmed in Bern, where they were handed over to a locomotive engineer who hid the film in a secret compartment above the steam engine's firebox. In the event the train was searched by the Germans, the OSS engineer would open the trap door, destroying the microfilm. In that event, he would be given a duplicate copy of the microfilm and the process would start over. Once the train safely traveled to Lyon, France, the microfilm was given to an agent who bicycled to Marseille. From Marseille, the film was transported by ship to Corsica, and then by plane to Algiers. The entire exchange took about 10 or 12 days.[6]

Switzerland was the ideal vantage point to monitor other German technological advances. One of the most important agents to visit the outpost was Renaissance man and super-agent Moe Berg. After roaming through Italy and France and charming Italian and French scientists into revealing what they knew about the German atomic bomb program, Berg traveled to Zurich to listen to Germany's top physicist, Werner Heisenberg, lecture on something called the matrix theory. Armed with a pistol and an L-pill, Berg posed as a student to determine how close Nazi Germany was to developing the atomic bomb. If Heisenberg was close to a breakthrough, Berg would have to assassinate him with the pistol. He was ordered the take the L-pill if captured.

During Heisenberg's lecture Berg took copious notes and interviewed other German scientists. According to a recently declassified cable Berg sent to Donovan, the Germans were not even close to developing the atom bomb. "Timed entry [into] Switzerland to attend Heisenberg lecture and discussion . . . separation of U235 isotope ab-

solutely hopeless after experiments . . . Flute [German scientist] pre-
dicts at least two years probably ten for successful AZUSA [code word
for atomic bomb]."[7]

Berg later asked Heisenberg a series of oblique questions, determined that the German scientist was not a threat, and let him return
to Germany and survive the war.

Berg also returned home after the war, leaving spy craft and employment altogether. He became a drifter and for the next twenty-five
years never owned a home or rented an apartment. Berg moved from
place to place but never owned a car, and he would show up unexpectedly at a friend's home for a meal. Moe Berg's life ended as myste-
riously as it was lived.

In February 1943, the prime minister of Hungary, one of Germany's eastern satellite countries, dispatched an emissary to OSS Bern
to establish a confidential line of communication with the United
States. The Hungarians were looking for a way out of their relationship
with the Germans, and hoping Washington would guarantee their
sovereignty against a Russian takeover. The Hungarians wanted to create a de facto state of neutrality, provided the U.S. gave them certain as-
surances regarding their borders and Russia. The U.S. could not enter
such negotiations without antagonizing Russia, but Dulles wanted to
test the good faith of the Hungarians, and proposed that they receive
an OSS agent who would transmit military intelligence.

The Hungarians agreed in principle to the operation but, for various reasons, stalled its execution for months. Finally, on March 15,
1944, a three-man team, code-named "Sparrow," parachuted into
Hungary near the Yugoslav border. The plan called for the Sparrow
agents to turn themselves in to the Hungarian authorities. Their cover
story was that they were part of a military mission heading for Tito
but their plane was hit by flak and they were forced to bail out over
Hungary. Once in Hungarian custody, they would go through routine
questioning but instead of being interned they would operate out of a

secret location and transmit intelligence information.

The Sparrow operation ended in disaster. Less than 48 hours after the team dropped into German-occupied Hungary, the Gestapo uncovered elements of the operation, and the Germans swiftly sent three armored divisions toward Budapest. Shortly afterward, the Hungarian authorities turned the Sparrow agents over to the Germans, as Sparrow team leader Colonel Florimond Duke recalls.

"On Sunday morning, the 19th of March at 5 o'clock, we were awakened with the request that General Ujszaszi wanted to see us immediately. We dressed hurriedly, went upstairs and found him in a very nervous state. He had not slept all night—practically had tears in his eyes—as white as a sheet—and informed us that three German Panzer Divisions had crossed the border from Austria into Hungary and were occupying the country and surrounding Budapest. He asked if we could send a message, but we informed him that we could not until about eleven o'clock because it would take us that long to set up our equipment. Actually we could not send a message before that time because eleven o'clock was our call time. The General then said that eleven or twelve o'clock would be too late. We asked him if he had an airplane hidden on some large estate outside Budapest that we could all get on and get out of there. He said that he had not made any such preparations. We then told him that if we worked fast he could get us down to the Yugoslav border and we would then make our way through Yugoslavia to join the Partisan Resistance forces and in that way make our escape. He replied that it would be impossible because the German troops were already practically surrounding Budapest. In other words, the Hungarians offered no resistance whatsoever to German occupation and they did nothing to help us get away.

"The next morning, the Gestapo representative took me again, handcuffed, to the Gestapo headquarters. Here were the 'big shot' interrogators, as the questioning in Belgrade by the Gestapo had been rather second-rate. These men in Budapest were clever, smooth oper-

ators, well dressed in expensive civilian materials. On my first interview, I still held to the story that we were to join the Partisans and after
sparring around for about ten minutes, my questioner looked at me
and said, 'You look like an intelligent guy—there is no use kidding each
other and beating around the bush—here is the story.' With that, he
tossed over to me twenty type written pages, a signed statement by
General Ujszaszi, telling the entire story. I looked at this dossier and
saw that it told the whole story. I then told him enough to confirm
what Ujszaszi had already told him, but was very vague as to where we
had come from—that is, what organization. I said we were Air Corps
Intelligence and that I had volunteered for a special mission for the
Joint Chiefs of Staff and State Department. On returning to the jail, I
had an opportunity to tell Major Alfred Suarez and Lieutenant Guy
Nunn [OSS agents] that the story had come out on the part of the Hungarian general, so that on their interviews the following day they could
confirm the story. After about a week, when we had told our individual
stories, they moved the three of us together in one cell in the jail.

"About two weeks later, a special representative from the OKW
came from Berlin to see me. He was a specialist on the American
Army from the OKW Intelligence. He particularly wanted to know
how many troops we had in England. Although I had no idea, I told
him that we had about two or probably three million who were getting ready for the invasion of France any day. I told him the invasion
would be timed with the great push from the south of Italy and a big
drive on the part of the Russians from the east, so that Germany
would be squeezed in from all sides. He could hardly believe that we
would ever make a landing in France and could not understand it. But
I had a great time with him, and my statements to him are exactly
what did happen, so he must have thought I had all the inside dope."[8]

Duke and his teammates were eventually transferred to Colditz
Prison where they sat out the rest of the war.

Sparrow was blown partly due to security breaches in the Cereus chain, an OSS intelligence network that operated out of Istanbul. Through late 1943, Cereus furnished over 700 reports on order of bat- tle, industrial targets, and resistance groups—most of it incorrect. The network was heavily penetrated by German intelligence, which planted most of the information.

Several of Cereus's agents were Hungarian double agents working for Germany. The careless handling of the agents on the part of OSS re- sulted in the arrest of many of OSS's contacts in Europe, including members of the Hungarian general staff, and the OSS agents on the mission. OSS's failure to compartmentalize operations is a prime reason for the failure. In one aspect of the operation the Hungarian general staff requested that OSS participate in an exchange of liaison officers. Accordingly, an OSS agent was infiltrated into Budapest. However, the Hungarian military attaché who arrived in Istanbul turned out to be working for the Gestapo. The enemy agent gained access to OSS oper- ations and contacts in Istanbul, helping to bring about Cereus's collapse.

The biggest problem was "Dogwood," the key spy behind Cereus, who was a double agent. Dogwood was a Czech businessman who worked with British intelligence. Shortly after OSS arrived in Istanbul, the Brits passed him off to the Americans. Dogwood provided reams of intelligence, most of it planted by the Germans. He never revealed his sources, merely assigning them code names, making the intelli- gence he provided impossible to verify. OSS counterintelligence later uncovered the leaks in Cereus, but it would not be until mid-1944 that OSS was able to salvage operations in Istanbul.

While the Sparrow mission ended in failure, it did confer a signifi- cant strategic benefit. Two of the German armored divisions used to crush Hungary were taken from France and were not fully opera- tional or in the right place on D-Day. Sparrow also set the ground- work for another mission. In October 1944, OSS infiltrated agent "Molly" into Budapest bearing messages from AFHQ (Allied Forces Headquarters) and dissident Hungarian groups urging Hungary's regent, Admiral Horthy, to turn his forces against the Germans and surrender to the Russians. Molly gained a personal audience with Horthy and convinced him to deliver a declaration of armistice the day after their meeting. Once more the Germans had to divert a large number of troops to crush the Hungarians. Molly, actually a male agent, went into hiding and survived the war. Once again the action of a single individual agent had had a bearing on the course of the war.

The Dulles organization also established contact with the German resistance. Despite years of oppression and a totalitarian apparatus that killed or incarcerated political dissenters, pockets of resistance still existed within the Reich. Described by Dulles as the "Breakers," the resistance was comprised of various German intellectuals from military and government circles who maintained their foreign contacts through the Abwehr, the German military intelligence corps. Dulles described the Breakers in his report to Washington on January 29, 1944.

"These groups are made up of well-educated and liberal individuals, but nevertheless, they do not have rightist tendencies and are confident that in the future the Government will have to be really leftist. The Fat Boy [Göring] of Germany is popularly considered the German Ciano, and as I see it, he currently commands no support in reputable opposition circles. I believe that Gorter [a member of the resistance] may be considered trustworthy for existing purposes, but like the majority of such Germans, he is acting for the future welfare of his own country, and hence his opinions may not always check with ours. I am satisfied by the evidence before me that he wants to wipe out every element of the current Nazi group. Recommend that you use Breakers for my contacts except for the Fat Boy's group. . . ."[9]

The Abwehr was headed by Rear Admiral Wilhelm Canaris. Even before the war started, Canaris and several of his lieutenants had secretly turned against Hitler. At the war's outbreak, Canaris sent Hans Bernd Gisevius, an Abwehr agent, under diplomatic cover to maintain contact with the Allies on behalf of the German resistance.

At 6 feet 4 inches tall, Gisevius was a hulk of a man, who squinted through tiny spectacles. This comic look earned him the nickname "Tiny" from someone in OSS. As Gisevius had trained as a lawyer and served in the Gestapo, Canaris was able to assign him to be the German vice-consul in Zurich without raising suspicions about his qualifications.

Gisevius first approached British intelligence, MI6, in 1939 and furnished information. But after being stung by a series of self-proclaimed "anti-Nazis" the British stopped dealing with him, fearing he was an opportunist, or worse, a double agent.

After receiving the cold shoulder from MI6, Gisevius turned to the Americans and contacted one of Dulles's top lieutenants, Gero von Gaevernitz, a German-born American who prior to the war had managed his family business in Switzerland. In his first meeting Gisevius provided Dulles a window into the German resistance movement. Gisevius disclosed its plans to overthrow Hitler and seek a separate peace with the West.

Despite insistence from British intelligence that Gisevius was a double agent, Dulles trusted Tiny, writing that "I have seen many men in my lifetime, but this one is extraordinary. I've never quite met anyone like him. My office is piled with denunciations of him as a double agent. That doesn't bother me."[10]

Gisevius established Dulles's trust by informing him that the Germans had broken the U.S. State Department's diplomatic code in Bern. The code was broken after a janitor, who was a member of the Swiss Nazi Party, retrieved carbon copies of secret messages that were carelessly thrown in the office wastebasket, and delivered them to German agents. After Gisevius's revelation, the code was changed.[11]

Gisevius became Dulles's primary contact with the Breakers, providing otherwise unobtainable information from the highest levels of the German resistance movement. In this report, Dulles describes the July 20, 1944 bomb plot against Hitler from information provided by Gisevius:

"Apparently Breakers are breaking. In all probability the movement is the one explained in my #4110 and earlier Breakers communications. It was planned that certain men in the inner circles, such as Theta, our 3432, would be at the meeting when the bomb went off because the only chance for planting the bomb was in conjunction with a conference attended by many of the chief military leaders. . . .

"The outcome of the revolt at present rests with the Reserve Army and their willingness to follow Himmler as their chief or whether they will stick to their old commanders, some of whom, as pointed out in my #4110, appear to be involved in the plot. Naturally, the blood purge will be unmerciful."[12]

As Dulles predicted, Hitler's revenge was swift and merciless; thousands were executed or incarcerated. The event marked a turning point for Dulles's organization, since several of his key contacts were exposed and executed. Networks that he had carefully stitched together collapsed. Gisevius escaped the Gestapo dragnet and remained a fugitive in the Berlin area for six months. After Gisevius contacted Dulles, a bold plan was devised to get him false Gestapo officer identity papers, and most importantly the Silver Warrant Identity Disk, serial numbered and made from an unknown metal alloy, that gave a Gestapo officer virtually unlimited power within the Reich. Working with the British, OSS produced a counterfeit medallion and false papers that bore Himmler's forged signature. Using an elaborate set of couriers, Dulles got the counterfeit material from Switzerland to Gisevius's girlfriend's apartment, where he had been holed up. With medallion and papers in hand, he safely fled to Bern in January 1945, and revealed the full story of the failed July 20 putsch.

Despite the near collapse of its networks in the aftermath of the failed coup, OSS Bern would continue to play a prominent role in OSS's intelligence war in Europe. Fritz Kolbe, unconnected to the plotters, remained undetected at his Foreign Service job, and continued to furnish valuable intelligence to OSS until the end of the war.

Into the Balkans

Yugoslavia and Albania

"I shook hands with the RAF dispatcher, gave our 'thumbs up' signal, and when the light went green, shoved off. When the chute blossomed, I immediately saw the fires, realized I was way off to one side, and landed in a pile of rocks, hurting my hip slightly. I found myself on a cool mountainside and in a few minutes was surrounded by a group of big bearded Chetniks who tried to smother me with kisses, yelling 'Zdravo, Purvi Amerikanec!' [Greetings, first American]"[1]

Walter Mansfield's parachute jump marked the beginning of the American presence in Yugoslavia—and the plunging of OSS into the middle of a vicious civil war between the Chetniks, loyal to the exiled King Peter, and Tito's Partisans, whose loyalty lay with Moscow.

Initially, a truce existed between the two resistance groups, but soon they were engaged in open civil war. As in other European countries, Allied policy was to support both Communist and royalist resistance groups as long as they fought the Germans.

The principal OSS goal in Yugoslavia was to tie down as many German units as possible, so that they could not link up with the 26 German divisions in Italy, or be redeployed to face the Allied landing in Normandy. OSS also conducted covert espionage and sabotage missions, and rescued hundreds of Allied fliers. Unfortunately, OSS operations were complicated by turf wars with the British SOE, which had been given preeminence over the Balkans by the Donovan-Hambro Accords.[2]

The Donovan-Hambro Accords placed covert operations in the Balkans under the tight control of the British. It essentially carved up the world between the two organizations. SOE had preeminence in the Balkans and Allied missions in the region were planned and staffed by SOE Cairo. The agreement stipulated that the parties were co-equals, but in the Balkans the SOE treated the OSS as a junior partner. Donovan became obsessed with establishing an American presence in the region.

Donovan set about this task in the late summer of 1943. Citing the Quebec Conference, where the Allied leaders agreed that subversive operations should be intensified in the region, Donovan launched an ambitious crusade to run independent missions and raise OSS to an equal footing with the British.*

Moving quickly, and without consulting the British, Donovan dispatched the three-man Jadwin Mission to Bulgaria. Led by Colonel C. C. Jadwin and Colonel Angel Kouyoumdjisky (formally a banker in the region with ties to the royal family and the Bulgarian army), the team managed to lure representatives of the Bulgarian government to Istanbul for talks. The Allies tried to twist the Bulgarians' arms by launching a couple of bombing raids, but the talks broke down, and Bulgaria remained an Axis satellite for most of the war.

Undeterred by the failure of the Jadwin Mission, Donovan stepped up OSS efforts to play a larger role in the Balkans.

Mansfield parachuted into Draja Mihailovic's headquarters in the third week of August 1943, where he spent several months surveying the Chetnik army and political environment. A few days later his counterpart, Captain Melvin Benson, parachuted into Marshal Tito's (Josip Broz's) headquarters.

---

*Donovan's strategic goal was to induce the Axis satellites Bulgaria, Hungary, and Romania, to switch sides.

OSS Operations in Yugoslavia and Albania

Two weeks after his drop, Mansfield received his first taste of war in Yugoslavia.

"Two spies were captured and I had the unpleasant experience of seeing them get their throats slit. . . .

"On the following morning, 6 September, the Germans let us have it and I had my first taste of combat. In the early morning mist a force of about 200 Germans came up the mountainside while we were asleep. All of a sudden all hell broke loose, with heavy machine [gun] fire 'dum-dumming' and light machine[gun fire] rat-tatting in all directions, right close by. Bailey [a British liaison officer attached to Mihailovic] and I threw on our pants and shoes, grabbed our rifles and 'quick-packs,' slit a hole through the back of our tent and jumped into the woods. We could see the Jerries coming up over the hills at about 400 yards in their blue-green uniforms with rifles, and opened up fire ourselves. But there did not seem to be any front. Machine guns, Sten guns were being fired from all directions, both in front and in back of us, and were cutting branches in the trees overhead. Bailey suggested we back further into the woods, which we did. Finally we did a semi-circle about a half-mile back. The firing continued another hour and a half. We learned that the Germans had been driven back down the mountain. We then went back, got our horses and things and returned to Mihailovic.

"Several were killed on both sides and some prisoners taken. I saw one prisoner being alternately questioned and then kicked and beaten. Later I was told that he had had his throat cut."[3]

After several months in Serbia, Mansfield and 10 other men made the long and dangerous trek across the mountains of central Serbia, avoiding German soldiers, Ustashe [Croats aligned with the Germans] patrols, and the Gestapo. The group made it to the coast where a ship brought them to Italy.

Even while Mansfield was still working with the Chetniks, a series of pro-Partisan reports from Allied officers assigned to Tito accused the Chetniks of refusing to fight, and even of collaborating with the Germans. In reality Mihailovic was practicing a policy of "accommodation," a series of temporary "live and let live" arrangements with the Germans to buy time for his own agenda.[4]

Reports written by the British officers attached to Tito overstated Partisan exploits and inflated their troop strength. The reports persuaded the British government to reduce supplies to Mihailovic to a trickle, making it very difficult for the Chetniks to mount operations against the Germans. The British were pulling the plug on Mihailovic.[5]

OSS contended that both the Partisans and Chetniks were valuable allies, and proposed that the country be divided into two separate operational zones: Tito would control the western portion of Yugoslavia and Mihailovic would operate in the eastern sector. If either camp did not fight the Germans they would be boycotted by the Allies. Courageously, Donovan even proposed parachuting into the country to propose a truce between the rival groups. The scheme died before the Allied conference at Tehran in late November 1943.

At Tehran, Churchill, backed by Stalin, demanded that Roosevelt sever U.S. ties with Mihailovic, and commit American support exclusively to Tito. OSS disagreed with the policy mainly since it did not want to put all of its intelligence eggs in one basket, and it still viewed Mihailovic as a viable ally capable of fighting the Germans.[6]

While Donovan was fighting to increase the OSS presence in Yugoslavia and keep OSS operators in Chetnik territory, he also continued to battle the British for functional control over American missions. Even OSS radio communications were tightly controlled by the British. Slowly the situation began to change. OSS operations expanded from individual agents to teams.

Shortly after Christmas 1943, the first OSS teams permitted to carry their own radios, Alum and Amazon, parachuted into Yugoslavia. Alum was led by American Lieutenant George Wuchinich, an officer with deep roots in Yugoslavia. While Wuchinich was viewed by some of his peers as biased in favor of the Partisans, the Alum team provided a bumper crop of intelligence. "A German intelligence officer of ack-ack Regiment No. 76, stationed in Vienna, deserted to the Partisans. He gave us . . . the whole ack-ack and locator defense system of southern Austria between Udine in Italy and Vienna in Austria. All in all it was a complete picture beyond our fondest wishes."[7]

Another Alum intelligence coup was obtaining information on a new German secret weapon. "We were on the lookout for new weapons and were the first to report the development of the flying bomb and gave the location of the proving grounds, description of the bomb, and location of one factory making them. This was gotten from a Nazi party member who deserted to the Partisans."[8]

Along with Alum's intelligence responsibilities, the team somehow found time to aid scores of Allied fliers who bailed out over Yugoslavia. In a single four-month period, Wuchinich's team rescued 90 fliers.[9]

Many of the fliers went through remarkable trials while trying to avoid the Germans and, sometimes, even the Yugoslav resistance groups. Allied flier Frank Gilly was bedridden in a Partisan field hospital when it was raided by the Chetniks. "About noon we heard one shot fired and about five minutes later, shots rained from all directions. There were about twenty patients from the buildings in which I was housed lying out in the sun. Those who could walk got up and ran. Those who could not walk started crawling. I had crawled about fifty feet together with two Partisans when we encountered face to face a band of Chetniks about 150 to 200 strong. They completely overran the buildings, that is, about twelve or fourteen buildings. Two Chetniks stopped to talk to us. These Chetniks talked first to the two Partisans. Then one of them came over to talk to me. He asked me if I was Italian and I told [him], 'No, I am American.' His reply was, 'Good.' I asked him what the insignia on his cap was and he told me 'Chetnik.' He told me to follow him which I did for about ten feet and then I told him that my leg was hurting me too much. He took my watch and then it looked as if he was going to leave, but another Chetnik from the road shouted something at him and he shot the two Partisans who had been with me. The first one was shot through the chest on the left side. The second was hit just below the mouth so that pieces of his head flew in all directions. I noticed that as the Chetnik shot each Partisan he shouted, 'Ustashe, Ustashe!' I consider that may have been to make me believe that the persons shot were not Partisans but actually Ustashe. The Chetnik who did the shooting was standing no more than eight feet away when he shot them. They left me then to go on and complete their raid on the village.

"Fifteen minutes or so later two Chetniks returned with one partisan. During the following few minutes I could see the Chetniks going back with loaded horses and hospital personnel and a few Partisan patients. Almost all of the Chetniks had gone back when one stopped and asked this Partisan who was sitting beside me for his blouse. The boy stood up to take it off and just as he got it half off the Chetnik shot him through the right lung from about fifteen feet.

"A bearded man approached wearing a similar type of cap to that already described and wearing crossed bandoliers of bullets over both shoulders and another two around his waist. He asked me who I was. I replied, 'American.' He said, 'Dobro, Dobro,' and proceeded on his way. The next Chetnik who approached was carrying about 20 stolen blouses. He asked me how I was. I replied, 'Cold.' He gave me a blouse and told me to get into the sun. That was the last Chetnik I came in contact with."[10]

In February 1944, the British ordered all Allied units attached to Mihailovic out of Yugoslavia. By the spring only one OSS officer remained in Chetnik territory, Captain George Musulin, a tough former college football player of Serbian ancestry. Donovan saw the value of having someone on the ground and requested Musulin be allowed to stay. Roosevelt approved the plan, but Churchill personally intervened. "We are pressing King Peter to clear himself of the millstone . . . if at this time an American mission arrives at Mihailovic's headquarters, it will show throughout the Balkans a complete contrariety of action between Britain and the United States." Roosevelt had no choice but to order Donovan to cancel the mission.[11]

In contrast, OSS operations and teams sent to Tito steadily increased in 1944. In November 1943, only 6 men were assigned to the Partisans, but by October 1944, 40 men were attached to 15 missions in the country.[12] Each mission had unique characteristics and objectives.

Team Cuckold was sent into Yugoslavia to blow the main rail line leading into the Reich. As Cuckold leader Major Franklin Lindsay recalled, "The first objective of the operation was in connection with the Anzio beachhead. We were to cut the main double track rail line south from Vienna over which the Germans were moving troops in support of their attempts to contain the beachhead.

"We had several members on my team, and a lieutenant who was not part of the team [also] dropped in with us. He was a weather officer and he brought with him weather observation equipment. His mission was to set up as near to a German airbase as he could get safely, and take observations at the same time of day that the airbase reported its weather reports to German central command. The mission was performed for the British codebreakers. They would intercept the German transmission, in cipher, but if they had the exact same information they had the key to breaking the German weather code. After the war, I found out the Allies read all of the German weather reports from occupied Europe as soon as they were sent.

"We crossed the frontier into the Third Reich, and finally made contact with the Fourth Zone of the Partisans, which was a relatively small group in the Karawanken Alps. We arranged for a parachute drop. The Partisans were really gung ho about attacking the rail line. This first attack was made against a bypass line and shortly afterward we attacked the main double intake line that went to Italy.

"We received the British version of plastic explosives. We had to organize a group of 50 to 75 men to carry the explosives down from the drop area to the track. The target was a stone viaduct. There was a German garrison about a kilometer away. So the operational plan was that the Partisans would set up roadblocks in order to protect us as we loaded explosives in holes we dug below the columns of the viaduct. It would take a couple hours time.

"Partisans with Bren guns were placed on a ridge overlooking the German garrison. Another group formed ambushes on the paths leading to the bridge. We spent a couple of hours at the base of two of the stone viaduct columns, loaded the explosives, and retreated down the track a short distance. They also decided that there was a tunnel near the viaduct that they wanted to attack but it was largely unsuccessful since large rocks were just blown on the track, which the Germans easily removed. We blew the charge which made one hell of a racket. The German garrison, thinking they were under attack, tried to defend themselves. The air was filled with tracer bullets. We went back and the viaduct was still standing. We had not placed a significant charge at the base of the two columns. Fortunately, we had enough explosives left to reload and we blew it again. This time after the sound of the explosion we heard a separate crash. That line was broken and never repaired during the war."[13]

Farther north, the Alum team headed by George Wuchinich was monitoring traffic on the same rail line. Along with two Partisan guards, Alum's four OSS agents penetrated the Third Reich, sidestepping unsuspecting German soldiers and moving into Austria. Wuchinich recalls what happened. "On the way we had to cross main highways and railroads, and often passed German barracks where we could plainly see them drinking beer and singing. Fortune smiled on us because it rained heavily every night and deadened the sound of our steps.

"As soon as we reached the point from where we could see the main railroad line leading from Zidani Most to Ljubljana, we planted our operations base deep into the side of a mountain. We hauled the logs up the mountains ourselves, and the two guards cut the wood and dug the cave. The hole was bunkered with boards and earth strewn over the top. The original moss and grass was laid over the roof, and not a single tree had been moved. At ten feet no one could tell whether a bunker had been built. It was here we buried our transmitter, battery, and foot-driven generator. We only visited this place to broadcast to our mission radio, from where the reports would be transmitted to Italy.

"Contacts were made with the local people, and food was brought to us secretly. Twice a day a basket of food was left beside a certain thicket or tree and we would send two men down to pick up the bundle. We changed our position often and in this way did not violate security. The people knew that we were Partisans, and I dressed the same as the two guards. I left my Army cap and insignia behind since traitors would quickly disclose to the German garrison (which numbered 700 men) that American officers were in the mountains nearby. The garrison was at Litija and I went down to within 300 yards of the town to observe life and the activity. There were no Partisan units in the vicinity and we were the only organized group. The few people who were trusted took great courage from our presence and helped us lay plans for the work. Within a few days we had made contacts with the railroad workers and began to get daily manifests of traffic both east and west on the main Zidani Most–Ljubljana line. Within ten days we had workmen from Maribor sending us traffic information along the Maribor–Zidani Most line which gave a total picture of all the trains traveling both into Italy and into Greece. This line is the throat of Balkan traffic.

"All my men, with one exception, were up on the mountainside sending the reports that had been accumulated and ciphered during the night. . . . My sixth sense made me certain that matters were not right, so I left the hollow in which I was resting, taking my tommy gun and field glasses to have a look around the valley into which the hollow emptied. In a sense I was the rear guard while my men worked on the mountainside, since the hollow was the approach to their position. I went down the valley to view the open spaces for any sign of life. While I scanned the forests from behind the thicket I saw a man coming up a path running full tilt. He cried, 'We killed a Gestapo man just about 200 yards from here.' I went with him and learned that a German, who had not suspected any armed unit close by, stumbled upon the two Partisans who were staying at a nearby house, and after learning that they were not Germans but Partisans, began running away shouting, '*Achtung, Banditten!*' The chase was short and even though the German had two bullets in him, he kept running until a third broke his thigh and tumbled him into a thicket. He hid until his head jerked up out of the bushes at the wrong time and bullets were pumped into the location from where he began to scream, '*Nicht Schutzen—Nicht Schutzen.*' He was lying in the branches quite bloody, and realizing that no hope existed for him, pointed his finger at his heart and mutely asked to be shot there. He was only 26, and completely Teutonic—fair hair and blue eyes. One of the men shook his head as if to say 'no' and calmly pointed the pistol at the German's forehead about three inches away and shot him between the eyes. The dead man's papers showed him to a member of the railroad Gestapo police. We took away all his valuables and threw earth over him.

"Somehow I was not convinced that this was an accidental meeting with the Gestapo. I warned my men we should move constantly and that someone must have blown our position. Even though the German had no gun he still was out nosing for us.

"We did keep moving, and during the three weeks I was there we were chased twice, but it was of no consequence. When I was certain that all had been properly organized and that the three men I would leave behind would do their work well, I decided to go back to the mission with my radio operator to see that all was in order there."[14]

Wuchinich's station continued to send reports on the rail traffic, but the British protested the existence of the independent station that was getting information "through its own sources." To resolve the issue Wuchinich decided to leave the outpost and take the matter up with OSS and the Allied command. It was a fateful action that may have saved his life. "Before any action could be taken we received a cable that the Germans had solved the problem by wiping out the station, killing the radio operator and scattering the rest."[15]

Frustrated by the Partisan activity, the Germans launched an offensive to crush the Partisans during the winter of 1943 and the spring of 1944. The centerpiece of the German offensive was Operation Rösselsprung (Knight's Move), which attempted to capture Tito and his staff. Knight's Move went into play on the morning of May 25, 1944, when German paratroopers and gliders landed only 300 yards from Tito's headquarters and the Allied mission. Tito and the Allied agents took to their heels in a deadly footrace to escape the German troops.

OSS radio operator Arthur Jibilian was with the Partisans during the German offensive. "I can safely say it was the most rugged two months of my life. Our mission was primarily to gather intelligence. Farish and Popovich were working with the Partisans and found out the strength of the German army in that area.

"[Near the end of May, the Germans attacked Tito's headquarters.] We had to run for our lives; for six nights and five days they were on our tail. I remember it was hot and sunny during the day and freezing at night. After about three days, I was just numb. Fortunately, the Germans couldn't use any mechanized equipment. We were in such rugged terrain it was just a footrace. The terrain was all mountains and densely forested.

"We were with 75 to 100 Partisans and constantly on the move. We moved through enemy lines five or six times. I'll never forget we were crossing through the lines in this mountainous area and there was an outpost, I think it was Bulgarian or German. We had to pass through it or take a more mountainous route that would take us six or seven additional days, [so] we opted to go through the Bulgarian camp.

"The Partisans supposedly bought off the Bulgarian guards. There was a bridge that we had to cross. We crept up to it and could see a little garrison they had there. Everything was nice and quiet until we got halfway across the bridge and all hell broke loose. Flames went up, lights came on, searchlights probed. It was the first time I fired my Marlin submachine gun. Glass shattered and the searchlight went out. We crossed and amazingly, only one person was killed."[16]

To ease the pressure on the escaping Partisans, OSS OGs and British commandos launched raids on German garrisons in the Dalmatian islands of Brac and Solta. Andy Mousalimas was a member of the Greek OG group that raided Solta Island. "Before we got to the village, we started firing on it. Then they told us to back up. Allied P-40s came in and dive-bombed the village. Our group split up. Two squads went one way and the third and fourth squads went around the other side of the village. The other group took casualties. One man was killed and several others were wounded.

"We kept moving. There was nothing but silence. We were skirting this brick wall and all of a sudden five German officers jumped over the wall. We backed away and two members of my squad put up our guns and they put their hands up. I called out to our group sergeant and asked him what to do. He growled, 'Bring 'em up.' He was right at the end of the wall and ready to go into an open area so he grabbed one of the German officers who balked about entering the open area. He pushed them out, all five of them. The German officers started to scream out. All of a sudden, a platoon of German soldiers who were camouflaged came out. When they came out of the camouflage I never saw anything like it. I was shocked because you couldn't see them until they emerged [and] gave themselves up. What was interesting is why would these German officers give up when they had these men camouflaged so well?

"When we finished up we went out and started to clean out the whole village. We heard voices coming out of the ground. Some were hollering. We had several German POWs with us and we told them to start digging. The Germans thought it was a Yugoslav native who had been buried by the bombing raid.

"This shows you something about human nature—the Germans reluctantly started to dig. When the P-40s hit, a German got knocked off a building and buried alive. The only thing that saved him was a small air hole that allowed him to breathe. When the Germans realized it wasn't a Yugoslavian they started to dig like hell. They were concerned about getting the guy out. One of my guys remarked, 'Shoot the son-of-a-bitch.'"[17]

One of the men in Mousalimas's squad barked at fellow OSS agent Alex Phillips, "Why don't we just kill him and put him out of his misery?" Phillips said this part of the war has haunted him for decades. "We got into a big argument that you couldn't do that since this guy was a prisoner of war. They tried to get me to do it but I wouldn't. This guy is a POW and one thing led to another, finally, I reached down and lifted up what looked like a piece of sidewalk and released him. Remember in *Private Ryan* when they captured that German and let him go? It came back to haunt them. After seeing that movie all of these memories that I buried came back in my dreams. I keep seeing that man under the rock, he comes back in my dreams every night."[18]

Mousalimas remembers what happened after they pulled the soldier out of the rubble.

"When we got him out he was white and from what I understand he died from shock."[19]

The OGs performed well. Thanks to their diversionary attacks, and to merciless strafing and bombing of the pursuing German forces by Allied aircraft, Tito narrowly managed to escape capture.

The small country of Albania borders Yugoslavia to the south. The Allies gave only limited aid to the Albanian guerrillas since the groups were primarily engaged in fighting among themselves and not Axis troops. But beginning in November 1943, several SI teams infiltrated into Albania, gathering information on the resistance groups and the Axis troops in the country.

OSS operative Lloyd Smith arrived a few days after SI set up shop. Armed with only a pistol, and with zero knowledge of the culture or the language, Smith was on a mercy mission to rescue 26 unarmed nurses and medical personnel whose plane disappeared over occupied Albania.

"I arrived at the small town of Dukati and was met by about 50 armed Ballists [a guerrilla group in the country] who tried to persuade me not to enter Partisan territory. I told them this is a mission of human compassion. 'We have people in your country that are by themselves; they are not soldiers but medical personnel. Right now, our president knows that they are in your country. I am sure that he trusts you people. He expects your help.' It turns out the president was very much interested in the mission and getting the people out. Reluctantly, the Ballists provided me with three guides and we started out for Partisan territory.

"After traveling some distance, we encountered a group of 30 armed Partisans. One of them would accompany us to our destination, the town of Terbaci. At Terbaci we were taken to a house where I met a girl who was acting as an interpreter.

"The Germans were active in the area. I noticed the Partisans coming back down the pass with captured German boots, seven K98 rifles, one MG-34 machine gun, and three pistols. The next morning the Ballist guides had been taken prisoner by the Partisan commissar. I was told that they would not be allowed to accompany me. I went down to his headquarters.

"They seemed to be very glad to see me but showed disappointment that I was accompanied by three Ballist guides. They also embarrassed me by asking, 'Why aren't the Allies making good progress in northern Italy?' They were very quick to point out how well the Russians were doing on their front. Here also for the first time they wanted to take my three Ballist guides prisoner. I told them that I had guaranteed the safety of my guides and would go nowhere without them.

"On the afternoon of December 17, 1943, word was received by W/T [radio] from Cairo that we heard from the group and they were on the move and expected to be at Kue on the 21st. The next morning, I left the base for Kue. I was using the coastal trail since the Germans were still very active around Dukati and Terbaci . . . this was a hell of a rough trail.

"It was still raining and since my clothes were wet I decided to stay in Dhermi that day. I received word that over 100 Germans were making a house-to-house search of a nearby village for Partisans and weapons. Suspecting that Dhermi would be next on their list, I moved to a house at the extreme western end of town and made ready for a fast getaway. Before they arrived I moved to a cave and spent the remainder of the night sleeping there with a shepherd and his flock. This is standard operating procedure with the Germans. They move into a village, kill a few Partisans, and after a few days move out again.

"The following day I contacted an English-speaking friend and made arrangements for six men to start out in three different directions in search of information about the American party. The men were to travel in pairs and should the party be met, it was agreed that one of the two men should stay with the party and the other should return to me with information.

"The next morning [January 6] I left and met the party just outside of Kue. I cannot remember any group of people looking happier."[20]

Smith and the downed medical personnel avoided numerous German patrols and eventually made the long trip to the coast, where a ship picked them up and brought them back to Italy. A few weeks later he was sent back to Albania to find another group of three nurses. He brought them safely back to Italy, forever winning their gratitude and the Distinguished Service Cross, America's second highest decoration.

By the summer of 1944, Tito's forces were on the move. Their attacks focused on Mihailovic's weakened forces as well as the Germans. Frank Lindsay recalls how a German double agent tried to infiltrate Fourth Zone Partisan Headquarters.[21]

"Early during the summer an Austrian arrived in the Fourth Zone Partisan Headquarters. He said that he was from an Austrian group outside of Graz and represented a resistance cell. He claimed that he was from a group of Austrians who had gone to the forest to resist and he had heard that there were Allied officers with the Partisans in southern Austria. He was sent to contact us to get radios and a radio operator, in the hope of receiving air support. I thought, here's an opportunity we had been looking for, and sent messages back to headquarters asking them to send a radio operator with equipment. A week or two passed without direction from headquarters. We finally received a favorable reply but it would take two or three weeks to drop the radio and operator. In light of this, the man from the Graz group decided to return and send another group back to us when the radio operator and radio arrived. A couple of weeks later, a second man arrived and said he was from Graz and ready to pick up the radio and operator. A few days later a Partisan patrol came in.

"One of the men in the patrol spotted the man and said he was a Gestapo agent. They were from the same village. We immediately interrogated him. Apparently there was a [resistance] group outside the mountains near Graz. They had sent a courier and the courier had been captured on his way to us and the German SD [Sicherheitsdienst] had decided, quite intelligently, to substitute one of their own people for this fellow they captured. He was to come, appear to be the courier, and try to induce us to provide a courier and radio operator which he would take back. That way they would control the entire operation. It would have been a classic double agent operation."[22]

In the summer of 1944, OSS found the pretext it needed to reestablish contact with Mihailovic. Hundreds of downed American fliers were trapped in Chetnik-controlled territory. OSS approached the Partisans and British about the problem. When they failed to provide a solution, the Americans formed the Air Crew Rescue Unit (ACRU). Staffed primarily by OSS, ACRU officially rescued fliers. Covertly, Donovan once again directed it to reestablish contact with Mihailovic. In August 1944, the Halyard Team, led by Captain Musulin, parachuted into Pranjane, about 80 kilometers south of Belgrade, where the Chetniks were caring for 250 downed Allied fliers. After parachuting into Pranjane, Team Halyard supervised construction of a runway, which C-47 transport planes would use to evacuate hundreds of airmen.

Art Jibilian, who had recently returned from Linn Farish's mission with Tito, was asked to join Halyard. "I was contacted since I was an experienced radio operator behind the lines. They asked, 'Would you like to go in again?' I said, 'Sure.'

"It took us almost a month to get in because the British didn't want us to go in. . . . [They didn't want] Mihailovic to get credit for helping American airmen.

"After about a month we finally got into Pranjane. When we landed we found not 50 but 250 airmen. They were in pretty bad shape. Some of them had wounds; they had been force-marched, et cetera. Many did not have boots in the parachute jumps but the natives made sure they had something on their feet. These people fed the men; 250 take up a lot of resources and those people fed these men at the expense of themselves and their children.

"Directing about 300 laborers, we built the airstrip. When we were with the Halyard Mission, preparing an airfield to evacuate downed fliers, the Partisans were shelling us with our own ammunition that we had dropped to them.

"About a week after we arrived, the first C-47s landed and started taking the men out. We got these airmen back to Italy. It was beautiful. The men were so grateful for the help the Chetniks gave them. They gave their clothes, jackets, and anything they could spare to these people since they were in such desperate need of them."[23]

The six-man Team Ranger, led by Lieutenant Colonel Robert McDowell, arrived in Serbia in late August. Officially McDowell was rescuing fliers, but unofficially he was there to continue OSS intelligence operations with the Chetniks. McDowell surveyed Chetnik and Axis forces and witnessed firsthand the Partisans' systematic efforts to destroy the Chetniks. First Lieutenant Ellsworth Kramer, the junior officer on Ranger, recalls the aftermath of a Partisan attack on a village friendly to the Chetniks. "[On the] morning of [September 18], the Partisans put up a heavy counterattack. The Chetnik commander of the brigade [I was observing], Captain Gordich, asked me to counterattack or retreat, and I replied that I was not the commander of his troops, and therefore, could not advise him but was solely here for observation. In the Chetnik ranks are weapons of all calibers and makes. Many men go into battle unarmed and wait for a man to get hit and then take up the dropped rifle. The majority have no shoes at all [and] are dressed in peasant clothing. The only reason they fought so stubbornly is to prevent the Communists from occupying their villages.

"[A few days later] in a small village eight miles north of Drenova, I saw the bodies of eight men (civilians) who had been tortured to death by knife. The older men had been slashed about the face with a knife and then their skulls bashed in with a rifle butt. One young man who refused to join the Partisans had been carved up pretty badly by the orders of a Partisan woman who stood by.

"I also found out from Partisan prisoners that they had specific orders to kill or capture the American officer with the Chetniks. Also upon my arrival back at Bela Voda, the peasant at whose hut I had been staying told me that two hours after I left the place, a Partisan lieutenant, two women and nine guards came to his hut and asked for the whereabouts of the American officer.

"I never have had much time to interrogate Partisan prisoners because if I get to them within half an hour after capture, they are executed by knife. Prisoners are killed by both sides. All Partisans, dead or wounded, are relieved of their boots, shoes and serviceable clothing immediately, if they have any. . . . Hatred runs so high that I have seen men kick the dead after a battle."[24]

Fear of a Soviet takeover of Eastern Europe motivated several high-ranking Germans to contact the OSS to discuss the potential surrender of their forces in the Balkans. During September 1944, McDowell, in the presence of Mihailovic, met with Rudi Stärker, a messenger from General Hermann Neubacher, military governor of the southeast Balkans. However, no surrender agreement ever materialized. Politically the Allies were in a delicate situation. The Russians, massed on the Yugoslav border, would have perceived a German surrender to the United States as a separate peace, one of Stalin's greatest nightmares. Mike Devyak, McDowell's radio operator, broke nearly 60 years of silence to recall a secret meeting with the Germans. "We were at Mihailovic's headquarters that consisted of only a couple hundred men. Ninety-nine percent of the time we were walking, sometimes we were on horseback. I recall one incident where it was still daylight and we were getting ready to eat and the perimeter guards suddenly were under attack and they ordered us to get the hell out of there.

"I remember we went about 26 hours without stopping. We crossed a German convoy, just before an individual truck would come around a bend we would pass through them.

"My most vivid memory is regarding one of the radio messages I was asked to send out. It essentially said we made contact with the German high command in the Balkan area and they wanted to surrender their troops. At the time the Russians were closing in on Yugoslavia and the Germans wanted to avoid being taken by the Russians.

"I spent hours coding the message. It was King Peter's birthday, September 4 or 6, I don't remember. They were having a big celebration. Everyone went to it except me and my guard. I spent all day on the radio encoding the message and I had to wait for the reply. We had a preset time when I could make contact with them. On the other hand they could call me whenever since they had powerful radios.

"They responded by telling us to 'get out of the country any way you can.' They weren't going to negotiate with the Germans. It was politics. Several of the British liaison officers were full-fledged Communists. Yugoslavia was controlled by the British. Tito was their man. They didn't want to give anything to Mihailovic."[25]

McDowell was ordered to break off contact with the Germans and return to Italy. Churchill again personally persuaded Roosevelt to recall McDowell's mission, for the sake of preserving the appearance of Allied unity. The decision effectively conceded Yugoslavia to Tito. But McDowell's mission was not the last time the Germans tried to contact the Allies about potential surrender discussions. Franklin Lindsay describes the most promising proposed meeting that might have altered the course of the war.

"On October 24, 1944 we received an operational priority message from OSS headquarters asking me to go to Croatia to try to make contact with a senior German general, Glaise von Horstenau. OSS Switzerland had made secret contact with him and explained he wished to discuss surrender and asked for a meeting with an American officer.

"Getting to him took much longer than expected. It was nearly 100 miles away as the crow flies and twice that distance on foot, plus this was during the winter and we had to travel through German-occupied territory. Three of us and our liaison officer and a patrol of 10 men and a machine gun left Zone Headquarters. . . .

"Several days later we crossed a river and moved along the courier lines and arrived in Croatia.

"As we approached Zagreb the Partisans sent a courier in to establish my meeting with him and [we] found out that Glaise von Horste-

nau had been arrested by the Gestapo. I later found out after research-
ing it that he had been recalled to Hitler's headquarters at Berchtesgaden and relieved of his command. This was getting close to the end
of the war when the German armies surrendered. He was in Austria,
was picked up, and sent to an officers' prison camp and killed himself
a few months later. Hitler probably did not know of Dulles's contacts.

"I was not given much information at the time. I later found Allen
Dulles's [OSS station chief in Switzerland] message at the National
Archives. Apparently, von Horstenau had contacts with the German
general who was in charge of German Army Group Southeast. He
mentioned another German general and that the two together represented the German high command in the Balkans. He indicated that
in their name, he was prepared to negotiate surrender. But they
weren't going to negotiate with the Partisans or Communists. Hitler
probably felt he was not aggressive enough against the Partisans and
that's why he was arrested.

"I always regretted that we never made contact. If we had it could
have opened up the whole of the Balkans. It would have given the Allies the opportunity for a landing at Istria, [a] move through the Ljubljana Gap, [a]cross the Hungarian plain. This probably meant that
Allied troops would have been in Vienna before the Russians. So it
could have changed things considerably."[26]

During the fall of 1944, Soviet troops overran Romania, Bulgaria,
and most of Yugoslavia. Coinciding with the Soviet drive, Tito
launched his own offensive into Serbia, crushing most of Mihailovic's
forces. At the time, the OSS was running 15 intelligence teams attached
to Tito. The U.S. teams were finally under their own command, designated the Independent American Military Mission (IAMM). As the end
of the war approached the Allied teams working with Tito were ex-
pelled. Almost a year later, the Communists captured Mihailovic and
placed him on trial. He was found guilty of treason and executed by a
firing squad. Perhaps most telling are Franklin Lindsay's final words

with Marshal Tito before the IAMM left Yugoslavia. Lieutenant Colonel Lindsay, then in command of the IAMM, asked Tito if other political parties could coexist independently with the Communist Party. According to Lindsay, the Partisan leader responded, "Prewar parties represented the collaborators and were the enemies of the people. Surely you don't propose that they be allowed to be revived? Other new parties could of course exist, but who would they represent? And what would they do? The Communist Party represents the people."[27]

In the end, the Chetniks and Partisans took a heavy toll on the Germans. Germany was forced to deploy 15 German divisions and 100,000 well-armed native troops in order to maintain control over Yugoslavia. While the Allies achieved their goal of tying down large numbers of German troops, they did so at considerable expense: the tilt toward Tito's Partisans contributed substantially to the postwar Communist takeover of Yugoslavia.

SEVEN

"SMASHEM"

Greece

Life for the average Landser in Greece was a nightmare. Firefights and ambushes by the guerrillas were a way of life. Even the generally highly trained, battle-tempered Waffen SS veterans were feeling the strain . . . exactly as the Allies had hoped.

OSS operations in Greece began in August 1943, when SI (Secret Intelligence) agents began to be infiltrated into Greece by submarine. Throughout most of the war, insertion of agents presented the greatest obstacle to clandestine operations in the country. Agents were parachuted in, or more typically, arrived in caïques, small fishing vessels. The agents would depart from Alexandria and sail to Cyprus in cargo ships. From Cyprus, the ships proceeded to secret bases in Turkey, which operated with the blessing of the Turkish government. The final leg of the journey was made in tiny two-ton caïques that surreptitiously slipped the agents into Greece.

One of SI's highest-priority missions was the Simmons Project. Organized by the OSS Special Projects Office, a department created to "carry out special assignments and missions approved by the Director," Simmons was intended to secure intelligence on a radio-guided bomb, the HS-293. German pilots had used the HS-293, a precursor to modern-day smart bombs, to destroy several Allied ships. After an OSS informant, a German officer, claimed that a bomber grounded at a Greek airfield was carrying the bomb, OSS recruited several men to gather information. One of those agents was a former Greek army officer, Lieutenant Nikolaos Sotiriou. Spirited into Greece via caïques, Sotiriou recalls his odyssey to find the bomb.[1]

"I reached Tsagezi the same day, and left there in a small canoe belonging to black marketers. That evening, we were caught in a storm and were in great danger of capsizing, so we stopped at a lonely point on the coast about thirty miles north of Tsagezi, waiting there three days for the weather to clear. During the three days, we repaired the damage to the canoe.

"On the 29th, the weather cleared and we continued our journey, traveling by day only and stopping at night at various lonely spots on the coast. We were approached the following day by an armed German caïques which was prepared to search us, but thanks to our miserable appearance and good manners (we offered them some drinks), the Germans' suspicions were allayed and we were allowed to proceed without even an examination of our papers. The morning of October 1, we reached the coast of Aretsou, three kilometers outside of Salonika. As we landed, I observed a German NCO with field glasses on the terrace of a single-story building, following the movements of all craft. At the moment I was disembarking, I discovered that he had trained his glasses on me."

The Germans didn't question Sotiriou, and he began searching for the plane with the bomb, or for workmen who may have seen it up close.

"I personally visited the area of the Mikra Airdrome three times. The first time, disguised as a shepherd, I approached the northwest part of the airdrome with a flock; the second, I hid in the garden of a house very close to the east side of the airdrome; the third time, I approached by sea in a canoe, pretending to fish. From this personal observation, I made certain of the following: in the northwest section of the airdrome, there was an abandoned glider. A small training plane

OSS Operations in Greece

was in the smaller hangar; three other small training planes were half-hidden under trees in the northeast part of the airdrome. The main hangar, in the center of the airdrome, contained barrels of gasoline. In general, except for the guards, there was no movement observable. From the above observations, I decided that the bomb for which I was looking was no longer there.

"During all this time, I had sent trustworthy people to the vicinity of the airdrome for the purpose of making friends with the Germans working there. The Germans were then invited to parties, where by indirect questioning, attempts were made to get information regarding the baby. It was impossible to learn anything from all the Germans contacted. None of them seemed to know anything about it. At the same time, my cousin and I repeatedly approached a German NCO by the name of Johann Kiellner who was a radio operator. He had been in Greece about two years, at the airdromes of Athens and Salonika. We finally succeeded in bribing him, but either because he deceived us once he was paid or because he actually had no information, we learned nothing from him. He professed never to have seen such a bomb in Greece.

"Through one of my relatives who speaks German, Clio Mesirli (who was absolutely trustworthy), I approached a German officer named Oberleutnant Hans Guntner, who had been stationed in Athens and later Salonika. I questioned him when he was slightly under the influence of liquor, but he seemed to know nothing. I signaled Cairo of my efforts with the NCO and officer, and that I was continuing my search.

"From all the above I decided that the bomb was no longer in Salonika, and wired Cairo to that effect a few days later."[2]

The principal buildup of SI teams took place between May and October 1944. Eventually 30 teams, totaling 80 U.S. agents, were gathering intelligence throughout the country, from Athens to the Aegean islands. Teams worked directly with the royalist, anticommunist EDES, as well as the Communist and Leftist EAM and its army, ELAS.[3]

In late 1943, seven German divisions were stationed in Greece; as in Yugoslavia, the Allies wanted the German garrison to stay put. OSS and SOE devised a bold plan, known as Operation Noah's Ark, to keep the large German garrison far away from the upcoming Allied landings in France.[4]

Noah's Ark continued the fiction promoted by earlier Allied deception plans that the Allies would attack Germany from the Balkans. The plan called for extensive sabotage operations throughout Greece. Remarkably, fewer than 400 SO, OG, and British SOE agents would be responsible for destroying bridges, trains, tunnels, and truck convoys on an epic scale. They executed a classic guerrilla campaign that yielded spectacular results.

Noah's Ark also had a political dimension. The plan called for unifying the Royalist, Communist, and religious resistance groups; not an easy task considering the political complexities and rivalries among the parties.

Noah's Ark went into action in January 1944. The first major achievement was not military but diplomatic. Under the "Plaka" agreement, SO was able temporarily to halt the blood feud between the anticommunist EDES and the Communist and leftist EAM.* By directing both groups' energies against the Germans and not against each other, the Plaka agreement made a crucial contribution to the success of Noah's Ark.[5]

SO quickly got back into the business of blowing things up. The first major mission was an impressive one. At the request of the State Department and Joint Chiefs, OSS was tasked with cutting the flow of vital chrome ore from Turkey to Germany. OSS's R&A (Research and Analysis) Branch recommended targeting two bridges for destruction: the 210-foot Svilengrad Bridge, code-named "Milwaukee," and the

---

*The EAM's army was known as the ELAS. This book refers to both units collectively as the EAM.

100-foot Alexandroupolis Bridge, "Joliet." A four-man team led by Captain James Kellis, dubbed the "Chicago Mission," infiltrated into Greece the end of March.[6] Chicago's only surviving member, Spiro Cappony, recalls the early phase of the operation, which involved gathering information on the trains in Istanbul, Turkey, a hive of espionage activity. "I accepted the mission and was joined by two other team members, A. Georgiades and Mike Angelos, and they said 'Gus (they called me Gus), how the hell are we going to get to Istanbul?' This is how new we were. 'Who's going to meet us?' 'A guy by the name of Spurning, he's a professor from Yale University.' One of them said, 'How the hell are we going to know who the guy is?' I said, 'Well, my orders say he's going to show a ruby ring on his finger.' 'Man oh man these guys are crazy,' remarked one of the guys.

"We traveled to Istanbul. The train stopped and we got our luggage. Walking down the gangway there, George says, 'Where the hell are we going?' I said, 'Come on, just keep walking. I have no idea either.' George was assigned to me as my bodyguard because I knew the codes and they let him be my right-hand man. Here comes this guy in a trench coat. I said, 'George, I bet you that guy in the trench coat, he's our contact.' Sure enough, as soon as he passes by, he raises his right hand and shows his ruby ring. I said, 'George, that's the guy.' He said, 'Turn around and follow me.' So we turned around and got into a black car and ended up in the embassy there. We spent about two months in Istanbul. We went to try and find out different things about the rail lines. At the rail yards, we talked to people and learned which trains shipped the ore and when they left.

"Before the mission, we were given cyanide pills. In the event we were captured we were supposed to take them. I put mine behind my belt, and put it out of my mind. I didn't want to think about that possibility."[7]

After gathering intelligence on the trains, the Chicago Mission team crossed the Greco-Turkish frontier into the Evros area of northern Greece. The men walked to the local EAM headquarters, which was located in the side of a mountain. They found the Communist guerrillas, or Andartes, to be like an "organized mob, armed mainly with 19th-century muskets."[8]

Spiro recalls their first encounter with the Andartes: "All of the sudden we encountered the guerrillas; they held us up. We put our hands up, and identified ourselves as Americans. I had an American flag on my shoulder. They were surprised to see us. Captain Kellis negotiated with the guerrillas, what he wanted them to do and what we were going to do. In the meantime, the Greek guerrillas, in order to work with us, made their demands. They wanted ammunition, guns, they wanted whatever we could give them because they were preparing for their own little tid-bit later on I guess. Kellis reported back to base and the British started dropping arms."[9]

While Kellis's group was rearming the guerrillas, large German patrols actively attempted to wipe out the team and the EAM contingent. Kellis remembers one close call. "The enemy lost no time making it as uncomfortable for us as possible. They started making arrests in order to terrorize the Greek populace and thus prevent them from supplying us with food, but they soon sensed that those measures only strengthened the morale of the population. Eventually, the governor of the district requested and received a special reconnaissance battalion from the Olympus district, which was assigned the sole duty of eliminating the guerrillas. This battalion, although it was composed mostly of second-rate troops, was very well equipped and thus put us on the defensive. In one case, this battalion surrounded [me], Angelos and twelve Andartes near the village of Lefkimi. We fought them for a period of seven hours and finally escaped, although three of us were slightly wounded."[10]

During the first week of May, the caïque St. John dropped off three new team members: Lieutenant Athens, Sergeant Curtis, and Specialist 3rd Class Psoinos. The team went into "overtime" to train the guerrillas on the use of U.S. weapons and demolitions, and destruction of the bridges went into the final planning stages. The Svilengrad Bridge, "Milwaukee," the larger and tougher target, was located in Bulgaria, and "Joliet" near the northern Greek town of Alexandropoulis. Chicago sent a team against each target. Sergeant Curtis and Angelos led a group of 40 Andartes against the Alexandropoulis Bridge, while Lieutenant John Athens, Captain Jim Kellis, and 170 Andartes hauling 1,400 pounds of explosives set out for the Svilengrad Bridge.[11] Kellis remembers the trek to the bridge and its destruction. "For the first two days, we traveled through mountainous and relatively safe country, but later we crossed into the Maritsa or Evros Valley. There we had to take several security measures. We walked only at night and always followed a zigzag course so as not to give away our direction of march. Our guides were excellent and even though we passed nearby German and Bulgarian posts, they never noticed us. It is worth mentioning that during this march only three persons knew the destination and purpose of this mission. For example, the sabotage crew, which was in the advance element, did not know that the main body carried explosives. Also the main body knew nothing of the presence with us of a sabotage crew.

"On 29 May, we assembled the Andartes and explained our mission. They were very enthused and immediately proceeded to prepare the charge.

"The Germans were caught napping and did not interfere until the last five minutes of the operation. They fired a flare and opened up with a machine gun and submachine guns in the general direction of the bridge. Luckily the bridge was already mined and we were making the connections with primer cord. Steps two and three were easily carried out. . . . Mining of the bridge started [late in the evening of] May 29 and was completed at 0010 [12:10 a.m.] May 30. The slow-burning fuse was set for five minutes delay and the bridge was completely demolished by the explosives."[12]

The Alexandropoulis Bridge assigned to Sergeants Curtis and Angelos met the same fate as the Svilengrad Bridge.[13]

A new phase in the OSS campaign in Greece began on April 23, 1944, when the first OG (Operational Group) team infiltrated into Greece. During a period of 219 days, seven OG teams consisting of 1 or 2 officers and 20 to 22 men entered Greece by small boat or parachute. The OG teams sowed an enormous amount of destruction, as their final report states: "Trains attacked 14, Locomotives destroyed 11, trucks destroyed 61, bridges destroyed 15, yards of rail blown 9,920, enemy killed and wounded 1,794."[14]

The Greek Operational Group was made up of volunteers from the 122nd Infantry Battalion. Formed at the request of the Greek government-in-exile, the battalion was composed almost entirely of men of Greek ancestry. About half the enlisted men in the cadre were Greek-Americans and the other half Greek nationals who one way or another entered the United States and wanted to fight Germany. Some of these Greeks even had their ships torpedoed by U-boats, were picked up in the water, and brought to the United States. Almost twelve hundred men volunteered, but a withering selection process weeded out over a thousand. The volunteers were powerfully motivated to become part of the unit, as the commanding officer of Group II, John Giannaris, recalls.

"The spirit within the unit was tremendous. They were ready and eager to get back to Greece to undo what the war had done to their people. They trained hard and were focused and determined. We pared the unit down drastically. All in all, we had over 1,200 men come into the unit but it was pared down to 182. The ones that were left out or sent to other units would break down and cry."[15]

Ted Russell also noted the men's morale while embarking for Europe from Camp Patrick Henry, Virginia in December 1943. "At the camp our boys would march and sing, both in English and Greek, and the entire camp would say, 'Who are these guys?' We were dressed smartly, had new experimental clothing including jump boots, and we were the first unit to be assigned the new Eisenhower jacket. We looked good, acted good, and the biggest thing, we felt good. Officers from other outfits would ask me, 'Who are you guys?' Security told us to say that we [were] truck drivers; they knew that wasn't the case.

"As I speak now, I vividly recall a dreary day in Virginia when many units were marching, including the 88th and 45th Divisions, who were slated for combat duty in Italy. Standing aside as communications officer I could see these poor soldiers in these infantry outfits scared and ill-prepared for combat duty. Our group was marching with joy; we were hyped up and ready for combat; we wanted to go into battle; we were not forced to go into battle; we were prepared to go into battle."[16]

The first OG team to enter Greece was Group I, led by Captain George Verghis. On April 23, 1944, Verghis's band of 22 men made the dangerous journey across the Aegean, barely avoiding the searchlight of a roving German E-boat. Once ashore, the group began operations in the Epirus region of northwest Greece. A veteran of three wars, Verghis is still haunted by his first successful roadblock. "I spent twenty years trying to get rid of these demons. It was decided to go to the horseshoe [a bend in the road shaped like a horseshoe] and hit anything that would come along. We reached the position at 2030 [8:30 p.m.]. By this time we were all extremely tired. We had averaged two meals a day and sleep was hard to get during the day. A couple hours later, five headlights were seen approaching from the east and 10 minutes later seven more were seen. We knew that if this truck did not stop at Versinaw we would hit them. We had taken our positions hastily and everyone was making last-minute preparations on their emplacements.

"No man in the group was more than 30 yards away from the road and some were only a few feet from it. The second section was on the right flank and the first section was on the left. We did not have long to wait and soon we heard the sound of approaching motors. The first truck rounded the horseshoe past the second section and was in front of my section when four more trucks started to round the horseshoe. By this time all weapons were fully loaded, safeties were off, and all ears strained for the signal to fire. As the last truck rounded the horseshoe, [I gave the signal to fire]. The bazooka, operated by Technician Fifth Grade Leonardos, missed on his first shot at the fourth truck, and by this time four trucks were in the group's sector of fire. The enemy was taken completely by surprise and it was some seconds before he could come into action. The bazooka was again brought into position to fire, but the first shot had revealed its location and that of a BAR [Browning Automatic Rifle] manned by Johnson. There were five Germans, two in the cab and three in the rear. The driver was killed instantly and the other man was shot up badly. One of the men in the rear of the truck was in an empty barrel and was armed with a Schmeisser (MP-40 submachine gun). He had located the BAR by its fire and with the help of the bazooka flash. He opened up on the BAR, which had just jammed, but missed. At that moment, the bazooka fired again and scored a direct hit on the fourth truck. Immediately it burst into flames, for it was loaded with gasoline and ammunition. The driver had been killed by bullets; two men manning an MG-34 were killed by concussion and did not fire a shot. The man with the Schmeisser saw the BAR out of commission, switched his fire to Sergeant Apostolatos, who was armed with an M1 rifle, then, upon seeing the bazooka fire, tried to knock it out also.

"As the firing died down, Apostolatos and Papastrat rushed to the road and started removing the bodies from the vehicles."[17]

The OG teams blended into the countryside, growing beards, carefully planning their operations, and swiftly striking German targets at night. By the middle of the summer, over 150 OG personnel were roaming Greece, destroying bridges and barracks, mining roads, ambushing convoys and trains. Troop trains were a primary target; 14 were attacked. Angelo Lygizos, a BAR gunner with Group V, remembers attacking their first German troop train.

"I just got back from a trip to Greece and I found the spot where we set up the ambush 58 years ago. As the train, about 50 cars long, came in, we immediately blew up the tracks, derailing the engine. Someone fired a bazooka which scored a direct hit on the engine's boiler creating a big explosion and a lot of steam. We opened fire on the boxcars, spraying everything that moved for about 10 minutes, turning the train into Swiss cheese. Next we charged forward pouring on the fire. Eventually the order came down, 'Cease fire!' and the Germans and Italians began to surrender. We started rounding up the Germans; they were SS. There was a German lieutenant and a couple of big sergeants and about 200 Italians. The Italians started crying, 'Take us with you.' We couldn't take them. There was no place to put them so the guerrillas took care of them. The train was loaded with medical supplies, mules and trucks which the guerrillas started taking.

"We got the signal that German tanks were coming in from the highway towards us. The order came down, 'Withdraw.' Lieutenant Payton said to me, 'Get that officer and move him up into the mountains.' I got him and told him to move. He was tough and looked like a stereotypical German officer. Those SS soldiers were the best soldiers in the world. He had a gold ring. I wanted it and told him to take it off. He said, 'Nix! Nix' and wouldn't do it so I almost cut his finger off trying to get it. I got it off along with his watch and ribbons."[18]

Shortly after destroying the train, Group V moved the prisoners into the mountains. Pete Photis has an incident seared into his memory. "We had a couple of German prisoners and passed through a village. One of the kids recognized a soldier that had killed his mother and father. They had it coming. The guerrillas gave a pistol to the 12-year-old kid and said, 'Here, kill the two German prisoners.' We told them that wasn't our way and took the pistol away from the kid." But the reprieve was only temporary.

The Greek people had suffered tremendously under the German occupation. Aiding the Andartes led to swift reprisals from the Germans: villages were burned to the ground and there were mass executions. Captured guerrillas were also shot on the spot, so naturally the Andartes were unforgiving, as Lygizos recalls.

"Eventually we turned them over to the guerrillas and they killed all of them. They put them in a ravine or canyon, lined them up and shot them."[19]

Shortly after the POWs were executed by the Andartes, Lygizos attempted to visit a young woman he had met earlier that week, a mistake that has haunted him for 58 years.

"There was a girl that I had met outside the town of Edesa, which was garrisoned by the Germans. Stupidly I took off from the group to see the girl. The German guards were stationed outside the town. I never told this to anyone including the officer. I went out to see the girl, [and] a guard surprised me from behind. He took my grenades, tommy gun, and knife away and ordered me to 'move!' As I started to walk forward I turned around and I kicked him. Hitting him squarely in the stomach with the back of my shoe, he fell over and I scrambled for a large rock. I grabbed it and hit him on the back of the head, killing him. Blood went all over the place."[20]

In the middle of August, Lieutenant John Giannaris of Group II remembers the German reprisals and a military operation that turned into a mercy mission. "That night the Germans started torching the homes in the villages as the people slept. It was in reprisal for something, I don't know what.

"When I first got there, we found the Germans would take hostages. They would take civilian hostages and murder them. I saw the mass graves. I asked about it, a villager told me, 'Whenever there is a mission, they pay us back in that manner.' So I told the men, 'Don't throw your empty cigarette packages away, give them to me.' This was so they would know it was Americans and not Greeks that conducted the raids. They knew we were there, so many people saw us already. I wanted them to know that the Americans were doing it and not the Greek guerrillas [hopefully to minimize reprisals].

"They would periodically go through, burn, pillage, and kill. There was one mass grave that contained 103 civilians. After I got there I made a recon of the area. It was night and I saw this little white picket fence and the villagers said, 'It's a mass grave with 103 bodies.' It was for some mission the guerrillas had conducted so the Germans rounded up the most educated people in the town, including women and children, and machine-gunned them and dumped them into a pit.

"The day before, we crawled down into the valley on our bellies for hours to set mines in the roads [for] when the Germans headed out of the village the next day. As we crawled to this one place we heard Germans talking. One of the soldiers lit a match and we could see we were less than twenty yards from them. We stopped and they got into a truck and pulled out. Right where they were smoking, that's where we planted the mines. It worked and several trucks were burning after they ran over the mines.

"When we came to the high ground the following day, women, children, and the elderly were fleeing their villages in the face of German fire. I saw them through my field glasses. They were fleeing across a wide expanse, fleeing from the Germans up to a mountain, trying to get away. These people didn't stand a chance, so I deployed my men on our only daylight mission. We moved down behind any cover and concealment we could find and started firing at the Germans who were firing at the people.

"We gave the Germans a firefight to give these people a chance. I exposed my men in the daylight, [even though] all of our missions were carefully planned and at night. Thank goodness none of my men were killed or wounded. We started rounding up these people and told them, 'We are going to help you.' We took them back to our base camp at Pappas. They were there for several days and we shared our meager rations with them.

"This one lady had a baby. Oh, the poor baby. She couldn't breast feed him because of the trauma, the milk stopped. So we gave her sugar and she put it in a handkerchief and she was feeding the baby sugar on this handkerchief to survive. The baby had to be baptized according to the Greek Orthodox religion. The child had 22 godfathers. We passed the child from hand to hand within the group. We named the child Eleftherios, which in Greek means freedom. Sadly, we found out the baby died a few weeks later."[21]

Meanwhile, Lieutenant Johnny Athens and Spyriolon Cappony of the Chicago Mission found that the Communist EAM were sometimes as dangerous as the Germans. Cappony is still troubled by his brush with death. "When we were on the move, they tried to kill us a few times. Their families were in prison and they were told by the Germans that if they wanted their families out of prison to go up and join the guerrilla bands and find the Americans and kill them and then, with that, they would release their families. Even though they fought with us shoulder to shoulder, they sometimes had another agenda.

"I had given my .45 to a guerrilla who I thought was a pretty damn good fighter. He was right next to me the whole time we were fighting. He said, 'Can I clean the .45?' I said, 'Sure come over. I'll show you how to take it apart.' I leaned over to get my cleaning brush by this little river and goddamn, he had the gun in his hands. It had one bullet in the chamber. He aimed it at me and pulled the trigger. The bullet came real close to my left ear. I reached for my bodyguard's gun and was about to shoot the guy. My bodyguard ran over and said, 'I apologize. It should have been me! I should have been watching. I should have been more careful.' These bodyguards, they were assigned to me with their lives. In case something happened to me, they were dead. They were told that if I die they die too. I was the only contact to Cairo and to . . . the airplane supply drops, so they wanted me around. The bodyguard took him back to the camp, and they interrogated him. He admitted his family was in jail and he wanted to release his family, and the only way to release his family was to kill an

American. They made him dig his own shallow grave and he laid down in it and they shot him. I felt sick."[22]

Most military experts agree that men in continuous combat for more than two months without rest begin to suffer combat fatigue. Constantly on the run and in daily firefights with the Germans, the Chicago Mission was behind the lines in Greece longer than any other SO or OG team. The long days in northern Greece with the ELAS were starting to take their toll, and the men were getting burned out. Spiro Cappony looks back on his worst day in Greece. "One time we were being chased by the Germans and I was kind of out of it; pooped, kind of tired. I grabbed the BAR and got my bodyguard to handle the ammunition. I started picking spots here, picking spots there. I wasn't sure if I was hitting anybody, but if I saw any type of movement out there, I would shoot at it. I wanted to kill everything in sight. I got so damn entranced. I was pissed off and tired of running. I was tired of everything. I was tired of this damn war and this was going to be my last drop. Johnny comes up to me and says, 'Gus, goddamn you! Let's get the fuck out of here!' 'Johnny,' I said, 'piss on them. I'm going to blow up them goddamn bastards.' He grabbed my head and smacked me. He knew I was out of it. I kind of woke up and said, 'Johnny, you hit me.' He said, 'Yeah, you son-of-a-bitch. Let's get the hell out of here.' I said, 'Oh shit! I'm sorry sir.' I grabbed my stuff and away we went."[23]

By September 1944, all German units in Greece had begun to withdraw northward to Yugoslavia. September was also the high-water mark for Allied sabotage operations. Operation Smashem called for the systematic destruction of rail lines and highways to impede the German withdrawal. Most of the German soldiers would have to travel over the critical Athens-Salonika railway and the rail terminus at Lamia. Known as the "five-mile run," the area was a beehive of German activity. Thousands of German soldiers defended the rails and bridges.

Group II, credited with blowing over four miles of track, played a key role in Smashem. On September 8, Group II was performing its tenth operation. For Lieutenant John Giannaris, it would be the last mission. "The line was guarded by machine-gun posts every 50 yards, followed by concrete flak towers. As we approached our target, there was a machine-gun burst that cut down the forward scout. Then they started shooting their flares. We all hit the dirt. I called out, 'Rendezvous! Don't take the ravine.' They had their guns trained on the ravine. Guys later told me that I saved their lives since they were all inclined to go for the ravine. The rendezvous was a predestined spot we determined before we started the mission. I ran forward to the scout [Michael Tsirmulas] and stepped on a mine. It blew me sky high. I was stunned but eventually made it to him; he was dead. With that, I started crawling out of there. I got maybe 50 yards. Flares kept going up and machine guns were spraying the whole area.

"At one point, I did a stupid thing. I saw where the machine-gun fire was coming from and with my carbine, I fired. All hell broke loose. Bullets were ricocheting off the boulder I crawled behind. I started crawling and crawling and crawling, trying to get to the high ground. I crawled all night. I could feel blood oozing out. There was a bad odor and one of my wounds ran parallel to my rectum. Blood was oozing out of me. Both legs, both arms and my back were hit. Miraculously, I made it to the high ground and I looked down and here comes a patrol, slowly coming up the trail. I got my carbine and it wouldn't work. Blood had coagulated on the working parts. But I had four hand grenades and I put them in front of me and said to myself, 'I'm not going to be captured and I'm going to take somebody out.'

"They came up the trail within 100 meters, 75 meters, 50 meters, and then they stopped and turned away and went back down. So I took my grenades and started crawling and got out of there. I crawled the whole next day and crawled into a small shed used by German railroad workers. I wouldn't allow myself to sleep so I took my officer's bars off my uniform and I was pricking myself to stay awake.

"Later on I started crawling, I was becoming dehydrated; I had no water. I crawled until six or seven o'clock in the evening and I heard some cowbells. Twenty minutes later, there were two young ladies and I called to them in Greek that I needed help. They had a blanket and tree limbs and made a handmade stretcher and carried me to a burned out village. There was a doctor there and he said, 'I'm going to clean you up.' I asked him to send word to my men.

"A couple of my men came with the plasma, which wasn't any good, like so much of our equipment. Women would take me on a stretcher from village to village; all risked their lives to get me to the landing strip. I was in and out of consciousness. A Lysander [light aircraft] came in and took me to Italy. I had quite a few surgeries. I still have dozens of pieces of the mine in my feet and posterior and both arms. They are still there and painful. I got wounded on September 8, 1944 and didn't leave the hospital until January 20, 1947."[24]

On September 8, 1944, the last OG, Group IV, parachuted into Macedonia. Shortly after arriving, the group destroyed a railroad bridge. Alex Phillips was there. "I remember that baby going up in the middle of the morning. It was a loud and thunderous roar. There was a big flash and a massive explosion just before it went up. We took up a security position on one side of the bridge and after it went up we started to move. The Germans pursued us immediately.

"As we were going through this little town, an old lady grabs me as I passed by her house. She spoke to me in Greek: 'Please don't leave us.' The Germans typically executed innocent civilians who aided the partisans, even if we simply passed through the village. I said, 'Yaya (which means grandmother in Greek), we have to go. We have to go, we can't stay.' She said, 'You have to stay.' I'm moving fast and she has her arm on my shoulder holding me. I'm moving and carrying her with me and saying, 'I can't stay, Yaya.' She persisted and I kept moving and kind of pushed her off of me but she hung on to my .45 holster and then she grabbed my foot. I kicked her off. It was the most horrible feeling I've ever had in my life [chokes up]. I had to move, I would be far behind because we were really moving fast, and everyone was in such good shape.

"The experience stayed with me for years; it's still with me. After the war, I could only sleep four straight hours. Eventually I got out of it but I saw *Saving Private Ryan,* which brought everything back."[25]

With the Germans now withdrawing, Group II, operating in the "five mile run" area, launched its final mission. Captain Nick Pappas was brought in to replace the critically wounded John Giannaris. Pappas's final mission, to destroy a section of track, brought him into conflict with the Panzer Zug, a German train encased in armor plate and bristling with machine guns and cannons. The Zug rode the rails, protecting German troop trains by steaming into hot spots and defeating ambushes. "The only way to approach the town without being spotted by the Germans was to go right through their lines in broad daylight. The terrain was flat for 10 miles and there was no cover for concealment. So we had to go in broad daylight in disguise; it was a suicide mission. The British provided the sappers and helped plan the mission of laying 400 pounds of explosives in 2,000 yard intervals. The plan called for two parties of guerrillas in addition to our group.

"We rode through the German lines in two farmer's carts that were loaded with hay; the men rode in the back under the hay. I was in front with the driver wearing a farmer's cape or smock over [my] uniform.

"As we moved through the German lines, we approached a destroyed town that still had a church steeple. I wanted to send a man up in the steeple so he could recon our target area, a rail yard over a hill. The place was crawling with Germans, about 2,000 to 5,000 were in there since they were withdrawing north. As we approached the town, we had to cross a bridge that spanned a ravine near the town.

"This is where we got in trouble. One of the carts tipped over and since everyone had their weapons cocked and ready one of the weapons discharged. The Germans heard it. The driver of my cart started to panic. But I had a feeling that they wouldn't do anything other than do a quick scan since they were more concerned about withdrawing.

"I told the men to slowly get out of carts and hide in the ravine but not to shoot. Four Germans in motorcycles and a German or Italian light tank approached the carts. I stayed with the carts and assumed correctly that this was their flank security force and they wouldn't bother us. I spoke eight languages, including German, so if they came closer I was prepared to give them some story that the wagon was kaput. They got within 75 yards, made a quick scan, and pulled away.

"We got the wagon back together and moved toward the rails. I was able to make a recon from the church steeple and we hid there until it was dark. After a general recon of the area, we moved into position about 200 yards from the tracks. I put a BAR man at 150 yards on each flank and in the center of our approach to the tracks. Our demolition party of five men moved down the track with a tommy gunner on each flank for protection.

"The first flares went up. I told the men to hold their fire since this was only their attempt to draw our fire [the muzzle flashes from the weapons] so they could see where we were. I knew the first German fire would be high, since they didn't know exactly where we were. As the demolition party reached the tracks, all hell broke loose and they were pinned down by fire from pillboxes. They came close to setting the charges but the fire was too intense and they were forced to pull back, leaving the blasting caps on the tracks. We needed them for our secondary objective. I said, 'We got to get them.' Planas, a skinny kid who didn't look like a commando, said he knew where they were and went back out. By this time the Panzer Zug pulled up and it was the worst fire that I'd ever been in. It was really hot. They were lobbing mortar shells. It seemed like we were out there for over an hour before we were finally able to safely pull back to the rendezvous area."[26]

By the second week of October, Group II had completed its fourteenth mission. The bulk of the German forces had already left Greece, and the British had begun to land troops in the country. OG, SO, and SI agents were gradually being withdrawn. The uneasy alliance between the EDES and EAM was also crumbling. As civil war was breaking out, Pappas's Group II became the first and only OG to enter Athens. "We commandeered a German or Italian vehicle to get into Athens and eventually left Greece. The civil war was starting. On our way to Athens, we ran into the leader of the Greek Communists. He looked like Mussolini, a tough guy, bearded. He was making a speech: 'We got to continue on and keep fighting. We got all our commanders down here. We aren't going to put our guns down, we are going to keep going.' I remember telling our commanding officer that these Communists are going to take over the whole place.

"As we entered Athens, crowds of people were euphoric and greeting us. We saw Greek flags and even a few American flags. After entering the city, we were greeted by the British Red Devil paratroopers who jumped into the city and took a picture of us. We had nothing, no money or food or a place to sleep. The British wanted to put us in a jailhouse outside the city. They were clearing bombs left in the hotels by the Germans. But we came this far and we wanted to stay in the city. While we were there, fighting broke out between the Communists and the Royalists. They were starting to shoot here and there. Eventually, they came in with a C-47 and pulled us out."[27]

After many long months in Greece, the Chicago Mission was also finally pulling out of the country. The group also got a bitter taste of "appreciation" from the EAM, as Cappony recalls. "Johnny Athens said to me, 'Gus, these Greeks are going to kill us. They won't be satisfied with the weapons Jim is going to bring up.' He said, 'You are a pretty good shot with that .03 [Springfield rifle], so why don't you climb up that little hill over there.' At that time we were on the coast waiting for Kellis to arrive in the caïque. 'Take your rifle and pretend you're taking a piss just in case something happens, I want you to be away from the group.' My bodyguard started to follow me. I called him Cue Ball. I said, 'Cue Ball, get out of here.' In Greek he said, 'No, no. I know what's going on. Those guys may hurt you and Lieutenant Athens. I'm with you and want to go back to America with you. I want to be on your side.' I said, 'Cue Ball, please leave me alone. I've got things to do.' He picked up my radio and went with me. So I got on this hill about 100 yards away. Athens was talking with the Greek guerrillas. They were saying some things. Johnny looked up at me. Here comes Jim Kellis in a caïque. The guerrillas were all excited. They came onto the shore. Sure enough, right away arguments started that there wasn't enough weapons and ammunition.

"So Johnny Athens turned to the guerrilla leader and said, 'See Gus up there?' I had my rifle pointed right at him. Johnny looked at the guerrilla leader and sternly said, 'Take what you got.' They hushed up.

"I came on down. I was tired, exhausted, down to 118 pounds. I was in there nine months. Cue Ball was on the shore crying, saying, 'Gus, please take me to America. Please take me back with you.' I just couldn't do it. I got on the caïque and we sailed away. I've been to Greece three times, but I never went back to the northern area, I just couldn't bring myself back there."[28]

EIGHT

From Frogmen to SEALs

The OSS Maritime Unit (MU)

The U.S. Navy SEALs, Army Special Forces Combat Divers, Ranger Scout Swimmers, and Air Force Pararescuemen all trace their heritage to a common source: the Maritime Unit (MU) of the OSS.

OSS maritime training began in August 1942. SO and SI agents were trained in destruction of cargo and dock facilities, small boat handling, and basic seamanship. OSS was also busy designing specialized equipment such as motorized floating mattresses and underwater rebreathers for use in covert operations.

As OSS's maritime capabilities developed, Donovan decided that these functions should be placed in a separate branch, so, in the summer of 1943, the Maritime Unit was created. Its primary mission was the "infiltration of agents and operatives by sea, the waterborne supply of resistance groups, execution of maritime sabotage, and the development of special equipment and devices to effectuate the foregoing."[1]

MU's first officers were shipped to the Mediterranean, where they took over boat services set up by SI and SO. A significant operation involved running the German Adriatic blockade to supply Tito's forces in Yugoslavia. Known as Operation Audrey, a fleet of 14 schooners evaded German patrol boats, delivering guns, ammunition, and over 2,000 fully equipped guerrillas to the Partisan-controlled island of Vis.[2]

One of the first schooners to make the journey left Bari, Italy on October 29, 1943. The mission: to determine what aid Tito's forces needed to hold the Peljasac Peninsula in Yugoslavia. Lieutenant Robert Thompson describes one of these voyages, which afflicted him with postwar nightmares and flashbacks. According to his family, after the war, Thompson would never again set foot on board a sailboat.

"Mountainous seas and fog made the crossing difficult. The vessel nearly grounded on Catsa Island. While we were approaching Vis, the seasick interpreter for the pilot quit his post on the bridge. I was forced to hold a gun at his back to make him return to duty. At 0100 hours [1:00 a.m.], the vessel became hemmed in by reefs off Vis, and after an hour's battle [we broke free] and rode out the storm until dawn. The boat was severely damaged.

"German patrol planes made it necessary to remain under camouflage until dusk. A new pilot and interpreter were found and [we] proceeded to Hvar to rendezvous with the Partisan naval commander. During a five-hour conference, the commander reviewed the battle positions in minute detail. The conclusion was that the Peljasac would be in danger of falling to the enemy within 48 hours unless Allied support was obtained.

"We were all taken to Korcula aboard a crash boat from where [we] proceeded to Peljasac to visit the front. . . . The pilot mistakenly led the craft down the wrong side of the island, through the main enemy E-boat route, and up against a shoal. [We] once again skillfully extricated the [boat] and lay off [shore] until dawn . . . [we] then dashed for open sea to get out of range before the first enemy air patrols arrived."[3]

Back in the United States, the OSS was creating "Operational Swimmer Groups" to plan and execute special marine missions. The groups ranged in size from 12 to 36 men. Swimmer Group training included underwater sabotage, hydrographic work for amphibious beach assaults, reconnaissance work, and a host of marine special operations.

Using special equipment developed by MU personnel, the swimmers enjoyed the unprecedented ability to swim underwater undetected. The Lambertsen Amphibious Respiratory Unit (LARU) enabled a swimmer to approach a target underwater without leaving breathing bubbles. The groundbreaking system, developed by OSS veteran Dr. Christian Lambertsen, saw decades of distinguished service; an upgraded version remained in service with the navy SEALs until 1982.

Along with LARU, OSS developed a variety of specialized devices for the swimmers, including underwater compasses, watches, depth gauges, and ordnance. The men also trained on one-man submersibles and a two-man surfboard with a silent electric outboard motor.

Training bases were set up on the West Coast at Camp Pendleton, California, in November 1943, and later on Catalina Island. At Pendleton, the swimmers received Marine Raider–type combat training, which the men would need out of the water. Three Swimmer Groups were formed (Group I or Group L, Group II, and Group III). The men were handpicked from volunteers from the navy, coast guard, marines, and army. They were all in outstanding physical condition, and many were world-class swimmers. A large number of the men were "beach rats," lifeguards and divers from southern California, such as James Eubanks.

"I was a lifeguard in L.A. County. If you've seen *Baywatch* on TV, it was *Baywatch* minus the babes. We had a boat named *Baywatch* but we didn't have girls in the lifeguard towers. Prior to the war, I was a diver who won quite a few rough-water swim meets.

"The coast guard put out a call for expert swimmers to help with operating landing craft since we knew surf conditions. Two of us volunteered. They gave us a second-class boatsman rating since we understood surf conditions. After boot camp, they placed me as a swimming instructor and I couldn't get off the base camp.

"After several months of boring duty, we received notice that the OSS wanted volunteer swimmers for extra hazardous work, with a 10

OSS MU Training Areas and Operations in the PTO and Far East

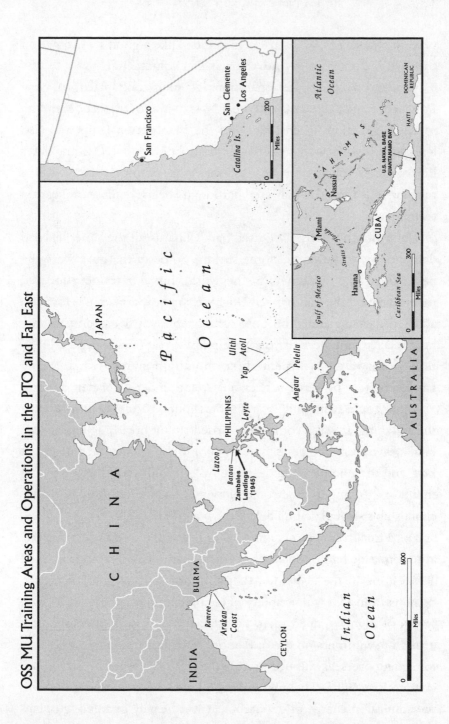

percent chance of coming back. It sounded like a good way to get off the base and a way to get into the war, so I volunteered."[4]

Advanced underwater-operations training took place on New Providence and Salt Cay Islands near Nassau in the Bahamas. Here the men trained more extensively with the Lambertsen Units and also learned to work with underwater demolitions, first C-2 and later limpet mines, magnetic explosive devices that swimmers could attach to ships. The men also mastered harbor and beach defense infiltration techniques.

John Booth recalls: "We used paddleboards all the time, learned demolitions, and even did some surfing. Some of the guys were the best surfers and swimmers in the world, but our training focused mainly around the Lambertsen Unit; we were experts on it. How you adapted to it depended on how comfortable you were underwater, how relaxed you were. If you were relaxed you could spend a lot of time underwater. We spent three months training with it, using kayaks, battery-powered rubber boats, and underwater demolitions.

"You could swim underwater for an hour wearing the unit. Unlike the aqualung, it was a completely closed circuit breathing device that didn't leave breathing bubbles. A lot of time was spent attaching C-2 at first, and then limpet mines, on the hulls of old wrecks and blowing them up."[5] A limpet mine could blow a 25-square-foot hole in a merchant ship's steel plate hull below the waterline.

As a final training mission, Group II was selected to test the U.S. antisubmarine harbor defenses at Guantánamo Bay. The tests marked a milestone in the evolving MU infiltration and demolition tactics, demonstrating the vulnerability of Guantánamo's defenses to a small group of highly trained men. Lieutenant Booth was in charge of a group of swimmers on the operation. "Our last training exercise before going overseas was penetrating the U.S. harbor defenses at Guantánamo Bay, Cuba. The only one who knew we were doing this was the admiral in charge of the harbor. It was heavily guarded, gun batteries, submarine nets, and everything. Convoys used to come in there and anchor because it was considered so safe.

"We went in there at night in an old submarine. The sub surfaced just outside the nets. When we got out of that thing the waves were lapping over the sides and we got into rubber boats. We went and camped overnight without being detected. Using the Lambertsen Units, we swam underwater and penetrated the sub nets, no problem. We could have swum in and destroyed everything in there. They had an old barge in the harbor that the navy didn't want so we placed live charges on it, blew it up, and got out of there."[6]

Starting in January 1944, OSG swimmers were sent to three different combat theaters: the Pacific (Group II), Burma (Group III), and Europe (Group I). In Europe, Group I, also known as L-Unit, was detailed to the OSS London office, where it joined a small group of OSS swimmers who had been training in the cold waters of the upper Thames near Oxford. Group I, which had a total strength of 17 men, was tasked with the spectacular operation of disabling U-boat pens in France. Scheduled for four days prior to D-Day, Operation Betty called for four intrepid operatives, "X, Y, Z, and Q," to "reduce the striking power" of German submarines based in massive reinforced concrete pens in the French port of Lorient-Kéroman. The pens were impervious to Allied bombing raids and shore bombardment; they still survive intact today.[7]

Agent X was Gordon Soltau, who after the war became an all-pro receiver and kicker for the San Francisco 49ers. "We trained for weeks in a river outside Cornwall where the tides were close to the tides at the pens. Everything was done at night since that was when the mission would take place and to avoid the locals.

"The plan called for a surface craft to drop us off near the pens. Using these things called 'flying mattresses' or 'Water Lilies,' we would ride into shore. They were teardrop-shaped rubber rafts that had a buffer on the bow. Two men could lie on it comfortably and two

12-volt batteries powered a silent electric motor. The thing had a speed of about three knots. Since they were rubber and riding low in the water, German radar would have a hard time detecting us.

"My mission was to swim underwater using the Lambertsen Units [and] plant explosives on these big iron gates [locks] that swung out when the subs would enter or leave the pens. Another swimmer would plant a limpet on the waiting sub. About 15 minutes later both the limpet mines and charges on the gates would be blown. The sub would sink into the cradle in the pen and the gates would be destroyed. We'd swim back to the safe house and make [our] escape on foot and link up with the advancing Allied armies that had landed at Normandy.

"Right before D-Day, we got word that the mission was scrubbed."[8]

Several other proposed missions never got beyond the planning stage. Operation Sampson involved blowing up a ship in Germany's vital Kiel Canal. The half-baked plan called for three men from L-Unit to be infiltrated onto a Swedish ore carrier and place a charge in the ship's hold. At the right time, "one [agent would] create disturbance and confusion at the moment of attack by using smoke bombs and explosives on the ship's bridge; one would call for full speed ahead and to starboard the helm at the required moment, and a third agent would detonate the charges at the right second." According to the plan, the sunken ore carrier would obstruct the canal for 14 days, causing the loss of two million tons of imported materials, and "ships in the canal would provide a great target for Allied planes.[9] Sampson was a true suicide mission; no escape plan was proposed for the unlucky agents.

A variety of factors led to cancellation of these missions. Water temperature frequently dipped below 50 degrees, making swimming for extended periods of time difficult. The practical distance that a swimmer could travel underwater ranged between 150 and 200 yards. And, perhaps most revealing, the fact that "at the present time the Allies have an overwhelming air and naval superiority, and can reach almost any shipping targets they wish in this theater, both easier and with greater devastating effect than the group of swimmers could possibly do."[10] While it appeared that their services were obsolete, the swimmers' tactics actually evolved as the war progressed.

Not long after MU abandoned underwater operations in the European Theater of Operations, and after Italy surrendered, OSS Italy retained the services of their former adversary, the elite Italian amphibious operations unit known as the San Marco Battalion.

One element within the San Marco included the men of Grupo Mezzini d'Asalto, a unit formed from veterans of the celebrated 10th Light Flotilla, which pioneered underwater demolitions. On many of the 10th's operations, special assault teams entered harbors riding underwater torpedo-shaped submersibles known as Chariots, and attached explosives to the hulls of Allied ships at anchor. The crack assault teams wrought devastation in Crete's Suda Bay and Alexandria harbor, sinking or severely damaging several British capital ships, including the battleships *Queen Elizabeth* and *Valiant*.

The group's most audacious coup was its campaign of sneak attacks against Allied shipping in Gibraltar. A derelict freighter, the *Olterra*, was seemingly abandoned off the Spanish coast. But the *Olterra* was a Trojan horse. Her hold served as a clandestine workshop where the frogmen could repair and rearm the Chariots. Access in and out of the ship was afforded by a sliding door six feet below the waterline. All told, the Italians sank 42,000 tons of Allied ships anchored at Gibraltar; the British never discovered the secret of the freighter.

Following the surrender of Italy, OSS arranged with the Duke of Aosta to acquire the crack unit, along with the latest in Italian maritime gadgets.[11] Equipment included two-man mattresses, high-performance MAS boats, and the Chariots.

The first joint San Marco–OSS mission, Ossining I, took place in June 1944. The swimmers destroyed a train 100 miles behind enemy lines. The commander of OSS MU operations with the Eighth Army, Lieutenant Robert Kelly, recalls the character of San Marco men and their first OSS mission. "They are an elite volunteer unit made up of highly skilled, physically and mentally superior men. . . . Ossining I was accomplished on 19 June 1944. A railroad train was blown up between Fano and Pesaro, destroying the engine and four cars and blocking the line completely. Shortly afterwards the Air Force bombed the blocked traffic and blew up an ammunition train on the same stretch."

MU executed several other important operations, including Operation Packard, as Kelly describes. "Packard . . . involved the infiltration of a San Marco officer, two enlisted men and a partisan engineer who was brought out with the complete plans of the Gothic Line defenses from the coast to thirty kilometers inland. This information, much of it from pictures, was extremely valuable to the Eighth Army which broke through the Gothic Line at this point shortly thereafter."[12]

One of MU/OSS's Eighth Army Detachment's most important missions involved the infiltration of several San Marco commandos deep behind the lines to work with the partisans, reporting important artillery and bombing targets and gathering valuable intelligence. Using high-performance Italian MAS boats, the men were infiltrated deep into German-occupied northern Italy. Once ashore, they set up Radio Bionda. Frank Monteleone, a veteran of OSS's Eighth Army Detachment, worked closely with MU and the men of Battaglione San Marco. "The mission was planned with three agents from the Battaglione San Marco. We took them up to an area just south of Venice, a big swampy area.

"The San Marco guys had balls. They were tough sons of bitches. They were like our paratroopers or Rangers. These commandos did everything and were extremely reliable. We trained them but they hardly needed to be trained. We mainly trained them on our weapons and procedures.

"We landed the San Marco guys after seeing the flashlight signal. As we were landing these guys we could hear German boats in the distance and voices; voices carry on the water; they were German voices.

"We didn't hear from them for a couple of days and we began to worry. With the German voices and boats we figured maybe the jig was up and they got captured. But then we started getting the messages. It turned out that these guys had all kinds of problems. Initially the partisans didn't contact them since they thought the mission's cover was blown. Nevertheless, the guy who was in charge of this mission found a way to survive and made contact and started sending valuable intelligence back.

"The mission lasted several months and we had to resupply them and we brought back several Allied POWs. I'll never forget going in at night. Naturally, we had to avoid all types of contact; it was exciting. I could hear the Germans talking in the background in patrol boats. They were looking and listening. They saw the flashlight on shore.

"I had to go in to deliver codebooks and crystals. I went in on the Tattrougia, Italian for "Turtle;" it was a two-man motorized rubber mattress. I had to lay down on this thing, it was messy and wet.

"I was getting wet and asking myself what the hell am I doing here? I made it to shore and dropped off the codebooks and crystals. I went back on the mattress and got the hell out of there real fast.[13]

As the war in Europe drew to a close, OSS seriously considered sending the special equipment and men of the Grupo Mezzini d'Asalto to participate in clandestine operations in the Pacific. While the men were willing, the order never came. However, their specialized equipment was shipped to the United States for further evaluation, and San Marco personnel provided consulting services to the navy's postwar underwater operations program.[14]

In contrast to Europe, OSS operations in the Pacific theater were minimal. Despite Donovan's most persuasive efforts, neither Admiral

Nimitz nor General MacArthur welcomed OSS operations. Nevertheless, a few OSS units quietly saw action, including MU Operational Swimmer Group II. The swimmers were placed on temporary duty with the U.S. Navy's Underwater Demolition Team (UDT) 10.

The Navy formed UDTs after the bloody battle at Tarawa, where scores of landing craft were destroyed as a result of poor reconnaissance and a lack of hydrographic (water depth and beach gradients) information about Tarawa's beaches. Hundreds of men were killed because the landing craft could not clear reefs that surrounded Tarawa. To remedy the problem the navy rapidly created camps to train men in underwater demolition, hydrographic surveys, and reconnaissance.[15]

After training on the West Coast and the Bahamas, 29 officers and men from MU Swimmer Group II joined the navy's UDT training program on Maui, where they were integrated into UDT 10, bringing the team up to full strength.

Lead by OSS Lieutenant Commander Arthur Choate, a multimillionaire who made his fortune on Wall Street, UDT 10 completed its training and set sail on an old four-stacker destroyer, the USS *Rathburne,* in early August 1944. The *Rathburne* was part of large convoy heading southwest, toward the Solomon Islands.

As the team was heading for the Solomons, five volunteers from UDT Team 10 and several men from the UDT training school were assigned to the submarine *Burfish.* Embarking on one of the most difficult recon missions of the war, the men would conduct beach reconnaissance on the islands of Peleliu, Angaur, and Yap. The mission represented a milestone, the first time American swimmers were actually deployed in maritime special operations.

The first recon mission took place on August 11, 1944, when the *Burfish* surfaced off the southeast tip of Peleliu. Blackened with face paint, the men paddled to shore in a rubber boat. Avoiding numerous Japanese patrols, the men surveyed the beach, finding it suitable for landing craft. When their work was completed a team member tapped a prearranged signal on a large coral rock with his fighting knife. The sonar operator on the *Burfish* picked up the signal and the sub recovered the men.

August 18, 1944, would prove to be a fateful night for three of the men. That night, the *Burfish* surfaced 3,000 yards off Gagil Tomil, a small island near Yap. Five swimmers—John Ball, Robert Black, Emmet Carpenter, Howard Roeder, and John MacMahon—blackened their faces, armed themselves with grenades and combat knives, and set out in a rubber boat for the team's final beach-recon mission. The mission report reveals the chronology of events. "At 2110 [9:10 p.m.], the two teams left the boat and headed for the beach—the high point of which was plainly visible. Ball was left as a boat keeper. At about 2130 [9:30 p.m.], Carpenter and Black returned to the boat because Carpenter was in distress and too tired to swim further. Black then oriented himself, took another compass check, and headed back alone for the shore. At 2315 [11:15 p.m.], which was 30 minutes past the deadline time, Ball and Carpenter manned the boat and rowed to within 100 yards of the beach. They then returned to a point inside the surf line and then rowed in a general northwest and then southwest line until 0015 [12:15 a.m.] at which time Ball was forced to make a decision to return to the ship, it being 45 minutes past the deadline given the boat to depart from the rendezvous with the ship and one and half hours past Roeder's time for rendezvousing with [the] boat. The boat went through the surf without much difficulty and once through, they abandoned all caution and flashed their flashlight all around in hope of picking up the other three men. They had no success. . . . It is believed that the three men [Roeder, MacMahon, and Black] saw something interesting near the shoreline, decided to investigate and were captured [and likely beheaded by the Japanese]."[16]

Meanwhile, UDT 10 had been cruising the Pacific on the *Rathburne* for several months and was finally gearing up for its first mission, in support of the navy's landings on Peleliu and Anguar. The team's Lambertsen Units, silenced High Standard pistols, and other high-tech spy gear were permanently shelved, replaced by K-Bar knives, swim trunks, and plastic pads and wax pencils to record hydrographic data. Since the men had received highly specialized underwater sabotage training and considered themselves agents or special operators, functioning as beach demolitions men and hydrographic surveyors did not sit well with many of them. Nevertheless, the OSS men went about their dangerous and important duty.

After a final briefing on September 14, 1944, the swimmers departed the *Rathburne* and headed to Angaur's Blue Beach. Robert Kenworthy remembers his first mission.

"After 57 years I guess I can still see myself propelling into the air. I jumped up like on a diving board, curled my body, and dove into the water. This was in broad daylight; we were at least 300 yards from the beach, all the while avoiding getting shot.

"As we were approaching the beach, we were expecting them to open fire but they were waiting for us to get closer. You are looking at the beach expecting to see a flash.

"We were perfectly at home in the water, if it was two or three miles out, it wouldn't make a difference. There were four landing craft. I was with Platoon Number 3. I'm looking out at my 500 yards of beach. The water was mighty cold but crystal clear. But we were used to it. fifty-four-degree water after several hours becomes very untenable. Your testicles climb up inside, it's later when they come down that it is not very nice.

"On the left of the section I had to cover a concrete pillbox. Just remembering it makes the hair stand up on my arms. The Japs knew that this was the best beach for a landing and accordingly set up a pillbox. We were about 75 to 125 yards away from it when all hell broke loose. I turned my head and from the right end of the beach I saw three Jap soldiers push palm fronds aside and open fire. We were caught right between the two machine guns. Then came several F4Fs (Wildcats, our own planes) firing, accidentally strafing us. Bullets were hitting the water all around us. Our CO broke radio silence and told the admiral, 'Get your goddamn cowboys out of there!' Luckily, they broke off the attack and none of our guys were killed.

"After we made our way back with the data [measured angle of inclination and soundings and other measurements] we gathered, [and] it was concluded that demolition work was needed. I remember taking a few sacks of tetrytol and placing them on a reef. We also used a small block to destroy a mine. I remember taking two sacks of C-2, 22½-pound green sacks, one on each shoulder, and placing them on a spot on the reef. We had to place it so the craft could clear it. I held my breath over two minutes so we could go down and stay down and set the charge. Boom! We detonated it. Coral shot into the air. It was sickening because thousands of fish were also killed by the explosion. I still remember their white little bellies.

"On D-Day as these landing craft were coming in, we would stay about five or six feet below the surface and help guide them to avoid the coral. This was a powerful thing as you looked at the clenched faces of these 18- and 20-year-olds and in another 15 or 20 minutes they were dead. It's a visual thing you carry with you all your life."[17]

After a brief interlude, the men joined a massive convoy steaming northwest toward the Philippines. Team 10 would play an important role in the invasion of Leyte, the first major island liberated in the Philippines. At 10:00 a.m. on October 19, a day before the invasion, the big guns of the battleships *Mississippi, Maryland, Pennsylvania, California, Tennessee,* and *West Virginia,* along with numerous cruisers and destroyers, began a devastating shore bombardment of the Japanese beach defenses on Leyte. About an hour later, the swimmers scrambled down cargo nets into waiting landing craft and headed toward the beaches. Armed only with combat knives, the men conducted their work in broad daylight, directly in the face of Japanese sniper, machine-gun, and mortar fire. The Allied shore bombardment helped keep the Japanese buttoned up, but a stray 14-inch shell could easily eliminate most of the team. Les Bodine, a marine prior to joining the OSS, was swimming toward the beaches. "At about 400 yards we dropped off the side of the boat and loaded up with the amount of tetrytol that we anticipated we would need to level the beach so the LSTs could land, open their doors, and tanks could roll out. As we swam forward the water around us was being peppered with machine-gun, rifle, and mortar fire. Water was splashing up around me from the rounds. I noticed that the Japanese had fish traps in the water in front of the beach. They turned out to be markers that allowed them to direct their mortar and cannon fire.

"A mortar round practically dropped on top of Bob Scoles and me. It wasn't until about 50 years later when we were at a reunion that I found out the whole story. A concussion from the mortar forced me to the bottom. I went about 10 feet under the water. Bob was pushed upward. When you get hit by an explosion like that water goes into every orifice: the ears, nose, rectum and tears things up a little bit. I was spitting up blood and blacked out.

"As I recall, we all wore an inflatable bladder inside our trunks. So if any of us got hit, someone could blow up the bladder and tow us back to the boats. Somebody inflated it and brought me back. Doc Gibboney—we had our own doctor—gave us something, I think it was whiskey. It burned. My eardrums and stomach have scar tissue, but the next day we went back in."[18]

The climax of Team 10's work was providing surveys and putting troops ashore on Luzon. Before and during their mission, the men nervously witnessed kamikaze airplanes hit ships in the invasion fleet. The men participated in one other amphibious landing in the Zambales area of Luzon; the operation effectively cut off the Bataan Peninsula from Japanese retreat. As the Philippines were being secured, the frogmen were then moved to Guam where they trained for the proposed invasion of Japan. The team was disbanded in early 1946.

The final group of swimmers, Group III, was sent to Burma, where they were joined by men from the terminated Group I program in Europe. The swimmers were assigned to the Maritime Units of Detachments 404 and 101, mainly conducting reconnaissance missions along Burma's Arakan Coast. Group III swimmers also dropped off agents and conducted a few specialized operations with 101's Amphibious Recon Battalion, an Operational Group specially trained in amphibious operations. A typical mission would involve the swimmers reconnoitering an island or beach. Once a landing beach was established, the OGs would follow up with a raid or operation.

The men were equipped with the latest underwater equipment in the Allied arsenal, including a submarine, fast patrol boats, motorized mattresses, kayaks, and the newest generation of Lambertsen rebreather units. The British-designed one-man submersible, known as the "Sleeping Beauty," was also available for maritime sabotage missions. John Booth piloted the submersible.

"Our wetsuit was a pair of longjohns underwear. We donned the Lambertsen and got into the 'Beauty.' We completely submerged in about eight feet underwater, achieving negative buoyancy. It ran pretty good but it wasn't good enough to risk my life with it. The batteries leaked acid and the currents were too strong in Burma. The British, of course, had two-man models and used them with great success in Norway. In our training, we used the 'Beauty' to plant fake charges under boats. These days, most high school projects are more advanced. However, the missions and the tactics we were developing helped pioneer underwater demolition."[19]

Booth and his fellow swimmers started conducting scores of reconnaissance missions up and down the Arakan Coast. He recalls one of his first missions.[20]

"The British were hopping down the coast of Burma and had planned an invasion of the Arakan Coast. We went along with them. Our job was to survey beaches that they were considering landing on.

We had four double kayaks, all paddle power. On one mission, we paddled 18 hours straight. We were in pretty good shape back then. We had a compass bearing to a line of blackness [laughs]. So we paddled and found the spot and went up a *chaung* [tidal river]. We were looking for Japanese activity. About that time, a Japanese patrol boat approached our position. We were along the banks in our kayaks, they missed us as they went by. We scanned the area for activity and did a recon of the beach. Our goal wasn't to shoot 'em up. When we got back we had a real bunch of cowboys running the operation. The British officers who were in charge asked, 'Why didn't you put a grenade in that Japanese boat?' Somewhat annoyed, I said, 'What does clandestine mean?' We weren't there for a shoot 'em up, we were there to get information. These were second generation British officers who were trying to make a name for themselves, earn medals, and they died by the bushel.

"We had to go in the next night and the guy who was with me couldn't make it since his hands were so raw from the paddling. I remember checking out the beach, taking soundings for a possible beach landing. That night we ran into natives in an outrigger. We were going into a country where they spoke Burmese and Japanese and we were supposed to get intelligence [laughs]. I put my .45 to the native's head and asked him a few phrases in Burmese that I memorized like, "Where are the Japanese?" I could ask questions but when I got the answers, I was lost. It was kind of ridiculous. A lot of stuff we did, the Special Forces refined. Modern Special Forces these days have at least two men on a team who speak the native tongue."[21]

As the British, Chinese, and Americans overran Burma, operations slowed down dramatically. In the summer of 1945, MU launched its final missions, to recover coast watchers in Sumatra and insert a number of agents into Burma or Thailand in support of the Free Thai Army.[22] All of the operations required exceptional seamanship and boat-handling. Walter Mess was a skipper of one of the fast patrol boats that dropped off agents bound for Thailand, but more frequently dropped off swimmers or OGs on coastal or behind-the-lines recon missions.

"Shooting wasn't our mission. Our mission was taxi driver, our mission was not to fight, but we were prepared to do it. We would take them to a point on the Arakan Coast or [a] *chaung,* to a point that they determined. What I would do would be to lay out that course on a dead reckoning basis since we would be working in the dark. So it meant all of these azimuths had to be memorized. We may be changing course every three or four minutes.

"Many of the missions were 50 to 70 miles behind the lines, moving up shallow *chaungs.* Try picturing running a patrol boat up Washington, D.C.'s Rock Creek Park River without attracting attention. That was what it was like. It was a river war like the movie *Apocalypse Now.* The boat required at least six feet of water to operate so that meant we needed a sailor on the bow of the boat taking measurements. We moved silently at night right through Japanese gun emplacements and encampments. I still remember going by the Japanese camps at night seeing the soldiers and their fires.

"Most of the time, we would [pick them up from] the place where we would put them in. If they were in trouble, we would have to pick them up with outboards. If we were under fire, we would use a bicycle tire to snatch the men. They would stick their arms up, and we'd hook them with the bicycle tire and swing them into the boat, using the bicycle tire as a hook.

"We got them back aboard and they would be out on the mission for 72 hours without sleep. That was a group of men that I had a healthy respect for; just the way they carried themselves, and their ability—everything about them, they were having fun. . . .

"You are not alive, unless you are living on the edge. And living on the edge like these swimmers and the rest of those men, you are alive. I mean you are *alive.*

"I think that was the most fun I had in my life."[23]

During the spring of 2002, U.S. Navy SEAL Team 10 honored the men of UDT 10, officially tracing their lineage to the World War II unit. On March 6, 1998, OSS veterans of the Maritime Unit were inducted into the Special Forces as honorary members. Each man was awarded the Green Beret and a ceremonial stone was erected at Fort Bragg, home of America's Special Operations—*De Oppresso Liber* [Free the oppressed].

NINE

Infiltrating France

North Africa and the Mediterranean provided OSS with a valuable proving ground, demonstrating that the fledging intelligence agency was moving closer to performing on an equal footing with its British counterparts. But both the Axis and Allies considered these theaters to be mere sideshows. The main theater in Europe was France. Millions of Allied soldiers would land on France's Atlantic coast, making it the front where OSS, and its counterpart, SOE, concentrated their efforts. Gathering intelligence and coordinating the forces of the French resistance were OSS's primary goals.

By January 1943, the French resistance, or Maquis (a name derived from dense undergrowth found on Corsica) were farmers, students, former soldiers, butchers—men and women representing all walks of French life. Politically, and ideologically, the Maquis were divided into three major factions. The strongest, Forces Francaises de L'Interieur (FFI), was aligned with Charles de Gaulle. The other main groups were the Communist-controlled Francs Tireurs et Partisans (FTP), and the supporters of former French army General Giraud, organized as the Organisation de Résistance de l'Armeé de l'Armistice (ORA). By March 1944, through Herculean efforts, de Gaulle managed to unite most of the resistance groups under the FFI.[1]

France and all occupied governments in exile had their offices in London. More importantly for OSS, London acted as a base for their intelligence organizations. To facilitate cooperation with FFI, OSS set up London support desks to handle counterintelligence, research and analysis, communications, Special Operations, and Secret Intelligence.

However, OSS chose Algiers, not London, to serve as its first gateway into France. Since Algiers, the major OSS base in the Mediterranean, was located in an American-controlled theater, the city provided greater access to American supplies and transport. The British could not limit OSS operations as they did in London. Also, Algiers provided an ample supply of recruits from France's former colonies and from France itself.

It was in Algiers that OSS found its first agent to infiltrate France, Frederick Brown. Brown had an eclectic background: he was a Ukrainian Jew who claimed to be raised in Luxembourg by Canadian parents. Since 1938, Brown had run a radio shop in Algiers. From his shop Brown facilitated radio communications for Robert Murphy's Twelve Apostles prior to the Torch landings in North Africa. He also gained some experience leading an OSS mission to Corsica, but most importantly, he had extensive personal contacts in France.[2]

The sophisticated Brown, who was assigned the incongruous code name "Tommy," was first ordered to create a wireless telegraphy (W/T) radio network in southern France for OSS. Tommy and a small team were spirited into southern France by the French submarine *Casablanca*. They set up intelligence networks in Toulon and Marseille, and a sabotage station in the Alps.

Ultimately, Brown conducted four separate missions in occupied France. Brown's description of his final mission displays the courage of the French agents operating in harm's way in spite of their disappointment with the level of support they received from OSS. "[I was staying in a] house with a prostitute in Madrid, and was able to take my first bath. In the afternoon, it was Sunday, Mitchell came back carrying a package in his hand, and a telegram. I saw the message: 'Your friends are in danger in France; take new codes and signal plans and 1,000,000 francs and go back into France to change the codes of the three sta-

Initial OSS Missions into France

tions.' I got the package with 1,000,000 francs, 20 crystals, four code-books, and four signal plans, while going back to Barcelona in the car with Mitchell.

"In Barcelona I asked Mitchell for money and equipment for the journey, to enable me to get back. Mitchell now gave me 1,000 pese-tas, with which I bought new clothes with the help of his two Spanish Red Guards, and the next day the guards drove me out from the same villa in a taxi. This was around the 25th of September [1943]. Ten miles south of the Spanish-French border, at a place called Ribas, the two guards told me, 'In this direction, to the north, lies France.'

"At 10 o'clock at night, in very rainy weather, in complete dark-ness, I stood with a package of one million francs in my hands, with two pounds of food, with crystals, code books, plans, etc., and aban-doned in the country. During the next three days, I never saw such days in my life; I climbed up and down, 9,000 feet and back again, to get into France to a spot where I had an appointment with one of my men, arranged via Madrid and Algiers OSS radio.

"This friend was the chief of the Texas station. I was so glad he was not a man like Mitchell; he was just one of the French Maquis men, named Claude. I was starving and cold. I had gone eighty-five miles on foot in very mountainous country; Claude told me that my best man, Vincent Dick, had been arrested. This was a little of his own fault, be-cause he hadn't heeded the warning I had given before leaving France.

"I remember, however, that it was OSS's fault not to have sent supplies to my friends, and after that everything had gone badly and they had become disorganized. One need only see the messages sent from the York station in Toulon, in which the operator begged for money; the operator didn't even have money to buy his own food with. So I was coming back with one million francs, but I also heard, two days later, that the York station had been abandoned or caught. So I was obliged to organize everything once more, with no supplies, only some money.

"Another agent was arrested on the Cannebiere in Marseille. Some of his men were arrested with him at the same time. They were tortured by the Gestapo immediately, and so the Gestapo heard about the Boston station with which Dick was in liaison, so on the same day I changed the position of Boston. This station had been operating in a castle in Crest; just one hour after we moved it, the Gestapo came up with 62 men, armed with mortars and machine guns, but I had escaped, and Boston, now Ohio, operated on without hindrance. I escaped to a spot five miles south of that place, and hid the station and the operator, Dick, and myself in a little farm, surrounded by a wood. I could not leave because everything was controlled and barricaded. One day later, I heard about the arrest of ten people; they were all best friends of mine, who had helped the OSS Boston Station. Count Dandingé, they took 5,000,000 francs cash away from him, and all his possessions, amounting to more than 10,000,000 francs in all. The garage proprietor Isard; the businessman Latard; the owner of the castle in Crest, and his two sons. Some days before this, Max was arrested, also Vincent Dick, and three of their friends. I do not have an exact report of how this happened, but I am firmly convinced that if we had had the supplies which had been promised in July from OSS, and later canceled by London, I will guarantee that this would not have happened.

"OSS Algiers asked me to keep on working and to send intelligence reports; they promised me supplies monthly; I was now on the fourth month without supplies, money, or new sets. The money I had brought back from Madrid, plus the million I had borrowed from Count Dadinge, was not enough. We needed not only money, but supplies. The supplies would help the morale of the people, to place them in relationship with America, which they liked very much; the failure to deliver these supplies lowered their morale greatly. When the people found out that OSS was a simple, ordinary spy organization, which liked to take but not to give, the morale of my people fell very low, and this greatly endangered our security. . . .

"In Vercors, I received an order to return to Algiers via Spain. Below Montelimar, at a crossroads, I was stopped by four Gestapo men with a radio car; this was October 4, 1943. One of the men approached my car and began to talk; he ordered me out of the car; I had my tommy gun right between my legs. I shot across the window and killed him, in two seconds, all three men whom I could see, one in front of my car, and two in the middle of the road, and I shot a second load into the radio car, and I don't know what happened; certainly I wounded the fourth man, but of one thing I am sure, and so was Philippe [resistance leader]: three men were dead.

"I left Philippe in Valence. Philippe told me, when I saw him the last time in Valence—his last words to me were, 'Perhaps this is the last time that I will see you, so goodbye. Tell the OSS to be sure to furnish supplies, and to be gentler with the French underground than they have been until now.' Philippe was killed ten days later by the Gestapo.

"Philippe was the most respected underground leader in the Rhone Valley. He was not a Communist. He was non-political. He was a Frenchman. . . . The car left us some 40 miles in front of the Spanish border, and with great difficulty, we crossed the frontier; we had a narrow escape from a German patrol, and it was good luck for us that the Germans didn't have a dog, as they usually do. We were hiding only a few yards from the patrol. We crossed the last electric railway 10 miles before the Spanish border."[3]

Frederick Brown pioneered OSS's first secret intelligence work in France, but after returning from his final mission he was accused of being a double agent. One of his stations, Dartmouth, was later determined to have been under enemy control. Dartmouth had arranged for four agent teams to drop into France. Each team was captured by the Germans and executed shortly after landing.

In an attempt to clear his name, "Tommy" first went to London, where his peers largely absolved him of blame. But the suspicions per-

sisted. He was recalled to the United States and initially detained on
Catalina Island and told he was a prisoner of the OSS. Tommy protested
with a hunger strike. In consequence, the major in charge of his detention phoned Washington and Tommy was given liberty to travel the
United States for seven months while he awaited permission to return
to Algiers. Later X-2 (counterespionage) confirmed, through captured
German documents, that Gestapo direction-finding (D/F) efforts, and
the capture of other OSS agents, led to the doubling of station Dartmouth. Nevertheless, the name of Frederick Brown, OSS's first agent
into France and a true hero, has yet to be cleared.[4]

Building on the efforts of Tommy and others, OSS slowly established additional intelligence networks inside France. Agents were infiltrated into the country via Spain, Switzerland, Algeria, and finally
England. One of the more significant intelligence networks, Penny
Farthing, was formed late in the summer of 1943. Flying out of England, the team parachuted blind (without friendly forces waiting for
them at the drop zone) outside Lyon. The mainsprings of the intelligence chain were Jean de Roquefort, code-named "Jacques," and
Mario Marret, "Toto." Both men were French agents recruited from
General Giraud's army by the OSS SI Algiers office, which was headed
by a 29-year-old spymaster named Henry Hyde.

Lyon acted as a hub for the resistance. The city was not far from
the Swiss border, and all the resistance movements had their general
staffs located there. In order to build a secret network of agents, Jean
de Roquefort recruited a variety of personalities. One of his first recruits was a Jesuit priest, Father Chaine, who was able to provide motivated young men who could be trained as agents.

Through de Roquefort's father-in-law, a doctor for the bordellos of
Lyon, prostitutes were recruited to glean information from unsuspecting German clients. Every German soldier carried a *soldebuch,* or pay
book, that denoted his unit. By copying the information in the books,
the women were able to determine when a new unit came into the

area. Ultimately, through the efforts of the prostitutes and other agents, Penny Farthing was able to reconstruct portions of the German order of battle (the military units in a given region) in southeast France.[5]

Toto and Jacques had no formal training on how to gather information or instruct others on what to look for, so they ingeniously created a "how to" pamphlet that they distributed to the prostitutes and other agents, as Jean de Roquefort recalls:

"It is noteworthy that my teammate and I had to procure in France, with enormous difficulty, all of the pieces of information, in particular the makeup of the larger units and the tactical identification signs of the German units. Our work would have been greatly accelerated and improved if the service [OSS] would have been in position to provide us with [knowledge of how to obtain] this information. . . . We ourselves published a little brochure quite similar to that of the service, although unfortunately less complete. . . . It by itself made possible worthwhile work by agents who had no military training or any personal knowledge of the German army."[6]

Penny Farthing agents gathered an impressive array of intelligence. On February 4, 1944, they reported the arrival of 18 German divisions in the south of France. Just after D-Day, Captain Jean Lescanne, who headed up a Penny Farthing station in southwest France, alerted the Allies that German reinforcements were on the way to Normandy: "Number 67 Division SS Das Reich has left region Garrone is heading north via National Routes 20 and 126 since 7th of June until morning of 9th."[7] The division, badly needed by the Germans to stem the Allied advance off the beaches, was harassed, delayed, and damaged by Allied fighters as it made the long journey to Normandy.

Mario "Toto" Marret was nearly captured about ten times before he was finally taken by the Gestapo. "Jacques" Jean de Roquefort remembers one close call.

"The incident took place from seven in the morning until eleven at night[. A] large force of SS men took over the Perrache [rail] Station, bottled up the exits and forced everyone to show their identity cards. Some were carefully examined with a magnifying glass and all names were looked up in a dictionary of suspected persons which contained many thousand names. They rummaged in everybody's belongings except those of old people and women with babies in their arms. All arriving trains were shunted off to certain secondary platforms so that travelers getting off had to enter the station through underground passageways. These passages were blocked off shortly after the arrival of each train in such a way that the people in them were bottled up and taken by complete surprise. In spite of this Toto and his agent were able to drop their packages in the crowd and get out without being discovered—a great accomplishment in view of the strict control. . . ."

Another close call occurred a few week later. "Toto and Roger were working late in the afternoon in a new location, a factory along the Saône. They had never worked in this section before and we had thought the security would be excellent. However, since the preceding alerts the time we allowed ourselves on the air was strictly limited. The contact that afternoon lasted for sixteen minutes. But as the two operators came out of the factory, two men called to them from across the street while others appeared from all sides and rushed to surround them. Toto and Roger started running, but their followers were close behind, using their revolvers. Toto knew a house in the neighborhood through which a stair mounted directly to the next parallel street. They ducked into this passage and a battle of revolvers ensued. Toto shot and killed the first of the men who ventured in. This allowed a short respite, in which time they managed to turn into the next street and disappear."[7]

Toto eventually had one close call too many. "On the 11th of April 1944, Toto made a rendezvous with a member of the Petit Jean's group, Jean Forat, through a young girl who acted as liaison agent. This Jean Forat had been given the job, during the preceding months, of finding locations for broadcasting in the region of Roanne, which mission he had not accomplished with much success. We had cut off all contact with him when, through this young girl, he asked for a rendezvous with Toto.

"The meeting took place in a café in Lyon and while they were sitting there, German agents burst into the room and seized Toto and the girl, both of whom put up strong resistance. In the meantime Jean Forat escaped. Toto succeeded in giving a false address, which made it possible for me to save myself and clear out of our apartment, taking with me all that was important—military papers, signal plans, and money.

"Jacques II and Petit Jean were immediately warned and they in turn made all their agents take immediate security precautions of the severest nature, since we did not know where the leak had started and thus did not know whom to guard against. Unfortunately, a liaison agent was arrested before he could be alerted, and the following day Jacques II, on his way to the station to wait for a friend whom he wished to warn, was himself seized before he had a chance to swallow the poison pill which he, like all of us, carried constantly with him.

"This was a tremendous blow to the network, but the excellent security and absolute isolation which had been established among the personnel of the group prevented any further leak and the damage stopped there.

"Toto was taken under such conditions that the Germans knew he had been parachuted into France; the papers later seized at my apartment confirmed this fact. After the arrest, his first and foremost thought was to stall for time so that we would get away. He did this so well, with his cool courage and constant lucidity, that it is not untrue to say that it was Toto who had the upper hand during all the interrogations. He was the only prisoner at Fort Montluc who refused to sign his deposition because he did not know German, the language in which his story was presented to him for signature. From the beginning and without a definite or binding word being said between them, there was a tacit understanding between Toto and one of his interrogators who knew the importance of his prize. Under Toto's influence this man agreed to try and save his prisoner's life in return for which Toto was to attempt to do the same thing for him later in the game. In this way Toto was able to avoid hours of interrogation and torture.

"Special interrogators were sent from Berlin to question him as much on the Allied invasion of North Africa, in which he had participated, as on technical radio questions. On the latter he managed to say nothing, while giving the impression that he was answering their questions. By his adroit answers he succeeded in getting from the enemy valuable information on the methods of the Gestapo. The testimonies of his fellow prisoners were all in accord in stating that Toto exhibited an extraordinary courage during the whole period of his imprisonment. Of the thousands of men and women who had passed through that terrible prison, he remains the one who is held up as an example."[8]

In the end, Toto managed to escape execution. "He was condemned to die, but the interrogator who was on his side managed each time to delay the execution and to avoid having him chosen as one of a group of hostages who at regular intervals were shot without trial. The excuse used was that there was more information to be extracted from such an important prisoner. On the 24th of August, a few hours before he was to be shot, his Gestapo agent and one of the latter's colleagues grasped him as if taking him to his execution and, as soon as they were in the car, untied his hands and declared themselves to be his prisoners and handed over their guns.

"Toto drove them around the German lines to a Maquis some 40 kilometers from Lyon. His odyssey thus ended, he immediately put himself at the disposition of an American division for intelligence missions through the lines.

"As for Jacques II, he adopted toward the Germans an extraordinary attitude, refusing purely and simply to answer any questions put
to him, even such simple questions as ones concerning his identity.
Terribly tortured, he continued to maintain this silence. Twice he
tried to kill himself. The last time, paralyzed from the poison he had
swallowed, he was taken to the hospital of the prison, where his interrogators and torturers persecuted him until the day of his disappear-
ance from the prison, after two months of detention. He left no trace
and he was certainly among those shot."[9]

On September 21, 1943, Algiers-based SI/France inserted their
second agent team, Mutton Pork, into southwestern France. After
parachuting from an Algiers-based British plane, the team organized
three intelligence chains and two radio stations. Mutton Pork sent a
number of valuable intelligence reports before a clever Gestapo agent
penetrated the Bordeaux chain, resulting in the arrest of several
agents. However, Mutton Pork's chief agent, Jean I, avoided arrest and
continued to send intelligence pouches through Spain to Algiers.[10]

Louis, the team's radio operator, was unable to avoid the Gestapo
dragnet. Here he recalls his arrest in Toulouse in April 1943: "The
Gestapo set a trap for me in my own quarters. I arrived, walked
through the yard, opened the door, and was immediately arrested by
two Germans in civilian clothes, each with a [sub]machine gun.

"I was violently shoved, with my face to the wall and searched.
The house had no rear exit. I thought of how I could get out. Without
letting me move, the Germans questioned me. 'Do you know so-and-
so?' Naming agents already arrested. I denied everything. They
laughed, and did not mistreat me at the time. No doubt they saw no
use to, feeling they already knew too much about me from the others
who had been arrested. I stood there for an hour with my hands
raised, my face to the wall. Then a German police car arrived. They
put me in the back with one of the Germans beside me. The other got
in the front beside the chauffeur.

"Passing through the Place Arnaud Bernard, a very busy square filled with trams, cars, and people buying at the market, I tried to execute a plan I had thought out. I pressed strongly on the door handle of the car hoping to open it and throw myself out. Unfortunately, the handle worked the other way. This was a piece of bad luck that I immediately paid for. I got a blow to the head that almost split my skull, then in the face, until I was blind. I was immediately handcuffed with my hands behind my back. No doubt the Germans would have killed me on the spot except that they wanted to reserve this pleasure for later. After this I was in pretty bad shape. The car sped up and arrived in front of the Gestapo headquarters in the Rue Maynard. I was taken by the throat and violently snatched out of the car. Then the Krauts pretended to open the iron gate by knocking my head against the bars.

"With my hands still cuffed behind me I went up two flights in the apartment house, kicked at every step. Then they gave me the works: rawhide whips, clubs, and fists rained on me. They spread my radio equipment out in front of me and tried to force me to acknowledge it, and to admit my relations with the others who had been arrested. I denied everything, or remained silent, not having time to say anything but 'No.' Then they took me by the hair and beat my head against a radiator. I could not ward off these blows because my hands were still cuffed behind me. Then they took me upstairs to the top of the apartment where they had another nice trick. I was hung by a strong rope tied around the middle of my body and run through a pulley in the roof just over the stair shaft. Then I was whipped hanging in space with nothing to hold on to. My feet, my face, my head, my back were beaten until I was unconscious. They broke several clubs on my back. From time to time they let me down to the bottom and between whippings interrogated me. My 'friends,' arrested before, certainly must have had a long tongue. It was difficult for me to deny the truth of certain facts in the Gestapo's possession.

"Choking, my head and jaw aching, I had about all I could stand at this point. I admitted that I was an American agent for no other reason than to gain time. I must say that at this moment death would have been pleasant.

"The wife of one of our agents who had been arrested was in a cell not far way from mine. Through the hallway I heard her cry and scream, 'Where is my husband? Where is Francois?' Francois was myself. That fool woman certainly must have talked in order to save her husband, and part of the deluge of precise questions which they were putting to me must have come from her.

"I was taken out of my cell several times that day and on the following day to be interrogated. These sessions showed me the extent of the disaster. I was cooked, hog-tied, and betrayed. It was impossible for me to deny the evidence of my activity. At least I didn't do very well at denying it. Then I suffered more morally and physically. Death would have been very easy to stand.

"In order to test me out the Germans gave me a revolver. I put it to my head and pulled the trigger. It was not loaded. That little trick immediately earned for me an SS guard day and night. They thought they might lose me. I was still handcuffed. I asked to shave and they sent me a barber. They didn't want me to shave alone. They sent me excellent food but sent it by SS guard. No civilian was allowed to see me. I was physically weak and in pain. Then I began to play dumb in order not to be 'dragged on the carpet.' I made myself out to be stupid; I changed my opinions; I became almost Nazi in conversation with the Germans and told them that having been betrayed by my friends there was no reason for me to pay for them all. I pretended to have no conscience. I set to learning German again with a perseverance which touched these brutes. I pretended to be astounded at the unexpected power of 'Greater Germany.' I pretended to abjure 'the errors of my youth.' I feigned the most salutary fear. All this brought me sleepless nights of bad conscience, and during the day I was extremely dull. Nevertheless, I would go calmly into my cell as if it were the most natural thing in the world. I would go up to be handcuffed so docilely that they finally would put the cuffs in my pocket instead of putting them on my hands. In reality I was thinking of nothing but how to escape, how to murder my guard. But the roofs were inaccessible, the doors were locked with electric locks controlled from a distance, and the Gestapo had requisitioned this whole section of town. In the end all that my feigned good-will got for me was a room without windows and an SS guard day and night."

Jean I had learned of Louis's arrest through one of his chief cut-outs, René. Then a few days later Jean I received though F-10, his Spanish chain contact, the curious news that Louis was not under arrest but hiding at the home of a friend named Bonal. Suspicious of this contradiction, Jean I asked for three separate confirmations, and finally sent René to make contact with Bonal and see who he was really working for. René made the dangerous contact and returned with the information that Bonal was in reality a Gestapo agent holding Louis under arrest. The Germans tried to use Louis as a double agent, but Louis managed to turn the tables.

"Two days later we met René in town. I was accompanied by Bonal. Five civilian policemen about 20 yards away never took their eyes off me. We went to a restaurant. I stated from the first that anybody who talked shop would have to pay a fine, that we were there that evening to have a good dinner and a good time.

"René, Bonal, and I, somewhat against Bonal's wishes, shut ourselves off in a little room on a small courtyard behind the main dining room. I knew the waiter. The room was quite small and had only one table so that my Gestapo followers had to sit in the common dining room. Every chance of escape now offered, through the stairs, hall, houses and streets. Also, with the aid of René I could have murdered Bonal. I had the situation in hand, but I refused to use force. I wanted to avoid a row that would perhaps gain nothing. I had better things to do than shed blood and perhaps spoil everything by rushing.

"I ordered the best wines, I ordered an enormous dinner, I filled the glasses time and again and led the drinking. Bonal, half drunk, went to the toilet. During this time I told René that I was under arrest by the Germans, that Bonal was a Gestapo agent, I told him the game the Germans were trying to play with me. René offered to help me murder Bonal. I ordered him to continue laughing and drinking and do nothing of the sort. I told him and all our friends that it was better to get out of this affair in some natural way. I told him to imitate my own behavior. He was finally convinced.

"Bonal came back and I continued to set the tone of the conversation, joking and drinking. Finally, after many rounds of the bottle we all three went out. Bonal was stewed; René, who was imitating everything I did, pretended to be drunk. The dinner lasted two and a half hours. The Gestapo agents sitting in the large dining room were also drunk, having passed the bottle to kill the time and keep face while waiting for us.

"I decided to go to the street carnival, and got permission to do so. It was night, 9:30 or 10:00. We stopped at the shooting gallery. Without seeming to do so, I gave René details on what he should do and how to alert Algiers. I managed to get alone with him on a roller-coaster and while laughing and joking I told him everything he needed to know, under the very noses of the five Gestapo agents leaning on the fence waiting for us. Bonal was at the exit. We said we were tired and drunk. We would meet again a couple of weeks later. It was better not to continue now because the Gestapo agents were getting closer and were probably worried. Bonal and I said goodbye to René and in a very natural manner picked up the Gestapo agents. I was now completely sure that René would not show up at the next meeting we had arranged, and that it would mean the end of me. Still I was able to tell funny stories. It is true that I was actually quite happy that evening. René had been able to get away, and I put myself back into the hands of the Gestapo in the most natural manner, to avoid all suspicion of duplicity. I went back to the prison and took my place."[11]

Louis courageously agreed to operate his radio under German control and play the *"Funkspiel,"* literally, "radio game."

By controlling, or "doubling," the agent, the Germans typically hoped to control the chain and gain additional information on OSS activities or limit the number of agents OSS would send to that region of France. But OSS was not fooled. When Louis went on the air, OSS Algiers nonchalantly acknowledged that he was under German control by signing off with SK instead of VA (SK is a German signal). Fortunately, the Germans did not pick up on the sign-off discrepancy. Armed with the knowledge that OSS knew he was being forced to work for the Germans, Louis kept up the transmissions, playing for time. Louis's clever handling of the situation managed to deceive the Germans for four and one-half months. He later escaped and joined the Maquis, eventually linking up with the OSS.

Tommy, Penny Farthing, and Mutton Pork were only a few of the intelligence networks established by OSS in France. These networks gathered intelligence crucial to the impending Allied invasion.

Paving the Way for Overlord

The staccato drumbeat of machine-gun fire pierced the air as bullets kicked up dirt on a nearby hedgerow. William Donovan whispered to Colonel David Bruce, head of OSS London station, "I must shoot first." "Yes sir," Bruce responded, "but can we do much against machine guns with our pistols?" "Oh you don't understand. I mean if we are about to be captured I'll shoot you first. After all, I am your commanding officer."[1]

Against the direct orders of the secretary of the Navy, Wild Bill Donovan took part in Operation Overlord, the Normandy landings on D-Day. Donovan did not lack courage. But allowing himself to be captured by the Germans would have been unthinkable; Donovan knew too much. By June 6, 1944, Donovan was leading a complex machine that was playing a key role in the effort to drive the Germans out of France.

Only months elapsed between OSS's first missions into France through Algiers, and the beginning of pre–D-Day operations in Normandy. But in that short time, OSS grew markedly in professionalism, particularly in regard to selection and training of agents. In the early days, recruitment was largely ad hoc and training skimpy, but by early 1944, both selection and training became rigorous for OSS agents sent into France.

OSS feared that most agents recruited in the United States would be out of touch with what was going on in France, so many agents were recruited from de Gaulle's forces. Most of the operatives were Frenchmen who escaped from France to England or Frenchmen liberated in North Africa. Candidates went through a multiweek assessment and parachute course, culminating with the candidate operating for one week undercover as an agent within Allied areas of control such as England. If caught, the trainees were subjected to an intense interrogation, and if they cracked and blew their cover story they were dropped from the program.

As the agents completed their training, they were given false identities and cover stories. Using their own backgrounds as much as possible, the agents fleshed out their identities, making them as realistic and watertight as possible. The best covers corresponded to their actual backgrounds and professions.

In England, a special French Document Section was established, furnishing the agents everything from ration cards to identification papers. Papers were aged by rubbing them with ash or placing them in a room and letting people walk on them. Most of the documentation was only temporary. Once in the country, the agents typically obtained original documentation issued by the proper authorities.

An agent's clothing had to come from French civilians living in North Africa. British clothing "screamed spy"; it could not be used because it was so well made, unlike similar French garments. As a final refinement, if the agent was American, dental work was even redone to correspond to French style. Next, the agents were briefed on their target areas. Last-minute checks ensured that agents did not possess contraband articles.

Most agents were transported into France by plane, but OSS also used other means such as small boats or overland travel through Spain or Switzerland. A parachute drop, either "blind" or to a reception committee, was the most common form of agent insertion.

Paving the Way for Overlord

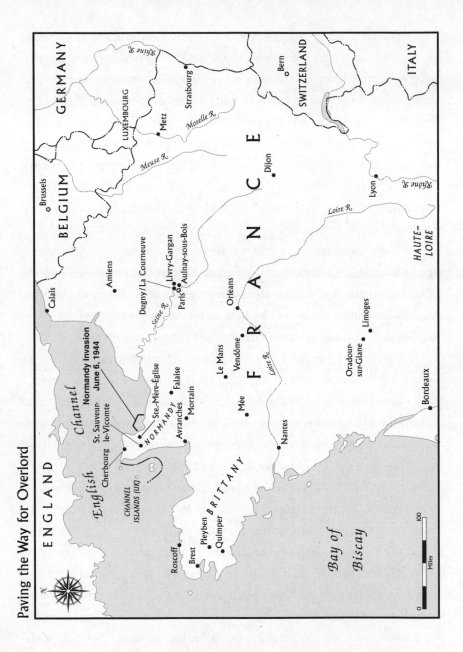

Many agents were inserted by the Royal Air Force or the American 801st/492nd Bombardment Group (H). Better known as the "Carpetbaggers," this special unit of the Eighth Air Force was designated for agent infiltration, supply drops, and other clandestine operations. Flying specially modified, black-painted B-24s, A-26s, C-47s, and British Mosquitoes, the Carpetbaggers were America's transport arm of the secret war.

Agent infiltration was delicate work. Once the coordinates for a drop zone were selected, the agents were typically dropped when the skies were clear and there was enough moonlight for navigation. If a reception committee was on the ground, they typically used Morse code by flashlight or lamp to signal the plane. If the signal was correct and the winds favorable, the dispatcher in the plane flashed the green light and gave word to the agent to jump.

A significant aspect of the covert campaign for Normandy began in June 1943, when the British and the OSS agreed to enter a joint intelligence mission known as Sussex. Sussex was intended to supply strategic and tactical intelligence to the Allied armies once they landed in northern France. One hundred twenty French agents, organized in two-man teams (radio operator and observer) were parachuted into key rail hubs, communication centers, enemy headquarters, and river crossings in northern France to watch the German army.

Sussex agent René Joyeuse succeeded in his mission through deceptiveness and sheer audacity. "I dropped through the 'Joe hole' with my radio operator, Georges Ducasse. We parachuted in the environs of Chartres in a wheat field, where we were taken in by a farmer and his wife. Our base of operation was northeast of Paris, so we took a train to Paris. The train was called the Train de Haricots [the 'Green Bean Train'—a train used by the people in and around Paris to travel to the countryside to buy vegetables]. We dressed as farmers. All the seats were taken except for some seats next to a few German officers. I placed potatoes and green beans over the top the equipment and asked the German officers if I could place it under their seat [they did not want any Gestapo agents patrolling the train to see him with too much luggage.] They were very polite and agreed, so I put the crates with our radio equipment right under their feet [laughs].

We traveled to Livry-Gargan [the northeast suburbs of Paris] where we met the local postmaster, who was a member of the resistance, and were given employment papers for PTT [Postal-Telephone-Telegraph]. We were referred to the Girard family who offered us their home as a safe house in Livry-Gargan. We began operations in the backyard of the Girard's house next to the ruins of the Château de la Marquise de Savigne, where the Germans had a group stationed.

"We started gathering information but we could not send anything out, as the original radio was damaged in the parachute drop and did not function. Eventually another radio set was sent.*

"We were transmitting right next to a German position, right in their backyard. I wanted to be right next to them so my signal would be mixed up with theirs and they couldn't triangulate my position with direction-finding trucks. I remember seeing their trucks going around but they thought it was their own signal.

"Through 27 subagents we gathered intelligence, mainly troop movements from Germany through Paris to Normandy. We were near the main highway that convoys would pass down to Normandy. They were traveling on it day and night. The whole town was with us. They were helping me, protecting me. I had people looking for unit numbers on trucks and gathering other information.

"I sent reports on the Le Bourget Airfield and an underground V-1 factory. On July 9 we sent back valuable information on a powder factory at Sevran. Based on this information, the following night the factory was heavily damaged by Allied bombers. On August 3 we

---

*The original radio was hidden and kept in France since the war at the Girards's home. It is now on permanent display in the CIA museum in Langley, Virginia.

sent back complete plans and details of the oil refinery at Dugny La Courneuve, which was completely destroyed on August 11, 1944 by Allied bombers. We were sending back information mostly on the Klaxon phone to a plane that flew overhead.

"By August, the Germans were getting closer, so we decided to move to Alunay-Sur-Bois, as we did not want the Girards harmed. Despite our precautions Jacques Girard was arrested and taken to a German prison. He was tortured but never talked.

"At Alunay-Sur-Bois we moved to an abandoned house which was owned by a doctor who went into hiding prior to our arrival. I sent messages via a Klaxon system.

"I believe someone tipped off the Germans to our position. It was early in the morning of August 18 and we were trying to send information back to England. The transmission was interrupted by a large group of SS troops. We all opened fire. I was firing my Colt as I ran, and in the confusion escaped. I ran out the back door and just ran.

"It was the courageous efforts of these young men that allowed me to escape, but they gave their own lives and were executed by the SS, who also burned the house down. The area is now a park in honor of the two men. The inscription on a small grayed monument reads: 'Here killed on the 18 August 1944 Louis Barrault 23 years old, Pierre Gastaud 20 years old assassinated by the Germans—FREEDOM in HONOR of our Martyrs Louis Barrault and Pierre Gastaud.'

"I ran through a garden and made my way to another safe house but was hit in the foot in the process. The Germans were searching everywhere trying to find me. I stayed there until the next morning and they called a butcher who brought up a car and took me to a doctor who patched me up. I was in hiding for 10 days and later linked up with Allied forces when they overran the area."[2]

Sussex, although perilous, proved a success. Of the 52 agents OSS dispatched, six were captured and executed. However, the information they provided was invaluable. A G-2 SHAEF (Supreme Headquarters Allied Expeditionary Force) report summed up the contributions of Team Vitrail, which was representative of the Sussex program. "The series of reports transmitted to G-2 SHAEF by OSS from Chartres in the early stages of Overlord were exceptionally able and useful . . . a Sussex agent was the first to identify the movements of the Panzer Lehr Division, on maneuvers in western France, and the value of this piece of information was sufficient to justify all the work that had been put into the Sussex project, even if nothing else was accomplished."[3]

Meetings between the Free French, SOE, and OSS in early 1943 determined that building up the Resistance before D-Day was the top priority. The goal of the Resistance would be to reduce the flow of war matériel to the Germans, by sabotaging factories, fuel dumps, and power plants. The Resistance would mount a classic guerrilla campaign, relying on hit-and-run raids. Seizing and holding ground was considered counterproductive.[4]

Throughout 1943, operations and planning for the upcoming invasion accelerated. OSS and SO/SIS moved toward integrating their efforts in France, with SO/London becoming a full partner with SOE under the formal title of SOE/SO. A month before the invasion SOE/SO went through another name change and formed a partnership, called Special Force Headquarters (SFHQ). SFHQ was directly responsible for coordinating the Resistance in the upcoming invasion.

SFHQ came under the command of General Eisenhower, who focused its efforts on preparation for the invasion. The responsibility of OSS and SOE agents in France would be to organize and coordinate the Resistance forces, making them an effective element in the Allied invasion.[5]

The plan adopted by the Allies called for an all-out behind the lines attack on the Germans. Maximum paramilitary assistance and supplies would be furnished to the Resistance in order to cut off major north-south arteries that the Germans would have to use during the

invasion. Disabling command and control, especially by cutting telephone lines, was a priority.[6]

The first OSS SO agents parachuted into France in civilian clothes.
Recruited from the United States, they were attached to SOE teams or
"circuits" headed for France or already in the country. These circuits
were code-named RF Section for circuits supported by General Charles
de Gaulle and F Section for circuits that were non-Gaullist and non-political and organized as "closed" circuits, that is, their existence was not
directly reported to de Gaulle. There was also a smaller section, DF,
that ran escape lines. Most SO agents went to F Section circuits.[7]

SO's first agent in France was E. F. Floege, code-named "Alfred."
Alfred was a resident of Chicago who had lived in Angers, France for a
number of years before the war. On June 13, 1943, Floege parachuted
"blind" into France and used his extensive contacts to set up the Sacristan circuit located in the Le Mans–Nantes–Laval area.

About two months after Alfred jumped into France, his W/T operator, André Bouchardon, known as "Narcisse," joined him. For six
months operations went well, including several successful arms drops
for the burgeoning Resistance groups Alfred was nurturing.

Working out of Meé, a base camp, Sacristan relied on two couriers for communications. One of the couriers was Alfred's son, who
was caught in a Gestapo *ratissage,* or literally, a rat hunt. Young Floege
broke during the interrogation, resulting in the arrest of 45 of Sacristan's members. The SO war diary describes the breakup of Sacristan
and the capture of Narcisse.

"On the 23 of December, seven of the Gestapo came to the house
where Narcisse was staying, during dinner, and arrested him and his
host. They handcuffed him [Narcisse] and while they were doing this
[a Gestapo agent] threatened one of them with his revolver. [Narcisse]
kicked him in the groin with both feet, upon which the man shot him
in the chest. He pretended to be dead and three of them immediately
bundled him off in a car, leaving the other four to deal with his late

host. Two sat in front discussing the affair, the third was with the 'body' in the back.

"They had searched his trouser pockets but they had not searched his jacket, in the pocket of which he still had his revolver. While in the car he managed to ease this out of his pocket and shoot in rapid succession the man beside him and the two in front. The car went into a ditch, whereupon Narcisse abandoned the car and made his way to the house of some friends nearby, intending to warn Alfred as soon as he was sufficiently recovered. On the following day, early in the morning, Alfred was in the garden of his house when several men whom he took to have been Gestapo appeared on the garden wall, brandishing revolvers. Within a few minutes the house and garden were surrounded. On the fourth side there was a fairly high wall which the Gestapo evidently thought was too high for escape, but Alfred managed to scramble over this unobserved and made his way to the same friends where Narcisse had taken refuge. They thus found themselves together and able to compare notes. Realizing that the game was up, they decided to leave.

"At Laval they contacted a Free French group through whom they sent their messages to London."[8] Both agents escaped to Spain and eventually returned to a different region of France on another mission.

On June 6, 1944, the great crusade to liberate Europe began, as tens of thousands of men stormed ashore at Normandy. Like all American army commands, the invading U.S. armies were assigned OSS detachments, and OSS personnel were attached directly to some of the units making the landings to provide tactical intelligence.

Both SI and SO units were attached to Allied army groups. SO units were referred to as "Special Force Detachments." Four were created: Special Force Detachments Nos. 10, 11, 12, and 13. One of the most productive detachments, No. 10, operated with the U.S. First Army. No. 10's first mission involved smashing German phone lines behind Utah Beach, forcing the Germans to use their radios for communication. Days later, Detachment No. 10 harnessed FFI Resistance groups near the beachhead and destroyed a key section of rail a few miles inland, forcing exhausted German reinforcements to arrive on foot.

However, Detachment 10's operational successes failed to overcome First Army's reluctance to cooperate with OSS. The OSS SI detachment assigned to First Army was actually denied transport on D-Day. Once the SI team finally arrived, it began to provide valuable tactical intelligence. Nevertheless, an unsympathetic G-2 (intelligence officer), who did not understand irregular warfare, eventually banned both units from operating with First Army. The decision would prove disastrous when First Army, after depriving itself of its own eyes and ears, was surprised at the Battle of the Bulge.

OSS's greatest contribution was made through its independent operations behind German lines. OSS Special Operations provided personnel to the 40-plus SOE/SO circuits active prior to the invasion.

"Salesman" was one of the more successful circuits. Salesman's greatest coup before D-Day was sinking a 900-ton warship using a three-pound plastic charge strategically placed below the waterline. The ship sank in six minutes.[9]

After the landings, Salesman's agents turned their efforts to harassing one of Germany's most powerful panzer divisions. Salesman delayed and considerably damaged the 2nd SS Panzer "Das Reich" Division as it struggled from the south of France to counter the Normandy landings. Jean Claude Guiet, Salesman's radio operator, at times found himself serving as an infantry officer against the SS.

"We fought a pitched battle against elements of Das Reich and some Bulgarian troops. We had about a two-day running battle mainly because we wanted to preserve our drop zone. They hit us about two days after a supply drop. We were fighting them all over the place. I grabbed a Bren gun and ammunition and joined the fight. The

Germans quit around sunset and again we were moving containers.

"The next morning they attacked again. I would guess we had about forty guys. I was a second lieutenant, I had basic training and that was about it. But I was the American who jumped in. I had sort of a de facto leadership role.

"We had two days of pretty constant fighting. They had mortars and machine guns; they just overwhelmed us with firepower, but we still held. They would go, come forward, we would stop them and hit them on their rear flank. Night would come. We had no entrenching tools, obviously, but people would bring ammo, food, and water. We just held. The worst part was this was in a forest, we didn't have a clear field of fire. The worst part was when mortar shells would hit pine trees and shower shrapnel and splinters down on us.

"Anyway, at the end of the second day we were being pushed back and just about wiped out. They overran the roadblock that we had built. I was thinking, 'How are we going to get out of this?' All of the sudden another Maquis group of about 400 or 500 guys hit their flank. I left about three smoldering trucks and over a hundred dead. Nevertheless, as far as we were concerned, we cleared the drop zone of supplies and we were willing to let them have the area.

"Patton was circling around and heading east from Normandy. We continued to ambush German convoys. One of my most memorable ambushes wasn't really even an ambush. . . . we came up near a castle. We attacked and cleared the Germans out of the castle which was a strong point for them. We were getting together and about to move back and all of a sudden we found out that Bob Maloubier, our demolitions expert, was missing. What had happened apparently is that he had wandered off down to a road below the castle.

"He saw three Germans pushing a bicycle with the sunset behind them. He stepped out on the road with his Marlin submachine gun and said, 'Hands up gentlemen!' At that time he noticed that there was an entire convoy coming up a hill behind those three guys. He was taken prisoner after being slightly wounded in the arm. They treated him fairly well and stuffed him in a truck behind two 50-gallon drums of gas and a stack of artillery shells.

"When they got to the nearest city the German commander had so many wounded men that he approached Bob and asked him as a British officer if he was willing to take charge of his wounded and take them into his car in exchange for his freedom, and get them treated as prisoners of war. Bob agreed. He took care of them and turned them over to the local FFI group and the next thing I know I'm sitting in Limoges and the phone rings and it's Bob on the other end and acting as if nothing happened: 'Hi, I'm at the café such and such, pick me up.' So my other teammates and I got a car and picked him up and that was that."[10]

The "Hermit" circuit operated in the Loire region of France. Herb Brucker, the team's radio operator, recalls the day he almost lost his life.

"We fell in a roadblock, complete with radio and everything. I was on a tandem bicycle. We shot our way out of there. Naturally we lost the radio and the frequency. Something had happened in the area. The Resistance became very active and the Germans reacted . . . they were out in force and they had roadblocks everywhere and they were looking for one particular guy whom they eventually caught up with. There must have been a whole battalion in the woods because it was an operation. It was a rat hunt and we were just caught in the end of where they were actually located.

"They shouted for us to come forward to which we made believe we did not understand. We asked them by gestures if they wanted us to turn around and leave. They shouted more than the first time, and judging us very stupid, scared, and not dangerous, they came forward themselves.

"We kept cool and leaned our bicycle on the side of the road and practically asked them to ask us for papers, which they did. While we searched our pockets for our papers, one German started looking over our baggage [radio] while another, lowering his rifle, inspected Raymond's pockets. He soon found that Raymond had something hard on his chest [.45 automatic]. Not exactly sure, he asked if it was a gun; the answer was 'No,' of course. He insisted. Seeing that the attention was on Raymond, I folded my papers again, reached into my pocket, and pulled out my .32 automatic. They asked for my papers. I showed them my pistol! To make a long story short we had to shoot them. When that happened the Germans were popping out from everywhere in the woods. I just kept on shooting right into the mass of bodies and kept moving on foot.

"My buddy and I wound up in a hole behind a bush. Aside from the .32 I also had a .45 but since we didn't have any holsters we kept these weapons sort of stuck in our belts. In order not to lose the pistol I tied parachute suspension line to it. When I jumped from the road there was a ditch so I'm jumping over the ditch and as that happened the .45 slid between my leg and my pants and it kept banging on my knee which made me limp so I presume the Germans thought I was hit. We wound up in a hole and I thought that was it. I had to lift my pants leg in order to get at the pistol and there must have been 25 knots in that goddarn thing and it wouldn't come off. I still had two bullets left in the .32 so I decided to shoot the suspension line and I missed. The second one I put the barrel right on the suspension line and fired and of course it came off. Now I had the .45 which also had an extra bullet. Of course, by now, bullets were flying all over the place from Germans. I was in a prone position taking aim at one of the guys and it suddenly occurred to me that 'you're stupid,' these guys got rifles with a range of 300–400 yards. A pistol is good for about 20 feet. So I decided we should just move out of there. I was talking with my buddy and we decided on the count of three we were going to bound out of that hole and run like hell for 10 paces and hit the ground and bounce up again and hit the ground and so on and so forth and that's exactly what we did.

"The other thing that also should be mentioned is the mentality—
I had now geared myself for immediate reaction if I was hit anywhere.
As long as I'm hit anywhere but the feet I will continue running. If
they hit the feet, I take the pistol and blow my brains out so I kept on
running and eventually found a safe house whose owner was part of
the Resistance."[11]

"The woman who limps is one of the most dangerous Allied
agents in France. We must find and destroy her," declared an abrupt
order issued by the Gestapo.[12] The order was referring to OSS's most
decorated female F Section agent working in France, Virginia Hall.

From her compatriots in the French underground she earned the
nickname "La Dame Qui Boite" (the Limping Lady)—her limp was
caused by the fact that she wore a wooden leg. (Hall lost part of her
leg before the war in a hunting accident, when a firearm she was carrying discharged.) Hall never let her disability hamper her actions. She
nicknamed the leg "Cuthbert." In 1940 she was recruited by SOE after
working as a code clerk in the U.S. embassy.

Hall's first mission to France with SOE was in 1941, under the cover
of a reporter for the *New York Post*. Hall openly reported on conditions
in France while she covertly organized an SOE F Section. Since the
United States was not at war with Vichy France at the time, she was still
able to operate freely until the Allied invasion of North Africa. After the
invasion, German troops occupied Vichy France, forcing Hall to flee to
Spain, where she was assigned to an SOE circuit that acted as an underground railroad, maintaining escape lines for agents and downed
fliers out of France. Bored with her new assignment, Hall transferred to
OSS with the rank of second lieutenant in late 1943.

A few months after Hall's transfer, OSS infiltrated her back in
France on a small boat as the radio operator and co-organizer of the
Heckler Mission, which set up sabotage and organized Resistance op-
erations in the Haute-Loire region of central France.

"The arms received went to the Maquis and I financed them, for there were a couple thousand men already in the mountains and I hoped to be able to arm them and to 'do in' most of the several thousand Germans then in Le Puy.

"The fact that I did not receive officers or materials as promised put me in a very difficult position. The three plane loads that came at the end of July helped tremendously and enabled the Maquis to do a lot of bridge and tunnel wrecking and eventually force the Germans out of Le Puy by sheer bluff and finally to make them surrender in conjunction with the FFI forces of the Loire—some five or six hundred of them surrendering.

"In the middle of August, a Jedburgh team, Jeremy, arrived from Africa, but this was after the Germans had been liquidated in the department of the Haute Loire and Le Puy had been liberated. I was told that in reply to my repeated clamoring I would be sent a team from Africa, so when the Jeds came I assumed that they had come to work for me. I told them what I wanted done, and what was impossible to do for myself. . . .

"Meanwhile, the Jedburghs had done a very nice organization job at Le Puy and formed, under their own officers, three battalions, 1,500 men, and I continued to finance them and give them what arms I could get."[13]

Building on the SOE/SO circuits established in 1943 and 1944, the three-man Jedburgh teams had begun to parachute into France, just as Overlord was beginning. Jeds, and the larger uniformed Operational Groups, were purposely held back by direct order from Eisenhower, who feared that their capture would reveal information on the proposed landings. Though trained and ready, no Jeds or OGs entered France before June 5, 1944.

The Jeds took their name from their training grounds near Jedburgh, Scotland. Each Jedburgh team consisted of two officers and one radio operator. Staffed along multinational lines, 83 were American, 90 British, and 103 French.[14]

Major General William "Wild Bill" Donovan, director of the Office of Strategic Services and architect of America's version of unorthodox warfare. (*National Archives*)

OSS's legendary hand-to-hand combat instructor, William Fairbairn, also known as the "Shanghai Buster." Fairbairn was the creator of the deadliest form of jiujitsu and street fighting ever devised, called "Gutter Fighting." During WWII, the Shanghai Buster was in his fifties, but he could easily crush any recruit that he trained. He often described his hand-to-hand system to new recruits this way: "There's no fair play; no rules except one: kill or be killed." *(National Archives)*

Wedding picture of OSS super-spy Elizabeth Pack, code-named "Cynthia," who seduced men in the line of duty. Cynthia's greatest coup involved helping acquire the first Enigma machine model from Polish intelligence and securing Italian and Vichy French codebooks. (*Library of Congress*)

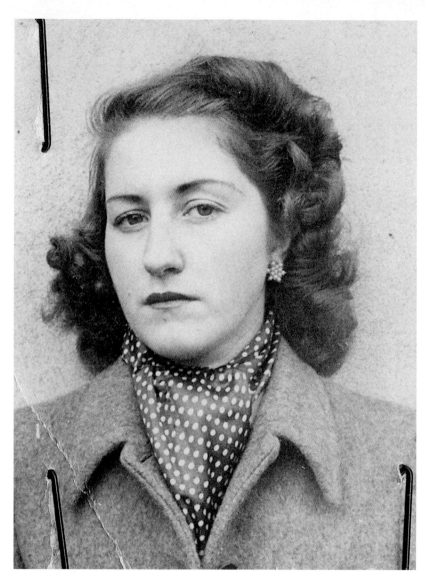

Maura Bertani, a former circus acrobat, parachuted into Germany in February 1945. (*National Archives*)

Materials used by OSS's Cover and Documentation unit to make false identification papers: captured German stamp pads, typewriter, and identification papers. (*National* Archives)

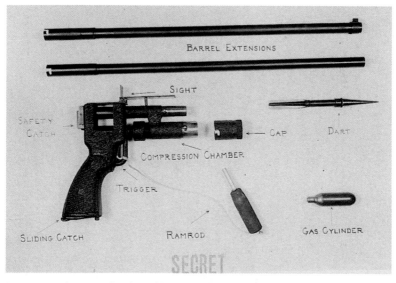

Top-secret dart gun developed by OSS's Research and Development division. (*National Archives*)

Altered German postage stamps from Operation Cornflakes. The stamp shows Hitler with part of his face eaten away, revealing his skull. The stamp has been altered to read, roughly, "Reich shot to Hell." (*National Archives*)

Fake German mailbags employed in Operation Cornflakes, an attack against German morale delivered via the German postal system. (*National Archives*)

OSS Assessment Party. After training was ostensibly completed, some OSS recruits were treated to a "relaxing" party, where they were plied with alcohol to see if they would reveal their cover stories. (*National Archives*)

Destroyed viaduct and wrecked train in Yugoslavia. The photo was taken by OSS's Alum team. (*National Archives*)

Lieutenant Johnny Athens of the Chicago Mission distributing weapons to Greek guerrillas. Chicago destroyed two critical bridges and temporarily disrupted Germany's vital chrome supply. (*National Archives*)

alian OGs. OSS's commandos were organized into 15- to 30-man Operational Groups (OGs). All volunteers, the men were highly trained in a variety of special operations, such as planning and raising guerrilla forces, demolition, sabotage, gathering intelligence, and "hit-and-run" raids. The OGs, who worked in uniform behind enemy lines, were the forerunners of the U.S. Army's Special Forces. Many OG operatives were drawn from the ranks of America's airborne units. (Photo courtesy of Nick Cantgelosi)

Frogman John Booth, of OSS's Maritime Operational Swimmer Groups. The swimmers, trained in underwater demolition and sabotage, were forerunners of the U.S. Navy SEALs. Booth is wearing the OSS-developed Lambertsen Amphibious Respiratory Unit, which enabled a swimmer to approach a target without leaving breathing bubbles. (Photo courtesy of John Booth)

Italian frogmen riding underwater submersibles known as Chariots. After Italy changed sides during the war, veteran Italian operatives carried out missions for the Allies. (*National Archives*)

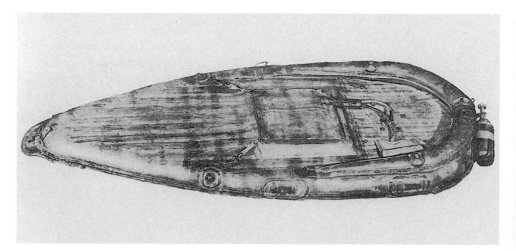

A two-man surfboard or motorized mattress used by OSS agents for seaborne insertions behind enemy lines. (*National Archives*)

OSS agents don specialized camouflage jumpsuits and parachutes. (*National Archives*)

Battle-tested OSS OGs with a band of Maquis in southern France. (*National Archives*)

Bridge and a locomotive sabotaged by the OSS and French Resistance.
(*National Archives*)

A specially blackened B-24 bomber is prepared for a mission to deliver agents deep into Germany. (*National Archives*)

OSS officer assisting a Polish agent deep behind the lines in Germany during Operation Eagle. OSS employed Poles exiled to Britain and former German prisoners of war as agents. (*National Archives*)

ABOVE: Hammer Mission agents Toni Ruh (left) and Paul Land were the first OSS team to parachute into the outskirts of Berlin. (*National Archives*)

LEFT: OSS OGs from the Rype team, led by William Colby, future director of the CIA, parachuted into Norway to destroy a vital bridge, preventing the redeployment of thousands of German troops. (*National Archives*)

OSS officer Howard Chappell of OG team Tacoma, which operated in northern Italy, is awarded the Silver Star by Wild Bill Donovan. A German manhunt captured Chappell and two members of his team, but he managed to escape by dispatching a German guard. Later, Chappell's team and Italian partisans forced the surrender of hundreds of German troops. (*Photo courtesy of Howard Chappell*)

Italian partisans organized by OG team Aztec. OSS organized and supplied tens of thousands of partisans in northern Italy, who played a key role in the Allied offensive in 1945. (*Photo courtesy of Nick Cantgelosi*)

Partisans salute their dead comrades and the end of the war in northern Italy. Through secret negotiations, OSS facilitated the surrender of several hundred thousand German troops in northern Italy a week before Germany's official capitulation. (*Photo courtesy of Nick Cantgelosi*)

Like most OSS personnel, Jeds were extraordinary individuals skilled in a variety of disciplines—Renaissance men in a sense. Each Jed was handpicked and went through a rigorous training program. The commandos were skilled in demolitions, communications, training of partisans, and intelligence work.

The teams took on an advisory role, supplementing the existing F and RF circuits by supplying additional arms, and conducting attacks on German targets. They acted as rallying points for the Resistance. During June and July they attacked German units entering Normandy. A total of 276 Jeds parachuted into France.[15]

Jed team Ammonia dropped into France on the night of June 10. Ammonia member Jacob Berlin recalls helping to slow a crack German SS division making its way to Normandy.

"Most of the work we did involved leading the Resistance groups. We blew up bridges or railroad tracks, slowing down the Das Reich SS Panzer Division that was trying to reach Normandy. They were so mad at what we were doing that they tried to wipe us out. The day we jumped in they massacred scores of people in a church at Oradour-sur-Glane. I remember the smoke, but we didn't know where it was coming from. At Tulle they took about one hundred men in the village and strung them up on lampposts. They left them there as a warning. Instead of taking two days to get to Normandy we (including the other teams) held them up until practically July. We are very proud of that.

"My most vivid memory involves driving down a road in a Citroën. All of a sudden a car zoomed up behind us. There were five of us in the car including the driver who was the local head of the Resistance. We noticed it was a German military car. It had been raining earlier and the road was still wet, causing us to get into several accidents. I was sitting in the front passenger's seat and I had a tommy gun out the window. As we went around a bend, I saw that we were going to hit a cow sideways. I had tried to pull the tommy gun inside the window but it was too late and we hit the cow. I hit the cow near the gut with my fist but I didn't feel a thing. The cow crushed the side of the car, and we flew several feet in the air but it didn't hurt me for some reason.

"Luckily, we were near another car and we pulled the people out of it and took off again. We left our car in the middle of the road; that slowed them down some. They couldn't get by it until they moved it. During the chase they were shooting at us but we weren't shooting at them. My tommy gun didn't have the range so I didn't see the point. They got fairly close to us a few times when we went around a bend.

"Near the end of the chase, we went around a curve in the road and there was a little path that went up into the mountains. Our driver noticed it and slowed the car down and drove up the path. The Germans just kept going and we took the car up the path.

"I've been back three times. Twice I went with my other teammate. This last time, I went alone since I'm the only one on my team left. The Resistance is now in their seventies and eighties. Each time they greeted us with their children and grandchildren. They would come up to us and say, 'Thank you for what you did for our country.'"[16]

The Allies broke out of the Normandy beachhead in late July. Montgomery drove east while the Americans pushed south, seizing Avranches. Ten days after a disastrous German counterattack at Mortain, most of Army Group B was trapped and destroyed at Falaise. With the German army in the west in tatters and retreating across the Seine, the road to Paris was left open. In the south, one corps of Patton's Third Army was assigned to clear Brittany and seize the port of Brest in order to relieve the strain on Allied supply lines.

In Brittany, 14 Jed teams worked with the British SAS (Special Air Service), analogous to OSS's OG teams, to organize 20,000 members of the Resistance. With the help of the Jeds and SAS the Resistance tied down large numbers of German troops in open battles. Rail cuts and ambushes forced the Germans to move their troops largely by foot.[17]

"Giles" was typical of the teams that dropped in Brittany. This Jed team was tripartite, consisting of American captain Bernie Knox, French captain Paul Lebel, and English sergeant Gordon Tack. Its mission was to organize a small army of Resistance fighters, and upon receiving a prearranged signal broadcast by the BBC, engage the Germans and help open the way to Brest for the advancing Allied army.[18]

Knox's team also brought in several additional Jed teams, including Ray Trump's Team Ronald, which caught the Germans in a devastating ambush in the streets of Quimper.

"Before we set up the ambush there were reports of a large German contingent in Quimper. I decided to try to talk to them. So I wrote a letter to the German commander telling him that I was in command of an advance guard of an armored unit and we were ready to attack the town and we would like to arrange the terms of his surrender. I gave the letter to a French policeman who delivered it to the German headquarters. They sent out patrols and realized that we were bluffing and said they would only surrender to the Americans when they arrive.

"We set up an ambush for the Germans we knew were heading north. [C. G.] Blathwayt [British head of Jed team Gilbert] and I went into the third story of a big old apartment house. We were situated on a corner and the streets kind of split and we were in that triangle. We had about 60 Frenchmen across the street on both sides. When the convoy got there we immediately started firing. Blathwayt had never fired a bazooka and he wanted to shoot it. So I wired him up, loaded a shell. In the meantime he closed the door in the room he was in. I moved to the room next door.

"The Germans appeared and we all opened fire. I heard the bazooka go off. I ran to the next floor and the blast knocked him on the floor. I looked out where he said he had fired and sure enough a house on the left had a large hole in the roof. It was one of the funnier things that happened during my war. Anyway we killed over 100 Germans that day.

"They were coming right in front of us and we were spraying everything that moved with rifle, machine-gun fire. They kept on coming and we were involved in street fighting for three days and the Germans eventually tried to retreat to Brest. Very few reached their destination."[19]

Team Giles also engaged the elite 2nd Parachute Division. Captain Bernie Knox (who after the war was director of the Harvard Center of Hellenic Studies) recalls their first significant ambush, which netted scores of prisoners.

"In the course of these attacks, a considerable number of prisoners were taken. I along with Legal interrogated them. They were all from the 2nd Paratrooper Division. Most were battle-hardened veterans in their twenties and confident and cocky. They served in Russia and some served in Crete. Most of them only gave their name, rank, and identity number.

"I approached an older *Feldwebel* who, after seeing I was an American, said, 'Now international law has arrived.' They all feared what would happen to them in the hands of the FFI. We started searching them for weapons and intelligence. Several had bloody wedding rings in their pockets. French women never removed the rings and the only way to get them off the finger was to cut them off.

"They admitted to the atrocities they had committed, refused to believe that the Americans had taken Rennes, refused to discuss the Hitler regime, and refused to explain why they had French jewelry, money, and identity cards on them. They were all very young (one of the worst was only 17), and they were all subsequently shot by the FFI. Even if we had wished to prevent this shooting we would have been powerless—these men had burned farms and farmers with the wives and children all the way along the main road."[20]

When a presence larger than a Jed team was required, the Allied High Command sent in the OGs. Operational Groups typically consisted of 15- to 30-man teams led by two officers. 356 Americans assigned to 21 OG teams parachuted into France dressed in full military uniform.[21] Most of the men were bilingual. All were trained in a variety of advanced infantry tactics and guerrilla warfare. Armed with automatic rifles, machine guns, bazookas, mines, and explosives, the OGs were the most military units in the OSS.

The OGs worked alone or with the Maquis and Jed teams, blowing up bridges, ambushing enemy columns, cutting communications, and destroying rail lines. The OGs conducted "anti-scorch" operations by protecting vital installations such as bridges or hydroelectric plants from destruction.

Team Donald executed a typical OG mission, facilitating the Allied advance on the Brittany peninsula by organizing the Resistance and seizing bridges, railroads, and highways. One of Donald's officers, 1st Lieutenant Rafael Hirtz, recalls the capture of a German casement.

"Before we captured the casement, one of my most vivid memories involved finding a Buick automobile in France. Occasionally, we used it to move around. On one occasion we approached a German checkpoint. Rather than stop we blew through it at about 70 miles an hour. They had about a squad of men. The Germans were so stunned that they weren't able to even give chase.

"We had one operation where we moved into the town of Roscoff. The French Resistance [leader] had about 200 men [and] asked us to join his force. We went in three coal-burning trucks. They could do a good five to ten miles an hour. We didn't have any artillery, just basic infantry weapons. I went with another Frenchmen who spoke German. We approached a German fortified blockhouse that was surrounded by water except for one easily defended approach. The place could not be taken without artillery. We set up positions around a curve that offered natural protection outside the blockhouse.

"Shortly afterward, a German on bicycle was coming from the town (I think he had a girlfriend in town that he was visiting). He had some rolls of bread and when he saw us he tumbled over the handle-bars. He was panic-stricken but he understood French and we sent him back to the blockhouse to arrange the surrender of those inside.

"They said they would be happy to talk to one of the American officers but would not surrender to the French. I approached the German blockhouse and told them that Germans were surrendering in Brittany and that if they didn't come out we would shell the blockhouse with artillery. I don't know what would have happened if our bluff had been called since we didn't have anything to shell them with.

"About 30 Germans came out but made the mistake of carrying their weapons. The French opened fire and they made a hasty retreat back into the blockhouse. We told them they had 20 minutes or we would shell the casement. Luckily, before the time limit expired they came out with their hands up. We made a real effort to protect the prisoners from the Maquis. None of us believed in taking human life if we could avoid it. We captured about 200 German prisoners and put them in a French jail and eventually turned them over to advancing American troops."[22]

With the assistance and guidance of hundreds of OSS personnel, the French Resistance became an effective covert and overt strike force. Resistance fighters disabled German command and control, and delayed and degraded German units being rushed to the front. General Eisenhower acknowledged that "the Resistance had been of inestimable value to the campaign."[23]

By the middle of August, Allied troops were advancing toward Paris and the Allies were planning for the invasion of southern France. OSS would play a key role in the landings.

ELEVEN

Dragoon

"A violent blow broke two of my teeth and I was once again kicked to the ground. My mouth was full of blood and I was in pain. I was once again asked to reveal my identity and I kept on denying the name Frascati. They changed the system and I was made to lie down on a bench while one of the men took hold of a pick ax which was lying around. For three hours they held me there, while I endured the most violent lashing with this instrument. One blow cut my scalp open and I was drenched with blood. I thought they were going to kill me and I waited for the moment, saying to myself they could do anything they want, but they could not force me to talk. Arneux, who knew nothing, was beaten as hard as I was despite his age, but not one word escaped his lips. We were placed against the wall and threatened with being shot, at which time we decided that if we had to die we would die with courage."[1]

This is the nightmarish story of OSS agent Walter Lanz, who was captured by the Gestapo before he could complete his mission.* Lantz was one of hundreds of OSS agents who provided intelligence for the Allied invasion of the French Mediterranean coast. OSS was the deciding factor in making Operation Dragoon (initially code-named Anvil) one of the "best briefed" invasions of the war.[2]

---

*See page 182.

Operation Dragoon was spearheaded by the U.S. Seventh Army, which seized the key ports of Marseille and Toulon on August 15, 1944. Originally planned to coincide with the Normandy landings, Operation Dragoon was delayed by a lack of landing craft and by disputes at the highest levels of the Allied command. In the end, supply problems stemming from a lack of ports in northern France, and the desire to draw German units away from Normandy, compelled the Allies to move forward with the invasion.[3]

OSS worked closely with the Seventh Army and G-2 AFHQ (Allied Force Headquarters), watching main rail and transportation hubs as well as principal ports in southern France for enemy troop movements, and reconstructing the German order of battle. The primary intelligence target was the German defenses in southern France, such as minefields, gun emplacements, road blocks, and supply lines. OSS generated over 8,000 intelligence reports prior to the invasion.[5]

About 2,000 reports came from OSS's most successful network, Penny Farthing. Penny Farthing reported troop movements, fortifications, and the transport of supplies and ammunition prior to the

---

*Lanz endured unbelievable suffering, first in a French prison at the hands of Gestapo torturers, and later at the infamous Dachau concentration camp:

"We arrived at Dachau after a [train]ride which lasted three days [892 prisoners died from suffocation or were murdered by the Germans on the overcrowded trains] and were forced to walk through the town itself, surrounded by the hostility of the people. The children even shook their fists in our faces and the women laughed and pointed at us. The SS amused themselves and the crowd by throwing their dogs upon us. . . . We were nothing but criminals who did not want to be slaves of this 'great' nation. . . .

"Our heads were then shaved as well as the other hairy parts of the body and testicles painted with a caustic solution which produced painful burns among a great many.

"The construction of the camp at Dachau used up thousands of human lives. . . . One of the favorite distractions of the SS consisted of throwing a Jewish or Communist prisoner into the concrete mixers while he was still living. The man was crushed to death and was poured out with the concrete. The gas chamber was also working and yielded its share of dead. The survivors of this outrage became, in large majority, the unconscious auxiliaries of the tormentors." Miraculously, Lanz survived Dachau and was liberated by the Seventh Army at the end of the war.[4]

OSS Operations in Southern France, 1944

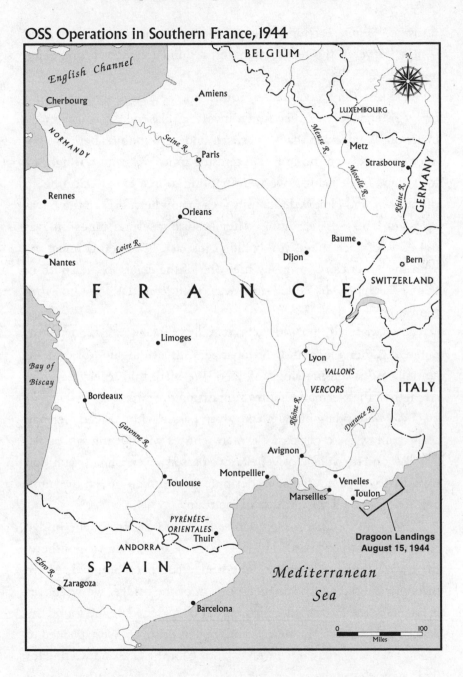

invasion. Penny Farthing agent Helene Deschamps, code-named "Anick," covered the territory in and around Avignon, Montpellier, and Marseille.

"I was in the French underground since the beginning in 1940. I had a sister who was very much involved, like me, who was killed in action. We decided that the French underground was being so political that we were no longer interested in it. We were not fighting for Giraud or de Gaulle, we were fighting to free France. So I heard of the OSS, and I knew that in our area in southern France there was an agent who was recruiting. After inquiring several times—it was not easy to reach them, you couldn't just ask, 'Can you connect me with the American?'—I finally met one of the chiefs in the south of Penny Farthing. His code name was 'Petit-Jean.' I started to work right away.

"I worked with my sister who was also an agent and we were ordered to gather information on a panzer unit heading up from the Atlantic coast as the invasion unfolded. We were told to estimate the strength of the German infantry supporting the tanks.

"We were riding bicycles and given passes with falsified German seals to allow us to get past German sentries without much trouble.

"Beyond the village of Venelle, we passed a German ammunition train that was camouflaged under pine trees. I memorized the number of boxcars and the location of the train.

"We knew we had to get across the Durance River. The bridge was supposed to be guarded by the Germans but, when we got there, there wasn't anyone there and the bridge had been bombed. As we carefully crossed an undamaged portion of the bridge, we were surrounded by the French underground. They searched us and found the papers with the German stamps and took us prisoner. We explained to a Colonel Beaugard that we were working for the OSS and waiting for Petit-Jean. He laughed at us and said, 'OSS? Petit-Jean? What kind of nonsense is this?'

"The Resistance took us prisoner and locked us in a pigsty and put an armed guard at the door. They agreed to wait until morning for Petit-Jean to arrive before they did anything with us.

"At about 1:00 a.m. there was a violent struggle outside. The guard was knocked down by the butt of a rifle and men wearing the Communist FTP armbands crashed through the door. We explained who we were.

"Less than an hour after the FTP showed up, the local leader of the FFI, Martin, appeared with about a dozen men armed to the teeth and furious. They launched a barrage of obscenities and threats and tight-fisted gestures. The Communist leader made the mistake of pointing his weapon at Martin and he was quickly disarmed and kicked savagely to the ground.

"After a long pause, we were back in the hands of the FFI. The FTP hissed at us, 'We'll meet again. I'm not finished with you bitches.'

"Meanwhile we told Martin our story and they agreed to wait for Petit-Jean. It was eight, nine, and finally ten o'clock passed and he didn't show up.

"They put us in front of a makeshift tribunal and decided that we were going to be shot. They said we have proof that you worked for the Germans and therefore you are traitors. They paraded us into the streets and people were spitting on us. We waited to be executed.

"Suddenly, the parachute-drop-section ringleader [in charge of supply drops] arrived on the scene and recognized me. He said, 'I've been looking for you all morning.' He was with Petit-Jean when he was coming to meet us but rather matter-of-factly explained that Petit-Jean was killed by a German sniper.

"We decided to try to stay in the town for the night. I wasn't in bed more than an hour when I was awoken by a loud explosion. I looked out the window and German tanks were entering the town. We escaped the town in our bare feet. Outside the town we encountered a group of FFI that were in a truck who were coming into the town to celebrate the American landings. We told them about the tanks, so they took us back to their camp and we stayed there. Meanwhile, we were unarmed but they gave me a Sten submachine gun and something to my sister.

"We knew the Americans had just landed and the chief of the FFI told us to cross the German lines and notify the Americans who just landed about the German tanks. They also felt if we got the information to the Americans, there was a chance we could save the town (it looked like they were going to demolish the place). We felt that we were at least accomplishing part of our mission if we did this.

"They gave [us] a small car, a Simca. It's a tiny little car. They gave us a driver, a former air force lieutenant, since I didn't know how to drive at the time. We left at about 11:00 p.m. at night. There was no light, of course, on the roads. First, we met a German patrol and we passed through them. They were so surprised to find someone on the road, and fortunately their shots missed.

"Maybe 20 minutes later, the shots rang out again but this time only from a single machine gun. My sister who was crouching in the back said, 'I'm hit!' We reached an intersection and I reached back and she was dead with a bullet through the heart. I learned after the war that it was the FTP.

"We reached a town, dug a hole in the side of the road, and buried her. There is no way to express how I felt.

"Shortly afterward, I was given a new driver with a motorcycle. He took me to Forcalquier where I notified the G-2 about the tanks and the ammunition train I had seen at Venelle. I then left for the coast and joined the Strategic Service Section, OSS agents that had landed with the Seventh Army during [the] landings."[6]

SI agent Jacques Snyder also had a run-in with the FTP that nearly cost him his life. Snyder parachuted into southern France in June to expand an existing *réseau* [the French word for network, and OSS/SOE's term for an intelligence network].

"We fell into an ambush. Hell, we weren't shot by the Germans but by the Communist underground. We were some of the first casualties of the Cold War. The FTP got their orders from Moscow and turned out to be more of a hindrance than anything else. They knew damn well who we were. They were trying to beat us to the drop zone and get the containers before we did.

"We even had hospitals that were working for us. When my radio operator was shot in the arm, we took him to one of the hospitals working for the underground. This was before the southern invasion and the place was crawling with Germans. I had to go [to] the sanitarium, [where] all the doctors worked for the underground. So I wheeled him in there. They took an X ray of him and said, 'The bullet is right here, we'll have it out in five minutes.' They got the bullet out and put him in a Spanish cast. You've heard of a Spanish cast, haven't you? They just put some sulfa powder on the wound and then wrapped the arm in a cast with the open wound. The idea was that the wound would get infected and maggots would eat all the rotten flesh. This works and cleans up the wound. The only problem is the smell—you couldn't get within 20 feet of that son of a gun.

"I left the sanitarium and said, 'Aren't you in danger trying to hide all those people from the Germans?' He said, 'Well we've got a special room with a big red sign that reads "Highly Contagious Cases of TB."'

"What people forget is we make a big deal on the heroic stuff, parachuting in and ambushes that the Resistance conducted. It was the daily heroism of the common people. Those people would help and they were risking their lives every day."[7]

Landing along the Riviera, the Seventh Army quickly pushed off the beaches. Battle lines changed daily as the Americans swiftly moved north. OSS intelligence agents supplemented the advance by providing tactical intelligence to each division within the Seventh Army. Second Lieutenant William Duff, head of an OSS tactical intelligence team attached to the 45th Division, describes a typical mission.

"Upon receiving the mission, I selected Minet, Gaston, Roger and Marianne, briefed them and gave each a map of the city which they memorized. The plan was for each of them to go into the town, cover one fourth of it and the surrounding fields and return with the desired information before dawn. . . .

"Proceeding cautiously, we entered the town over garden walls and discovered a house which showed a gleam of light. The occupants proved to be French, old people and children, but they were so upset by the shelling that they could not tell us anything about the Germans, except that there were troops in the hospital near the center of the town, where Marianne entered the building, spoke with some German soldiers and nuns, and came back with information that the town's garrison consisted of twelve men and non-coms billeted at the hospital and that four officers and a few enlisted men were staying in another building a few blocks away. While standing in the street discussing our next move we noticed a German sentry about two yards behind us, but he took no exception to our presence.

"[With this information I returned though our lines to the command post] and recommended that a patrol be sent to capture the twenty men. Colonel Cruikshank agreed to this proposal. . . .

"Leading the patrol across the same fields we entered town as light was breaking. Two Germans were seen in the street but they escaped before they could be shot. Marianne, Minet and I reached the hospital some distance ahead of the reluctant patrol and Marianne [weapon in hand] again entered the hospital, this time shaking the Germans out of their sleep and telling them to surrender for the Americans had arrived. They did. Minet and I turned the prisoners over to the patrol and started up a [German] Horch weapon carrier which had a 20 mm flak gun in tow. . . . We had no difficulty driving the weapons carrier back to American lines, where we immediately reported the additional information that the Germans had tank and troop concentrations. . . . The mission was a success and [the town] was taken three days later."[8]

Despite the difficulties encountered by individual agents, the intelligence-gathering effort for Dragoon was extremely effective. According to a memorandum from G-2 AFHQ, "The intelligence for Operation Dragoon was probably the fullest and most detailed of any provided by G-2 AFHQ." OSS played the crucial role in the invasion; based on rough estimates, 50 percent of the ground intelligence for the invasion was provided by its agents.[9]

Behind the lines, Special Operations would also play a key role in the invasion. SO Algiers and SOE combined to form the Special Project Operations Center, another alphabet soup abbreviation known as SPOC.

As in Normandy, SPOC held back most of the Jed and OG teams. Security concerns and the on-again-off-again nature of Dragoon prevented the Green Beret–like units from entering southern France until about a month before the invasion. Nearly a dozen teams would finally drop after July 15, 1944. And while their impact was felt, they should have been dropped earlier for maximum effectiveness. Nevertheless, the OGs knocked down 32 bridges, caused almost a thousand German casualties, and bagged ten thousand German POWs.[10]

One of largest catches came from OG team Louise, which dropped on the night of July 18. A few days later, Louise destroyed a key bridge over the Rhone River, obstructing barge traffic for days. Next, a rail overpass and bridge were destroyed. By late August, Louise was relentlessly tracking and harassing elements of the retreating German army. Ultimately, the team tricked the Germans into believing they were surrounded by thousands of Allied troops, and arranged for the surrender of nearly 4,000 soldiers. Louise team leader Lieutenant Roy Rickerson remembers how the team convinced the Germans to lay down their arms.[11]

"After the invasion of southern France by Allied troops on August 15, 1944, the Germans began retreating from the south and we began pecking at them as they were coming along. We had two 37 mm antitank guns and we would set them up on the side of a mountain and would hit them and then run.

"On the 25th of August, the Maquis told me that there were 1,500 Germans at the town of Vallons and they said if we would loan them the two guns they could show the Germans that they had artillery and would be able to convince them to surrender. Well we did not agree to give them the two 37 mm guns but we did agree to go with them to the town and fire some rounds down into the village.

"The French left a zero off the number of troops: there were 15,000 Germans, not 1,500. We pecked at them and they started to put mortar fire on us. The mortar rounds were hitting closer to the French than to us [Louise]. We were up on a knoll. The French went home and forgot to tell us, they just took off. The next thing we know the Germans were above our position and firing down on us from higher ground. The French had a gun up there and were supposed to provide close security.

"We turned our guns around but soon ran out of ammunition, so I started crawling off to get a bazooka and to tell someone to get more ammunition. I crawled about 50 yards, I had to go about 100 yards to get to the bazooka and other men. I said at that point, 'Well the sons of Bs are just going to have to kill me, I can't go another inch.' Right then they shot about three rounds [makes sound of machine-gun fire], three bursts right across my hands. My name bracelet disappeared, my wart disappeared, and blood shot up into my left eye from the rocks flying. I found out I was not too tired at all. I took off and got to that bazooka about the same time as one of my sergeants [Collette] got there and we knocked it out [the machine-gun nest] and got out all right.

"We had captured a German captain and he asked us if we [would turn] him loose so that he could go back to his unit and get them to surrender. He did not have but 15 men or so left. The air corps was doing a tremendous job of scrapping everything that moved in the

Rhone Valley, including us. If we got there and heard a plane coming, we would hide or they would get us even with the white star we had. We told the captain that we were not interested in just a few men but if there were more than a few we would be interested in it. He did not know how many troops were there but I asked him if he could take us to his headquarters and maybe we could do something. Well something kept nudging me, so four of us, including the captain, got into an old Model A Ford and we stuck an American flag out of one window and a white flag out of the other window and went down to the village of Chomerac. Our first contact was a German major. Well, if you see a major you know a good many troops are there (about 300 according to the team report). He wanted to know what we wanted and I said we are here to take some prisoners of war on behalf of the Allied armies and if you do not surrender I will have to wipe you out and said we were in a hurry. He said he did not have the authority to surrender and would have to talk to the colonels. Well now you know this is getting bigger and bigger. I figured it would be 30 to 40 men and I already had seen over 150 to 200 troops. He sent for the colonels. In about 10 minutes or so, two full colonels come down. One looks like Colonel Klink of *Hogan's Heroes* but he did not act like Colonel Klink. The colonel's men stayed at attention in his presence and he was the boss. There was also an SS major and the major actually ran the whole thing. The colonel asked me what I wanted. I told him I wanted to make them prisoners of the Allied army and if he did not surrender we would wipe them out.

"He said, 'Where are the Russians?' I had not even thought about the Russians in what, about a year, and I did not know where they were but I told him that they had crossed into Austria and were making their way to Berlin and we were in a hurry to get there ahead of them. The colonel said, 'We will keep you here as hostages because the Americans will not move in with some of their own people down here, so we will keep you hostage.' Well the answer was obvious: 'We have a deadline to meet. If we don't get back in time, they will move in thinking we are either dead or captured and we are expendable.'

"The German colonel said he could not surrender because his officers, battalion commanders of various units, may not want to surrender. He would have to send for them and ask them. I said, 'How long will that take?' He said, 'It [will] take a little while because they [are] dispersed.' I said, 'Your deadline is almost up.' He said, 'Can you delay it?' I said, 'I do not know but I will try,' so I walked off to the side of the road while they talked and tried to make up their minds. I pulled out this little testament. I would always do that when I got in trouble. It would tell me what to do. I would do what it told me to do, if it told me to go, I would go, if it told me to stay, I would stay. I opened it up to the fourth chapter of Ephesians and here is what it said: 'I, therefore, the prisoner of the Lord, beseech you to walk worthy of the calling with which you were called. With all the lowliness and gentleness, with longsuffering, bearing with one another in love, Endeavor to keep the unity of one Spirit, just as you were called in one hope of your calling. . . .'

"Well I read that and I asked Collette, he was my interpreter, I said, 'Hank, what do you want to do? Do you want to take these jokers or do you want to go?' We could go back because we were under truce. Collette said, 'What does the little black book say?' I passed it to him, he was a devout Catholic, and he read it and said, 'Well I am going to stay because I know that is what you are going to do.'

"So we sent the other two men back on the pretense of extending the deadline (I recall and it is in the report they were also to try to contact Colonel Al Cox because the Germans were not sure they wanted to surrender to a lieutenant). Hank Collette and I stayed down there, and at 3:45 P.M. we took the surrender of 3,824 Germans. A few things happened during the conference held by the German unit commanders. Firing erupted and a few moments of chaos ensued as an old French tank rolled up. [Richardson and Collette had to explain how they were trying to take the surrender of troops and convinced them to stop.] But we did not really do it [get the column to surrender], the little black book did it. We do not take any pride in it. Hank will say the same thing, but we put that many people out of the war and saved their lives and many American lives as a result. Later on, the two full colonels and the SS major were killed by the French after a kangaroo court. They took them off and made them dig their own graves before they shot them. I felt badly about the executions."[12]

Team Louise's capture of thousands of German soldiers was arguably one of the single greatest achievements of the Operational Groups in France. It would also prove to be the final great achievement of the French OGs. By August 27, 1944, Paris was cleared of enemy forces and the German army in northern France was in full retreat toward Belgium and Holland. The south of France was being freed even faster. Within weeks of seizing Toulon and Marseille, the Seventh Army drove 270 miles inland and linked up with Patton's forces in the Rhone Valley. By September 21, the Seventh Army had crossed the Moselle River and was less than 50 miles from the borders of the Reich. With the liberation of all France at hand, OSS turned its attention to the Low Countries, and to Germany itself.

TWELVE

X-2

Counterespionage

At a small Victorian estate 40 miles outside London, the Allies kept the greatest secret project of World War II. Hundreds of people were working around the clock at Bletchley Park, analyzing and cracking Germany's most sophisticated codes and ciphers. The intelligence gathered from Ultra was crucial to winning the war. Remarkably, nearly three decades would pass before word of Ultra would become public.[1]

OSS was initially kept out of Ultra, and code breaking in general, due to turf battles with G-2 (army) and ONI (Office of Naval Intelligence). The army and navy viewed procuring and analyzing enemy signals as their exclusive domain, a position backed up by the Joint Chiefs of Staff. The armed services also doubted whether OSS was secure enough to be trusted with the secret.[2]

In early 1943, Donovan overcame this resistance, and dispatched a four-man team to England for the purpose of sharing Ultra and counterespionage information between the British intelligence services and OSS. The work of this team eventually gave rise to a separate branch of OSS, known as X-2 or Counterespionage. Modeled on British Counterespionage, X-2 quickly developed into a full-blown counterespionage service, establishing field stations around the globe with independent lines of communication that reported back to

Washington. The new department attracted some of OSS's best minds, and eventually received authority to veto operations in other OSS branches. X-2 gained a reputation as an elite unit within OSS.[3]

Counterespionage not only protects a nation's intelligence assets, it also attempts to control and manipulate the intelligence assets of the enemy. As OSS states in its own history, counterespionage "performs a dynamic function in discerning [another nation's] plans and intentions, as well as deceiving them."[4]

A few months after X-2 became operational, the British invited X-2 to join one of the most sensitive counterespionage institutions of the war, the XX or "Twenty Committee." Ultra had unmasked all of the German agents in England, allowing the British to "double" them, or turn them into double agents. Given the choice of changing sides or losing their lives, most opted for self-preservation, and agreed to work for the Allies by feeding carefully selected intelligence to Germany. The Twenty Committee coordinated the strategy for controlling the agents, with the goal of completely controlling the intelligence the enemy received from a given area, and preventing uncontrolled agents from being sent to that area.[5]

Controlling enemy agents was a delicate process that required imagination, creativity, and careful planning. Elaborate deceptions were conceived to influence Germany's plans. Controlled enemy agents were fed false information, or in some cases actual facts that were screened by SHAEF and considered harmless to the Allies, but advantageous for the Germans to know. This type of leak was considered essential for establishing the credibility of the agents, and came in handy, when attempting to deceive the Germans, for example by selling them on the existence of the phantom U.S. First Army Group (FUSAG).[6]

Enemy agents were often captured by Special Counter Intelligence (SCI) units, consisting of small groups of X-2 agents attached to Allied field armies. The SCIs operated at the front lines or, in some cases, just behind the lines, collecting and examining captured enemy documents, providing information on enemy intelligence organizations and implementing counterespionage activities. Signal intercept trucks within the SCIs triangulated enemy agents' radio transmissions, pinpointing their locations. OSS, in cooperation with other Allied units, apprehended 1,300 enemy agents, primarily German "stay behinds," agents who had stayed behind after the German army withdrew and began to report intelligence once Allied troops occupied their area.[7] In France, two SCI units landed in Normandy, and a third landed in southern France. The 31st SCI was the first X-2 unit ashore at Utah Beach. Major Charles Hostler was part of that advance unit.

"We landed on the evening of D-Day on Utah. Our task was to gain control of the targeted enemy agents before our troops overran them or could disrupt them. My first actual case was a fellow who was sort of a grocer that lived in the vicinity of Ste.-Mére-Église. The next day I went over there accompanied by my helper and driver.

"I went up to this house where he was located and tried to be cool and calm and not attract attention, so we didn't have our guns drawn. I knocked on the door. He opened the door and looked at me and without saying a word, he just reached behind him and grabbed a meat cleaver. He hit me with the blunt end. He hit me across the forehead. I still have the dent in my forehead to this day [laughs]. Fortunately, the driver stepped in and we overpowered him. This was a Frenchman who was sympathetic to the Germans.

"We made it clear to him what his options were, which were limited. We made it clear that he either cooperate with us or we would turn him over to the French. The French had no sympathy towards these people and would have maybe taken action against their families. In most cases, we got good cooperation and he cooperated."

Hostler and his group moved on to Vannes, Cherbourg, and finally toward Rennes, just south of the Normandy region, where they overran a large Gestapo headquarters.[8]

The first Abwehr W/T agent doubled by the SCI units in France was Juan Frutos, a Spanish national living in Cherbourg. Frutos, code-named "Dragoman," was controlled by OSS case officer, poet, and Rhodes Scholar Edward Weismiller.

"Counterintelligence found this guy and searched his apartment, when his mistress was out, and found a letter with his code name: Eikens. Counterintelligence confronted him with the letter and he broke down and confessed that he was a German agent. That led to a tremendous complication. The British wanted him sent back to England for intense interrogations. The Americans wanted to get [him] on the air as soon as possible. It turned out that he had been on the air for about 10 days after the invasion but then he had gone off the air. It was by now July.

"They called for me to be sent over as his case officer. The day that I arrived Frutos reestablished contact through his radio with the Germans. Dragoman continued to work his job as an interpreter at the Cherbourg harbor. He told his mistress that at night he had been given special work as an interpreter in Cherbourg.

"The port was very elaborate and destroyed by the Germans before they left. But it was being rapidly rebuilt by the Allies. Meanwhile, the Germans were flooding us with questions. Our first job was to convince the Germans the port wasn't being rapidly rebuilt. It was part of a larger deception plan.

"The problem was that most of the G-2 sections in the American army were scared out of their wits about giving the Germans information, but it had to be done. They were immensely reluctant to let the Germans have anything.

"The Germans were obsessed with a fuel pipeline that ran from Cherbourg into Normandy. G-2 wouldn't let us give any details on it, even though there were huge signs completely out in the open with 'Pipeline' or 'Pumping Station 2,' so we had to say we couldn't get close to it. Through disinformation we convinced the Germans that it was too closely guarded and not subject to sabotage. I think the Germans brushed it off as kind of timidity on the part of Dragoman. This was one of the challenges on the part of the missions. We had to keep to the character that the Germans knew.

"We would send [information] to G-2 to have it vetted. In many cases it was harmless information but they would still refuse to let us send it or say send it later in the week. We were fighting to send as much harmless information as we could to the Germans. This may sound weird but we were trying to build an accurate case. They got other means of finding out this stuff, such as photo reconnaissance, but one of the ways to make them trust you is when your agents reveal accurate information.

"The Germans started asking us about naval matters and the British picked up on this. The Admiralty started feeding us false information that they were feeding other double agents elsewhere. We began building up a network of subagents. This fit into a larger plan.

"You are constantly trying to figure out what will they think. You read everything into a mirror and then back into another mirror, and then back into another mirror. You can lose your goddamn mind. You read these possibilities in one mirror which reflects from another mirror. It's tremendously complex and can be a mind-shattering business."[9]

Through Weismiller's outstanding casework the Germans remained convinced of Dragoman's loyalty. They unwittingly revealed other German agents in the area by calling upon Dragoman to check on their status.

Weismiller also initially handled the casework for "Skull," another German stay-behind agent doubled by OSS. "Skull was a marvelous guy. He was an old sailor and he had been one of the many people who the Germans had tried to enlist who had been on fishing vessels. The Germans found out who they were, and they would corner them in some way. These people would try and get another job, but when they couldn't get another job, the Germans would fence them in and finally they would come to them and say, 'Would you like a job? A harmless job, just sending weather information.' Then after six months they'd say, 'Okay, you've been working for the German intelligence service for six months. If you think that anybody would believe that you didn't know what you were doing, you're out of your goddamn mind so you will now really work for us.' If you were in his position, what do you then do? You had no choice. They were merciless. But they were also fools 'cause it didn't occur to them somehow that they would ever lose, that it would ever really happen and that then these people would not turn against them.

"So this old guy, he had a young wife and he was just madly in love with her and they had a little son and he was just devoted to the little boy and he had throat cancer so he wasn't going to live very long. All of a sudden his wife and the little boy disappeared and he went to the local commandant and said, 'Where's my wife?' They said, 'We don't know.' Then he went again and they said, 'We're sorry to have to tell you this but she ran off with a German officer. She fell in love with this young German officer and they ran off. We can maybe help you find her on certain conditions.' That's how he got in and he never found his wife and child. She wouldn't have done that, he knew she wouldn't have done that. So he was trapped. He was very glad when we came along.

"Skull had no loyalty to Germany. But he did have some loyalty to his German case officer, code-named 'Georges.' Skull forged a relationship with this guy."

"Georges" was Friedrich Kaulen, the Abwehr officer in charge of Skull and several other stay-behind agents in France. When Kaulen arranged a meeting with Skull, X-2 devised an elaborate operation to snare him.

"Georges proposed to come down a river by boat and meet Skull at a certain location and bring him money and equipment. We wanted to take Georges prisoner since he was high ranking and he could have given us tremendously detailed information that we could not get any other way.

"Skull consented to be a party to this, but only if we guaranteed him that no harm would come to Georges.

"The story as I remember it was that Skull and several armed men were in a field near a river waiting for Georges. They heard the sound of oars hitting the water and people looked at one another and thought, 'My God, this is actually happening.' Georges got out of the boat very carefully, looking around. He was very security conscious.

"Before the mission, a desk clerk in Paris who had never been in the field begged to be taken along. The stupid little jerk got so excited when he saw Georges that he popped up from behind a hedge. The entire capture team was hiding behind a hedge. Georges saw his face and realized that it was a trap. He started to run. The capture team included a large group of French soldiers. Kaulen was cut down by machine-gun fire and died within minutes."[10]

Even though the operation was blown, documents found on Kaulen included instructions to German agents in the area and confirmed that the agents under Kaulen's command were already under Allied control.[11]

Putting sensitive Ultra intelligence in the hands of field armies was the role of Special Liaison Units (SLUs). Only 28 SLU teams operated in the European theater. The SLU agents reviewed decoded Ultra intercepts and determined what should be placed in the hands of field commanders. Then they repackaged the information in order to disguise its source.

Betty Lussier was assigned to an SLU that took part in the invasion of southern France. She was also a pioneering woman pilot

whose contribution to the war effort began with flying newly manufactured planes to airfields in England.

"They announced that they would not use women aircraft pilots
on the continent. They would stay in England. That sort of annoyed
me. It was an integrated service, men and women pilots; we were all
treated the same. I was looking for some way to go to the continent
and get involved in the fight. I joined OSS through my father's contacts with Sir William Stephenson.

"Sir William Stephenson was like a member of the family, and
part of my father's squadron in WWI and he was my reference into
OSS. They sent us to St. Albans for training. We learned about Ultra.
They only wanted a few people to know so they would send these
trained people into a headquarters such as Third Army or Sixth Army.
That person would be the one that would go over the messages in the
morning with the British and carefully reveal pertinent information to
the armies we were assigned to.

"We were trained on how to read and evaluate the code. I worked
a lot on the middle European codes for Belgium, Yugoslavia—the
messages the Germans were sending from there to Berlin.

"I was trained with five men and five women. The men happened
to all be from Yale. For security's sake they more or less recruited
friends and people they knew.

"First, we were sent to Algiers. There, I worked with the British to
determine what Ice [the term used by Americans to describe the information acquired through Ultra] they wanted to give to the Americans. Then we had to find a way to disguise it so it didn't look like a
radio intercept. We would sometimes say we found it in letters or
some agent observed it, stuff like that. We repackaged Ultra so they
could not tell where it came from. What was remarkable to me is they
held the secret for the entire war."

Later Lussier was sent to Nice, France, to work with a counterintelligence unit on the Franco-Spanish border. Lussier worked closely

with Ricardo Sicre, whom she later married. The team ferreted out stay-behind enemy agents and organized a group of double agents.

"I got a call from Holcomb that they needed a unit to uncover whatever spies were left behind. I reported to Roger Goiran and Ricardo Sicre. We worked in the Pyrénées-Orientales province of France. He was in a chateau in Thuir.

"We had at least a dozen people. They said, 'We have German agents all along southern France and we'd like you to find them.' We would move into a town such as Nice and then we would contact the post office and find anyone that had recently moved into the area in the past five years or so. We would go to the police and see if they had information about anyone that was a new arrival. Typically, the Germans wouldn't recruit people that had been there all their lives. Usually they would insert people.

"We would also look for anyone that didn't have a French profile—Tunisians, Algerians, people who would generally have a beef with the French. Many of the agents were Algerians.

"As we were going through the post office list of residents and police we found this guy who had moved there three or four years before. He fit the profile. He was our first big bust. It was initially just a shot in the dark. Ricardo had a hunch. We were in the jeep one day and he had gotten the address from the post office so we just drove up to this farm he was living at. We knocked on the door and he answered the door himself. Ricardo just said to him quickly in French, 'Where is the radio?' The guy turned white, sort of stammered and pointed out to the barn; he just collapsed. He led the way out and showed us the buried radio. He buried it behind a bale of hay. We took possession of the radio right away since the first thing an agent will try to do is send a distress code. We had to be careful that he didn't send the code. So we took the set and handcuffed him. He had a wife and child that we took into custody and said if anything went wrong we would kill them; he spilled his guts. I remember he told us that he

thought the Germans were right. We were shocked about his attitude
that he thought the Germans were on the right side, and were on the
'right path in purifying the races.' We put him with a case officer and
we planted valuable misinformation with him on where the troops
were going, et cetera. He was a very credited agent and the Germans
put a lot of stock in what he said so we gave him a lot of disinformation. For example, troops would be going up one route so we gave
him information that they were going up another. The case officer
had to live with the agent 24 hours a day. Our case officer was an interesting character who was gay and was always falling in love with his
cases. We eventually got another case officer.

"The key to the entire chain was this little German guy who happened to be a paymaster. He was captured as the German army retreated from Toulon; he was captured kind of accidentally. They
thought he was a soldier and the French kicked the shit out of him.
He didn't break. So they handed him over to the British. There was
great rivalry between the American, British, and French intelligence
agencies. And everyone tried to get as much [as they could] out of
someone before they turned him over to the other. The French
couldn't get anything and the British didn't try much since they evalu-
ated that he was pretty low on the totem pole. So they passed him off
to us. It would seem they were doing us a favor, but they thought he
didn't have anything to give so they gave him to us as a courtesy. So
Ricardo sat down with this guy. Ricardo was really good at eliciting information and he talked [to] him. He was really shaken up because
the French beat him so badly. Ricardo asked him, 'What do you want
to do after the war?' He confessed that he wanted to go to Hollywood
and be a comedian like Charlie Chaplin. Ricardo said, 'That might be
possible, but you have to have something you can trade for it.' So the
guy's eyes lit up and he said, 'Well I'm the paymaster for the German
intelligence network.' He didn't have it with him but he took us to a
book that contained the names and addresses of the German agents in

the area. Here were the names of 35 agents the Germans had left behind. We got this list and started uncovering the network. The poor guy, we gave him back to the French and they shot him."[12]

X-2 field personnel also participated in special task forces that seized key enemy personnel, equipment, and files. Charles Hostler commanded one of the special teams responsible for recovering very sensitive materials in Paris.

"When the Allies were getting close to Paris, General Bradley's Twelfth Army Group realized that there were a lot of intelligence objectives in Paris. They wanted to go about getting them in an organized way so they established Paris Task Force [sometimes called T-Force]. They picked as team leaders people like myself who had some intelligence experience. I was assigned to the fifth [Pantheon] and sixth [Luxembourg] arrondissements on the Left Bank of the Seine. We were given a team of people and tried to plan an advance, and then we would go for each objective. One of our objectives was the organization that Polish-born scientist Marie Curie founded which was conducting research in atomic theory. We were also tasked with protecting her safety. Another objective was protecting the Hôtel des Monnaies; this is where they kept the engravings for printing French currency. If the Germans had the engravings they could disrupt the French economy with counterfeit currency. You may remember that the Germans had used people in concentration camps to make engravings for counterfeit British money. So we got those. There were also enemy agents there that were high on our list to turn into double agents.

"There was a lot of action in Paris. We found ourselves racing down streets and we frequently passed truckloads of German troops in vehicles going in all directions. Their trucks were loaded with loot and wine, everything. They were absolutely intent on getting the hell out of there and we were intent on our target. Often we zipped by each other in a weird way.

"The people I had on my team I divided up into smaller groups so we weren't all stampeding off to one objective and missing the other. I did go Curie's labs to collect information and take the scientists into custody. That was interesting. There was a team [already there] that had been put together by the people who were working on the atomic bomb. They had not told anybody about it. They just showed up at the same time we did. It happened [that] a major named Pasha was the head of the team. By an absolute coincidence, he had been a high school teacher of mine. It wasn't a case where it was a trick. I knew the guy. I didn't know he was in the military or what he was doing, but I felt certain he was reliable. We argued about who should take possession of the things in the lab. In the end we were convinced and got the agreement of our superiors that it should be turned over to his people. They took the documents and also took into custody the scientists who were working there.

"We also entered the Hotel Lutetia, which was the Gestapo headquarters in Paris, and it yielded a great deal of useful documentation."[13]

In existence for just about two years by war's end, X-2 developed into a world-class counterespionage service that would prove to be a crucial instrument of national security during the Cold War.

THIRTEEN

Approaching the Reich

The approach of the Allied armies toward Germany created a pressing new need for tactical and long-range intelligence. With most of France liberated, the intelligence chains cultivated by OSS in 1943 and 1944 were no longer useful. French-speaking agents were generally unsuited for operations in Germany, one of the most tightly controlled police states in history.

Seventh Army commander Lieutenant General Alexander Patch called upon SI France's intelligence chief, Henry Hyde, to come up with a solution. Hyde recommended utilizing his most readily available source of German agent candidates: POWs.[1]

Use of POWs as agents was strictly prohibited by SHAEF and illegal under the Geneva Convention. However, the need for intelligence outweighed the risk, so the rules were broken. Seventh Army officers turned over POW records to OSS so it appeared that POW agent candidates had never been taken into custody.

Recruitment began in the fall, when OSS started combing the POW cages for suitable candidates. The OSS was looking for men who fell into a variety of categories: anti-Nazis, Socialists, opportunists, and even noble Germans who wanted to bring about a better Germany. One Seventh Army POW recruiter, Peter Sichel, belonged to a family that owned a prominent winery before the war, but was forced to flee Germany with other Jews to avoid persecution.

"Things moved so fast. The Seventh Army couldn't have moved faster. They were finally halted by the Germans in the Alsace about 30 miles west of Strasbourg where we got stopped. We had a very cold winter. We were near the Rhine, but we couldn't get across it. That is when I got involved in intelligence. Suddenly, my being a German became valuable.

"Our first operations were as straight tourists. In other words, the agent would walk through our lines and the German lines and gather intelligence by staying behind the lines. Eventually, the Allied front would overtake the agent or he or she would exfiltrate back to friendly lines.

"My specialty was recruitment. I somehow had an ability to do that. The interrogators would select people they thought were motivated against the Nazis: intelligent, possibly willing to do something to shorten the war. Muecke, Viertel, and I went into the PW camps and if we felt they were the right kind of person we would pitch them. If they were willing to do it we would check them out as much as we could and get them out of there and put them in safe houses.

"There were some Socialists, people that were in penal battalions, but most of them were businesspeople. They were all intelligent. Their motivation was not so much that they were anti-Nazi, but this is a hopeless war and any additional day of war would destroy more cities and more people. Some of them were rather good patriots but they felt this was total madness, and were convinced that there wasn't a chance that Germany could win the war. Some of our finest agents were motivated by a higher cause.

"One of the best was a young 21-year-old medical student who had been conscripted into the German medical corps. I recruited him. When I spoke to him, he very simply stated that he hated the Nazis. He said, 'The war was slaughter' and anything he could do to shorten the slaughter the better. He was a very impressive young man, who was trained extremely well. We sent him in with a radio operator who was a Russian, who OSS sent in with the Maquis into France earlier in the war. He was by profession a lion tamer.

"Tragically, they were triangulated by the Germans and captured and they got killed. Later, this mission was made into a movie called *Call It Treason*. They asked me to help with the film so I decided to try to find his parents. I knew they lived in Berlin. I was able to track them down and visit them. Although they were sorry that their son had died, they totally understood it. I've never seen such total acceptance and maturity."[2]

Agent candidates underwent a crash course in espionage and radio communications at a secret mountain training camp established by the Seventh Army. Agents helped devise cover stories, and received suitable clothing and equipment, in preparation for infiltration behind German lines.

The Seventh Army OSS detachment's most audacious mission was directed at the OSS's chief rival, the Sicherheitsdienst, or SD. The SD was a small, elite unit within the German intelligence apparatus. Cloaked in a veil of secrecy, the SD guarded the most sensitive military, political, and diplomatic secrets of the Reich.

The opportunity to penetrate the SD was provided by Youri Skarzynski, a cocky, 21-year-old former SD agent who was earning a living in the black market in Paris. Youri offered his services to OSS.

Youri was born in Berlin to White Russian parents who had fled the Russian Revolution. While he was considered an opportunist by OSS, Youri was also viewed as an anticommunist who did not want to see a red Germany. He also had an ailing mother in Berlin whom he wanted to visit and care for.[3]

To persuade OSS to send him on a mission against the SD, Youri stressed his close personal connection to Michel Kedia, president of the Georgian government in exile in Berlin, who was working directly with the SD to send agents into Russia. While the Nazis were using Kedia's organization for their own ends, Kedia was hardly pro-Nazi;

he was violently anticommunist, and was working to break his homeland away from the Soviets. With the demise of the Third Reich imminent, Kedia was looking for a way to save his skin, clinging to the
hope that his anticommunist leanings and personal prominence might
be valuable to the West. He could be trusted to vouch for Youri and
maintain his secret.[4]

Weighed down by $10,000 worth of jewelry sewn into his clothes,
Youri passed through Seventh Army lines into Germany, planning to
present himself to the SD with a fabricated story that he had escaped
from the Allies. Once in SD hands, he hoped to secure employment at
the SD's main headquarters in Berlin. If he managed to penetrate SD,
he was to communicate by letter with OSS Bern, which was jointly
working the operation with OSS Seventh Army. Youri recalls working
his way through the heavily guarded German lines:

"At the divisional Command Post, high ranking officers fired a
thousand questions at me concerning the location and movement of
Allied troops. It was easy for me to reply, since the night before I visited a number of sectors with the Americans who authorized me to
reveal certain items for this specific purpose. This information was not
new for the Germans, since there was a fairly constant stream of civilians crossing the lines in both directions, but my reports were checked
with the maps they had before them, and served to establish my bona
fides as an employee of the SD.

"During lunch many more questions were put to me about
France and Paris. It is noteworthy that what interested them most was
the effects of rising communism in France upon the Allies.

"During the afternoon I was introduced to the general. Everything was prepared for my arrival, that is to say that this sector of the
front was expecting the return of an SD agent from Paris on that day,
but did not know his identity. The coincidence was very strange since
they never discovered that I was not the one they expected."[5]

Youri was taken to an SD headquarters at Strasbourg and grilled for days by the senior leadership, who took detailed notes on dates, places, and people he had met during his journey back to Germany. Youri also provided harmless intelligence on units he passed. Convinced that his story was legitimate, the SD permitted him to return to Berlin.

"I left for Berlin on the 6th of November and arrived after having changed trains fourteen times. Rail communications were very disorganized."[6]

On November 7, Youri arrived in Berlin and contacted Michel Kedia. The next day he received a knock on the door. "At 7:00 a.m. on Wednesday 8 November the Gestapo came to my address and arrested me. They had heard I had just returned from Paris and that I had brought mail with me. Naturally their greatest interest was to know what I was doing and what was contained in the letters. I was escorted to their offices at 17 Lutherstrasse where I was interrogated. It is noteworthy that up til now I had passed myself off elsewhere as an agent of the SD, knowing that Kedia would cover me with the service, which was of course very interested in my journey. The only paper I had was one certificate signed by Bickler [SD chief at Strasbourg] authorizing me to travel to Berlin. Naturally not wishing to discuss my real mission I pretended that I was authorized to speak only upon the authority of my chief, and if they wanted further details they would have to refer to him."[7]

As Skarzynski predicted, Kedia vouched for him. After a lengthy Gestapo interrogation, Youri was offered a sensitive SD position dealing with the eastern front, complete with a salary of 500 marks and a bonus of 5,000 marks for the information he provided about his journey through France.[8]

Youri was hardly out the woods. He was closely watched, and all his phone calls were recorded by the Gestapo. He was denounced by a number of people as a foreign liaison agent, but none of the accusations stuck. In spite of the close monitoring, he managed to get a let-

Approaching the Reich

ter out to OSS Switzerland, stating that he was in Berlin and indicating that "everything is alright, but cease all contact."[9] It was the beginning of five and a half months of intrigue and danger in the heart of the German intelligence apparatus in the capital of Nazi Germany.

Like the Seventh Army, the Allied armies farther north were also running up against the Rhine. The commander of the British First Army, Field Marshal Montgomery, proposed a bold plan to hurdle the Rhine, seize Germany's industrial heartland, and bring the war to a swift conclusion. Operation Market Garden called for airborne troops from the First Allied Airborne Army (FAAA) to descend upon and hold over 50 miles of Dutch highways and bridges. Simultaneously, ground forces would push north from Belgium, race over the freshly captured highways, and cross the final bridge over the Rhine at Arnhem. The Germans managed to hold the final bridge at Arnhem, dooming Market Garden to failure, and blunting the momentum of the Allied armies.

A few OSS units were attached to the FAAA, leading the airborne phase of the attack. Jed team Edward was attached to airborne corps headquarters. Edward landed in a glider with the 82nd Airborne Division outside Groesbeek, a small town near the important city of Nijmegen. Captain McCord Sollenberger recalls the mission: "On the journey over, we didn't encounter enemy fighters or flak and at 1410 hours a perfect landing was affected at the landing zone near Groesbeek. After landing, the mission made its way along a predetermined route to an assembly point. Enemy opposition was slight. Some prisoners were taken. . . . Later that night first contact was made with the local resistance and the strength was determined to be at 300.

"A reported underground telephone communication with Arnhem was investigated but proved unsuccessful. Telephone communication was established with the center of Nijmegen which was in enemy hands and valuable information on the local military situation, defenses of the railway and road-bridge across the river Waal was obtained and passed on to Corps Headquarters. . . . at the town hall in Malden some 200 members of the resistance group were addressed, their activities with the forces of the 82nd Division organized and internal strife settled. . . .

The Jeds organized the Resistance, which acted as guides, guarded key areas, and, most important, gathered crucial intelligence used by the 82nd Airborne Division to capture the bridge at Nijmegen. "On D+3 in the link up with 30th Corps, which was established firmly on that day, 30th Corps was brought in contact with the chief engineer of water-works and ferries in Nijmegen through underground channels. Very detailed information on possibilities of river crossings and bridges in the Nijmegen area was obtained. . . ."[10]

As the front lines grew closer to their homeland, the German army's resolve stiffened. The Germans destroyed scores of dikes in northern Holland, turning the terrain into a quagmire reminiscent of the battlefields of the Great War. At the same time, the civilians in areas near the Reich were often hostile to the Allies. For Allied agents, concealment and use of the traditional bulky radios was becoming more challenging.

During the fall of 1944, OSS engineers developed the "Joan/ Eleanor," an early cell phone–like transmitter that allowed agents in enemy territory to communicate with planes circling overhead. Unlike the bulky S-phone or Klaxton, which had to be strapped to an agent's back, the Joan was only six and a half inches long and weighed less than four pounds. A larger set, known as the Eleanor, was installed in a plane along with a recording device.

The compact size of the unit meant agents did not have to carry around hard-to-hide suitcase radios. Also, while German radio vans using direction-finding equipment could hone in on the traditional radio, the Joan/Eleanor (J/E) was immune to direction finding.

It was in northern Holland that OSS dispatched their first Joan/Eleanor operation. The first agent to use a J/E in the field was Anton Schrader. Code-named "Bobby," Schrader was a 27-year-old engineer from the Dutch East Indies who escaped occupied Holland at the beginning of the war. Equipped with a J/E, and without any formal parachute training, Schrader dropped into Nazi-occupied Ulrum. Bobby's mission was to infiltrate Holland and establish a secret route into Germany. Bobby successfully provided important intelligence on German troop movements and defensive plans in the Arnhem area, before his mission was blown in a case of mistaken identity.[11]

An assassination team from the Dutch Resistance confused Bobby with another Allied agent, code-named "Bobby," who had become a turncoat and was working for the Germans. Before the team could kill the traitor, the Gestapo arrested the assassination team and Bobby too. Pretending to be outraged by the double-cross on the part of the Dutch underground, Schrader feigned working for the Gestapo as a double agent. Even while the Germans were "playing" him, Schrader was able to convey the control signal that he had been captured. Humorously, the control signal was the use of frequent profanity while talking on the J/E. Because of his cussing and other hints, OSS figured out Bobby was being run by the Gestapo, and fed him enough misleading information to keep him alive. In his own words, Schrader reveals several compelling memories from his mission.

"On 10 March there was a J/E contact. The preparations were the same as usual. The main point this time was that the Germans insisted on repeating the request for a new drop. They also gave me a good deal of 'intelligence' to read to Steve [Stephen Simpson, the OSS officer in charge of J/E missions]. I swore at the beginning of the contact, and Steve said, 'I understand, what can I do for you?' To which I replied, 'Try to have another damn drop at the place I mentioned to you last time. But be careful, they are trying to engage you.' By this last sentence I was trying to warn Steve that the Germans were trying to follow the course of his plane by radar in order to discover what other agents were using J/E. I believe that the main radar station was in Essen. As I then had to repeat the information prepared for me by the Gestapo, I managed to break one of the contacts inside the battery case. Thus, when my contact with Steve was abruptly broken off, I repeated what the Gestapo had given me, knowing that Steve would not hear it. I got the idea that the Gestapo might try to follow the plane from the casual remark made by me. This was the last time I saw both J/E sets together.

"After this contact the Gestapo became suspicious because they told me that my messages had been coming on the air at 1830. I explained that sometimes the BBC would change the time of their special messages and that the announcer would warn the listeners of this change. I told the Gestapo that they must have missed this announcement. It did not quite satisfy them, and I must say that the next and last contact with Stephen Simpson on 30 March saved my life.

"A few days before the last contact with Steve, my third series of interrogations was started. I was given two books to read: Alfred Rosenberg's *Die Mythus des 20. Jahrhunderts,* and Schopenhauer's *"Über die Richtigkeit des Daseins.* Schumacher was the sole interrogator. This interrogation lasted only a few days, and the main topics of discussion were Communism, the political differences between the Allies, and the attitude of the Americans and the British toward the future of the Jews.

"I believe that the main purpose of this interrogation was to make the final check to see if I had really turned. I behaved as a truly turned agent would act."[12]

Schrader was so effective in convincing the Gestapo he was working for them that during the final days of the war, they chose him to deliver a message to the Allied army. The SS staff in Holland wanted

the Allies to grant their forces safe passage to the east so they could
fight the Russians. In return, the SS agreed to stop their scorched-
earth policy in Holland and release all political prisoners. Naturally,
the Allies dismissed the SS offer and interned Bobby for several days
while OSS interrogated him and determined that he was not an Axis
agent.

In neighboring Belgium, OSS and the Belgian Sûreté (Resistance
movement) created a joint venture, code-named Espinette. Espinette
was created to recruit Belgians for intelligence work and establish
links with Belgian underground agents as they were overrun by the
advancing Allied armies. A total of six teams were eventually created
to penetrate Germany and gather intelligence. Ray Brittenham, a
lawyer from Chicago who grew up in Belgium, was in charge of Espinette.

"Espinette was my hometown and where I went to school. As a
kid I went to the coast in Belgium. I remember going there in civilian
clothes and reporting information on what the Germans were doing.

"One of the things they wanted us to do was send agents into occupied Belgium and Germany as civilians. Recruiting potential agents
was difficult, and I handled it carefully. I told them that they would be
involved with the Americans in extremely hazardous work. Many of
them thought they would be interpreters. We put together several
teams that would be used in Germany and Belgium. Once they got
into the program and realized that many of these missions might cost
them their lives, they didn't flinch and felt honor bound to continue."
The Belgians' most important missions would come later with the direct penetration of the Reich.[13]

While the Allied armies were advancing rapidly toward Germany, OSS was expanding the scope of its operations even faster.
American covert operations spread beyond the western front to assist anti-German partisans fighting in Czechoslovakia.

FOURTEEN

Catastrophe in Czechoslovakia

The autumn of 1944 brought the Allied armies to Germany's borders. To the east, the Russians were sweeping through Poland and moving toward the foothills of the Carpathians in eastern Czechoslovakia. In the midst of the maelstrom, six B-17s slipped through German air defenses and gently touched down in a grassy airfield in Czechoslovakia, only miles from the front lines. The Flying Forts were crammed with 20 tons of munitions, including Marlin submachine guns, Brens, bazookas, explosives, medical supplies, and over 200,000 rounds of ammunition. The flight, the second of its kind in three weeks, was part of an OSS operation to support several thousand partisans and two divisions of the Slovak Independent Army, who had revolted and set up their headquarters in the city of Banska Bystrica.

Nearly two dozen OSS personnel were devoted to the operation, code-named Dawes. Led by Lieutenant Holt Green, Dawes was designed to act as a liaison with the Czechoslovak army and partisans. Dawes was also an intelligence mission designed to gather order of battle information. In addition, over a dozen weary American aviators who had bailed out over Czechoslovakia were evacuated through the Dawes mission.[1]

The Germans recognized the danger of the uprising behind their lines and rapidly sent a patchwork of SS units to crush it. OSS expected that the Red Army steamroller would reach Banska Bystrica before the Germans. But it didn't happen that way; the Germans moved too quickly.

OSS realized the seriousness of the situation and tried to evacuate the Dawes personnel before the Germans recaptured Banska Bystrica. Rescue flights were ordered, but the missions were grounded by bad weather. Eventually, the Germans overran the partisan airfields at Banska Bystrica and Tri Duby.

With one of Europe's coldest winters in decades setting in, Lieutenant Green decided to split up the party and hide in the Tatra Mountains, with the hope of eventually linking up with the advancing Russians.

The team, accompanied by several downed airmen and even an AP reporter (who had stowed away on one of the B-17s), had to filter through a massive exodus of partisans who were throwing away their weapons and fleeing through snow-covered mountains to the Russian lines. Hundreds froze to death in the bitter weather.

It was bone-chilling cold, as 24-year-old Maria Gulovich recalled. The blond, blue-eyed former schoolteacher had joined the partisan revolt just months earlier, and was recruited by the Dawes team to act as their interpreter and guide.

"We were on the run and had no place to sleep. On the side of a mountain we tried to build some shelters when it started raining. We were soaked to the bone. Constant rain, mud and you couldn't keep straight up on your feet. You don't want to carry anything heavy, so you drop it. Eighty-three partisans went to sleep and froze to death. Eighty-three people dead.

"During one of the ice storms, men's beards froze, eyebrows and hair became icicles, clothes and shoes became as stiff as boards. And the wind was bitter. The flesh on my right leg started to flake away as gangrene started to set in. I still have the scar there, and when it gets cold I can still feel it. Even here in California I can feel it. When I lived

OSS Operations in Czechoslovakia

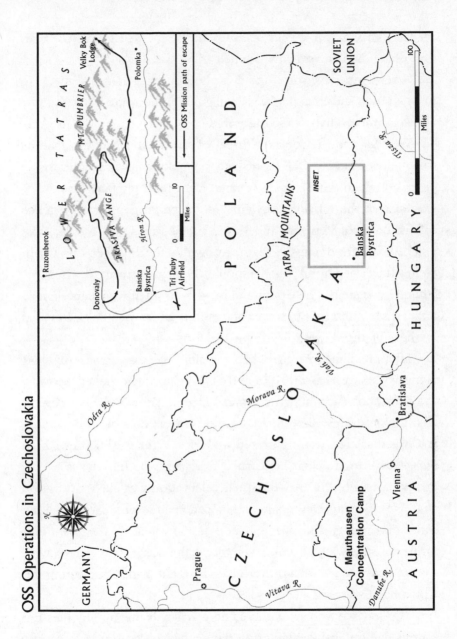

GERMANY

POLAND

CZECHOSLOVAKIA

AUSTRIA

HUNGARY

SOVIET UNION

Prague

Odra R.

Morava R.

Vltava R.

TATRA MOUNTAINS

Váh R.

Banska Bystrica

Bratislava

Vienna

Danube R.

Tisza R.

Mauthausen Concentration Camp

INSET

0   100
Miles

Inset

Ruzomberok

Donovaly

Banska Bystrica

Tri Duby Airfield

Hron R.

PRASIVA RANGE

MT. DUMBRIER

Polomka

Velky Bok Lodge

L O W E R   T A T R A S

0   10
Miles

→ OSS Mission path of escape

on the East Coast it would open up and fester, years after the war. One of the men had sulfa, which helped.

"I remember Nelson, the navy photographer, had bad feet. He just sat down and cried. He was a tall guy. His feet were black and just as bad as mine. That was so miserable."[2]

Weather and the constant threat of starvation started to take its toll on the exhausted OSS agents and fliers. But an even greater threat emerged, when the Germans learned from captured partisans of the existence of the mission. Abwehr 218, a special counterintelligence unit made up of SS troops and Slovak and Ukrainian fascists, was dispatched to hunt down the team. Known as the Edelweiss unit, Abwehr 218 was led by an Austrian noble, SS Major Erwein *Graf* (Count) Thun-Hohenstein. The Count and most of his men were experienced antipartisan hunters with scores of missions under their belts. Pursued by the *Graf,* the Dawes mission pushed forward.[3]

After a killing march, what remained of the Dawes mission, along with several British SIS and SOE agents who linked up with the team, holed up in a mountain lodge at Velky Bok. For several days the group rested in the lodge and life took on a bit of normalcy. A Christmas tree was decorated and Holt Green even brewed up *Sumadinsky caj,* an elixir he learned to make from his days with Yugoslav partisans.[4] But the Christmas celebration was cut short by the *Graf,* as SOE agent Lieutenant Stefan Zenopian recalls: "We had done some decorating, and had a Union Jack as well as the Stars and Stripes on the walls. I will never forget the scene, and I have with me the penciled text of a prayer given by Lieutenant Gaul during the Christmas Eve party.

"'O God, we who are gathered here in Thy Name by Thy Blessing on this day of Thanksgiving do offer with deep gratitude our most heartfelt thanks for our deliverance from the blizzards and high winds of the wintry mountains and from the cruel snows fallen upon us, and from the perils of the black night and dark valleys. Gratefully we thank Thee for preserving our group together and for maintaining our physical health and strength and for buttressing our wavering courage and for providing food, even in our darkest days, and we ask Thy blessing on us and our Allies, particularly the Slovak nation, and Thy mercy on our comrades who are missing in enemy action and wintry storms. Amen!'

"On the morning of the 26th at 8:00 o'clock we were given a warning from below that the Germans were coming from the direction of Polomka and that we should be ready to move off. At about 10:00 o'clock, from a vantage point we could see the Germans as they came up the mountain. There were about 250, but it is certain there were many Germans in the group. . . .

" . . . The Germans started shooting. The Partisan guard put up a fight which lasted about three hours, and finally the Germans started firing artillery from Polomka at the house. When this started, the Partisans decided to move off and so did we. Immediately, after we left and gave up the fight, the Germans came on the house, which was burned and everything destroyed."[5]

A partisan collaborator informed Count Thun-Hohenstein where the team was hiding. Abwehr 218 captured most of the team and several partisans. Gulovich, Sergeant Steve Catlos, and Private Kenneth Dunlevy from the OSS team, and British operatives Bill Davies and Steve Zenopian were able to avoid capture only because they had been sleeping in a house farther up the mountain.

All the remaining OSS and English agents rounded up by Abwehr 218 were sent to the Mauthausen concentration camp, where inmates were literally worked to death—over 150,000 died within its gates during the war.[6]

Green and his men arrived at the camp on January 7, 1945. Shortly after their arrival, special interrogators from the SS and Gestapo were brought in from Berlin by direct order of the Führer's office to find out what the team knew.

Werner Müller, a bespectacled civilian employee of Amt IV, the German counterintelligence office, was dispatched from Berlin to interrogate the prisoners. He recalled what happened in a postwar interview with American war-crimes investigators.

"On the second day of our stay they brought in some beams into the building and three of them were erected in one of the rooms. Two beams high up along the walls and one across on top of the two underneath the ceiling. In the middle of the latter beam they fixed an iron chain. In the afternoon of the second day, we were asked to interrupt the interrogation of Gaul and were called over to Habecker's [a Gestapo interrogator at Mauthausen] room where Baranski [an OSS officer] was standing in the presence of Kommandant [SS Colonel Franz Ziereis, camp commandant of Mauthausen] and other SS officers. When I arrived we all went over to the room where this frame had been erected. Before we went over, I had to tell Baranski he would now be requested to give us information, and since I felt something dreadful would happen, I beseeched him to speak the truth. He replied he would do so, but when I translated that to the Kommandant, he replied, 'No, first he must be hanged so that he knows he can't tell any more lies.' I was the last to enter the other room with Baranski. When he saw the other people all crowded in the room and the chain over the table, he turned to me smiling knowingly saying, 'Oh, I know what they are going to do now.' I was so nervous and afraid I asked him once more to speak. He said, 'Yes, I'll speak.' I addressed the Kommandant that Baranski wants to speak, but he just laughed and said, 'No, first he must hang.' Baranski had to get on the table and they tied his hands behind his back and attached his wrists to the chain above, which they drew upwards. . . . The Kommandant requested me to ask him whether he was prepared to speak, whereupon I answered immediately myself, 'yes.' So, he told me he didn't want my answer, but wanted me to ask the prisoner. I asked the prisoner, and in the meantime they pulled the table away underneath Baranski.

Baranski answered me that he was prepared to speak, and although he must have been suffering terrible pain, he kept himself wonderfully. The Kommandant did not seem to like that and said, 'I think the fellow still enjoys himself.' Habecker touched him on the legs so that he got movement, and the Kommandant asked one of the SS guards to pull his legs down so that his backward bent arms on which his whole weight was hanging must have been strained. In the end Baranski couldn't stand it any longer. He cried and begged to be let down and told the Kommandant that he was willing to speak, but he insisted on keeping him still suspended in that dreadful position. Baranski started praying and the Kommandant asked me what he was saying. When I told him, he and the other officers laughed."[7]

Later one of the officers of the team, possibly Holt Green, was tortured by the SS, as Dr. Hans Wilhelm Thost, another interrogator from Amt IV, reveals.

"When I came in Arndt [a Gestapo interrogator] was holding a heavy whip in his hand and the American had on his forehead bloody marks from the blows he had received. Schoeneseiffen seemed to think that was a great joke and called it [a] 'Jesus halo.' The American chap was in a crouching position with his hands bound beneath his thighs behind his knees. It was apparent that he had been lashed on his buttocks. I was overcome and went into the first room where Habecker was questioning the English major in the presence of Standartenführer E [Colonel] Ziereis.

"As this officer did not want to give any information about the Allied service in Bari which had sent him to Slovakia, Habecker told him that he had another way of making him talk—the 'Tibetan prayer mill' . . . three or four wooden rings about the shape and size of a pencil which he pressed together hard, crushing the victim's fingers. This Tibetan prayer mill causes intolerable pain. Ziereis got intense pleasure out of that torture and slapped the English officer again. I myself was not able to leave the room since I was obliged to act as interpreter. That evening at mess I told Standartenführer Ziereis that I was incapable of hitting a defenseless prisoner. Ziereis answered me that an enemy was an enemy."[8]

The Allied prisoners were interrogated, beaten, hung, and tortured with the Tibetan prayer mill for several days. The Gestapo tortured the men with coldblooded composure. According to Thost, "The pleasure experienced by Ziereis and Habecker was apparent."[9]

On the last evening of the interrogations, Colonel Ziereis organized a drinking party in honor of the interrogation team. Before the festivities begun, however, SS Dr. Manfred Schoeneseiffen, a Gestapo interrogator at the camp, stripped the insignia and decorations off the prisoners and required them to change into prisoner uniforms. Next, the men were instructed to sign papers that stated they would be shot if they attempted to escape while being transported to another camp.[10]

But they were never transferred to a POW camp. Instead, Berlin ordered the Allied prisoners to be executed immediately. The group was taken to an underground bunker. The prisoners were ordered to strip so they could undergo a physical exam by a doctor. A dummy camera was set up on a tripod. The first prisoner in front of the camera was Major John Sehmer, a Brit from SOE. Sehmer was told to stand against the wall so he could be first photographed from behind. As he faced the wall Commandant Ziereis placed a carbine within inches of the back of his neck and fired. A total of five prisoners were ushered into the shooting gallery and executed in a similar manner. The remaining prisoners met the same fate on February 9, 1945.

After they were shot, the prisoners' bodies were dumped into a cold storage room and eventually moved to Mauthausen's crematorium. Wilhelm Ornstein, a prisoner working in the crematorium, witnessed the killings and the fate of Holt Green.

"The first shot did not kill the victim immediately. When we brought Green to the cold storage room, Schulz told Bachmayer [the deputy commandant of Mauthausen] that there was one still alive in the cold storage room, and that he should go give him a second shot. Bachmayer did this. The picture of that fellow remained in my memory until today, so that I am absolutely sure that he was Lieutenant Green."[11]

While their colleagues died in Mauthausen, Maria Gulovich, OSS agents Steve Catlos, Kenneth Dunlevy, and Steve Zenopian, and several other members of the team barely managed to avoid the German dragnet and flee toward the advancing Russian army, as Maria Gulovich recalls.

"The Germans were retreating and any day we thought they would be gone. So we hid in an abandoned antimony mine. It was huge. There was a collection of people. The Germans would use people to dig antitank ditches and entrenchments. After they dug them they would shoot them. So when the Germans came to collect people to dig trenches whoever was lucky enough hid in the mine. You had deserters such as Hungarians and families who were threatened by the Germans. We were there eight or ten days and in many cases we were laying on our backs.

"Oh. Oh. The lice. The lice were absolutely disgusting and they were half an inch thick—in the seams—that's where they congregated. On my arms, I still have scars from infections from the lice. We used to burn them with matches. You pull off a piece of clothing and burn them off. They covered everything and if you washed your clothes it made them worse.

"And then the Russians came. Our liberators, our Allies, that was a laugh. For the next two weeks we were threatened, abused, and accused of being spies by the NKVD [Soviet secret police]. They interrogated us over and over and treated us like POWs. Here's where my Russian came in handy. They shifted us from here to there. Finally, they put us in a hospital which was both a blessing and a nightmare. The front was moving very fast and they didn't have many supplies. Amputations were performed without anesthesia. They would get them drunk and start cutting. It was a scene out of a Civil War hospital. Eventually, they defleaed us and deloused us and gave us Russian uniforms."[12]

Eventually, Gulovich and her small band were taken to Romania by the Russians, en route to the port of Odessa and, ostensibly, a voyage back to the West. History, however, would show that many foreigners, and even Allied POWs, "liberated" by the Russians were never returned to their home countries. On the way the group was joined by several other foreign displaced persons who were also moving to Odessa. "Nobody wanted to go to Odessa; we knew we probably would never return. The Russians wouldn't let us contact the Americans or the British. So we made up a story that one of the displaced women that we met was pregnant and that we needed to stay in Bucharest. While we were in a train station in Bucharest a young boy spotted the Stars and Stripes on Catlos's sleeve. He gave Steve news that there were Americans in the city. Within 15 minutes, Catlos was able get the phone number of the American mission and made contact with U.S. Army Brigadier General Cortland Schuyler. The Russians wanted to transport us to Odessa but Catlos came back and said, 'We need to stall for time until the Americans arrive. Just don't get on the train.' They loaded us on a truck and sent us to a secure house. Our plan was to hole up in the bathroom, and we had one of the displaced women to pretend that she was in pregnant and in labor. Catlos said, 'Stall until I whistle "Yankee Doodle."'

"I never heard 'Yankee Doodle' before but we stalled for another hour until I heard that tune that I will never forget. The Americans and British arrived in jeeps and walked in the building and we sped away before the Russians realized what was going on."[13]

With the rapid advance of the Allied armies through France and Eastern Europe in the fall of 1944, the war in Europe appeared almost over. Allied armies straddled Germany's borders. Units and material assigned to Europe were being shifted toward the Pacific. In the hope that Germany would soon fall, OSS and British intelligence were postponing large-scale direct penetration of Germany. Insertion of long-range teams was fraught with peril and casualties were expected to be high.

The fall of 1944 also brought about a letter from President Roosevelt outlining the reduction and liquidation of OSS. The end of the war seemed in sight.

However, Allied hopes for victory in Europe in 1944 ended when Hitler unleashed his forces in operation *Wacht am Rhein*. The Battle of the Bulge forced OSS to resume efforts to penetrate Germany directly.

FIFTEEN

Psych Ops

Morale Operations (MO) and Origins of Psychological Warfare

MO is an intellectual weapon of the highest order.
It is not a weapon of crudity and of obvious purpose.
MO must cut to its target like a rapier
and not club its way like a bludgeon.[1]
        —"Morale Operations Student Handbook"

Allied efforts to defeat Germany went beyond the military campaign to destroy the Axis war machine physically. The Allies also conducted an active psychological campaign designed to undermine the German will to fight. The subversive aspects of America's psychological war were advanced by the Morale Operations (MO) branch of OSS.

Like most of OSS, MO was the brainchild of Wild Bill Donovan. Donovan held that "persuasion, penetration and intimidation . . . are the modern counterparts of sapping and mining in the siege warfare of former days." Propaganda represented the "arrow of initial penetration," followed up by sabotage, commando operations, and guerrilla operations that softened up an area before conventional forces invaded.[2]

Initially, Donovan envisioned an all-encompassing propaganda policy that would be coordinated by the Joint Chiefs of Staff and integrated into America's military plans. The predecessor to OSS, the Coordinator of Information (COI), had operated under a broad charter that covered the entire propaganda spectrum.

However, there were deep ideological disputes within the government over how America should conduct psychological warfare. While Donovan advocated the use of disinformation and subversion, the COI's deputy director and head of the Foreign Information Service (FIS), Robert Sherwood, contended that "propaganda broadcasts should stick scrupulously to the facts, and let the truth eventually prevail." Sherwood argued that America's image and prestige would suffer "if we emulated Axis methods and resorted to lies and deceit."[3] Sherwood also believed FIS should be controlled by civilians, not the military.

For a variety of reasons, including his respect for both Donovan and Sherwood, President Roosevelt decided that America's propaganda operations should be administered by two separate agencies. The same executive order that created OSS also created the Office of War Information. OWI, headed by Sherwood, was responsible for all "white" propaganda, or propaganda that admits its source and conforms to government policy. OSS was responsible for "black" propaganda, which is "subversive in every possible device, disguises its source, and is disowned by the government using it."[4]

The new branch got off to a rocky start. MO's roles and responsibilities were defined vaguely by the Joint Chiefs of Staff so that its activities could be publicly denied. Turf battles with the OWI over areas of responsibility ensued. In addition, MO received meager amounts of equipment and personnel in comparison to OSS's other branches, which were reluctant to work with MO since they perceived it as a danger to the security of their own organizations.[5] Despite these handicaps, MO managed to conduct an innovative and effective propaganda campaign against Germany.

MO employed a variety of methods to disseminate propaganda. The oldest and simplest method was to spread disconcerting rumors.

For instance, MO Rumor No. 109, cabled August 16, 1943, stated, "A wave of suicides is sweeping over the Nazi Party. The suicides prefer to die now in honor of the Führer rather than suffer the disgrace of collapse of the Nazi cause." Rumor No. 60 asserted that the plague was spreading in the Ruhr. "Because of bombings, garbage cannot be collected, sewers are broken and great hordes of rats are creeping through the cities. In one large city in the Ruhr the plague is spreading."

A rumor's success was measured on the "come back." A come back was an Allied or Axis newspaper, radio report, or intelligence service report that mentioned or disputed the veracity of the rumor. In the case of Rumor No. 60, the Axis chose to dispute the rumor in a large newspaper by retorting, "There is no truth in this report, we reply. There have been cases of typhoid fever, but in no greater number than last year."[6]

George Piday, an agent assigned to the MO mission in Bari, Italy, recalls his role in developing rumors and their devastating impact inside Hungary.

"My job was to keep close liaison with the Hungarian Section, and to attend weekly rumor meetings, and submit our own rumors to the board. At those meetings the rumors were checked and discussed individually. I do not know what methods [were] used to get the rumors into the respective countries; however, one thing was evident, the rumors hit the spot. The Hungarian newspapers were screaming their heads off, cautioning and threatening the population not to listen or believe in those rumors. It is my firm belief that rumors are one of the best MO weapons; it is easy to get one started from a neutral country or by agents inside the enemy country and [it] has a very damaging effect on the army and civilian population."[7]

MO also drafted leaflets, newspapers, and stickers that were crudely produced on cheap paper, creating the appearance that they had been fabricated by clandestine groups. One example included leaflets dropped on Fascist lines that claimed to be safe conduct

passes from the local partisans. Over 1,000 Italian Fascist soldiers surrendered.[8]

The July 20, 1944 attempt by German dissidents to assassinate
Hitler provided the opportunity for one of MO's more ambitious and
successful subversive propaganda schemes, an effort to undermine the
morale of German army units in Italy. Operation Sauerkraut passed
OSS agents, recruited from German POWs, directly through the front
lines to spread rumors and distribute leaflets, fake orders, and procla-
mations. Barbara Lauwers, one of the principal architects of Sauerkraut, recalls how the operation got off the ground.

"It was in July 1944. We learned that there was an attack on
Hitler's life. We had a planning session to see if we could capitalize.
There were the OSS men and one sole female private—me. I was the
only female in the unit. They used me to interrogate prisoners of war
since I was fluent in German.

"It was decided that we would disseminate propaganda to the
German forces up north that the war was over and spread rumors that
there was insurrection in Germany and there was no need to lose limb
or life for a cause that was lost. We decided to employ a novel approach: use German prisoners to spread the propaganda.

"At midnight on the 21st of July, Major William Dewart and I
headed down south to the prisoner of war camps. We went to Caserta
at 5:15 in the morning and put a musette bag down in the floor and
went to sleep. When I woke up, Major Newhouse was yelling at me,
'What the hell are you doing here?' I explained to him our plans to recruit POWs for the operation. Instead of reaming me out he said, 'If
you think it will work go ahead.' So I was taken to a POW camp,
Number 326, south of Naples that housed about 3,000 POWs.

"Many of the POWs were surprised to have a German woman
interrogate them. One of them [was] an absolute perfect specimen
of the Nordic race: tall, slender, blond-haired, blue-eyed, an SS man.
He was absolutely offended that a female would talk to him. For

these interrogations I always wore an officer's uniform without insignia. He was just furious and started vilifying America and vilifying President Roosevelt. He said, 'We'll be bombarding New York soon.' 'That Jew in the White House, we'll show him!' So I just listened to him for a while. But I'm half Czech and half Slovak. Slovak equals five Irishmen when it comes to temper, so I said to him in German, 'Say it again!' He repeated his statements in German so I gave him a knuckle sandwich right across the kisser. He was so stunned that I would dare touch him. The sentry outside the tent opened the flap and said, 'Did he say anything Madam?' in a very British accent. I said to the British MP, 'I'm through with this guy; take him away.' He could have hit me back but he didn't. He just staggered out of the tent."

The POWs eventually chosen for Sauerkraut were selected from a special dissident compound.

"They had a special compound that held dissidents who disagreed with Hitler and the German army. Out of those dissidents I selected sixteen that could be utilized to disseminate our disinformation.

"Talking to them, it became apparent that they disagreed with Hitler's policies. I remember one soldier telling me, 'I couldn't go on as I saw the atrocities they were committing.' He would say that the German soldiers would enter a village and grab a couple of women. Several soldiers would hold the girls down while the other soldiers would take turns raping them."[9]

The POW agents were trained, equipped, and given the proper papers and cover story. Wearing German uniforms, they were armed with rifles and Italian Beretta pistols. Each man carried ample supplies of cash and a brick of 3,000 sheets of propaganda material.

Altogether, the POW agents conducted four missions. One of their leaflets played on the homesickness and jealousy of German soldiers. MO introduced "The League of Lonely German Women" to convince war-weary German soldiers that their wives and girlfriends were sleeping with Nazi bosses, soldiers on furlough, and foreign workers in the Reich.

Lauwers remembers how she came up with the idea for the league.

"One day I was interrogating a POW. It was more of a conversation than an interrogation. I asked him, 'What bothers you the most when you hear from back home? Is it the air raids? The lack of food?' He thought for a while and said to me, 'What would bother me the most is if my wife was messing around with other men.' That gave us an idea and we created the 'Lonely Hearts Club' to which every German woman belongs: your wife, your sweetheart, your daughter, your mother, everybody. When a soldier comes home on leave, all he has to do is display this symbol of entwined hearts and immediately a member of our club will take him home, house him, feed him, and sleep with him. We want to make him happy since we want to be mothers again, since our men are gone and we want to bear children again. This we put in writing in German. It was done so well that the *Washington Post* bought it as a genuine story. It was quite successful. For instance, one fellow from OSS Research and Analysis found this leaflet instructing German soldiers on leave to be free to accept invitations from the homes of German women. This guy from R&A brought this leaflet to us and was raving about it and said, 'Can you imagine what the German women are capable of? Just copulating with just anybody?' So I listened to him for a while [and] said, 'Would you like to see the original blueprint?' He couldn't believe we were behind this type of morale operation."[10]

The propaganda distributed by Sauerkraut's agents induced the surrender of numerous enemy soldiers. Sauerkraut so rattled the Germans that the High Command was forced to issue an official proclamation denying authorship of the printed leaflets.

Scores of OSS agents worked MO field missions behind the lines, injecting doses of specific disinformation directly into enemy units, something that could not be accomplished with preprinted propaganda. In Greece, MO agents planted forged orders in German units, disseminated leaflets, and even committed acts of sabotage. Major M. W. Royse led a mission designed to create a mutiny among the German forces in Crete. Ultimately, Royse's men could not germinate a large-scale mutiny, so they concentrated on smaller units and prepped the area for preinvasion operations.

"In open and subversive work I operated as Major W. Bill. As Major Bill, I was sought by the Germans for treachery, subversion, etc., and there was little chance of their dealing with me on other grounds. I reserved my real name (with title of Major) mainly for negotiations with the Germans, written and parleys, in regard to surrender. How far this attempt at double identity succeeded is hard to say. In my parleys with the German commander and with his adjutant, both asked me whether I was Major Bill. In contacting the undercover men, in garrison towns, etc., a routine job, I carried the identity card of a sickly, half-senile man of about fifty, and was sometimes led by a small boy who could pass as a nephew and answer questions for me. A simple trick taken from the malingering propaganda was to make use of a local rash. My excuse for entering a town was generally to call on a doctor, if one was located there, otherwise to call on the priest, etc., for aid. An elaborate makeup was not necessary to get past German controls, but their Greek agents were sharp as well as ruthless. . . .

"Our political warfare work was devoted mainly to stuff based on local military data, directed at the troops as soldiers, although general propaganda on the lost war, annihilation of the homeland, maniacal bloodlust of the Nazi leaders, etc., was included. A German staff officer, a major acting as chief advocate general for the German Marine force of 2000 men, had joined us soon after we came into the area, and besides serving on intelligence work, did a good deal on war crime propaganda. A soldier's paper was set up and published weekly, and individual leaflets put out on specific subjects."[11]

Farther north, in the Volos region of Greece, the Ulysses Mission issued forged orders, printed anti-Nazi German newspapers, and distributed leaflets resulting in confusion and some German desertions. Ulysses also took part in Operation Hemlock, involving the dissemination of "poison pen" letters to Nazi officers in Greece. Crafted by OSS agents in Cairo, the letters capitalized on an SOE-orchestrated kidnapping of Major General Karl Kreipe, the German commander of Crete, and the death of Major General Franz Krech, who was ambushed by Greek guerrillas. Robert Knapp from the Ulysses Mission recalls planting the poison pen letter.

"The Krech letter was a forgery produced in Cairo during the month of May 1944, following the death of General Krech, German commander in the Peloponnesus. It stated that General Krech had been angered at the decision of the German High Command to sacrifice all German troops in Greece and had decided to make contact with the Allies and to desert to them in the hopes of saving his men from total destruction at the hands of the Greeks. His death was alleged to have followed the writing of this letter addressed to his officers, when the Gestapo found out about his intentions."

A portion of the letter stated:

I am in the most difficult moment of my life. I am joining the enemy. I believe that I have done my duty towards you and towards Germany. I can see that we are carrying out unsatisfactory plans which led us and Germany to destruction. Our troops in Russia have suffered a defeat unparalleled in the history of Germany. That is why I can see before me two roads. One leads to submission to the German Command, and the other to joining the enemy, with a hope that by doing I this may contribute to the salvation of Germany. The German Army is steadily marching towards destruction.[12]

Knapp continued: "The MO/Ulysses Mission into Greece was given three copies of this letter, which were taken by boat to the MO base near Volos. There, it was arranged to have one copy taken to the island garrison of the Sporades and another to Volos. In the case of the Volos letter, it was planted by an EAM [a leftist Greek resistance group] agent in the office of the commandant of the Volos garrison. This agent was employed as janitor and thus had access to the office."

The letters and Ulysses's other propaganda efforts resulted in hundreds of German desertions.[13]

Radio was one of the most powerful propaganda weapons of the war. Each of the war's great powers used it to convey its propaganda messages. MO operated several large radio stations, and MO radio operations had a significant impact on the war.

One of the more successful radio operations was Soldatensender-Calais (later Soldatensender-West), a radio station supposedly broadcasting from Calais, France but actually operating out of Milton Bryant, England. The station's purpose was to erode the morale of the German military and civilians by presenting news, unreported by German news agencies, on German military failures. The audience was further enticed with American songs that were put to German lyrics.

MO provided over a dozen writers and several musicians to the station, which broadcast anti-Nazi propaganda to civilians and Axis troops. The so-called black radio programs offered a mixture of truth and fiction, usually beginning by naming Germany's latest actual winners of the Knight's Cross.

In an effort to expand the audience, MO recruited Hollywood writers and popular singers such as Marlene Dietrich. Special lyrics were written and recorded for 312 popular German and American songs.

After the attempt on Hitler's life, Soldatensender broadcast the names of hundreds of prominent Germans whom it alleged were part

of the plot. Germans occupying influential positions, guilty and innocent alike, were targeted by MO in an attempt to decapitate Germany's leadership. Postwar records reveal that the Gestapo fell for
Soldatensender's reports.

Soldatensender achieved tremendous popularity among German
soldiers. According to U.S. Twelfth Army reports, 90 percent of POWs
taken during the summer of 1944 listened to the station.[14]

In the fall of 1944, MO put Operation Joker on the air, and in
doing so "resurrected" former German Chief of General Staff Ludwig
Beck. Beck was executed after the July assassination attempt on Hitler,
but the Nazis never publicly acknowledged his death. Before Joker
went on the air, an OSS rumor campaign laid the groundwork that
Beck was still alive. Then an OSS broadcaster who sounded like Beck
was put on the air. The phony Beck argued that the war was being lost
by the Nazis, who were interfering with Germany's generals, and
urged the German people to discontinue the war and liquidate the
Nazi leadership. The Nazis were horrified by Joker and jammed the
broadcast faster than any other radio program the Allies employed.
Other OSS black radio programs took its place.[15]

To complement the traditional propaganda leaflets, newspapers,
rumors, and black radio, MO devised several ingenious special projects to demoralize and confuse the Germans even further.

One of the most ambitious MO special projects began in early
1945. Operation Cornflakes was designed to bring subversive propaganda to the German breakfast table. OSS combed POW camps for
prisoners who had worked as mail clerks, in order to learn the inner
workings of Germany's mail system. The goal was to insert thousands of propaganda letters into the Reich's mail system, thereby demoralizing the German population and sowing defeatism within
Germany.

The plan was patterned after an earlier OSS operation in which a
few mailbags filled with subversive literature were dropped into Hun-

gary. But Cornflakes was far more sophisticated. From information gleaned from the POWs, OSS created identical Nazi mail pouches and postal stationery. Expert counterfeiters forged precise copies of Nazi stamps. The OSS master forgers outdid themselves with a stamp of Hitler with his skull bones exposed. They altered the header below the stamp to read: "Reich Shot to Hell."

Hundreds of German exiles took addresses from prewar phone books and addressed personalized letters to German citizens. Some personalized envelopes contained the OSS newspaper *Neues Deutschland* *(The New Germany)*, which claimed to be from a peace party operating inside Germany. High-ranking Nazis received poison pen letters.[16]

Cornflakes's most difficult problem was how to insert the letters into the Reich's mail system. OSS devised an ingenious solution: strafe trains carrying the mail and airdrop the fake sacks right on the wrecks. When the Germans cleaned up the train wrecks, the fake mail sacks, practically indistinguishable from the real ones, would be included with the original sacks, and the contents delivered to the German people.[17]

George Piday worked on Cornflakes. "I was called back to Bari to work on the German mailbag [Operation Cornflakes]. The envelopes were addressed in Siena, stuffed and sealed in Roma, we in Bari did the routing and canceling. After much work and experimenting with the Fifteenth Air Force, we had the whole operation running smoothly. The cooperation of the Fifteenth Air Force was excellent; they went out of their way to give us all the help they could. Until the day I left Italy, we had five operations with 50 percent success. I'm very proud of this MO project and glad I had some small part in the work of putting it together."[18]

Twenty missions dropped 320 bags of propaganda mail. OSS reported that the mail contributed to a decline in civilian morale and created confusion in the mail system. Postwar interviews revealed that many German soldiers received *Neues Deutschland* through Cornflakes mail.

The final MO operations involved "ghosting" German radio broadcasts. MO transmitters overrode Nazi radio broadcasts, heckling the speakers and interrupting with sarcastic comments on the air. MO broadcast fictitious claims that Allied tank formations had captured German towns and cities days before they actually fell. Bogus orders were issued activating German civilian and Red Cross units. The Germans denounced the broadcasts but could not jam them without disrupting their own programs. Joseph Goebbels, the father of Nazi propaganda, commented in his diary, "They are trying to play the same game with the German people as we played with the French during the western offensive in the summer of 1940. . . . They put out false reports of the capture of towns and villages, thus creating the greatest confusion among the German public."[19]

MO pioneered many of the psychological warfare tactics that are still in use today.

SIXTEEN

Penetrating the Reich

"Forward and over the Meuse!" German commanders barked Hitler's watchword to legions of Waffen SS and Wehrmacht soldiers—marking the beginning of one of the greatest battles of the war.[1] On December 16, 1944, eighteen German divisions, five armored, would punch a 65-mile hole in the American lines. The counteroffensive was Hitler's last desperate gamble to reverse the tide of war and force the Allies into a negotiated settlement.[2]

The Germans shrouded their preparations for the battle in absolute secrecy. Prior to the counteroffensive, Hitler ordered radio silence. Crucial communications were made over secure land telephone lines or delivered by messenger. Local commanders were issued orders specific to their area and were briefed at the last minute. During the day troop and supply trains traveled east, but at night they changed direction and moved west, dropping off men and equipment in camouflaged staging areas in the Ardennes. When the attack commenced on December 16, the Germans had achieved a surprise on the order of a European Pearl Harbor. For the Allies, the Bulge was one of the greatest intelligence failures of the war.

Contributing to this failure was the Allies' overdependence on Ultra. Bletchley Park had successfully predicted most of Germany's major actions throughout the war, but the Germans maintained communications discipline so perfectly before the Bulge that the codebreakers had only limited intercepts to decipher.[3]

Penetrating the Reich

North Sea • Kiel • Kiel Canal • Rostock • Baltic Sea • Hamburg • HOLLAND • Bremen • Alt-Friesack • Amsterdam • Berlin • Wünsdorf • POLAND • Oder R. • Arnhem • Operation VARSITY March 24, 1945 • Wesel • G E R M A N Y • Antwerp • Kassel • Halle • Leipzig • Oder R. • Brussels • Liege • BELGIUM • Cologne • Erfurt • Kerspleben • Dresden • Elbe R. • ARDENNES • EIFEL • Battle of the Bulge Dec. 1944–Jan. 1945 • Buchenwald Concentration Camp • Bastogne • LUXEMBOURG • Plauen • Prague • CZECHOSLOVAKIA • Frankfurt • Reims • Nancy • Regensburg • Abensberg • Strasbourg • Dachau Concentration Camp • Vienna • FRANCE • Rhine R. • BLACK FOREST • Stuttgart • Danube R. • Freiland • Freiburg • Munich • Dijon • Reichenau Labor Camp • Scheffau • Oberperfuss • KITZBÜHLER ALPS • Bern • LIECHTENSTEIN • Alpine Redoubt • AUSTRIA • Innsbruck • Brenner Pass • SWITZERLAND • ITALY • Klagenfurt • Geneva • Miles • YUGOSLAVIA

A greater factor was the crippling intelligence wound the U.S. Army inflicted upon itself. The U.S. First Army, upon whose front the Ardennes counteroffensive fell, had kicked out its OSS field intelligence detachment. Bad blood between the two groups began to arise as early as D-Day, when First Army bumped the OSS detachment off the landing craft, claiming a lack of space. When the agents finally landed in France they were denied transportation, rations, and quarters. Eventually, First Army personnel decided to dismiss the OSS detachment altogether, and rely on intelligence that was passed on to them from higher levels and their own organic G-2 sections. Had OSS

been permitted to operate routine "tourist missions" (agents who generally infiltrated behind enemy lines on foot, gathered intelligence,
and crossed back to friendly lines) in the Eifel, its agents would almost
certainly have spotted the movements of hundreds of troop trains, and
the massing of hundreds of tanks and tens of thousands of men. By ex-
cluding OSS, First Army cut out its own eyes and ears.[4]

While OSS field intelligence units were shut out of the Battle of
the Bulge, OSS's counterespionage branch, X-2, launched an important deception plan to screen the movement of Patton's Third Army,
which was moving north to break the siege of the 101st Airborne Division, surrounded in the key city of Bastogne.

Using German agents that X-2 "doubled," the basic elements of
the deception plan relied on convincing the Germans of the improba-
bility of moving the entire Third Army so fast under adverse winter
conditions. X-2 also wanted to convince the Germans that Third
Army units were being committed to the Ardennes in a piecemeal
manner, so the Germans would not redirect their attack to the south,
to encounter the Third Army on the road to Bastogne.

One of X-2's double agents was code-named "League." During the
start of the Bulge and again on December 24 the Germans wanted to
know the exact location of the Third Army's 80th Division. While the
80th was moving north into Belgium, League reported the division
was still in France, at St. Avold. Screened by the weather, which made
aerial detection impossible, the 80th achieved a complete surprise,
turning the flank of a stunned German division and taking 1,700 prisoners. According to the 80th's intelligence officer, "League's assistance
had in all probability aided materially in achieving this result."[5]

Another important role was played by "Witch," a 29-year-old
right-wing Frenchman who initially fought for the Germans in Russia
and later spied for them. Witch was doubled and controlled by OSS
captain William Browne, who recalls the key role Witch played in the
Battle of the Bulge.

"The [87th Infantry] division had come across France just prior to the 16 December offensive. The enemy, we knew, had followed its course with great interest and commendable accuracy. Then, largely because the division went into a period of strict radio silence, the German Order of Battle sections had lost track of it. This caused considerable dismay in C-in-C West, for at this point they were preparing to launch their diversionary thrust in the south. The plan called for the shifting southward of several divisions to attack in the Hagenau Forest area. What the enemy most feared was that this division they had lost track of would bob up to back up our defensive line just when the German attack emerged from the Hagenau Forest. Consequently, they were most anxious to learn anything which would indicate that this possibility would not occur. Twelfth Army Group on the other hand, was even more anxious to slip the 87th into the Ardennes line secretly. A full scale deception operation was planned, therefore, to indicate the presence of the 87th in the Metz [France] area. False bumper markings, false radio traffic, and Witch fixed the 87th in Metz." The Germans were so thoroughly taken in by Witch's misinformation that they awarded him the Iron Cross, Second Class.[6]

The Bulge proved that the war in Europe was far from over, and that Allied intelligence agencies would be forced to penetrate Germany itself. Some of the first OSS personnel to enter Germany were agents affiliated with the OSS detachments detailed to American armies. After the disaster in the Bulge, First Army was reluctantly shamed into taking its OSS detachment back. Meanwhile, the small OSS unit attached to the XVIII Airborne Corps (82nd Airborne, 101st Airborne, and 17th Airborne Divisions) was developed especially for innovative intelligence missions. After the Allied counterattack in the Bulge, the airborne divisions were pulled out of the line and trained for one last great jump, the largest single-day airborne operation of the war, Operation Varsity. Varsity was the airborne phase of General Montgomery's crossing of the Rhine at Wesel.

OSS Captain Stephan Vinciguerra was in charge of four OSS agent teams who were to drop with the 17th and infiltrate German lines immediately after landing. Two teams were in German uniform. "The operation took place on 24 March, 1944. One team was gliderborne, complete with a German Volkswagen [that they called a Kubelwagen], radio set, and uniform. A second team of German-uniformed personnel was parachuted. The third and fourth teams, civilian dressed, went in by glider. All had portable radios except the Volkswagen team, which had a regulation army set.

"Due to antiaircraft fire, one explosive shell tore through the glider carrying the Volkswagen, the best team was wounded and the Volkswagen damaged. I received shrapnel wounds also, but wasn't seriously wounded. My civilian team made a clean infiltration during the operation. Fifty-five Germans including two lieutenants surrendered to my party of four. I recommended a Bronze Star Medal for one of my sergeants who was with me during the skirmish and was extremely aggressive despite wounds more serious than mine. The second uniformed team arrived safely by parachute, properly infiltrated, but lost its nerve and returned to our lines during the same day. The last team was successfully infiltrated the following night, but due to a sudden breakthrough of the Allied forces, the team was promptly overrun."[7]

For agents who parachuted into Germany, one of the most difficult aspects of the mission was simply landing safely. The changing nature of the front, flak, enemy aircraft, and pilot and navigational errors made getting dropped on target a constant challenge. One of the most egregious blunders occurred when the air corps dropped the Seventh Army's Pitt Team directly on top of an SS unit.

Pitt consisted of two agents: "Red," Fritz Fischel, a naturalized American and second lieutenant in the U.S. Army, and "George," Ernst Georg Muller, a German. George went in with the cover of a Gestapo official, while Red was in the guise of a railroad official. Both men went in to report on an SS division that was stationed in the

Black Forest. Red recalls the debacle. "We were dropped right in the middle of an SS [barracks], about 1.5 miles away from where we were supposed to come down. I landed on the roof and George landed in a tree in the garden of this house. Everybody was still awake [watching an outdoor movie] and all lights were burning. Before the chute could completely collapse I jumped off the roof, but badly hurt my back. I tried to get rid of my suit without success. Almost at once, twenty men armed with rifles and pistols and a dog come out of the house and fired warning shots in the air. There was nothing else for me to do but surrender, the situation was hopeless. George was still trying to cut himself loose, as he too was arrested, still hanging from a tree. As one of the SS men told me later on, they were watching a training film outside the house and they saw the plane circling the field and were amused as they saw us come down."[8]

The Pitt agents were taken into the custody of the SD and played back (doubled) to OSS. Red, the radio operator, made as many mistakes as possible when he contacted OSS via his W/T. OSS realized that the men were captured and fed the men "chicken feed," or harmless information that kept them alive. Eventually, as they were being transferred to Dachau concentration camp by the SD, the Pitt agents convinced four of their captors "that the war was lost and that they would do better to cross the lines with us." The argument worked and the OSS and SD set out in two cars and were eventually overrun by Allied troops from the 42nd Division.[9]

While the agents assigned to the various army detachments concentrated on what was happening on the German side of the front lines, the Allies also needed to conduct comprehensive espionage operations deep in the Reich itself. Allied commanders needed strategic intelligence about troop movements far behind the lines, intelligence that could best be provided by agents on the ground. Agents could also furnish badly needed information regarding German production facilities and the effectiveness of Allied bombing raids.

However, British intelligence stressed the "prohibitive difficulty" of penetrating agents directly into the tightly controlled Reich.[10] Unlike in France, agents would not be welcomed by a friendly resistance group who would provide them cover and support. Agents would have to be dropped "blind." Moreover, the Gestapo was operating one of the most severely intrusive security regimes in history. Casualties were expected to be high.

British reluctance provided Donovan with the opportunity to take the lead in penetrating Nazi Germany. The responsibility for breaking into the German police state fell on the shoulders of a 31-year-old lieutenant who would later become Ronald Reagan's Central Intelligence Agency director. At the height of the Battle of the Bulge, Donovan told William J. Casey to "get us into Germany."[11] Casey quickly developed a plan for the direct penetration of the Reich. His plan was dubbed "Faust," after the Goethe character infamous for making a deal with the Devil.

One of the most daunting obstacles Casey faced was finding German-speaking agents who could blend into German society. OSS London's Labor Desk suggested exploiting one of the last untapped resources in England, hundreds of German Communists in exile. Most were part of the "Free Germany Committee," an organization with roots in the Soviet Union. Casey initially said no, citing the potential postwar risks of using Communist agents. However, Casey was ultimately overruled by the pragmatic Donovan, who said, "I'd put Stalin on the payroll if I thought it would help defeat Hitler."[12]

Two members of the Free Germany Committee performed one of OSS's most daring sallies of the war. The two-man Hammer Mission became the first OSS team to parachute into the suburbs of Berlin.

The two men selected for the mission were 34-year-old Paul Land and 33-year-old Toni Ruh. Both men were fervent anti-Nazis who had been involved in underground movements within Germany before the war. While living in England they had joined the Free Germany Committee. After undergoing a brief training program, the men were given the best false identity papers OSS could produce, and detailed cover stories. Before climbing aboard a blackened A-26 light bomber, they donned camouflage jump smocks, which they wore over civilian clothes. They carried .32-caliber pistols, a Joan/Eleanor radio, Reichsmarks valued at $700, and two diamonds each worth $200.[13]

Hammer's A-26 flew a complex flight plan that carefully avoided German flak defenses, using lakes as navigational aids. About 30 miles outside Berlin, the flight crew gave Land and Ruh thumbs up to bail out. Land recalled, "We jumped at 2:15 o'clock 50 km northwest of Berlin, near Alt Friesack. The plane crew did an excellent job in dropping us exactly on the point we had selected. When we made the landing we found that it was stormy and we were dragged against barbed wires and only then could release the chutes. It took two hours to get the chutes off these wires and to collect the package. We then dug in our material in three different places. It appeared that the landing place had been well chosen and could be used for further landings and deliveries. We separated our two sets and at the last hiding place left our weapons and everything that could have betrayed our activities. We arrived in Berlin during the night of 2 March. It was our intention to go first to Phil's home, a former leader, but because of the impossibility of checking the address at midnight, we changed the plan and went to the home of his parents. There we were most enthusiastically welcomed and every possible assistance was secured. We moved into an empty bungalow which was under the care of Phil's parents. We decided to stay there as the surroundings and assistance assured maximum security. Phil had never lived there before.

"Phil's parents, both 57 years of age, were in the past Social Democrats. Their attitude toward our sudden appearance and our mission can be best described in their own words. 'We knew that you would come one day to fight the Nazis.'

"We acquainted ourselves with the situation and conditions in Berlin. During the first week we systematically went through things we had to know about the town, the Nazis, the controls, etc. We went through large parts of Berlin, got used to air raid regulations, and to the raids, the behavior of the people, and learned to live like Berliners. With this knowledge we went over our papers and found them in order, but owing to local working conditions in factories we decided to remain illegal as it was the only way in which we would have sufficient time for our mission.

"We visited Toni's sister and found her willing to assist and advise us. From her we received information about a number of people we were looking for who were known to us as anti-Nazis and possible helpers. Most of them had died either in the Hitler armies or in concentration camps. We established one contact however, a woman aged 30, by the name of 'Dora,' who became our most active assistant. Her first task was to find out the conditions in the districts where our speaking points [locations to be used for contacting airplanes] were situated, the result of which was that Nos. 2 and 3 were occupied by the Wehrmacht and No. 1 was just good enough to be used.

"On March 8 we went to Alt Friesack, our landing point, in order to get half of our equipment, our weapons and other items such as coffee, cigarettes, etc. At the same time we made a thorough survey of the district and the surroundings of the field, and found out that it was good enough to take whole airborne units unobserved into the country. . . .

"On 12 March the first prearranged contact with the plane took place. Probably because of failure of our 'Joan Set' we were only able to contact the plane, but were unable to give our report. On 16 March we tried a new point about 1½ miles south of the original one because of better security: the time for contact given from base was already in daylight. We did not succeed in speaking with the plane but picked up their calling teams.

"During this week we collected information about troop movements, production details, etc., and prepared the first report on it. Furthermore, Phil went to his former teacher and her husband who was home on leave, and secured their assistance. They agreed to furnish a special report on conditions and troops in Wunsdorf, a Wehrmacht camp southwest of Berlin, to prepare living quarters for us or friends of ours and to find a doctor in case of emergency, all of which they later accomplished. . . .

"The British Air Force had changed its bombing tactics by that time and sent planes over Berlin from early night until the next morning. The result was that there was no traffic at all, everybody was sent to shelters, and all those on bicycles [were] controlled. It meant to us that traveling within the Berlin area became more and more difficult. The last contact we tried was on 21 April. Part of Berlin in the north-northwest area up to Alexanderplatz was already under heavy artillery fire. Toni lived there with Margarit and Warner since the end of March and had the Joan Set hidden there as well. We met there, both on bicycles, and went under fire to our speaking point. Chaos reigned in these districts. People were leaving their dwellings and Wehrmacht moving in. We took shelter in the woods near the field and waited some hours until the plane was to come. The villages around were on fire. The plane did not come, at least we did not contact it. When we left the field about 3:45 we were overrun by tanks one mile [from] where we came from. We thought at first they were German tanks and took cover. They rattled past us for about a quarter of an hour in a westerly direction. Immediately afterward heavy fighting broke out and it was then that we realized that they were Russian tanks."[14]

Rather than go into hiding or flee the doomed city, the Hammer Team remained in Berlin and later took part in the battle.

• • •

Another source of German-speaking agent candidates were the more than one hundred thousand Poles living in exile in England. Believing that the Poles could easily blend in with the tens of thousands of foreign forced laborers working in the Reich, OSS proposed Operation Eagle, which would use Polish spies to form the nucleus of an intelligence network. Forty Polish soldiers, "of the middle and lower labor type," were recruited and formed into 16 teams. The teams were named after popular alcoholic drinks such as Pink Lady, Highball, and Martini.[15] Martini agent Leon Adrian describes in excruciating detail his capture by the Gestapo a few days after his parachute jump into Germany. "En route to the police station I destroyed all incriminating evidence except one telegram which I could not destroy so I crumpled it up in my pocket and took it out of my handkerchief as if I was wiping my nose. Then I put the paper in my mouth and chewed it. The Gestapo noticed this and treated my body as only the Gestapo knows how. First, they gave me a shot to make me throw up what I had in my stomach, but that did not work. Then they gave me a solution to drink which I refused and immediately I was hit with the butt of a rifle in the teeth and I spit out three teeth. Then they forced the solution into my mouth and I still did not vomit. Next they used two cylindrical rubber rollers which were pressed against my body and rolled from my knees to my ribs. I vomited. They found small pieces of paper and I explained to them that I received two caramels from a woman on the way and could not remove the papers so I ate them with the papers. This helped me a little since they accused me of two things, either of being a deserter from the Army or an Allied spy. They threatened me with the Buchenwald concentration camp or death. Every day from 6 to 8 o'clock they questioned me continually about my story from the first to the last day. During these interrogations they continually beat me with rubber clubs giving me nothing to eat and all I received was a half liter of salt water each day.

"On the 6 April 1945 at 1400 [2:00 p.m.] hours, my sentence was to be decided. At 10 o'clock that morning an air raid siren had sounded and Allied bombers were overhead. From the burst of a bomb the doors and windows of the prison were blown out and two prisoners entered my cell and helped me escape. We ran on foot for eleven kilometers. Between Halle and Leipzig, I found out that they were deserters from the [German] Army. I no longer could run so the two of them left me lying in the woods and fled further. I slept for twenty-four hours and upon awakening I proceeded further. For five days I kept myself alive with turnips which I stole. After five days I met a group of foreigners who were clearing the ruins of a large gasoline refinery. They had taken excellent care of me up to the time the Americans arrived on 15 April 1945."[16]

After his liberation, Leon Adrian worked with U.S. Army Counter-Intelligence Corps (CIC) and helped track down former Gestapo agents. During the roundup he recognized the two Gestapo men who had tortured him. Adrian coolly removed a pistol from a nearby soldier's holster and fired two shots into each man, killing them instantly.

Despite its innovative aspects, Eagle was an operational failure. Not one of the 16 teams contacted OSS London. Poor training (conducted by the Poles) and an inadequate selection process were the main reasons for Eagle's breakdown.

OSS recruited a wide variety of people to work in Germany, ranging from priests to former Waffen SS soldiers. Some of its finest recruits were women. Female agents had clear advantages over their male counterparts. Most of Europe's male population had been pressed into Nazi work programs or drafted into the German military forces. Stray males, not attached to a military or work unit, generally triggered an identity paper check. Women did not have to carry the extensive documentation that the Reich required men to possess. They were less likely to arouse suspicion, and usually could blend into the civilian population more easily. Nevertheless, no clear OSS policy for recruiting women field agents existed. Many OSS women agents who operated behind the lines were foreigners and their recruitment was largely ad hoc.

The OSS's Seventh Army Detachment plucked one femme fatale out of a French detention camp. Code-named "Maria," she was a beautiful Alsatian French woman who spoke German as naturally as she spoke French. Maria was a woman with a past. She was in love with a German officer, Lieutenant Heinrich Berger, whom she had met in 1944. After being imprisoned as a collaborator by the French, Maria volunteered to work as a spy for the Allies. Joining OSS would free her from jail, and dropping behind German lines would enable her to search for her lover.[17]

As Seventh Army agent recruiter Peter Sichel recalls: "She came to us to whitewash her record. Maria was a collaborator, and had a German lover, she had been the mistress of a German officer and ostracized by the locals in a small mining town in the Vosges Mountains. We offered her a chance to make good. She was also two months pregnant. She was beautiful and very bright.

"She wanted to go on the mission but she also wanted to strike a deal—she wanted us [to] clean her record and also wanted us to perform an abortion."[18]

Peter Viertel, Maria's case officer, described Maria as "rather buxom, sexy looking, blond; the kind of a woman that was willing to take a chance.

"I told Maria that you don't have to do this. She said, 'I want to do it.' I think she feared the alternative of being sent back where they came from, a French detention center, but she was without fear when it came to the mission."[19]

After several weeks of training in the Seventh Army's mountaintop agent boot camp, Maria was ready for her assignment: to parachute into Stuttgart and travel disguised as a German army nurse. She parachuted into Germany in early February and helped care for German soldiers in Freiburg. Hitching rides in German military vehicles, Maria made her way down to southern Germany using the perfect fraudulent identification papers developed by OSS Seventh Army Detachment's excellent Cover and Documentation (CD) department.[20]

While traveling back to American lines, Maria mentally recorded German troop locations and information on a German headquarters. She never found her lover, but did contact his uncle, who informed her that he was at least alive. Upon her return Peter Viertel recalls Maria's exact words: 'I want to go back.'

Peter Sichel, as the OSS finance officer, performed a variety of odd jobs, including the heartrending task of upholding the second part of OSS's deal with Maria. "She had volunteered with the guarantee that we would arrange for an abortion. When she got back I arranged it by telling a physician in Strasbourg that she had given her body to find intelligence for us. He indicated his understanding and told me to leave her with him."[21]

Another beautiful Seventh Army agent, Maura Bertani, was an Italian circus acrobat who had been recruited by the Seventh Army Detachment in Strasbourg. On February 24, 1945, Bertani parachuted into Germany, where she gathered intelligence for a month before infiltrating back through the lines.[22]

One of the most secure areas in the Reich was Austria and southern Germany. The Germans claimed they were sending troops into the area, building factories inside mountains, and erecting fortifications for a last stand—the famed Alpine Redoubt. History would prove that the redoubt was largely a myth. Hardly any units moved into the area, and only a few fortifications were constructed. Nevertheless, the Nazis ruled the region with an iron hand. The Germans went so far as to send Gestapo agents into the area posing as Allied agents complete with Allied radio sets. If individuals provided assistance or housed the fake agents they were liquidated.[23]

Some of the first agents to penetrate Austria and southern Germany were four teams from Ray Brittenham's Espinette organization, a joint venture between Belgian resistance and OSS. Team Doctor's two young Belgians, Jan Smets and Alphonse Blonttrock, were ordered to gather intelligence on trains supplying the Italian front, and to report on military installations and German troop movements in the Alps. After a long flight from London, Smets and Blonttrock parachuted into the Kitzbühler Alps in Austria. Landing in five feet of snow, the men gathered their chutes and encountered an ironic twist of fate. The day before Doctor parachuted into their mountain drop zone, three Tyrolean deserters from the Wehrmacht spread a large Austrian flag (red, white, and red) on the exact spot of the drop zone. The deserters hoped to attract the attention of the Allied planes to the presence of partisans in the mountains, and obtain some sort of aid for the resistance group that they were forming. The deserters greeted Doctor with surprise and elation.[24]

With the help of the three deserters, Doctor recruited additional Austrians and set up intelligence and sabotage rings that gathered information on a Me-262 jet airbase, oil depots around Hall, and the Werewolves, a Nazi guerrilla movement then being organized. As the war neared an end, Doctor stopped blowing things up, and began to conduct counter–scorched earth operations, such as removing dynamite from bridges to keep them intact for advancing Allied troops.

Another Espinette team, Chauffeur, parachuted into southern Germany near the massive Messerschmitt assembly plant at Regensburg. The team was equipped with both a Joan/Eleanor and W/T suitcase radio for communication. Chauffeur's agents, Michel Dehandschutter and André Renaix, went in under the cover of being foreign workers. After parachuting outside Regensburg, the men made their way to a safe house only to find that the owner had left six months earlier. They were soon arrested by a Volkssturm patrol and questioned by the police. The local authorities bought their cover stories and released the two agents. The men eventually set up their base camp in a dairy staffed by Belgian POWs, placing their W/T in a cellar. The men fanned out and went into Regensburg, looking for new contacts. In Regensburg, Dehandschutter met two Frenchwomen who had been forced to prostitute themselves in a German brothel.

"April 17 André and I left for Regensburg, in order to find a contact in that town, as indicated to us by the POWs. Andre reentered Abensberg, in order to transmit the information obtained on the roads and on town of Regensburg itself. As for myself, I decided to return two or three days later, in order to obtain some more information on the town, and to find a contact in order to remain at that town. During my stay at Regensburg, I found two French civilians, and information I obtained myself as well as through the assistance of two prostitutes, who had good relations to German Army officers and also to members of the police." One of their "clients" was a German colonel who was fully informed on the defense plans for Regensburg.[25]

Chauffeur provided additional intelligence on the strength of German units in Regensburg, and even that the Hôtel du Parc was being used as German headquarters and as residence for four to six Nazi generals. With the Allied liberation of Regensburg, the team linked up with OSS field officers.

Most of OSS's missions into Austria and southern Germany originated from OSS's Mediterranean Theater of Operations (MedTO) branch, based in Trieste, Italy. Missions into this area were some of the most perilous of the war. Nearly all of the 12 teams that MedTO sent into the Reich would be captured or killed.[26]

Into this cauldron, five Jewish refugees boldly demanded to return. Fred Mayer, Hans Wynberg, George Gerbner, Alfred Rosenthal, and Bernd Steinitz all had fled Europe prior to the war. Several of the men had lost relatives in the Holocaust. All of the men had become American citizens, and upon the outbreak of war joined OSS's German Operational Group. The men had been idle for nearly a year, waiting for the OSS to send the German OG into Germany. After pleading with OSS operations chief Lieutenant Colonel Howard Chapin for a chance to return to Germany, the men were transferred to the Secret Intelligence branch, and trained to enter the Reich as spies rather than as saboteurs.

Close friends Hans Wynberg, a Dutch-American Jew, and German-born Fred Mayer were formed into a team. Wynberg recalls the chutzpah the pair displayed in an early training mission. "We had some practice missions. Freddy and I infiltrated Brindisi harbor, which was controlled by the British. We had no insignias on our uniforms. We both had German accents. Freddy had a really strong accent, nevertheless in plain uniforms without insignia, without papers, we entered the British compound, looked at the maps on the wall that showed the location of all the Allied minefields and Allied ships in the Brindisi and Bari harbors. We offered the sergeant in charge of the maps a bottle of Scotch and walked away with the plans for the harbor. This was security at its finest in September-October in 1944."[27]

The first two of the five to return to the Reich were George Gerbner and Alfred Rosenthal, members of a team known as Dania. The third member of the team was Paul Kröck, an Austrian who deserted from the German army and joined the Italian partisans before he was recruited by OSS.

The plan called for Team Dania to drop near the Austrian town of Freiland, Kröck's hometown, and establish an intelligence net to watch the roads for troop movements. As the team prepared to drop on the moonless night of February 7, 1945, Paul Kröck was certain he recognized the muted lights of Freiland through the "Joe hole" in their Halifax bomber. Only Kröck would ever reach Freiland. Gerbner recalls: "You go out and it seems an eternity before the parachute opens. The wind from the slipstream hits you like a hammer. As I was parachuting down I landed in a tree. And instead of an open field, I landed in a steep valley between two snowcapped mountains.

"I freed myself from the tree and found myself in about six feet of snow. We had snowshoes but they tore apart after I walked on them [so I] threw them away. I kept going downhill to the lights of a village. A truck passed by on the road to the village. I heard voices, they weren't German, I figured I was in Slovenia in northern Yugoslavia. I flashed my flashlight, to signal the other men on the team. All of a sudden the street lights went on in the village. I stopped flashing. I assumed the Ustashe [Yugoslav collaborators] must have seen the plane circling above the village. So I hightailed up the mountain several miles from the village. I was climbing as fast as I could, hours seemed like minutes, and I traveled several miles away from the village. I went as far as I could up the mountain, and strangely, I heard music. Lo and behold, it was a Partisan brigade with a brass band, holding a dance. They were having a wonderful time and weren't afraid of the Germans.

"I was in an American pilot's uniform and presented myself to the group. I just walked forward and spoke to them in German. They had seen quite a number of downed American pilots, so they were not that surprised.

"I wanted to go back to my base camp in Trieste. My cover story was that I was a pilot and my plane went down. Here I linked up with Al Rosenthal. They agreed to help us and assigned me a guide, a carrier."

Kröck , however, had disappeared.

Gerbner recalls what happened next. "They put me up for the night. I knew if the Germans found out they were harboring me they would burn down the whole village. I didn't trust anybody. I slept by the door so maybe I could get out.

"The next day they assigned a 16-year-old courier to us. We started out on a narrow mountain pass and traveled behind a waterfall, the path passed behind it. We kept moving at a breakneck pace. The courier kept going faster and faster, he was trying to lose us! Rosenthal was having a hard time keeping up. I told him, 'You stupid ass, we have to keep going!' He wanted to stop, he was complaining that he couldn't make it. I shook him and snapped him out of it. I re-member sleeping under the snow, it kept us warm.

"We avoided the German patrols. The last hurdle was crossing a major river. German sentries were guarding the main bridge. Eventu-ally, a man with a boat took us across the river about a half mile from the sentries. We got to Trieste and were assigned to a rest camp."[28]

Years after the war, Gerbner found out what happened to Kröck. The courageous German had made his way back to Freiland, where he holed up until the Gestapo discovered his whereabouts. When they came to arrest him, Kröck jumped out the back window of his home and broke his leg. Nevertheless, he managed to evade his pursuers. He remained in hiding until the end of the war.

Bernd Steinitz fared worse. Shortly after parachuting into Klagen-furt, Austria, with his partner, an Austrian deserter turned agent, Steinitz was captured by the Gestapo.

Team Greenup, in contrast, met with stunning success. The three-man team was led by 23-year-old Fred Mayer, whose family had fled Germany in 1938 and settled in Brooklyn, New York. Mayer's team-mates included Hans Wynberg and Franz Weber, a POW and former lieutenant in the Wehrmacht's 45th Division. The team would oper-ate around Weber's hometown near Innsbruck.

Greenup's mission was to monitor rail traffic moving through the Brenner Pass, the main route between Germany and Italy. Mayer, who "wanted to return to Germany to make a difference before the war was over" remembers the jump. "The actual jump was just beau-tiful, floating down over those alpine peaks. I had been sitting in the 'Joe hole,' which was the belly turret that had been removed and that became the hole to jump out of. It was so cold in the plane that I was happy to get out and the snow felt warm. I landed on top of a glacier and sank down to my hips in snow. I had a signal lamp that I was to signal if all was clear, red or green. So I gave the green light and the others landed within a few feet of me. I was wearing engi-

neering pants that were dark brown and a snow cape. We could have
passed as a German Alpine troop. After we landed we made our way
down to an alpine hut where we spent our first two nights, and from
there we went to the closest village and Franz went to see the mayor
of the village and said that we were alpine troops and we had to get
back to our unit. He lent us a sled to get down from the top of the
mountain. It was like a Santa Claus sled. Franz did the steering and
I was in the back with my ski stick trying to slow it down. That was
the scariest part of the whole trip. The sled was going about 60 mph.
The glacier was about 10,000 feet and we had to get down to about
3,000 feet. We had no weapons except I had a little .32. I didn't expect to get down in one piece; I thought we would turn over but we
didn't.

"When we got down into the valley we left the sled where Franz
had agreed we would leave it and the mayor could pick it up again and
then we hitched a ride aboard a truck (the driver thought we were
German Alpine troops and he gave us a lift) to the railroad station and
we bought tickets."[29]

While on the train the team had their first close call, as Hans Wynberg recalls: "When we got on the train we were still wearing American uniforms. They didn't give us German uniforms but our uniforms
were covered by these white snow capes. We still had uniforms with all
of our American insignia on them. So we are on this train and our papers were checked by Nazi officials. We had Franz, who was a local, tell
them that we had been in a ski event and that we lost all of our identity
papers. This guy passed us by. Then about half an hour latter the
Gestapo showed up and said, 'Show me your papers!' Franz responded
plainly, 'We have just been checked.' He passed us by. It was pure luck
at that point. We were in American uniforms, had our radio, codebooks, and no papers. If they picked us up, Franz was a deserter, they
would have shot us on the spot. It was all luck. We arrived in Franz's
town and started walking to his fiancée's house."[30]

Fred Mayer recalls what happened next: "In Innsbruck I met one of Franz's sisters, who was a head nurse in the hospital at Innsbruck, and she gave me my first real papers. I was supposed to be wounded in my hand; she said I was a wounded officer from the Italian front. I was an 'outpatient' at the hospital. The papers were under my real name. I then went to the officer's club and got officer's quarters. The club was like a cantina. The officers were on one side and the enlisted men on the other. I got into discussions with other officers and that is how I found out about the plans for Hitler's headquarters in Berlin [from an officer] who was there only a week earlier. He told me in great detail about the bunker and all that because he helped build it. I reported it all back completely."[31]

Excerpts from Mayer's message that Wynberg sent back read like a blueprint of the Führerbunker: "Located about 1½ KM Southeast of Station Zorsennager, Berlin. Pay attention to group of houses 5 each on parallel facing each other one length way in the center of east end. Roofs very steep and camouflaged black, white, green. Houses built of reinforced concrete. All walls one meter thick, 10 rooms per floor. Lowest 13 meters underground, under four ceilings one m [meter] each. Air warning tower in the center of the house group. Last attack hit officers club only. First house in southeast is Adolf. . . ."[32]

Mayer continues, "Every now and then I would have to go back to the hospital to have my hand 'rebandaged' and that's when Franz's sister introduced me to Colonel de la Roque, a French officer who was interned as a VIP prisoner at the Schloss Itter but needed treatment at the hospital. He told me that Charles de Gaulle's sister was at the same place he was interned and I sent that message back too.

"Everything was running pretty smooth. I went down to the railroad yard and that's when I started talking to the load master of the yard and he told me about these trains being assembled that were headed back into northern Italy. After some small talk, the yard master openly revealed that 26 trains fully loaded with tanks and artillery would pass through Innsbruck on their way to Italy."[33]

Accordingly, Wynberg sent the following message on his W/T: "Assembled at Hall and Innsbruck and west 26 trains 30 to 40 cars each loaded with ammo, tractors, ack-ack guns, gasoline, light equipment, leaving for Italy via Brenner April 3 after twenty one hundred GMT. Trains guarded. Source: loadmaster of the yard."[34]

Weather canceled the initial bombing raid on the Innsbruck rail yard, but the air force caught up with the trains when they entered the Brenner Pass.

"Two days later, I drove down in a Volkswagen to the Brenner Pass and saw the destruction. That was precision bombing, 26 trains destroyed after they came through the tunnel. They were loaded with tanks and artillery. That was the one part of the mission that I was most proud of. Someone in Eisenhower's headquarters later told me it shortened the war by six months."[35]

A request from OSS forced Mayer to change his cover. "I got a message saying they wanted information on jet production so I figured the easiest way to do that was getting a job at the Messerschmitt assembly plant in Kematen so I went to the labor office and I told them I was a French electrician from a town near Vienna and the Russians had already gotten there. I was escaping from the Russians and had lost everything so they issued me papers. I became a Frenchman.

"My first day I found out right away that production was zero because they couldn't get any parts in. The factory was inside a mine-shaft deep inside a mountain. It was well lit. It had hydropower from the river, which was flowing by so they were not dependent on the outside for lights. There was beautiful machinery in there. There were other Frenchmen. The supervisors were all Germans. There wasn't much going on. I was cleaning electric motors. I just spent a few days in the factory. Once I became a Frenchman I couldn't go back to the officer's club.

"After a long day at the factory I returned to my room in Innsbruck. Hans and Franz were still hiding out in another location. I remember there was a knock at the door and I heard them talking and I immediately pushed all my belongings under the couch. The SD burst into the room."[36] Mayer was betrayed by one of his own subagents, a black marketeer who had been picked up by the SD a few days earlier. Mayer was taken into custody by the Gestapo who tortured him for three days. Remarkably, it was while he was in the hands of the Gestapo that he accomplished some of his most significant work.

Lieutenant William Casey's Plan Faust initially called for 30 agents to penetrate the Reich, but by the close of the war nearly 200 agents would parachute, sail, drive, or walk into Germany. Inserting so many agents was a remarkable achievement, considering that OSS only had a handful of agents in Germany at the end of 1944.

SEVENTEEN

Backroom Negotiations

Sweden and Norway

Beginning in 1942, OSS maintained a field station in neutral Sweden. While geography made Sweden a natural candidate for an espionage base operating against the Reich, this potential was hamstrung by the State Department. Obsessed with keeping Sweden neutral, the State Department tightly controlled who OSS was permitted to bring into the country and also put the clamps on spying. During his first week after arriving in Sweden, the OSS station chief was warned by the State Department that if OSS conducted any espionage, they'd be sent packing back to the United States.[1]

The espionage ban was relaxed gradually over the next two years, and OSS operations expanded. OSS interviewed businessmen and sailors who traveled from Sweden into the Reich. From these interviews, OSS discovered that Germany was moving large numbers of soldiers and supplies through Sweden to German commands in Norway. Armed with this embarrassing information, American diplomats forced Sweden to honor its neutrality and curtail the transport of German troops.[2]

One of OSS Sweden's most successful agents was Eric Siegfried Erickson, code-named "Red." Erickson, who enjoyed dual U.S and Swedish citizenship, first worked for Standard Oil and later had his own oil business in Sweden. Early in the war Erickson was blacklisted for trading with the Germans. OSS gave him a chance to clear his name by approaching the Germans with an offer to build a synthetic oil plant in Sweden, an enticing prospect for high-ranking industrialists within Germany who saw the end of the war in sight and were looking for a way to shelter their money after the war. Red plunged into his work, cultivating German contacts, even spouting anti-Semitic remarks for realism. Erickson's most important contact was August Rosterg, a German industrialist who owned the synthetic oil firm Wintershall. Through Rosterg, Red gained a mountain of information on the German oil industry.[3]

The Germans were intrigued by the idea of operating a synthetic oil plant in Sweden. In October 1944, Erickson persuaded the Germans to permit him to make a weeklong visit to most of the synthetic oil plants in the Reich, "in order to provide the new Swedish refinery with the latest techniques." Ty Tikander, OSS station chief in Sweden, recruited Erickson for the mission. "Red Erickson is a fascinating character and his accomplishments have been grossly understated. . . . The climax to the scheme occurred at the moment when Heinrich Himmler signed the Special Permit for Red Erickson to travel in restricted areas in the entire Reich for the purposes of the mission. The fruits of this mission were the detailed reports which Erickson was able to bring back from an extensive tour of the German oil industry which in turn made it possible for the air intelligence in Britain (both British and American) to collate this material with reports from other sources and map out the destruction of the German oil industry. There is probably little doubt that in this instance Red Erickson achieved one of the truly great espionage coups of World War II."[4]

The Germans eventually grew weary of Erickson's activities and stopped working with him, but not before he persuaded the Japanese that he could furnish them with a large volume of ball bearings. Always in short supply, the small metal balls were crucial to both Germany's and Japan's war machines. Swedish plants turned them out by

OSS Operations in Sweden, Norway, and Finland

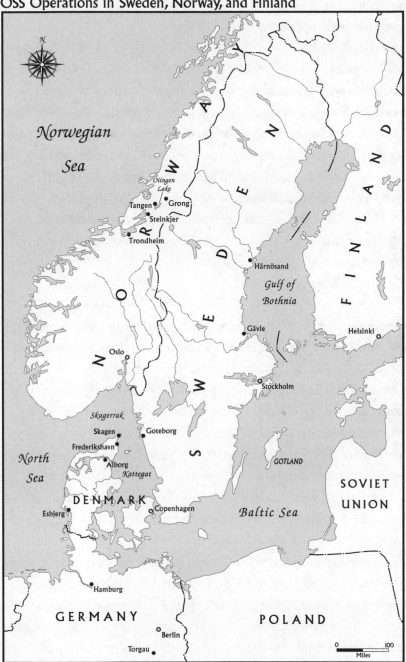

Norwegian
Sea

N O R W A Y

S W E D E N

F I N L A N D

Øtingen
Lake

Tangen
Grong
Steinkjer
Trondheim

Härnösand

Gulf of
Bothnia

Gävle

Helsinki

Oslo

Stockholm

Skagerrak

Skagen
Goteborg

Frederikshavn

Alborg
Kattegat

GOTLAND

SOVIET
UNION

North
Sea

DENMARK

Esbjerg

Copenhagen

Baltic Sea

Hamburg

GERMANY

Berlin

POLAND

Torgau

0   100
Miles

the hundreds of thousands. Erickson convinced a Japanese commission that he could easily obtain substantial quantities of ball bearings without raising the suspicion of Sweden's government. The closed-door negotiations broke down when Russia (which had a nonaggression pact with Japan at the time) refused to allow transport of the bearings through Russian territory. Nevertheless, Erickson gained valuable intelligence on Japan's ball bearing needs.[5] As the Allied bombing campaign targeted Nazi ball bearing production, by May 1944 the Germans were forced to covertly buy more of their supply from Sweden. An OSS mission gathered detailed intelligence, which the U.S. government used to persuade Sweden to stop selling the bearings to Germany. OSS Sweden would later play an even larger role in the earliest stages of the Cold War.

On September 21, 1944, three rusting coastal steamers emerged out of the early morning mist and docked in the tiny Swedish port of Härnosänd. The following day, another vessel pulled into Gävle, a port farther south along the coast. The ships were crammed with refugees fleeing Finland. That country had recently signed an armistice with Russia, knocking it out of the Axis. But the steamers' passengers and cargo were far from typical. Finland's entire intelligence service—one of Europe's finest—was on board.[6] Accompanying the "refugees" were hundreds of metal cases that contained the documents and equipment for unlocking the secrets of nearly a dozen countries. Everything was for sale.

For many months the operation, dubbed Stella Polaris, had been planned in great secrecy by Swedish and Finnish intelligence. The Swedes were shocked when, instead of a few senior intelligence officers, 750 cryptologists, commandos, and analysts, along with their families, arrived on the 22nd–23rd. The Finns went into negotiations with the Swedes for the keys to the codes and their expertise. Sweden hired the most talented Finns, while the majority of the refugees sat nervously in internment camps facing the prospect of deportation back to Finland, where they likely faced reprisals from the Russians. With their backs against the wall, the cash-strapped Finns went about selling themselves and their priceless cargo to the intelligence agencies operating out of Sweden.

The largest intelligence organization in Sweden was the 75-man OSS station in Stockholm. For most of the war the station had been working closely with the Finns. R. Taylor Cole, the director of secret intelligence from August 1944 through October 1944, wrote, "The resources of the entire Finish intelligence services have been largely available to OSS."[7] The Finns provided OSS with a bumper crop of hard intelligence on the German military, and, strikingly, on America's ally, the Soviet Union. Based on their past dealings, OSS assumed that except for the Swedes, they would be the only consumer of the material.

During their flight the Finns brought over hundreds of cases of intelligence and code material. The sensitive material was squirreled away in a variety of locations: the basement of the Hotel Aston, a castle in central Sweden, and at a private estate outside Stockholm.

Demand for intelligence on the Soviet Union was at a premium in Washington. "Ultra secret" arrangements had to been arranged for OSS to gather it, behind the backs of the State Department's diplomats, who vigilantly guarded the alliance with the Soviets.

During one of OSS's first meetings with the newly arrived Stella Polaris agents, Colonel Reino Henrik Hallamaa, commander of Finland's code-breaking services, revealed that the Finns had broken over 1,000 codes—including the U.S. State Department's diplomatic codes. The Finns read messages from American embassies in Helsinki, Moscow, Stockholm, Madrid, Tehran, the Vatican, Ankara, and Rio de Janeiro.[8] While their anti-American achievements were impressive, the Finns had devoted most of their efforts to breaking Russian codes. Hallamaa quickly got down to business and offered 200 cases of Russian material to the U.S., along with the Finnish experts to process it, for a hefty price tag.

State and OSS debated the proposition. Ultimately, State warned against purchasing the material—"We were not in favor of having anything to do with this material." For the time being the deal was off for the Russian material. But apparently the prohibition did not prevent OSS from purchasing a German Enigma machine for a suitcase full of cash.[9]

Unbeknownst to OSS at the time, the Finns had other customers besides the Americans and Swedes. They were also selling the intelligence to the Japanese, who in turn were transmitting it to the Germans. Months would pass before OSS would learn of the Finns' double dealings.

The issue of the Russian codes again surfaced. OSS acted in great haste, probably because the Finns had nearly completed negotiations with the Swedes over the Stella Polaris archives. It is likely that Tikander pleaded with Donovan to act and purchase the codes. The State Department was purposely kept in the dark on the details of the transaction.

A recently declassified handwritten document by Tikander, stamped "Top Secret" and kept in Donovan's personal safe, describes the deal: "In connection with the cipher matter which was discussed with you this morning. Permit me to inform you that I have sent a Top Secret cable today to Dick Huber and William Carlson instructing them to arrange for a meeting with our friends and accept delivery immediately of the materials previously rejected. Further, I directed that this material be photostatted and that the films be left in possession of Huber in Stockholm. . . . I authorized Huber to make a cash payment of 250,000 kroner."[10] For about $63,000, OSS purchased the material, and, in turn, Donovan informed the president.

Despite OSS's best efforts to keep the deal secret, the State Department found out about the purchase. Secretary of State Edward Stettinius protested directly to the president, who ordered Donovan to return the codebooks. A cover story was devised that OSS accidentally obtained the materials with other intelligence it was gathering and offered that "we would immediately make it available to the Soviet Government if they so desire."[11] OSS executive Ned Putzell returned the codes to a chagrined Andrey Gromyko, future foreign minister of the Soviet Union. "I went [to] the Russian embassy in D.C. and returned the codes to him; he was cordial but had a look of disbelief on his face and seemed shocked that we actually had the codes."[12]

While the OSS archives do not address the issue directly, OSS officials reportedly copied the 1,500 pages of Stella Polaris material before it was returned.[13]

This embarrassing incident did not prevent OSS from maintaining contacts with the Finns and buying more of the Stella Polaris documents. According to one recently declassified source, OSS bought four rolls of microfilm which contained the codes of ten different countries including the Vatican and Great Britain. Tikander later reported to Donovan that the transaction finally "drie[d] up the well."[14]

OSS continued to maintain contact with several Finns, who provided OSS with practically its only intelligence on the Soviet Union and on the activities of other members of Stella Polaris who were recruited by the British and French intelligence services to crack codes. Several Finns subsequently emigrated to the United States where they assisted American codebreakers of the Signals Security Agency (SSA).

The Russians had hundreds of different codes for their military, diplomatic, and espionage services. But remarkably, they did not change the codes that the Finns had cracked.[15]

If the Stella Polaris codes were actually copied, which seems highly probable, the material would have become part of one of the greatest secrets of the Cold War, code-named Venona. Venona represented a collection of nearly 3,000 partly decrypted Soviet secret messages sent between 1940 and 1948. The messages offered U.S. codebreakers an unparalleled glimpse into how the NKVD (later

KGB) and GRU (the Soviet military intelligence service) operated. The material was studied until 1980. Additionally, the Finnish material provided SSA codebreakers clues on new ways to crack other Russian codes.[16] Venona's massive database provided clues to the identities of thousands of Soviet spies around the globe, and confirmed the guilt of the Rosenbergs, Alger Hiss, and Klaus Fuchs. The material was so important that the U.S. counterintelligence community recognized it as the codebreaker's Rosetta stone. Venona would remain secret until 1996.

One of OSS Sweden's most interesting coups was establishing a backdoor diplomatic connection that could have changed the course of World War II. Through an intermediary, OSS conducted discussions with the second-most-powerful Nazi in Germany, Heinrich Himmler, about overthrowing Hitler. The intermediary, Dr. Felix Kersten, was known for his "magic hands"—he was Himmler's personnel masseur.

Before the war, Kersten, of Finnish citizenship, was the personal physical therapist for the Dutch royal family. Shortly after the Germans conquered Holland in 1940, they forced Kersten to treat Himmler, who suffered from excruciating stomach pain. Himmler became progressively more dependent on the doctor, both for his physical therapy and for his advice. Kersten accompanied Himmler throughout the day, even during many of his secret meetings and business trips, remaining at his side in case a stomach spasm occurred. As their personal relationship grew, Kersten was able to manipulate and influence Himmler. In late 1942, Himmler was becoming increasingly convinced that Hitler had lost the war. Influenced by Kersten, and his own instinct for survival, Himmler began to consider deposing Hitler and forging an alliance with the West so he could direct Germany's military might against the Russians. Himmler viewed Kersten as a potentially valuable middleman between himself and the West and authorized Kersten to contact OSS in Sweden.[17]

On September 30, 1943, Kersten traveled to Sweden to meet a "businessman" who was rumored to be connected with President Roosevelt. The businessman, Abram Hewitt, was indeed a close friend of the president, but he was also an OSS agent. Through a "very painful treatment program" that lasted six weeks, Kersten worked on Hewitt's back. More importantly, he described the inner workings of the Nazi party and key players. And, critically, he relayed Himmler's desire to seize power from Hitler and make a separate peace with the West.[18]

In a letter to Donovan, Hewitt wrote: "Himmler realized that Germany could not win the war. He was anxious to salvage as much as possible from the wreck and knew that the United Nations would not deal with Hitler on any conditions. I told the doctor that Himmler had very bad press indeed, both in England and America, and that it was very doubtful whether the American or British governments would deal with Himmler on any terms.

"The doctor urged me to come to Germany to discuss Himmler's position with him and to see whether a settlement might be possible. He indicated clearly that on certain conditions Himmler was prepared to overthrow Hitler and that he was the only man who had the power to do so in Germany."[19]

Kersten also revealed that the Russians were making separate peace proposals to the Germans, behind the backs of the Western Allies. The Russians proposed dividing Poland along 1939 lines. Germany and Russia would split the Baltic states, while Russia would get the whole coast of the Black Sea to the mouth of the Danube, and also a port on the Adriatic. According to Kersten, "Ribbentrop and Goebbels had been in favor of accepting these proposals while Himmler and Hitler were against them."[20]

One of Kersten's fellow conspirators was the powerful Brigadenführer Walter Schellenberg, head of Amt VI, the foreign intelligence branch of the Sicherheitsdienst (SD). Schellenberg also met with Hewitt, and confirmed that Himmler was thinking about overthrowing

Hitler. "I saw Colonel Schellenberg twice and he confirmed every-thing that Dr. Kersten had been telling me. He also pressed me to come to Germany to talk with Himmler."

Schellenberg recalled the meeting with Hewitt in a postwar inter-view with OSS's X-2 (counterespionage) while he was in captivity. "With complete frankness . . . I explained to Hewitt my view of the gen-eral situation in Germany, mentioning especially the ever-increasing in-ternal difficulties; the very critical position in state, party, and economics; the ever-increasing war-weariness of the entire population with all its consequences. . . . My plan was to persuade Himmler as soon as possible to make a proposal of compromise to the Western powers."[21]

Kersten and Schellenberg returned to Berlin and reported to Himmler, who appeared willing to talk with Hewitt. But as the weeks went by, Himmler appeared to lose his nerve, stating that he could not betray his idol, Adolf Hitler. Then later he had one more change of heart, telling Schellenberg, "For God's sake, don't let your contact be broken off . . . I am ready to have a conversation with him."[22]

It was too late. Roosevelt ordered OSS and Hewitt to cease discus-sions with Kersten and Schellenberg. Had the discussions gone forward and resulted in a Himmler-led putsch, OSS could have facilitated the collapse of the Reich at least a year before the war actually ended, cre-ating a mind-boggling array of outcomes. On the positive side millions of lives could have been saved, but at what price? A Germany with the SS in power was highly problematic and an East-West war between the Western Allies and the Soviet Union also could have ensued.

Direct negotiations could have fractured the Grand Alliance, and achieved one of the Third Reich's top diplomatic aims, to divide the Allies. A separate peace between Germany and the Western Allies was Stalin's greatest nightmare. Of course, Stalin had no compunctions about making his own separate peace overtures to the Nazis.

Stalin was fully informed about Hewitt's dealings with Kersten. The U.S. State Department, faithful to the spirit of the alliance, reported Hewitt's trip to Stalin. Another source was Kim Philby, a Russian mole operating at the highest levels of British intelligence.[23]

Despite the cessation of contact with OSS, Kersten continued to influence Himmler, and became one of the greatest unsung heroes of the war. He saved thousands of lives, by persuading Himmler to ignore Hitler's order to kill all the Jews in Nazi concentration camps before they were liberated by the Allies. Kersten even convinced Himmler to hold a secret meeting with a representative of the World Jewish Congress.[24]

OSS Sweden also facilitated the rescue of hundreds of Jews from occupied Europe through its ties with the War Refugee Board (WRB), a privately funded group within the United States that helped Jews escape from Europe. Ty Tikander became "ex officio chief of this extra-curricular activity" that required the expansion of OSS's fleet of trawlers for smuggling Jews out of Nazi Europe. This "Baltic Fishing Fleet" also smuggled Estonians, Latvians, and Lithuanians into Sweden. "Some wags amongst the Locals at times referred to [the fleet] as a branch of the American navy in the Baltic! In the summer of 1944 one of the War Refugee Board officials in Washington questioned [me] rather pointedly as to just how many Jews were amongst the refugees being smuggled to Sweden through the WRB-OSS activities in the Baltic. At the end of the war the Estonian cut-out [subagent] for this service advised me that over 7,000 refugees had been smuggled to Sweden. . . ."[25]

Near the end of the war, OSS agents began to make direct penetration missions into Germany from Sweden. Agents typically traveled by North Sea trawler to Denmark, and entered Germany overland. One of these agents was a Dane, Hennings Jessen-Schmidt, who traveled under the cover of a Swede buying electrical equipment. Code-named "Birch," Jessen-Schmidt was initially a member of the Danish underground. He was forced to flee Denmark when his underground ring was infiltrated by the Gestapo and his father imprisoned.

Birch's mission was to enter Berlin, gather intelligence, and deliver explosives to fifth columnists who would sabotage German industry. Once in Berlin, Jessen-Schmidt would contact "Maple," an agent living in Berlin, who would provide a safe house. Before Birch left Sweden, OSS established a courier chain that would smuggle in arms, explosives, and coffee and cigarettes for black market bartering.

On March 5, 1945, Birch traveled across the North Sea via trawler, evading the German and Swedish navies and landing in Denmark, where he traveled overland, smuggled in the back of a fish truck to Berlin.[26]

After contacting Maple, Jessen-Schmidt found himself haggling with a used car dealer to purchase two automobiles, even as Russian artillery rumbled in the background. Shortly after he consummated the deal, one of the cars was destroyed by an air strike. He used the remaining car to gather intelligence in the area surrounding Berlin.

On one such mission, Birch and Maple personally witnessed the carnage near the front.

"We got to within six miles of the Allied lines during the night, and the confusion in the German lines was beyond description. Corpses, dying civilians, and the stench of dead horses, burning tanks and cars were liberally strewn along the highways. We were under constant bombardment by Allied planes. . . ."

A few days later Birch returned to the front. "The Russians had already invaded the town [Bernau]. I was with a car at the time and must have been within a few hundred yards of the Russians, as the shells of Russian automatics and machine guns actually pierced the vehicle I was driving in."[27] Jessen-Schmidt remained in Berlin until its fall to the Russian army.

OSS Sweden also supported sabotage operations in Norway. The Norwegian resistance, known as the Milorg, was primarily supported by the SOE and SFHQ (Special Force Headquarters), who had had close ties with the group since 1940. The Swedish-based Special Operations mission, code-named Westfield, also helped supply Milorg through three supply and communication bases located near the Norwegian border in Sweden. The bases were officially labeled weather stations; the Swedes looked the other way.

Agents from OSS Sweden crossed the Norwegian border to help organize over 6,000 Norwegians in local resistance groups. OSS saboteurs were at work blowing up Nazi supply depots and sending a 1,500-ton steamship used by the Germans to the bottom.[28]

As the war drew to a close, Westfield dispatched five agents into Norway to coordinate with the Rype Mission, led by a man who would one day become President Nixon's CIA director, William Colby. Twenty OSS agents led by Colby parachuted into Norway to sever the Nordland rail line and prevent the redeployment of 150,000 German troops.

The mission got off to a rocky start when a plane carrying a quarter of the team drifted off course and dropped the men into Sweden, where they were temporarily detained by the Swedes. Colby and 14 men safely parachuted down to the Westfield reception committee. When SFHQ in London tried to reinforce the team, two planes crashed, killing 10 agents.

Undiscouraged, Colby pressed forward, as he recalls: "Our plan was lifted boldly from the history of the West. We would seize a train, board it, throw her into reverse and blow up every tunnel and bridge we could until ammunition had run out; then drive the train into a ditch. We hoped to succeed by sheer bravado. . . .

"Our usual luck was with us, and three hours after setting out we were plodding into a sleet storm, carried by the strong west wind and turning our clothing, equipment, and snow into a sheet of ice, making it almost impossible for the skis to take hold. We scraped along for fifteen miles, then took cover in one of the unoccupied summer huts, a *seter,* that dot the Norwegian mountains.

"The next day, we got 25 miles farther, stopping this time in the *seter* of a Nazi sympathizer who, therefore was well off. It took us three hours to find his liquor, cached in the baseboard behind his piano.

"Finally, we got to the peaks overlooking the Tangen bridge, somewhere north of Tangen, where the railroad skirts Oiingen Lake. The terrain was the most difficult I had ever seen.

"Picture the Hudson River, visualize the Palisades three times their true height. Place a railroad snug against the foot of the cliffs, and then crust the whole thing with four feet of snow and six inches of wet ice. Now place 23 skiers atop the mountain, and they are carrying revolvers, tommy guns, Garands, Brens, and 180 pounds of TNT plus other equipment on a massive sled.

"Helgeson said it would be impossible to get down. Men would break their legs, their skis. But I was a novice at skiing and knew motion is possible in positions other than upright. One patrol found an ice-logged waterfall that rambled in fairly easy stages in a deep, rocked-lined gorge. It ended in the lake. Perfect, I thought. Mad, thought Helgeson. We would sleep on it—and did, in a crevice in the rock. Next morning, we started, the men having been instructed to sit whenever they felt themselves losing control. . . .

"Sather and four men went north, snipping wires and smashing telephones. The remainder of the group took up battle stations as we waited for the locomotive. . . .

"Once again our plans went out the window, and quickly Farnsworth, Sergeant Myrland, Corporal Kai Johansen, and Sergeant Odd Andersen set the charges under the long, I-girdered bridge. They planted all we had, enough for four bridges that size. It was difficult to blow up steel—most often it simply bends out of shape. But the second Farnsworth touched the wires and the TNT went off, the structure vanished. The noise was awful, rocking back and forth between the hills. Even the softening lake seemed to jump, and it did crack like a boom like distant thunder. The happy men stood around with smiles on their grimy, weary faces. At least they had done something, and the Nordland railway was stopped."[29]

After destroying the bridge Colby and his team had to shake off German troops as they fled to a base camp on the Swedish border. After a brief rest, Colby's team cut another section of the railroad, reducing German redeployment plans to a trickle. Later they played a role in accepting the surrender of German troops in Norway at the end of the war.

With the war drawing to a close, OSS played a crucial role in the final offensive in northern Italy.

EIGHTEEN

Northern Italy

The Italian peninsula is nowhere more than 150 miles wide, but it offers some of the most defensible terrain on earth. Precipitous mountains, mud, bad weather, and skillful German deployments made fighting in the country a nightmare. After the Allies broke out of the Salerno beachhead, the Germans proved their mastery of the Italian topography by reducing the campaign to a slugfest. The Allies were forced to send one ponderous attack after another against well-constructed German fortifications.

After the fall of Rome in June 1944, two Allied armies pushed their way into northern Italy: the American Fifth Army on the western coast and the British Eighth Army on the east. OSS units supported both, supplying tactical intelligence and organizing local resistance groups. The drive was slowed by a lack of Allied troops. American divisions were transferred from Italy to southern France, while British troops were shipped to Greece to suppress the civil war led by Communist rebels. In the fall of 1944, the Allied drive ground to a halt before a belt of German fortifications known as the Gothic Line.

The war behind German lines was a different story. During the summer and fall of 1944, OSS successfully organized the Italian resistance into an effective "fourth arm," complementing the Allied land, air, and sea forces driving into northern Italy. Six anti-Fascist political parties, Partito d'Azione, Communist, Socialist, Christian Democrat, Liberal, and Republican, joined in a single resistance movement known as the CLNAI (Comitato di Liberazione Nazionale per l'Alta Italia). More than a mere resistance movement, the CLNAI also assumed the role of an underground government.[1]

OSS played a key role in coordinating and leading the CLNAI and other resistance groups. OSS SI built up CLNAI's intelligence staff, creating a robust intelligence organization that probed deep behind German lines, while OSS OGs and SO conducted sabotage operations and even engaged the Germans in open combat. One of the first OGs to parachute behind the lines in northern Italy was Walla Walla. Led by Lieutenant William Wheeler, the 15-man team organized partisan groups and ambushed German convoys on Highway 45, an important artery in the Genoa area.[2]

Walla Walla Technical Sergeant Fifth Class (T/5) Charlie Lotito vividly remembers the jump. "The green light came on and we started to jump. I was the last guy in the stick; we had 15 fellows. The red light came on. We overshot the field but one of the crewmen pushed me out of the hole in the belly of the Halifax. To tell you the truth, I'm lucky I'm alive. My static line, the cord that pulls out my chute, didn't work. I hit the back of the plane and got all caught up in my parachute shroud lines. I was getting thrown against the side of the plane. Boy, was I banging. The static line and shroud lines started to burn the side of my face, nearly taking it off. I tried to untangle myself but luckily the static line broke and my chute opened. I felt like I was dropping into a black hole. I couldn't see anything and 'boom!' I hit a tree.

"I landed in a 30-foot pine tree and right next to a German patrol. We were told you play dead. Here I am with my submachine gun swinging back and forth below me and I couldn't get a hold of it if I wanted to. There were about a dozen of them. They walked right below me and looked up. I was all bloodied up from the plane and the tree. One of the men in back took aim with his rifle and fired at me twice. My heart was racing. Then one of noncoms went up to the man and asked him, 'What are you shooting at him for? He's dead!'

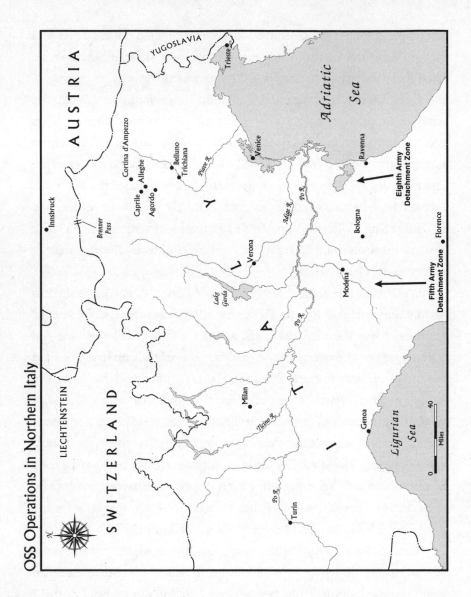

OSS Operations in Northern Italy

"Three or four minutes later they left. I reached for my knife and started to cut myself down. I got banged where the ankle bends with the foot and I slapped it against the tree. Blood was gushing out all over me. Blood was streaming down my face. I lost part of my face and I still have an indentation in my cheek. I was trying to feel the cuts with my tongue but luckily the cut didn't come through. I was slipping on my own blood as I wiggled down the tree and hit the ground. I started crawling since I couldn't walk on my ankle. Eight or ten hours later I found some of the other men."[3]

After the men regrouped they went to work training and unifying the local guerrillas into military brigades, each made up of hundreds of partisans. Tons of arms and ammunition were parachuted in, allowing the OG-led guerrillas to raid enemy garrisons and attack the highways. The force became a significant threat to the Germans, as corporal Chester Scerra remembers.

"It got to a point that we became wanted criminals by the Gestapo. We had a price on our head—dead or alive. We couldn't trust anyone and I remember trying to sleep with one eye open. Then we got a group photo; it was the stupidest thing we did. We were in a little town and this photographer was coming through. All 15 of us with our heavy clothing, machine guns, and beards. About a week later it was in the local newspaper. The photographer turned it in for a reward.

"But we did a lot of damage while we were out there. Every day was dangerous and they were really looking for us. We were always on the move, always on the run. We didn't know who would turn us in or help us. We would spot trains going in and out of Florence and radio the information back.

"We were in the mountains for about six months. We broke up the group so it would be harder for the Germans to find us. Six or seven of us were living in the attic of a house. We never had anything to eat; chestnuts, I remember eatin' lots of them. During the night we came across downed British pilots. The next morning the older woman who owned the house . . . hollered at us that a German patrol was coming; we rushed out the back door.

"I was carrying Fred Marchese, who had a terrible case of malaria. There was talk of leaving him behind because it was becoming very difficult to move around with him since we were always on the run. We all took turns carrying him, but he still thanks me for saving his life. Eventually, a British fighter dropped a belly tank with medicine that stabilized the malaria. We kept pushing forward and didn't look back but we heard the German machine-gun bursts. We didn't go back to find out what happened but I'm sure the old woman and her husband were lined up and murdered."[4]

German reprisals were swift. Captured guerrillas often had their eyes gouged out and were impaled on meat hooks in the village square. Captured OSS personnel did not fare much better. Orders were issued that captured commandos, even in proper military uniform, were to be shot on the spot. Eventually, German antipartisan operations became so heavy in the region that Walla Walla was forced to terminate the mission. During the winter of 1944, the 15-man OG team walked more than 100 miles south, avoiding numerous German patrols, to safety behind Allied lines.

The arrival of winter also diminished Allied command of the skies. Bad weather grounded Allied planes and halted the flow of supplies and air strikes. Accordingly, OSS directed the partisan groups to "lie low" for the winter.[5] The Germans took advantage of the lull by mounting counterattacks and mopping-up operations against the guerrillas.

To maintain the momentum of the guerrilla movement, additional OG teams parachuted into northern Italy. Team Aztec and Team Tacoma worked together in the Belluno area, not far from the Brenner Pass.

Over the next two months the teams armed and supplied the local guerrillas, and conducted operations against the Fascist and German forces in the area. The Germans countered the threat by bringing in thousands of additional troops. A collaborator told the German troops, commanded by SS Major Schroeder, the exact location of the OGs' hideaway, and on March 3, 1945 the Germans mounted a massive manhunt, known as a *rastrellamento*, to crush all organized resistance in the area.

Team Tacoma's radio operator, Oliver Silsby, vividly recalls the day the Germans launched the manhunt and a haunting incident that occurred a few days before it.

"It was very early in the morning. We were awakened by somebody running down there and saying the Germans are coming. We sort of got ourselves prepared and buried the radio, put straw on it and were just trying to figure out what to do when Benucci [leader of Team Aztec] and his two guys came by and said, 'Hey we got to get out of here.' Our escape route was over the mountains and supposedly the Germans were coming from that direction so we had to go down instead. Now we could see them coming down from the heights towards us. I didn't see that many of them in large numbers but you see one . . . it's like a cockroach, there a lot more out there! About 300 yards away from us. There were two or three or four. I didn't look anymore. Benucci said they were coming from where he came from, which was a path. We just stopped and started going down to the valley. There was a little stream down there. It was a steep slope from the valley into the stream. We slid down there and started running down this stream. The Germans were up ahead of us and behind us and there were shots all over the place. As we ran I was with Chappell and another guy and the Germans were in front of us shooting at us so we laid down in the stream and I had a carbine and I said, 'I'm going to shoot him, Captain.' Chappell said, 'Forget it, let's get the hell out of here.'"[6]

Captain Howard Chappell, a muscular ex–boxing champion and college football player of Prussian descent, led Team Tacoma. Before entering OSS, Chappell taught hand-to-hand combat to paratroopers at Fort Benning, Georgia. A natural leader, Chappell commanded OSS's German OG before he was picked to lead Team Tacoma. Chappell recalls running for his life and trying to save the lives of his teammates. "We moved down this creekbed in icy water, knee-deep, to keep from floundering in the snow drifts along the bank. There were five partisans, my five men, Benucci and I.

"We moved downstream about one kilometer and had almost broken through the ring encircling us, when from my position I noticed a machine gun being moved up over the crest of the hill. Fortunately, everyone but Silsby, Fabrega, Buchhardt, and I had gotten a short distance ahead around a curve. As the crew opened fire, both Silsby and Buchhardt seemed to be very tired. They were running like hell, but getting nowhere. I reached them and tried to help them some, gave them a quick pep talk, and we all reached the bend and temporary safety.

"Out of the corner of my eye, I had gotten a glimpse of Fabrega going down when the firing commenced. Waiting for a chance, I went back to see what had happened to him, but I was pinned down and couldn't find him. I cursed then, because he had gotten behind me, although I knew quite well that he was trying to protect me, in spite of the danger to himself.

"Moving down the creek another 400 yards I came upon Silsby and Buchhardt. The rest had dispersed up another creek that ran off at this point and had disappeared.

"Silsby was stretched out on the ground, apparently unconscious, and Buchhardt was trying to catch his breath and at the same time see if Silsby was injured and needed medical attention.

"As I moved to this point I saw two Jerries, both firing at Silsby and Buchhardt. One was only 30 yards from them and the other was about 100 yards away. I shouted, 'Kamerad!' a couple of times and then moved up a tributary about 10 yards with Buchhardt to a place where he could take over again. The last thing he said to me was, 'They are

going to get us now.' He was quite casual about it, but I am sure he
didn't feel casual!

"I went back to Silsby, who was still stretched out on the ground.
Strangely enough, he was not wounded, in spite of the short range the
two Jerries were firing from. Silsby is a long, lanky guy, and since it
was impossible to move him, I surrendered. I hoped at the time that as
soon as he was able to rest a little, we would be able to escape."[7]

Medic Eric Buchhardt remembers running for his life after seeing
Chappell and Silsby captured by the Germans.

"There was very heavy fire going on all this time, and so I moved
up the bank, found a hole in which to hide, and remained there. The
concealment was good because at least twenty Germans passed
within only a few feet of me, and I was not detected. Several minutes
later, however, one did spot me and came lunging at my hideout with
a fixed bayonet. I could not move more than a few inches, so I brought
up my knees to my waist to protect myself. The bayonet went between my knees. At this moment I grabbed the barrel of his gun and
pulled. As he tried to pull away from me, I let go. He fell over back-
wards giving me the time to get out of the hole to attack him. I dared
not shoot for fear of attracting attention, so I hit him over the skull
with the butt of my .45 over and over again. I am certain that he
wasn't living when I left him.

"I started to run up the valley when a partisan yelled to me that
there was a Jerry behind me, and a few feet away. I saw him. I made a
dash for a haystack about twenty feet from me and turned as I reached
it. At the same moment the Jerry who had followed me took a lunge
at me with the butt of his rifle striking me in the left ear. We scrapped
for several minutes, and I finally straddled him, again using the butt of
my .45 as my weapon. It was very effective, and after a little while I
left him and ran down the valley, found another hole in which to hide,
and dressed my wounds. My knee and ear were both bleeding now,
and I was very tired. I stayed in this hole till midnight at which time I

left it and went to a farm house to try to get some food and dry clothes."[8]

Chappell, Silsby, and eventually Salvadore Fabrega were captured by the Germans. However, Chappell was soon able to escape, as he recalls. "The two Jerries came in and disarmed me and ordered us to start walking. At this time I saw Fabrega again. It looked as though he was going to make an attempt to free us. Silsby was still too weak to walk and I had to support him. The area was crawling with other Germans, and I didn't want to draw their attention. I called out 'Raus' to Fabrega and he understood immediately and hid again. One of our guards became suspicious and began to look so we continued to move under the guard of one man only.

"Before surrendering myself, I had buried all my gold, hurriedly, and kept only a small amount of lira notes with me. As we moved along, I attempted to bribe the guard, offering him $5,000 if he would walk with us to a safe hiding place. I told him the war was almost over, his home probably destroyed, and of what he could do after the war with that much money, but he refused to listen. He [was] apparently getting nervous guarding us by himself, and attempted to get the attention of the other Jerries by yodeling. Each time he did so, I would yodel too, and he threatened to shoot us, but it served to make him stop attracting attention.

"When we walked about two kilometers, Silsby appeared to have recovered again, and I began looking for an opportunity to disarm the guard. He refused to come close enough for me to grab him, however. He had us covered with a pistol, and in his left hand he carried a potato-masher-type grenade, with a loop around his wrist. Not knowing whether or not the cord I saw was the detonation cord or not, I insulted the German grenades in general, while praising our own. He disagreed with me, showing me how the German grenade worked. I was then sure that the cord I saw was for carrying only.

"We reached a road that led to Trichiana, where I knew an SS garrison to be located. I realized by now that it would be impossible to disarm this wary Jerry, so I reached into my pocket and pulled [out] a little pistol known as a 'Stinger.' It is about as large around as a pencil, and not quite as long as a cigarette. He did not realize at first what it was until I threatened to shoot him if he did not drop his weapon. Unfortunately for us he did not lack courage, but just backed off about 20 yards, continued to keep me covered and threatened to shoot. The range of the Stinger is only two or three yards, so there was nothing I could do but throw it away, as it would not do to be found with it on my person.

"As we approached a house along the road I noticed a house with an open stable door and daylight through the other side. I told Silsby quietly, when we reached the house, to make a break through the stable and I would go around the house. When we were at the nearest point to the house, I made a break for it. I did not hear Silsby behind me and so I went through the stable door and down into a ravine in back of it. I moved down about two kilometers and ran into another group of Jerries. They fired a few shots at me, one of which ricocheted and hit me in the calf of my left leg. I moved away quickly and hid behind a snow bank from about 1200 hours [noon] until dark.

"After dark, I contacted a friend and learned that in addition to Silsby and Fabrega, five partisans had also been taken. One partisan, Brownie, had been captured while firing his BAR to cover the retreat of the rest of the mission. Later, we learned from villagers that he had been wounded and taken to San Antonio, where an SS officer had cut his hands off and gouged out his two eyes. Then they threw him on the pavement and one of the SS troops shot him.

"Through this friend, I learned that Captain Benucci was safe and sent a message to him. I also got an intelligence chain working to locate the rest of the mission. On the night of March 6, I got a pistol and ammo from a partisan family near Trichiana and went into town to see if it was possible to locate and liberate Silsby and Fabrega. A few

vigilant patrols made it difficult, and I failed to locate even the building they were held in. About 0300 [3:00 a.m.] on the 7th, I gave up and
moved about three kilometers to hide and sleep. I found 10 men hiding in this deserted stable, and they assured me that the Germans had
never come near the place. I lay down in the hay and fell asleep immediately. About 0600 [6:00 a.m.] one of the men woke me to say that a
German patrol was passing about 400 yards away. As they continued
on their way the civilians began laughing at their stupidity. Suddenly
our stable was caught in several bursts of fire! The civilians started
running out and I saw two go down and a few others were hit. I
waited inside to see where the fire was coming from, and then slid out
of the door and edged around the building. I backed right into a German who forced me to drop my pistol. What the Germans had done,
cleverly enough, was to send the patrol to draw our attention while
another group moved up behind the building. The soldier who caught
me started to march me to a knoll about 300 yards distant where their
commander, a lieutenant, waited. Between the two points it was necessary to cross a ravine. When we reached the ravine, I succeeded in
disarming the guard and in doing so I believe his neck was broken. I
then stuffed him in a culvert. The area was well covered with Germans. I estimated that there were about 70, although that figure is
purely a guess. It appeared impossible to hide from them, so I ruffled
my hair some and trying to look as German as possible (in English
battle dress!). I walked across a large snow-covered field, taking my
time though I wanted to run like hell. I was lucky and passed fairly
close to them without being questioned. I walked slowly into a house,
where I stayed for just a few minutes, and when an opportunity came
I moved out toward a creekbed, found an overhanging boulder, and
hid under it from about 0730 [7:30 a.m.] till dark. After dark I returned
to my informer near Morgan and learned the location of Buchhardt,
Delaini, and Ciccone. I sent a message to Buchhardt and told him to
sit tight and I would get him later. Meanwhile, I heard that Silsby had

escaped, but I also heard to the contrary and couldn't accept either story. I learned later that Silsby was supposed to be held in a schoolhouse in Trichiana. I went back into town but failed to get anything accomplished. I returned to the place where I had slept the night before but tried to sleep outside under cover. This was 8 March and the weather was still cold and the snow pretty deep. I fell asleep and awoke about 0800 [8:00 a.m.] to see three to four Jerries holding what I believe to be Belgian police dogs. They were near the stable where we had been surprised the morning before. I pulled out of my hiding place quickly and walked up a creek, keeping in the water for about three kilometers, and then hid again until dark that night. On the night of the 9th, I went back to Morgan where I learned that Fabrega had been sent to Belluno, but nobody knew of anything of Silsby. I stayed in Morgan, sleeping in a barn during the day, until March 11th, when it seemed impossible to do anything for Silsby. I also received word that Fabrega had been killed."[9]

In fact, Salvadore Fabrega and Oliver Silsby were both still alive, but captured by the Germans, as Fabrega remembers.

"I did see the Captain [Chappell] and Silsby being walked out of the valley under guard. I wanted to take a shot at the guard, but Captain Chappell must have seen me and yelled out to me to take off.

"The enemy kept firing at me and got as close as about twenty yards of me. There were too many for me to attempt to continue to fight them and perhaps in doing so, place the captain and Silsby in further danger while firing. Accordingly I surrendered to an SS lieutenant and a squad of six men. They escorted me to [their headquarters] in San Antonio in a school house there. There were about 100 soldiers and civilians herded together, each segregated from the other. They were trying to force the civilians to identify partisans they had already captured. They isolated me and sometime later took me into a room for interrogation. They applied electric wires to my tongue and ears and tried many other savage methods, such as beating me unexpectedly from somewhere in the circle they formed around me. They threatened to shoot me as a partisan if I did not speak freely. I kept insisting that I knew nothing but English. This continued for several hours at intervals and some time later I was sent by truck to Belluno. En route the truck stopped and Silsby was loaded into it. I surmised at this time that the captain must have escaped or was killed. Silsby and I managed to talk together, and we agreed to pretend that we were downed airmen."[10]

At the beginning of the German manhunt, most of the members of Team Aztec were hiding in a nearby house that was buried in snow. Nick Cantgelosi remembers the manhunt from his team's perspective.

"One of the guys goes out to take a leak and he sees movement on the crest of the hills. He becomes suspicious. He sees more movement on both sides of the crest and he runs back inside the house we were in and says, 'Tedesco!' meaning German in Italian and 'Rastrellamento,' they were surrounding us. The Germans came within several feet of our house and we could hear them talking in German, smoking and having a great time. Miraculously they passed the house which butted up against the side of a ravine. We couldn't be seen and we didn't know why. It snowed all night and apparently it covered the house and they couldn't see it as they were marching by. The house was buried in snow, thank God for that! At the time we didn't realize that so we decided we [would] try to make a run for it out one of the doors. One of the partisans tried to dash out the door when a guard came near the house and I whispered, 'Get back! Get back!' There were a hell of a lot more of them than us. We destroyed everything we could and hid it, we ripped everything we could to pieces. We waited until the last minute before destroying the radio, which had a self-destruct explosive on it. We needed the radio to communicate and it was the last thing to go.

"I held everyone back and I think it saved our lives. They were coming down the other side of the ravine and continuing to pass by the house. I would say that it was about a battalion [about 600 troops]. They started to search one of the other houses nearby; the house we slept in the night before. They went up to the haystacks and started to bayonet them. I was never more scared in my life. Sweat was dripping off my fingers on the trigger of my carbine [weapon]. I must have gained about 50 gray hairs and my throat was parched. That was fear and a memory that you carry with you. I was about to pull the trigger on the first one that came down but luckily I didn't. They knew my name. They knew my radio operator's name and they knew our officer's name. We all had prices on our heads.

"They didn't find us and they started climbing the other side of the ravine. They were led by a collaborator, that double-crossing son-of-a-bitch! Around six-thirty or seven o'clock that night Captain Benucci came through the door and he had blood all over him. His eyes were bright and large, filled with fright. He said, 'We got to get out of here.' He said to one of the partisans, 'Blackie, take 'em to the church.'

"Benucci left us. He went into hiding with a partisan woman we called 'Queenie.' Ten days later we met back up with him and he told us that he buried himself in a small hole in the side of the ravine and covered it with snow the day the Germans attacked.

"Meanwhile, Blackie led us into the attic of the local church. There was a trap door in the ceiling and they brought out a ladder. We stayed in the attic for about 10 days. We ate eggs, and a little pork, but mostly eggs. They would make a bird signal by whistling. We'd open up the trap door and lower a rope, and they put food in a basket. Everything was done by hand signals. We went back a few years ago and the bits of the egg shells were still there.

"There was nothing to do but sleep, eat, shit, and get dirty. We couldn't wash. We shit right on the floor on some hay. It stunk, let me tell you. There were cracks in the floor and some of the Germans even went to mass on Sundays and we could see them through the cracks in the floor in the pews below."[11]

Throughout the winter, *rastrellamentos* and a lack of supplies thinned the partisan ranks. But in the spring they reconstituted for the final Allied offensive, which began on April 1, 1945. Massive carpet bombing followed by artillery plastered the German lines. The bombardment was followed up on the ground by offensives spearheaded by the Fifth and Eighth Armies, who attempted to roll over the Alps into Austria. On April 5, in coordination with the offensive, about 50,000 Allied-led partisans attacked the Germans from the rear. Led by 75 OSS teams, the partisans blew up bridges, ambushed convoys, and cleared entire areas of Germans. The Germans could only move in heavily armed convoys, which were pounded by the Allied air corps.[12]

A few weeks after the start of the offensive, the Fifth Army and partisans captured the key city of Bologna. On the eastern side of Italy, the Eighth Army broke through the Argenta Gap, trapping a sizable German force before it could cross the Po River.

Bernie Knox was in command of a seven-man team operating in the Po Valley. Besides gathering intelligence and organizing partisans, Knox's team cut a road leading into the town of Modena. Several weeks before the attack, Knox's men conducted an eclectic variety of tasks, including escorting former German POWs through the lines.

"One of my most memorable experiences involved escorting a squad of fully armed Germans who had been recruited from the POW cages to work for us, through our lines. They were heavily armed with Schmeissers [MP-40 machine pistols] and when they pulled the bolts back with a resounding 'click' to put a round in the weapon I wondered if they were going to say to me, '*Sie müssen mit uns kommen* [You must come with us].' Luckily nothing happened. We took two lots through and most of them came back. Only a *Feldwebel* who had been with the Wehrmacht for 10 years didn't return. I suspect he turned himself in.

"Many of the prisoners were Austrians and they were hoping to get some kind of reward. But a lot of them seemed to be acting on genuine conviction."[13]

With the Allied offensive underway, OSS teams led the partisans in attacks to cut German escape routes north. Howard Chappell's Tacoma Team set up roadblocks to stem the Nazi retreat in the Belluno area, capturing a sizable German force.

"As our group neared the town, we dispatched scouts ahead on bicycles and the Germans came out to meet us. Our men, who had taken the high positions the night before, opened fire from their concealed positions. It soon became apparent that between the fire from this point and our roadblock that the enemy was pinned down. In spite of the large force they had, they too realized this and surrendered. The prisoners were marched to a large sanitarium, after we had disarmed them, and were placed under guard. On April 26, I moved with Ciccone near Serva, leaving the rest of the mission in charge of Sergeant Buchhardt. That night a large convoy was reported moving north from Agordo.

"We moved down the road and blew up a small bridge just north of Caprile, and set up a roadblock under the command of Ettore, the brigade commander. When the bridge was blown and the roadblock set, men were set to work preparing the material necessary to rebuild it for the Allies when they came.

"At this time I sent Quido, a partisan battalion commander, to set up a roadblock about eight kilometers to the south. He was also to prepare other civilians to take up German weapons against the enemy as fast as they were captured.

"We then sat back and waited for the Jerries to move into our trap, which they did on April 27, 1945.

"At this point a short description of the terrain is necessary in order to understand how small forces not only stopped but captured large numbers of the enemy.

"This area of which I write is well back in the Alps. The road, although it is a national highway, is narrow and tortuous. Many hairpin curves on very steep grades force traffic to a slow down to a point where it is barely moving. The roads in many places are cut into the mountainside so that it is impossible to leave the road to climb up or down. When we pinned the Germans down at these points, it was impossible for them to do more than one of two things: they could fight and die, or they could surrender. When the convoy had moved into the trap, they did both. As they reached our roadblock they tried to fight. One hundred thirty of them (SS troops) died in fifteen minutes, and the rest asked for a truce shortly afterwards."[14]

Fate was about to bring Chappell face-to-face with Silsby's and Fabrega's tormentor, SS Major Schroeder.

"Ironically, in making this truce, a Major Schroeder, who had commanded all SS troops and police organizations in Belluno, was included in the prey. Included, too, was his staff of officers and all his men. Schroeder was very Prussian looking, being tall with blue eyes and blond hair. At the time of the major's capture, he was carrying an American carbine taken from one of the partisans. Also included in the capture was a Captain Heim of the 504th Panzer Battalion, who represented about 600 men from the 26th Panzer Division. There were also 900 Todt [German construction and defense program] men represented by a captain whose name I do not recall.

"I didn't take my eyes off Schroeder and looking at him I remembered all the atrocities his men committed. Captured partisans hanging from meat hooks in public squares. British fliers shot eight times through the arms and legs, as he tried to get them to talk. After they gave up the ninth shot was in their head.

"We were asked our terms and I told them there were none, that they could surrender unconditionally, or be annihilated. Major Schroeder, then showing his customary pleasing character, told me that he had all civilians in Caprile in custody, and would kill them all if the convoy was not permitted to pass unharmed. He mentioned that they captured Fabrega and said they treated him well. I remembered how they tortured Fabrega with electrodes, but I didn't respond. I paused and I stated, 'If a single civilian was harmed in any way, we would accept no surrender from that time on.' All the commanders except Schroeder then agreed to surrender. We gave orders that the troops were to be reformed into organizations and all arms were to be placed in one place, along with trucks, material, etc. The commanders returned to their troops, and Schroeder, Sergeant Ciccone, and I went down to Caprile to talk with the remainder of the SS officers there. After a few very uncomfortable minutes in their midst, they decided to surrender.

"By evening of the 27th, all troops were disarmed and under guard. . . . Prisoners at this time numbered about 3,500 and with the material created quite a problem. I then placed Sergeant Buchhardt in charge of all prisoners and materials.

"On the morning of the 28th, German officers of the 504th Panzer and of other units requested to see me. They were very disturbed about being confined with SS and Police troops and asked to be segregated. I granted this request.

"After talking with them I called in Major Schroeder and other SS officers. We became quite friendly and even joked about how they had once captured me. We drank a little wine, and I learned the name of the spy who had disclosed my location prior to March 6. This man was later killed in an attempt to escape.

"We laughed about the fact that some of my equipment that had been captured was in his and some of his officers' possession. He told me at this time neither he nor any of his officers had ever committed any outrages and they regretted some of the brutalities that other Germans had committed.

"Before I left he told me that he was glad he surrendered to me because all of his staff felt I would treat them as they would have treated me, if they had the chance. All of them were killed that night trying to escape and they had some help from the partisans."[15]

Spurred on by the Allied military success, the CLNAI orchestrated a general uprising in the north, leading to the capture of Italy's industrial heartland cities of Genoa, Turin, and Milan. As the war was drawing to a close, the Italian campaign would ultimately end as it began in 1943, with OSS conducting behind-the-scenes negotiations to arrange a separate surrender in Italy.

NINETEEN

Final Missions
and Conclusion

Allen Dulles remembered Sunday, February 25, 1945, as a cold, sunless day. OSS's gentleman spy was dining on fresh trout at a small restaurant near Lake Lucerne with Max Waibel, his main contact with Swiss intelligence. Waibel informed Dulles that a visitor was trying to use Swiss intelligence to open a channel to OSS to discuss the surrender of the German forces fighting in northern Italy. It would prove to be one of the greatest OSS achievements of the war.

The visitor was a garrulous Italian baron and industrialist named Luigi Parilli. Parilli claimed that he was representing prominent Germans, including General Karl Wolff, the highest-ranking SS officer in the region. Dulles dispatched his right-hand man, Gero von Gaevernitz, to assess the situation. Peace feelers were nothing new, and Parilli was treated with suspicion.[1]

Five days later, two SS officers from Germany's northern Italian command appeared in Switzerland to open a dialogue with OSS. Dulles dispatched another aide, Paul Blum, to meet with the officers. To test the authenticity and goodwill of the German party, Dulles instructed Blum to request that the Germans hand over Ferrucia Parri, a senior anti-Communist partisan leader who had been captured by the Germans three months earlier, and Major Antonio Ushminiani, an OSS spy and resistance leader in German custody. Both men were high-profile prisoners whose release could only be arranged by the most senior German leadership in northern Italy.[2]

On March 8 the men were delivered to Switzerland by the SS, but Dulles was met with an even greater surprise. The prisoners were accompanied by General Wolff himself. The ensuing meeting marked the beginning of Operation Sunrise and talks between OSS and the German forces in northern Italy that eventually led to securing the surrender of Germany's forces in the region. In his report after the war, Dulles wrote: "Wolff gave the impression of a man of energy. He wasted no words and did not attempt to bargain for himself. He said he had committed no crimes and was willing to stand on his record. He did not dispute either the hopelessness of the German military position, or the fact that the German armies must surrender unconditionally. He said he was completely won over to the need for immediate action, and that he believed he could win over Kesselring [the overall German commander in Italy] to [the] plan and he would proceed immediately to try to do this." The next day, March 9, Wolff told Gero von Gaevernitz that "the time had come when some German with power should lead Germany out of the war to end useless material and human destruction, that he was willing to act and felt he could persuade Kesselring to join. . . ."[3]

Dulles informed the Allied high command of his discussions with Wolff and waited for their direction. Meanwhile Kesselring was appointed Wehrmacht commander of the western front. His replacement in Italy was General Heinrich von Vietinghoff, someone with whom Wolff had had only limited dealings. The SS general sent off a message to Dulles that he would need a few weeks to work on Vietinghoff.

Disposing of the German armies in northern Italy was a key factor in the overall Allied strategy. The threat of SS troops massing in the so-called National Redoubt in the Alps was forcing Eisenhower to divert troops away from the decisive battle on the Rhine. The Germans in Italy guarded the southern flank of the redoubt; their removal would remove the apparent threat. In reality, the redoubt was largely a myth, as information gathered by OSS agents in Bern and in the field revealed. But collectively, OSS failed to put all the pieces together and present it to the high command, so the myth endured. The surrender of so many enemy troops would strike a deep blow at Hitler's remaining faithful, myth or no myth.[4]

However, once Averell Harriman, the U.S. ambassador to Moscow, informed the Soviets that peace discussions in Italy were pending, the Soviets demanded direct participation. The U.S. Combined Chiefs rejected them and proposed that they only be observers. It was the wrong answer. The Sunrise discussions were a lightning rod, aggravating Stalin's fears of a separate peace. Over the next several weeks, terse cables went back and forth between Roosevelt and Stalin, including a sharply worded cable from Stalin who wrote: "[The German commander] has agreed to open the front and permit Anglo-American troops to advance to the East, and the Anglo-Americans have promised in return to ease for the Germans the peace terms." Eventually, Roosevelt maintained that no actual discussions had taken place and shot back, "I cannot avoid a feeling of bitter resentment toward your informers, whoever they are, for such a vile misrepresentation of my actions. . . ."[5]

Disrupting the alliance in April 1945 could have had grave consequences for the war against Germany and Japan, especially since the Soviets broke their peace treaty with the Japanese on April 5. Stalin responded by toning down his rhetoric. On the morning of April 12, FDR soft-pedaled the situation by calling it a "minor misunderstanding."[6] That very afternoon, the president, the creator of OSS, was dead.

Operation Sunrise meanwhile slowly crept forward, thanks to multiple meetings between Dulles and Wolff, who managed to win over Vietinghoff. However, at the end of April, the Combined Chiefs ordered Dulles to cease discussions immediately and break off contact with Wolff. Pressure from the Russians had finally hit home as the Truman administration refused to offend its ally.

Wolff took matters into his own hands. Accompanied by a few senior staff officers, he braved roving Allied fighter-bombers and partisans (OSS actually rescued Wolff from a partisan ambush that nearly cost him his life) and drove to Switzerland. The unexpected arrival of Wolff and his willingness to sign the unconditional surrender of his forces put the talks back on track. The Combined Chiefs authorized Dulles to accept the surrender of the German forces in northern Italy and Russian emissaries were invited to be present to calm Stalin's fears of a separate peace. Several German emissaries were flown to Allied headquarters in Caserta for the official signing ceremony. Gero von Gaevernitz describes what happened in their joint report: "The final meeting at which the instrument of surrender was signed took place shortly after fourteen hours [2:00 p.m.] on April 29. The German emissaries were obviously disturbed by the floodlights, and the clicking and grinding of cameras, which they had not expected. The instrument of surrender was signed by Lieutenant General Morgan for the Allies, and on the German side by Oberstleutnant von Schweinitz, signing for Vietinghoff, and Major Wenner signing for Wolff."[7]

With the conclusion of Sunrise on April 30, 1945, OSS secured the surrender of several hundred thousand German soldiers under arms more than a week before Germany's official surrender. It was a fitting final triumph for Donovan's men.

Indeed, if events had happened differently, they might have had one more shot at glory, in dramatic fashion. Before the Soviets overran Berlin, OSS Special Operations planned perhaps its most ambitious project of the war, Operation Cross. Cross called for the training of German nationals as mountain troops, who would penetrate the National Redoubt to assassinate Hitler and Himmler.

Nearly 100 German Communists or leftists interned in France were recruited, including several Loyalist veterans from the Spanish Civil War.[8] They planned to parachute into the redoubt and hunt for senior Nazis. They trained at a small manor house outside the French town of St. Germain-en-Laye, taking a crash course in parachuting, running, hiking, and night patroling. (In off hours, the Social Democrats played soccer against the Communists.) Their targets included "anyone wearing or having in his possession, the Golden Party Badge, the Order of Blood Medal, the Guerrilla Warfare Medal, or SS members . . . [who] should be disposed of without formality."[9]

On May 1 the orders were issued, beginning with an advance group parachuting into the drop zone the next day. Weather conditions delayed the jump—and then the Seventh Army overran Hitler's remaining territory, and shortly afterward the war ended. Political considerations helped influence Donovan to scrub the mission. With hints of a Cold War on the horizon, having nearly 100 armed German Communists under OSS control in Germany after the war ended was not worth the political risk.

Nonetheless, OSS agents played their part in the final days of the war in Europe. The five OSS agents inside Berlin at the end of the war felt the same fear and trepidation as native Berliners whose city was besieged by the Red Army. Block by block the city was falling to the Russians in some of the bloodiest fighting of the war. Some agents opted to wait to be overrun by the Soviets, while others attempted to break out. The Hammer Team's Tony Rah and Paul Land, who had parachuted into the suburbs of Berlin a few months earlier, chose to assist the Russians.

"On April 24 at 11 o'clock we saw the first Red Army men who were testing the area for defenses. We decided then to try to save a bridge from being blown. There were six of us. Phil, Phil's father, his brother-in-law, a neighbor who was the father's friend, and a half-Jewish boy of twenty who was a deserter.

"When we came to the bridge we found it still occupied by about thirty Wehrmacht men. We tried to talk them out of it, but they only crossed the bridge to the other side. The last two of them we dis-armed and took prisoners. With those rifles and an automatic rifle we had managed to get a day before we opened fire on the guards of the bridge. The Russian *grenatwerfer* [grenade launcher] gave a few rounds on the bridge. We had to pull back about a hundred yards, from where we continued to fire. Russian infantry then came around from the rear and took us for defenders, but stopped firing when we yelled and waved. They got the idea quickly and joined us. The bridge, however, blew up in spite of it. The two prisoners we had taken had already changed into civilian clothing. But the Russians let them go. They came and thanked us, rather ashamed. We did not forget to let them know what we thought about them. There was a lot of fraternizing then. Phil's father got a slip of paper on which a captain had written that the six men helped the Red Army. But they [the Soviets] 'frater-nized' with our Colts [pistols] as well, and 'liberated' our watches.

"On April 25 we went to the next Russian commander and re-ported as Americans. We were taken by jeep to a special detachment (counterespionage) where we gave the necessary information about our names and mission. We also handed over our local maps. The only question asked was whether we knew where Hitler was, but that we did not know.

They were not interested in any details about Berlin and its de-fense points, probably because of security. Our offer of assistance was not accepted. Because of experiences we had in the treatment of civil-ians, we thought it necessary to request the safeguard of some of our connections. Our request was refused and when we insisted, we were placed under strict arrest. We were then searched and our code books, the one-time pads, were found. They were the only important items we had not buried because we needed them up to the last minute. We had failed to destroy them in time. The Russian officers were rather cross that we had not handed them over voluntarily.

"We were with this unit from April 25 to June 16 when we were taken to the [American] 69th Division in Grisme near Leipzig."[10]

Youri Skarzynski, the White Russian who bravely crossed back into German lines in November and took a job with the SD in Berlin, was repeatedly denounced by people who worked around him. Nevertheless, Youri managed to survey every aspect of the SD, and make numerous contacts, including a woman named Maria Frankenstein who was a close friend of Hermann Göring, and high-ranking individuals in Himmler's headquarters. But with the Russians moving in from the east, he was trying to leave the city. "I had travel orders and a personal letter to the Polizei President of Erfurt, where I intended to cross the lines, knowing that the Third Army was in that sector. I also carried military identity papers. On the same day the Abwehr was evacuated to the south.

"Partly on foot, and partly hitch-hiking I made my way to Jena. On the way I met up with a group of officers who were returning to the front, and during the twenty-four hours I did not leave them, feeling more secure in their company than alone in a battle zone which was very closely controlled. My papers were in order, but a simple phone call to SD section in Berlin would have blown me completely. Therefore I had to remain very inconspicuous.

"Arriving in Jena on the morning of the 11th of April, I left my group of officers, and walked towards the Autobahn which led to Weimar, since no trains were running in that direction. I stopped a truck and got a ride to Weimar. The road was very difficult and we were continually attacked by Allied planes. I arrived at Weimar around midday but there was no means of transport in the direction of Erfurt since the road was constantly strafed by American planes. I therefore left on foot. I was continually stopped for verification of my papers, since my civilian status aroused suspicion, particularly since I was wearing military boots and breeches, and I was taken for a deserter. Nevertheless I had expressly kept these quasi-military clothes in order to support my military papers, and this was understood by the authorities. When I arrived at Erfurt, still on foot, I had no intention of presenting myself to the chief of police. I made enquiries and found that the Americans were encircling the town on all sides and [had put it] under artillery fire. I therefore left the town and crossed the fields in the direction of Nordpour and escaped from the trap which was closing around the town. For four hours I tramped the fields which developed into a battle ground for the small village of Kerspleben. By nightfall the Americans captured the village and continued on their way towards Weimar. Taking advantage of darkness, I entered Kerspleben and took refuge in a building containing French prisoners. I changed my clothes for English riding breeches. On the following day, not being able to make myself understood to an American officer, I bought a bicycle and started off in a northerly direction further to the rear of the American lines.

"About thirty kilometers farther on, recognizing the insignia of the Third Army, I arrived at the CP by following the markers. I showed my German papers and explained my case."[11]

Many miles farther south in Innsbruck, Fred Mayer of the Greenup mission was in the clutches of the Gestapo. Mayer's impressive string of intelligence coups would soon be crowned by arranging the surrender of the city of Innsbruck, but at the moment he found himself hanging upside down in a small cell.

"The beating started when I got to the headquarters. At first they tried to be polite. Then at one point they brought in another agent they captured and that jerk said, 'Okay, Fred, you better tell them everything. They already know.' That's when they started beating me because I refused to talk. They hit me, then stuck a pistol in my mouth and knocked out all my teeth. The more they hit me the less inclined I was to talk. I figured they were going to kill me anyways. I figured that if I could hold out for at least three days my people could get away and I did. They hung me upside down, took all my clothes, punctured my eardrums, stuck my head in a pail of water. I would come up gasping for breath.

"One of the torturers was a little man. I could have choked him with one hand. He was pretty vicious. He looked like he was enjoying it. He looked more tired than I was. The other ones were only interrogators. He was picked up after the war and sent to Nuremberg and then was freed because of lack of evidence. They couldn't find me even though I was working for the State Department! He got off scot-free!

"At one point Dr. Primbs [the top Nazi Party official for the area] was present and he told them, 'The man is unconscious, let him down.' A big guy in an SS uniform tried to break my instep with his boot but I pulled my foot away. After a while you don't feel anything. You are numb with pain. All I was thinking was that I wasn't going to talk because as long as I didn't talk they would keep me alive. The other OSS agent they captured talked and told Primbs that I was a high-ranking OSS agent that they could work with to save their own skins.

"They put me in an enclosure with no heat, no clothes and the guard was an older forced-labor Austrian. He offered me part of his sandwich and gave me his handkerchief to wipe off my penis which was bloody.

"The Gauleiter Franz Hofer [political governor of the region] wanted to meet me so Dr. Primbs took me over to the gauleiter's office. They cleaned me up and even gave me a pair of pants and a jacket and they wined and dined me.

"I remember them saying, 'Well, you may as well admit [it,] we know who you are.' There was one guy there who had been consul general of Germany in California and he said, 'If you tell me, I'll pass on your information.' I thought it might be a trick to reveal my other teammates but Ambassador Rahn, who was at the table, spoke up and said he was traveling to Bern, Switzerland and would deliver any message I wanted to deliver to Allen Dulles. The message I sent was that I am still in the hands of the Gestapo, but don't worry about me that I'm not that bad off and I expect to get out one way or another.

"I got the message out and discussed the deal. Hofer was still determined to make an appeal for a final stand.

"Next, they transferred me to a concentration camp at Reichenau. I was there less than a day. I came in one door and out the other. Dr. Primbs had arranged for me to slip out of the labor camp and his driver picked me up.

"Primbs took me back to Hofer's office. He wasn't sure what he wanted to do. I told him, 'There was no chance, why destroy Innsbruck? You have nothing to gain.'[12]

"We had another dinner meeting with Hofer. I told Hofer it was insane to make a last resistance and if you care at all for Innsbruck and this lovely city and all that, why do you want to destroy it all? You haven't got a chance. He saw my point. It took about 20 minutes to convince him. I told Hofer that I was willing, I'll take you prisoner of war. After a lot of soul-searching, Hofer agreed to make a surrender offer and declare Innsbruck an open city.

"I needed a way to get the agreement I reached with Hofer back to the outside world and OSS. I told Primbs about Hans [the Greenup radio operator] and we set out to find him in the nearby town of Oberperfuss. I went up to the village and got Hans.

"We had another dinner and Hofer told us that he gave the order for unconditional surrender of the city. He later went on the radio and urged no further resistance and announced Innsbruck's surrender. Next, I put Hofer under house arrest and Hans in charge of the regular police, who were working for me, and he secured Hofer's compound.

"From there I went through the lines to meet the U.S. 103rd Division. I was in Primbs's car with a bedsheet for a white flag. I went about 20 kilometers. There were German tanks and all kinds of artillery on the side of the road but none of it being activated. Nobody stopped me.

"I finally reached American lines. The MP [military police] that greeted me was confused, I was wearing pieces of an American uniform. I saluted and identified myself as Lieutenant Mayer of the OSS. He didn't believe me at first. I told him I was from intelligence and I needed to see the G-2. He took me to Major West and Major West got permission from General McAuliffe (the former assistant division commander of the 101st who retorted 'Nuts' when asked for the division's surrender during the Battle of the Bulge) to go with me through the lines and arrange for Innsbruck's surrender on May 3, 1945."[13]

A few days later, on May 7, 1945, at a redbrick schoolhouse at Rheims, General Alfred Jodl signed Germany's surrender. After the capitulation, OSS was assigned to help clean up Germany. X-2 and other OSS units hunted former Nazis and snuffed out postwar remnants of Nazi organizations. Special units tracked looted art and performed the tedious yet necessary duty of tracking German funds and physical wealth in neutral countries or some places in South America. OSS played a leading role in the Nuremberg war crimes trials.

Another issue of paramount importance to the Allies was Germany's secret weapons programs. German scientists pioneered V-2 rockets, guided rockets, and the latest jets; both the Soviet Union and the Allies wanted their expertise. OSS teams actively sought out the weapons and scientists. Personnel from the Simmons Mission, which had conducted operations in Greece to capture the German glider bomb, now were actively engaged in seizing the Reich's wonder weapons and the scientists who had created them. Major H. J. Rand's report was declassified 55 years after the end of the war: "I proceeded to Stuttgart and Dachau. Two interesting television tubes and laboratory details were discovered at Dachau in a boxcar being looted by slave workers. Samples of the anti-aircraft radio controlled rocket (Henschel) were discovered. . . . We proceeded from Dachau to Munich and Berchtesgaden. A sample of a television camera for guided missiles was obtained in a secret laboratory near Berchtesgaden."

Simmons also raced to determine how much the Germans knew about the American proximity fuse, a device that caused antiaircraft shells to explode when the shell came near an airplane. OSS wanted to find out if the Germans passed countermeasures and technical information on the top-secret fuses to the Japanese. After interrogating several scientists, Rand found out that Dr. Carl Mueller, an important German scientist, was trapped in a German-controlled pocket deep behind Russian lines.

"Captain Hoarth [SO officer] arranged to take a jeep and two German prisoners of war dressed in American uniforms to do this job. Seibert, G-2, Twelfth Army Group, concurred providing, if caught, Captain Hoarth state to the Russians he was on a private joy ride and not claim official business." The mission was a success and five days later Hoarth delivered Dr. Mueller to OSS. Mueller, later dubbed an "invaluable find," provided details on Germany's atomic research.[14]

While the OSS shadow war against Germany had come to an end, a new shadow war was beginning. OSS intensified its efforts to gather intelligence on the Soviet Union. The Cold War was in its infancy and a pared-down OSS started running intelligence missions against the Soviets. Dick Cutler, the Berlin X-2 station chief, reveals the race to save Nobel Prize winner Otto Hahn from capture by the Russians. "Most Germans hated the Russians, feared them after they saw what they did in Berlin. They did not hate the Americans equally; they would often volunteer information. One volunteer was a driver for a German Communist cell used by the Soviets to kidnap physicists that they wanted in Russia for the atomic bomb. They would give us the names of their next targets. I would send the names of the next target to Washington and they went to the Manhattan Project and asked, 'Does this German know enough to be important?' They would determine if he was important and if he was we were to frustrate the kidnapping. If he wasn't you'd let the kidnapping proceed since you didn't want to let them know there was a mole in their operation; you can't overplay your hand or you kill your source. In this case the Manhattan Project said, 'God' when the Nobel Prize winner for chemistry came in. He had been offered, we were told, a contract by Stalin for 100,000 American dollars a year to go to the Crimea and work in a wonderful laboratory; he turned it down. He lived in the British zone. They wanted to go in and capture him and give him work without the benefit of [free] will. He lived in a rural area, heavily forested, maybe 10 miles from the Soviet zone and the British zone border. They found a friend of his and had the friend say he'd love to come down and have a picnic with him and name a place in the forest in the British zone so this guy wouldn't feel insecure. We learned of this plan enough in advance that we could act. I went to the British major who was my counterpart in Berlin and asked him if he could help. The British arranged for a way to have them all arrested in a car without appearing that we had a tip as to who they were. So they arrested people all over the place. The British then went and captured the guy before he went on the picnic."[15]

OSS's learning curve was accelerated by Allen Dulles, who delivered one of OSS's last great intelligence coups. Dulles received information through his top agent, Fritz Kolbe, that 40-year-old General Reinhard Gehlen, who controlled an entire Wehrmacht intelligence unit directed against the Russians, wanted to work for the United States. Gehlen had on microfilm a complete set of his unit's records and a bumper crop of information about the inner workings of the NKVD and Soviet espionage. Soon Gehlen's men were housed in an OSS compound in Frankfurt and many of his former agents were working behind Russian lines for the U.S. In one fell swoop, Gehlen provided the United States with a working Russian intelligence unit that would have taken years to build from scratch.[16]

Alas, OSS's successes were overshadowed by politics at home. In the fall of 1944, at the request of the White House, Donovan submitted a proposal for a permanent "central intelligence service." The top-secret proposal was leaked to Walter Trohan of the *Chicago Tribune,* who dubbed the proposed agency a "super Gestapo agency." J. Edgar Hoover was the most immediate suspect for the leak, since he had the means, access, and motive (to eliminate a rival intelligence agency). Years after the war the CIA's chief historian, Thomas Troy, asked Trohan who his source was for the leak. The revelation was stunning: it was the president's press secretary, Steve Early, who told Trohan in 1945 that "FDR wanted the story out." The fallout from the article forced the White House to shelve the plan.[17] It was revived in April 1945, but the president's sudden death buried the plan again—until the CIA finally rose from the ashes of the OSS in 1947.

OSS always had its enemies at home, and in some cases, for good reason. Just before the end of the war it emerged that Stalin's NKVD had penetrated into OSS from its earliest days. OSS's X-2 branch did a yeoman's job of hunting German agents, and the Germans never penetrated OSS headquarters. But X-2 was not focused on the Soviets. Several OSS personnel passed important secrets directly to the Russians. The most prominent Soviet agent was Duncan Lee, who had worked for Donovan's law firm before the war. Donovan recruited Lee to be his executive assistant, and through this sensitive position Lee was privy to some of the organization's most important secrets. By 1944, Lee had become paranoid that he was going to get caught so he broke off contact with the NKVD, yet great damage had already been done.[18] Several sensitive operations had been revealed, including OSS peace feelers in Hungary and Bulgaria. Lee was hardly alone.

NKVD agents and other OSS personnel, some of whom were loyal Communists, willingly passed information on to the Soviets. In February 1945, a series of congressional hearings probed into suspected Communists in the OSS. OSS managed to escape the hearings relatively unblemished, but a cloud of suspicion remained.[19]

The new administration did not want the political baggage of an "American Gestapo." President Truman issued Executive Order 9621, which officially disbanded OSS on September 30, 1945. Two of OSS's operational arms, X-2 and SI, were transferred to a new organization called the Strategic Services Unit (SSU). The "chairborne" scholars of R&A went to the State Department.

OSS is often dismissed by historians as having been of little importance to the Allied war effort. Could the Allies have won the war without OSS? Very likely. But a balanced assessment of the agency's substantial achievements should conclude that the OSS shortened the war, and in the process saved the lives of thousands of Allied combat soldiers.

Thousands of reports were generated by the pathbreaking R&A division on everything from German tank production to the Reich's industrial capacity. R&A's Enemy Objectives Unit (EOU) helped pioneer strategic bombing analysis while extensive information gathered by OSS agents on the ground also contributed to the degradation of Germany's fuel industry.

In North Africa, OSS provided crucial intelligence for the Torch landings and undercut Vichy resistance. OSS helped subdue the significant Axis garrisons on Sardinia and Corsica with handfuls of men, allowing Allied troops to focus on other theaters. At Anzio, OSS agents pinpointed the date and location of German attacks that could potentially have overrun the beachhead had they not been anticipated.

Some of the best human intelligence was gathered by Allen Dulles and his office in Bern, which, through star agents like Fritz Kolbe, uncovered crucial information on German diplomatic efforts and war plans.

OSS operators in the Mediterranean pinned down numerous German divisions. In Greece in particular, the Germans paid a very heavy price as they withdrew north toward the Reich. Even the failed Sparrow Mission to Hungary drew German divisions from the front, degrading their operational effectiveness for the Normandy invasion.

In France, OSS's Jed, OG, and SO teams helped mobilize the Resistance, engaging thousands of German soldiers behind the main lines, and seriously interfering with the ability of the German army to move troops to the beaches during the crucial early days of the campaign. As the campaign in France unfolded, agents provided crucial tactical and strategic intelligence.

OSS provided the bulk of the intelligence for the invasion of southern France, pinpointing German defenses, supply depots, and order of battle information, helping make Dragoon one of the most successful Allied landings of the war.

In northern Italy, OSS created one of the most effective resistance movements of the war, tying down thousands of German soldiers, while behind the scenes the Sunrise negotiations effected the surrender of hundreds of thousands of troops six days before the official end of the war.

OSS effectively helped deceive the German high command during the Battle of the Bulge, enabling Patton's Third Army to smash the southern shoulder of the Bulge and doom the last great German offensive of the war to failure.

As the war drew to a close, OSS anticipated a need to gather intelligence on the Soviet Union. Allen Dulles's recruitment of General Gehlen and his anti-Soviet intelligence network saved America years of development time. Even General Eisenhower would declare,

"[OSS's contribution] has been so great that there should be no thought of its elimination."[20]

Of the roughly 13,500 personnel on the rolls of the Office of Strategic Services at the end of the war, only a tiny fraction served in the field. When one considers that the size of an average American infantry division in WWII was about 14,000 soldiers, this record of a few thousand men and women agents, operatives, and saboteurs is impressive. Did any single American infantry division (or regiment, when one considers the size of OSS's actual force in the field) contribute more to the final victory than did OSS?

OSS may have made its greatest contribution, not to winning World War II, but to winning the Cold War. OSS put an end to the shibboleths of "gentlemanly" intelligence that had reigned in the United States, and replaced them with a new paradigm: a democracy had to fight fire with fire and turn totalitarian weapons against the totalitarians. Even the recent American victories in Afghanistan and Iraq demonstrate the effectiveness of irregular warfare. As one CIA official close to the war on terror aptly put it, "What we are doing is all OSS."

In less than four years OSS developed from a fledgling amateur spy agency into an intelligence organization on par with its British counterparts. In the process, OSS pioneered many of the methods used in modern spycraft. Shadow-war strategies and tactics were created in most cases overnight and often from scratch. The agency was not averse to attempting new techniques, or afraid to fail in order to win. It fit into Donovan's mantra: "If you fall, fall forward." OSS was filled with risk takers, and as legendary citizen spy Fred Mayer put it, "If you don't risk you don't win."[21]

Donovan had a knack for recruiting the best men and women. His freewheeling, imaginative, bold agents created a record, though flawed at times, that speaks for itself, now that most of it has finally been released to the public.

On Sunday, February 8, 1959, Donovan passed away. At his side was his Dominican-robed brother, who administered last rites. When President Eisenhower heard the news he is said to have remarked: "We have lost the last hero." The heroes of the OSS are all slowly fading away but their legacy remains.[22]

Notes

PROLOGUE

1. Author interview with René Joyeuse, and his original mission report. Joyeuse used a radio and a special ground-to-air phone known as a Klaxton. His reports on the oil refinery and V-1 factory occurred over a period of several days.

2. Michael Warner, "Office of Strategic Services: America's First Intelligence Agency" (Washington, D.C.: CIA Public Affairs Office, 2000), p. 2.

3. "Commander John Riheldaffer to Special Intelligence Section ONI," National Archives (hereafter NA): Record Group 38, Box 1.

4. Norman Polmar and Thomas Allen, *Spy Book: The Encyclopedia of Espionage* (New York: Random House, 1997), p. 606.

5. Thomas F. Troy, *Donovan and the CIA* (Frederick, Md.: University Publications of America, 1981), pp. 10, 15.

6. Christopher Andrew, *For the President's Eyes Only: Secret Intelligence and the American Presidency from Washington to Bush* (New York: HarperCollins, 1996), p. 96.

7. The president's decision was heavily influenced by several letters written by William Donovan that outlined the concepts of the COI.

8. Troy, *Donovan and the CIA*, p. 423.

9. Richard Dunlop, *Donovan: America's Master Spy* (New York: Rand McNally, 1982), p. 102.

10. "The Army-Navy-FBI Agreements of 1942," NA: Record Group 226, Entry 146, Box 19.

11. "OSS Organization and Function" (June 1945), NA: Record Group 226, Entry 141, Box 4; "History," NA: Record Group 226, Entry 99, Box 75.

12. Dunlop, *Donovan: America's Master Spy*, p. 276.

13. OSS, *Assessment of Men: Selection of Personnel for the OSS* (New York: Rinehart & Company, 1948), p. 10.

CHAPTER 1. SPY SCHOOL

1. "OSS Training School History," NA: Record Group 226, Entry 99, Box 100.

2. William Stephenson, *A Man Called Intrepid* (New York: Harcourt Brace Jovanovich, 1976), p. 16.

3. Author interview.

4. Fairbairn is quoted from a script he wrote for an OSS training film called *Gutter Fighting.* NA: Record Group 226, Entry 90, Box 11.

5. Applegate, Rex, *Kill or Get Killed* (Boulder: Paladin, 1976), p. 97.

6. Author interview.

7. Author interview.

8. Author interview.

9. Roosevelt, *War Report of the OSS,* Volume I, pp. 223–24. This is an official history of the OSS produced by former OSS personnel shortly after the war. The study remained classified for decades.

10. Author interview. The official report of the action was also consulted. Source: author's collection.

11. As the war progressed, SI training school was conducted at nearby Area E.

12. Author interview.

13. Author interview.

14. Author interview.

15. Author interview.

16. Author interview.

17. Author interview.

18. "OSS Assessment Program, Attachment A" was used to supplement Buster and Kippy's dialogue. NA: Record Group 226, Entry 99, Box 102.

19. John Waller, *The Unseen War in Europe* (New York: Random House, 1996), p. 217.

20. Author interview.

21. Author interview.

22. "OSS Assessment Program, Attachment A" was used to supplement Buster and Kippy's dialogue. NA: Record Group 226, Entry 99, Box 102.

23. Robin Winks, *Cloak and Gown* (New York: William Morrow, 1987), p. 203.

CHAPTER 2. R&D AND "THE CAMPUS"

1. Stanley Lovell, *Of Spies and Stratagems* (Englewood Cliffs; N.J.: Prentice-Hall, 1963), p. 17.

2. Ibid, p. 39.

3. Author interview.

4. Author interview.

5. Lovell, *Spies and Stratagems,* p. 56.

6. Roosevelt, *War Report of the OSS,* Volume I, p. 159.

7. The TD report was recently declassified. The report is also rare documentary evidence that the OSS worked with the Mafia in Sicily. NA: Record Group 226, Entry 210, Box 361.

8. The OSS was ahead of its time in pursuing weapons of mass destruction. NA: Record Group 226, Entry 210, Box 361.

9. Lovell, *Spies and Stratagems,* p. 84.

10. OSS use of R&A was pathbreaking and provided structured methodology for analysis of data and information, compared to other spy agencies around the world at that time.

11. Winks, *Cloak and Gown,* p. 61.

12. "History of the Current Intelligence Staff," NA: Record Group 226, Entry 99, Box 76.

13. "Langer to Donovan," NA: Record Group 226, Entry 1, Box 1.

14. The source of this account comes from the CIA's OSS Oral History Project. Multiple accounts, mainly from high-level officers, are located at NA in CIA Record Group 263, Boxes 1–4. Since this book is an "agent-level" history, I found the material to be of marginal value; nevertheless, it is an important resource for other works on OSS.

15. "CIA OSS Oral History Project," interview with Charles Kindelberger, pp. 22–23, NA: Record Group 263, Boxes 1–4.

16. Winks, *Cloak and Gown*, p. 88. NA: Record Group 226, Entry 1, Citations: Alexander to Preston E. James, May 26, 1945.

17. Geoffrey Perret, *Winged Victory* (New York: Random House, 1998), p. 367.

18. "CIA OSS Oral History Project," interview with Walter Rostow, NA: CIA Record Group 263, Box 3. Also see Chalou, *The Secrets War*, pp. 49–50, for an additional account from Rostow.

CHAPTER 3. INTRIGUE IN NORTH AFRICA AND IBERIA

1. "Brousse to Admiral Leahy," NA: 701.511/1130 to 10-644, Record Group 59, Box 1843.

2. Personal Secretary's File Subject File "Vichy Material," FDR Library, Hyde Park, N.Y. The Donald Downs quotation on Ricardo Sicre was obtained from the author's interview with Betty Lussier, Sicre's wife.

3. Lovell, *Cast No Shadow*, p. 155.

4. H. Montgomery Hyde, *Cynthia* (New York: Ballantine Books, 1965), p. 151.

5. Ibid., p. 154. The full value of Cynthia's efforts will never be known, and evidence exists to indicate that British codebreakers cracked the Vichy naval codes prior to the break-in.

6. Winks, *Cloak and Gown*, p. 182.

7. Dunlop, *Donovan: America's Master Spy*, p. 369.

8. "Torch Anthology: My Part in the OSS Operations During that Period, 'Carleton Coon's Diary'" (May 1942 to May 1943), NA: Record Group, 226, Entry 99, Box 49. Coon kept the most complete and well-written diary of any agent in North Africa. It is preserved, in its entirety, at the National Archives in a collection of other personal accounts dubbed the "Torch Anthology."

9. "Clark to Eisenhower, Operation Lonmay Number 85" (October 1942), United Kingdom Record Office, HS 3/63.

10. Mark Clark, *Calculated Risk* (New York: Harper & Brothers, 1950), p. 84.

11. "Torch Anthology: Gordon Browne's Story," NA: Record Group 226, Entry 99, Box 49, pp. 1–9.

12. Darlan's intervention resulted in a cessation of fire on November 8 and a more general cease-fire two days later. A provisional settlement occurred on November 13.

13. Jay Jakub, *Spies and Saboteurs: Anglo-American Collaboration and Rivalry in Human Intelligence Collection and Special Operations, 1940–1945* (New York: St. Martin's Press, 1999), p. 73.

14. Winston Churchill, *The Hinge of Fate*, Volume 4 of *The Second World War* (London: Reprint Society, 1954), p. 159.

15. "Torch Anthology: My Part in the OSS Operations During that Period, 'Carleton Coon's Diary'" (May 1942 to May 1943), NA: Record Group 226, Entry 99, Box 49.

16. Ibid.

17. Author interview with Milt Felsen, who is in his nineties and still sharp as a tack. Felsen is the last surviving OSS field agent who was behind the lines in North Africa.

18. "Torch Anthology: My Part in the OSS Operations During that Period, 'Carleton Coon's Diary'" (May 1942 to May 1943), NA: Record Group 226, Entry 99, Box 49.

19. Author interview.

20. Bradley F. Smith, *The Shadow Warriors* (New York: Basic Books, 1983), p. 156.

21. Clark, *Calculated Risk*, p. 143.

22. "Torch Anthology: My Part in the OSS Operations During that Period, 'Carleton Coon's Diary'" (May 1942 to May 1943), NA: Record Group 226, Entry 99, Box 49.

23. Ibid.

24. "SI History of the Med USA Mission by O. C. Doering" (10/10/45), NA: Record Group 210, Box 313.

25. "Sicre: 'Operation Banana,'" NA: Record Group 226, Entry 136A, Box 2.

CHAPTER 4. UP THE BOOT

1. Quoted from Dunlop, *Donovan: America's Master Spy,* p. 399.

2. Quoted from Anthony Cave Brown, *Secret War Report of the OSS,* p. 190. Refer to the TD report in chapter 2 of this book for further documentary evidence. Material on the Mafia involvement with OSS was also exposed in congressional hearings during the 1950s.

3. "San Fratello Mission Report," NA: Record Group 226, Entry 99, Box 39.

4. "Bourgoin Report," NA: Record Group 226, Entry 210, Box 72.

5. Ibid.

6. Author interview.

7. "McGregor Papers," NA: Record Group 226, Entry 179, Box 286. The code name is spelled numerous ways in other publications. I chose the spelling in the official documents.

8. Ibid.

9. Obolensky's report can be found in NA: Record Group 226, Entry 144, Box 11. Also see Albert Garland and Howard Smyth, *Sicily and the Surrender of Italy* (Washington, D.C.: Center for Military History, 1965), pp. 258–61.

10. Ibid.

11. Ibid.

12. Ibid, p. 3.

13. M. R. D. Foot, *SOE in France* (London: Her Majesty's Stationery Office, 1966), p. 187.

14. Author interview. Additionally, the commanding general in that region of Italy who issued the final order to execute the Ginny team was tried for war crimes after the war and was executed.

15. Originally the mission was planned to be executed before the Anzio landings, but a number of issues delayed it.

16. Patrick K. O'Donnell, *Beyond Valor* (New York: Free Press, 2001), p. 81.

17. Carlo D'Este, *Fatal Decision: Anzio and the Battle for Rome* (New York: Harper-Collins, 1991), p. 7.

18. The author briefly spoke with Peter Tompkins but the text comes from Tompkins's wartime diary that is located at the National Archives in Record Group 226, Entry 99, Box 47.

19. Ibid.

20. Ibid.

21. Chalou, *The Secrets War,* p. 154.

22. Martin Blumenson, *Salerno to Cassino* (Washington, D.C.: Government Printing Office, 1969), p. 393.

23. D'Este, *Fatal Decision,* p. 306.

24. "Peter Tompkins Diary," NA: Record Group 226, Entry 99, Box 47.

25. Ibid.

26. The Italian portion of Berg's OSS mission was code-named Shark and had links to John Shaheen, who reported directly to Donovan in the OSS's Special Projects Office. Berg later went to Switzerland with the assignment of tracking down Werner Heisenberg, the leading scientist working on Germany's atomic bomb project. Berg's mission was to determine what Heisenberg knew and assassinate him if necessary. Based on limited information and a few questions that Berg asked Heisenberg and another scientist code-named "Flute," Berg determined that Heisenberg was not a threat and let him go. History would later prove that Berg was right and that the Nazis were far behind the Allies in the development of the atomic bomb.

27. Author interview.

28. "Peter Tompkins Diary," NA: Record Group 226, Entry 99, Box 47.

CHAPTER 5. ON HITLER'S DOORSTEP

1. Dulles ran perhaps the best OSS network in Europe. Recently declassified notebooks shed even greater light on the depth of his work, which included hundreds of agents and sub-agents.

2. "Telegram December 30, 1943," NA: Record Group 226, Entry 134, Box 274.

3. David Kahn, *Hitler's Spies* (New York: Macmillan, 1978), p. 344.

4. "The Story of George," NA: Record Group 226, Entry 190C, Box 7.

5. "Dulles Telegram Dated June 24, 1943," NA: RG 226, Entry 134, Box 307.

6. Roosevelt, *War Report of the OSS,* Volume II, p. 262.

7. "Berg to 106: AZUSA," NA: RG 226, Entry 90, Box 7.

8. Duke's report on Sparrow is located at NA: Record Group 226, Entry 99, Box 42.

9. "Telegram Dated January 29, 1944." This cable further describes the German resistance group "Breakers." NA: Record Group 226, Entry 210, Box 228.

10. Joseph Persico, *Piercing the Reich: The Penetration of Nazi Germany by Secret Agents During WWII* (New York: Barnes & Noble Books, 1979), p. 52.

11. This is not the first time the State Department's code was broken. During the early part of the war the Finish intelligence service broke several State Department codes. The problem was uncovered by OSS Sweden and State revised the codes.

12. "Dulles Telegram January 29, 1944," NA: Record Group 226, Entry 210, Box 228.

CHAPTER 6. INTO THE BALKANS

1. "Report from Captain Walter Mansfield" (March 1, 1944), NA: Record Group 226, Entry 99, Box 50.

2. Yugoslavia was garrisoned by roughly 15 Axis divisions and over 100,000 occupation troops. German troop strength in Italy varied, depending on the time period.

3. "Report from Captain Walter Mansfield" (March 1, 1944), NA: Record Group 226, Entry 99, Box 50.

4. The "live and let live" policy was coined and defined by David Martin in *The Web of Disinformation: Churchill's Yugoslav Blunder* (New York: Harcourt Brace Jovanovich, 1990). Martin describes the difference between "accommodations," which both sides practiced from time to time with the Germans, and outright collaboration.

5. Years after the war several high-ranking members of SOE operations were suspected of being Communists. An entire book by David Martin is devoted to the subject: *The Web of Disinformation*.

6. "Churchill to Roosevelt" (1 April 1944); and "Roosevelt to Churchill" (8 April 1944), Walter Kimball, *Churchill and Roosevelt: The Complete Correspondence*, Volume III (Princeton, N.J.: 1984), pp. 79–82.

7. "Alum Team Report by Wuchinich," NA: Record Group 226, Entry 99, Box 36.

8. Ibid.

9. Ibid.

10. "Gilly Report," NA: RG 226, Entry 99, Box 36.

11. Francis Loewenheim, ed., *Roosevelt and Churchill: Their Secret Wartime Correspondence* (New York: Saturday Review/Dutton, 1975), p. 482.

12. Anthony Cave Brown, *Secret War Report of the OSS,* pp. 276–77.

13. Author interview.

14. "Alum Team Report by Wuchinich," NA: Record Group 226, Entry 99, Box 36.

15. Ibid.

16. Author interview.

17. Author interview.

18. Author interview.

19. Author interview.

20. Author interview; Smith's wartime report was also consulted.

21. Author interview.

22. Author interview.

23. Author interview.

24. "Factual and Chronological Report by E. R. Kramer," NA: Record Group 226, Entry 99, Box 42.

25. Author interview.

26. Author interview.

27. Franklin Lindsay, *Beacons in the Night: With the OSS and Tito's Partisans in Wartime Yugoslavia* (San Francisco: Stanford University Press, 1993), p. 328.

CHAPTER 7. "SMASHEM"

1. "Report of the Simmons Mission: Lt. Nikoloas Sotiriou," NA: Record Group 226, Entry 99, Box 55. "Establishment and Organization of the Greek SI Section," NA: Record Group 226, Entry 99, Box 55.

2. Ibid.

3. "OSS History of the Cairo Office: Planta Agreement," NA: Record Group 226, Entry 99, Box 55. "Noah's Ark Plan," NA: Record Group 226, Entry 99, Box 56.

4. Elements of seven divisions were stationed in Greece during the first half of 1944.

5. "OSS History of the Cairo Office: Planta Agreement," NA: Record Group 226, Entry 99, Box 55.

6. "Chicago Mission Reports, James Kellis and Lt. Athen's Report," NA: Record Group 226, Entry 99, Box 55.

7. Author interview.

8. "Chicago Mission Reports: James Kellis and Lt. Athen's Report," NA: Record Group 226, Entry 99, Box 55.

9. Author interview.

10. "Chicago Mission Reports: James Kellis and Lt. Athen's Report," NA: Record Group 226, Entry 99, Box 55.

11. Ibid.

12. Author interview.

13. "Greek OG Report, Major Fred Bielaski" (December 24, 1944), author's collection.

14. Author interview.

15. Author interview.

16. Author interview

17. Author interview with George Vergis combined with his official report located in "Greek OG Report, Major Fred Bielaski" (December 24, 1944), author's collection.

18. Author interview.

19. Author interview.

20. Author interview.

21. Author interview.

22. Author interview.

23. Author interview.

24. Author interview.

25. Author interview.

26. Author interview.

27. Author interview.

28. Author interview.

CHAPTER 8. FROM FROGMEN TO SEALS

1. Roosevelt, *War Report of the OSS*, Volume I, p. 226.

2. Audrey was originally an SO project that came under joint MU control. The SOE later took over the operation.

3. "Reconnaissance Voyage" (29 October 1943–31 October 1943), Robert Thompson. This letter is courtesy of Peggy Stregel, Robert Thompson's daughter.

4. Author interview.

5. Author interview.

6. Author interview.

7. "Original plans for Operation Betty" (April 1944), author's private collection.

8. Author interview.

9. "War Diary: MU: OSS London England" (18 April 1945), p. 108, NA: Record Group 226, Entry 91, Roll 2.

10. Ibid.

11. Roosevelt, *War Report of the OSS,* Volume II, pp. 102–3; "Investigation of Special Equipment of the Mezzi D'Assalto Group of the Italian Navy," Ensign Kelly O'Neall (April 1945), NA: Record Group 226, Entry 143, Box 5.

12. "Operation Ossining, Report on Plan," R. M. Kelly (30 June 1944); "OSS/San Marco Group—Operational Activities of," R. M. Kelly (29 November 1944), NA: Record Group 226, Entry 143, Box 5.

13. Author interview.

14. "Investigation Report of Special Equipment of the Mezzini d'Assalto Group of the Italian Navy," Ensign Kelly O'Neall (April 1945), NA: Record Group 226, Entry 143, Box 5.

15. "UDT 10: The Brief History," unpublished history, UDT 10 Veterans Association, Langley, Va., 2000.

16. Action Report, USS *Burfish* SS-312, "Special Reconnaissance of Palau Islands" (24 August 1944), author's private collection.

17. Author interview.

18. Author interview.

19. Author interview.

20. "Operation North Carolina," Lieutenant John Booth (13 February 1945), author's private collection.

21. "MUR #3 MU Report," Lt. Comdr. D. A. Lee (7–13 January 1945), author's private collection.

22. "Report of Operation Caprice V" (4–14 August 1945), author's private collection.

23. Author interview.

CHAPTER 9. INFILTRATING FRANCE

1. "Brief History of the Resistance," Record Group 226, Entry 190, Box 741.

2. "Early Intelligence Chains by 'Tommy' Captain Frederick Brown," NA: Record Group 226, Entry 210, Box 72.

3. Ibid.

4. Ibid.; Roosevelt, *War Report of the OSS,* Volume 2, p. 176.

5. Chalou, *The Secrets War,* p. 253.

6. "The Penny Farthing Report: Jacques' Story," NA: Record Group 226, Entry 99, Box 45.

7. Ibid. Also see Chalou, *The Secrets War,* pp. 255–56.

8. "Jacques' Story," NA: Record Group 226, Entry 99, Box 45.

9. "The Mutton Pork Mission," NA: Record Group 226, Entry 99, Box 45.

10. Ibid.

11. Ibid.

CHAPTER 10. PAVING THE WAY FOR OVERLORD

1. R. Harris Smith, *OSS: The Secret History of America's First Central Intelligence Agency* (Berkeley: University of California Press, 1972), p. 185.

2. Author interview.

3. "SI Progress Report No. 33, June 1944, History File 3"; "Summary of Sussex Agents in France," NA: Record Group 226, Entry 99, Box 2; Roosevelt, *War Report of the OSS,* Volume I, pp. 210–11.

4. "Special Forces Plans, SHAEF," London: Public Record Office, Group 4967.

5. Foot, *SOE in France,* pp. 31–32.

6. Roosevelt, *War Report of the OSS,* Volume II, p. 193.

7. "Special Forces Plans: SHAEF," London: Public Record Office, Group 4967.

8. "London War Diary Book II, Vol. III, Report of Alfred" (12 April 1944), pp. 17–19. NA: Record Group 226, Entry 91, Box 20.

9. Foot, *SOE in France,* p. 289.

10. Author interview.

11. Author interview.

12. Pierre Fayol, *Le Chambon-sur-Lignon sous l'occupation 1940–1944* (Paris: L'Hamattan, 1990).

13. "Mission Heckler, Activity Report of Virginia Hall (Diane)," NA: Record Group 226, Entry 190, Box 741.

14. Roosevelt, *War Report of the OSS,* Volume II, p. 199.

15. Ibid.

16. Author interview.

17. "Jed Team Reports," NA: Record Group 226, Entry 103, Box 1. Roosevelt, *War Report of the OSS,* Volume II, p. 199.

18. Author interview and Knox's WWII mission report: "Team Giles," NA: Record Group 226, Entry 103, Box 1.

19. Author interview.

20. Ibid.

21. "Operational Report Company B 2671st Special Recon. Battalion (Provisional) Narrative History of the French OGs," NA: Record Group 226, Entry 99, Box 44.

22. Author interview; ibid.

23. Dwight Eisenhower, *Crusade in Europe* (New York: Doubleday & Company, 1948), p. 296.

CHAPTER 11. DRAGOON

1. "Walter Lanz Interrogation," NA: Record Group 226, Entry 210, Box 246. Before he was captured, Lanz provided important intelligence on German defenses along the coast of southern France.

2. Roosevelt, *War Report of the OSS,* Volume II, p. 238.

3. Jeffrey Clark and Robert Smith, *Riviera to the Rhine* (Washington, D.C.: Center of Military History, 1993), pp. 19–20.

4. "Walter Lanz Interrogation," NA: Record Group 226, Entry 210, Box 246.

5. Roosevelt, *The Overseas Targets,* p. 236.

6. Author interview.

7. Author interview.

8. "Report on Field Conditions Reported by Lt. William Duff," NA: Record Group 226, Entry 99, Box 36. I also interviewed Duff's key agent, Gil Pierrel.

9. Roosevelt, *War Report of the OSS,* Volume II, p. 238. Another G-2 report credits OSS with furnishing 79 percent of all order of battle material used by the invading forces.

10. "Operational Report Company B 2671st Special Recon. Battalion (Provisional), Narrative History of the French OGs," NA: Record Group 226, Entry 99, Box 44.

11. Ibid.

12. Rickerson eulogy/interview, from Robert Collete, who painstakingly transcribed the taped eulogy and provided it to the author. The author also interviewed all known surviving Louis team members.

CHAPTER 12. X-2

1. The crucial role of Ultra in winning the war is well known. For America's contribution to Ultra, see Thomas Parrish, *The Ultra Americans: The U.S. Role in Breaking the Nazi Codes* (New York: Stein & Day, 1986).

2. "The Army-Navy-FBI Agreements of 1942," NA: Record Group 226, Entry 146, Box 19.

3. X-2 snatched up many of OSS's top recruits, mostly from Ivy League campuses.

4. Roosevelt, *War Report of the OSS*, Volume I, p. 188.

5. The first book to reveal the existence of the double-cross system or XX Committee was by one of its key members, Sir John Masterman: *The Double-Cross System in the War of 1939 to 1945* (New Haven: Yale University Press, 1972).

6. Placed under the command of General George Patton, the First Army Group was a "phantom army" made up of fictional units designed to make the Germans believe that Allied forces were much stronger than they actually were. The plan was dubbed Operation Quicksilver and intended to trick the Germans into believing a second landing would take place at Pas de Calais.

7. "Certain Accomplishments of the OSS"; "Murphy to Donovan, November 20, 1944," Donovan Papers, Carlisle, Pa., Box 66B.

8. Author interview.

9. Author interview.

10. Author interview.

11. Roosevelt, *War Report of the OSS*, Volume I, p. 255.

12. Author interview.

13. Author interview.

CHAPTER 13. APPROACHING THE REICH

1. "Memo from Whitney Shepardson on Use of POWs," NA: Record Group 226, Entry 215, Box 2; "Penetration of Germany (6 February 1945)," NA: Record Group 226, Entry 99, Box 19.

2. Author interview.

3. "Mission Ruppert," NA: Record Group 226, Entry 210, Box 7.

4. Ibid.

5. Ibid.

6. Ibid.

7. Ibid.

8. Ibid.

9. Ibid.

10. "Team Edward: Book IV Jedburghs: London War Diary," NA: Record Group 226, Entry 91, Roll 7.

11. "Report of Bobbie," NA: Record Group 226, Entry 210, Box 56.

12. Ibid.

13. Author interview.

CHAPTER 14. CATASTROPHE IN CZECHOSLOVAKIA

1. "Gulovich Report to OSS HQ," NA: Record Group 226, Entry 108, Box 84; Roosevelt, *War Report of the OSS,* Volume II, p. 133.

2. Author interview.

3. Author interviews; also see James Downs, *World War II: OSS Tragedy in Slovakia* (Oceanside, Ca.: Liefrinck Publishers, 2002), pp. 225–28, for a detailed view of the count and his activities.

4. "Experiences of Sgt. Catlos and Pvt. Dunlevy, Members of an OSS Mission to Slovakia," NA: RG 226, Entry 210, Box 295.

5. "Zenopian Report," NA: RG 226, Entry 210, Box 295.

6. Konnilyn Feig, *Hilter's Death Camps* (New York: Holmes & Meier, 1979), p. 116.

7. The source of Müller's affidavit is NA: Record Group 226, Entry 146, Box 36.

8. Dr. Hans Wilhelm Thost's account is in "Report of Progress 'Dawes Case,'" NA: Record Group 226, Entry 146, Box 36.

9. Ibid.

10. Ibid.

11. Ibid.

12. Author interview.

13. Author interview.

CHAPTER 15. PSYCH OPS

1. "MO Student Handbook and Summary of Highlights" (July 29, 1944), p. 1, NA: Record Group 226, Entry 99, Box 88.

2. "OSS Organization and Function" (June 1945), NA: Record Group 226, Entry 141, Box 4; "History," NA: Record Group 226, Entry 99, Box 75.

3. Ford, *Donovan of OSS,* p. 124.

4. "MO Student Handbook and Summary of Highlights" (July 29, 1944), p. 1, NA: Record Group 226, Entry 99, Box 88.

5. Roosevelt, *War Report of the OSS,* Volume I, p. 212.

6. "MO Student Handbook and Summary of Highlights" (July 29, 1944), NA: Record Group 226, Entry 99, Box 88.

7. "George Piday Field Report," NA: Record Group 226, Entry 99, Box 37.

8. "MO Student Handbook and Summary of Highlights" (July 29, 1944), NA: Record Group 226, Entry 99, Box 37.

9. Author interview and Sauerkraut Mission Report. "Brief on Sauerkraut Missions: Final Conclusions" (December 19, 1944), NA: Record Group 226, Entry 99, Box 88; "Observed Results of Sauerkraut II," NA: Record Group 226, Entry 154, Box 51; "A Brief of Three Missions: Sauerkrauts I, II, III," NA: Record Group 226, Entry 99, Box 88.

10. Author interview.

11. "Final Report: Crete Operations by M. W. Royse," NA: Record Group 226, Entry 210, Box 410.

12. "An MO Example of a Poison Pen Letter; MO Achievements," NA: Record Group 226, Entry 99, Box 88.

13. "Robert Knapp, MO Cairo; Report on Krech Poison Pen Forgery"; "Mission Report: Ulysses Mission," NA: Record Group 226, Entry 210, Box 410. Many reports, such as Ulysses, were only recently declassified since they were labeled "sources and methods" by the CIA.

14. "Evaluation of Current Projects, Colonel K.D. Mann to the Board of Review," NA: Record Group 226, Entry 139, Box 172; "MO War Diaries," NA: Record Group 226, Entry 91, Box 5.

15. "Joker," NA: Record Group 226, Entry 99, Box 16.

16. "The Story of Cornflakes, Pig Iron, and Sheet Iron," NA: Record Group 226, Entry 99, Box 75.

17. Ibid.

18. "George Piday Field Report," NA: Record Group 226, Entry 99, Box 37.

19. Hugh Trevor-Roper, *Final Entries, 1945: The Diaries of Joseph Goebbels* (New York: Putnam, 1978), p. 223.

CHAPTER 16. PENETRATING THE REICH

1. Hugh Cole, *The Ardennes: Battle of the Bulge* (Washington, D.C.: Center for Military History, United States Army, 1965), p. 75.

2. Ibid., p. 72. Eventually the Germans would deploy 17 infantry divisions and 11 panzer and mechanized divisions in the battle.

3. Trevor Dupuy, *Hitler's Last Gamble* (New York: HarperCollins, 1994), p. 38.

4. Roosevelt, *War Report of the OSS,* Volume II, p. 217.

5. "X-2 History of Controlled Enemy Agents." The document was recently declassified and is located at NA: Record Group 226, Entry 211, Box 50.

6. Ibid.

7. "Field Report of Captain Stephen Vinciguerra," NA: Record Group 226, Entry 99, Box 15.

8. "Operation Pitt," NA: Record Group 226, Entry 210, Box 246.

9. Ibid.

10. Roosevelt, *War Report of the OSS,* Volume II, p. 305.

11. "SI Penetration of Germany," NA: Record Group 226, Entry 99, Box 19; Peter Grose, *Gentleman Spy: The Life of Allen Dulles* (New York: Houghton Mifflin, 1994), p. 211.

12. Persico, *Piercing the Reich,* p. 167.

13. "Report on Mission Hammer," NA: Record Group 226, Entry 115, Box 43.

14. Ibid.

15. "Eagle Project Final Report," Record Group 226, Entry 115, Box 39.

16. Ibid.

17. Interviews with the Seventh Army POW recruiters and "Seventh Army Matrix and Agent Dossiers"; "Report of Cover and Documents Branch of the G-2 Strategic Services Section" (May 1945), NA: Record Group 226, Entry 210, Box 246.

18. Author interview.

19. Author interview.

20. "Operation Dolly," NA: Record Group 226, Entry 210, Box 246.

21. Author interview.

22. "Seventh Army Matrix and Agent Dossiers"; "Report of Cover and Documents Branch of the G-2 Strategic Services Section, May 1945," NA: Record Group 226, Entry 210, Box 246.

23. The Germans employed the technique of sending SD agents masquerading as Allied spies on various occasions during the war.

24. "The Report of the Mission of Team 'Doctor': Jean Denis and Jan Block," NA: Record Group 226, Entry 210, Box 1.

25. "Report: Chauffeur Team: Renaix, André," NA: Record Group 226, Entry 210, Box 38.

26. "SI Penetration of Germany," NA: Record Group 226, Entry 99, Box 19.

27. Author interview.

28. Author interview.

29. Author interview.

30. Author interview.

31. Author interview.

32. Radio message: Gerald Schwab, *OSS Agents in Hitler's Heartland* (Westport, Conn.: Praeger, 1996), p. 90. The message is also located at the National Archives.

33. Author interview.

34. Radio message: Schwab, *OSS Agents in Hitler's Heartland*, p. 91. The message is also located at the National Archives.

35. Author interview.

36. Author interview.

CHAPTER 17. BACKROOM NEGOTIATIONS

1. "Summary of Westfield Activities," NA: Record Group 226, Entry 210, Box 30. "Outline of OSS Activities in Sweden," Wilho Tikander (November 19, 1945), NA: Record Group 226, Entry 210, Box 435; "OSS Activities in the European Theater—Based on Sweden, January–April 1944," NA: Record Group 226, Entry 99, Box 24.

2. Ibid.

3. "Wilho Tikander: Responses to Questionnaire" (May 1960), NA: Record Group 226, Entry 210, Box 344.

4. Ibid.

5. "Memo: Shepardson to Langsam" (July 24, 1945), NA: Record Group 226, Entry 99, Box 24.

6. Nigel West, *Venona: The Great Secret of the Cold War* (New York: HarperCollins, 2000), pp. 6–7.

7. Memo from Helms to Shepardson with "R Taylor's Report" (December 2, 1944), NA: Record Group 226, Entry 210, Box 435.

8. Source is an outstanding article by Mathew Aid, "'Stella Polaris' and Postwar Europe," *Journal of Intelligence and National Security*, Vol. 17, No. 3 (London: Frank Cass Publications): 28.

9. Ibid., p. 32.

10. "Memo: Tikander to General Donovan" (December 11, 1944), NA: Record Group 226, Entry 210, Box 362.

11. Robert Lewis Benson and Michael Warner, eds., *Venona: Soviet Espionage and the American Response, 1939–1957* (Washington, D.C.: NSA and CIA), p. 59.

12. Author interview.

13. Aid, "'*Stella Polaris*' and Post War Europe," p. 35. Moreover, there is the microfilmed copy of the material Huber was directed to make by Tikander in the December 11, 1944 memo to Donovan that remains unaccounted for.

14. Tikander to Donovan (March 28, 1945), NA: Record Group 226, Entry 210, Box 361.

15. Persico, *Roosevelt's Secret War,* p. 380.

16. West, *Venona: The Great Secret of the Cold War,* p. 10.

17. "Contact with Himmler: Memo: Donovan to the President" (March 20, 1944), NA: Record Group 226, Entry 1642, Roll 23. Felix Kersten, *Kersten Memoirs, 1940–1945* (New York: Macmillan, 1957), p. 75.

18. Ibid.

19. "Contact with Himmler: Memo: Donovan to the President" (March 20, 1944), NA: Record Group 226, Entry 1642, Roll 23.

20. Ibid.

21. "Schellenberg Statement to X-2," NA: Record Group 226, Entry 25-A, Box 2.

22. Walter Schellenberg, *The Labyrinth: Memoirs of Walter Schellenberg,* trans. Louis Hagen (New York: Harper & Brothers, 1957), p. 382.

23. John Waller, *The Devil's Doctor: Felix Kersten and the Secret Plot to Turn Himmler Against Hitler* (New York: Wiley, 2002), p. 153.

24. Ibid., pp. 186–88, 239.

25. "Wilho Tikander: Responses to Questionnaire" (May 1960), NA: Record Group 226, Entry 210, Box 344.

26. "Report of Birch," NA: Record Group 226, Entry 210, Box 30.

27. Ibid.

28. "Summary of Westfield Activities," NA: Record Group 226, Entry 210, Box 30.

29. The account is available from the National Archives is also in *Studies in Intelligence, Journal of American Intelligence, Special Edition for the 60th Anniversary of the OSS* (Langley, Va.: Central Intelligence Agency), p. 56. The document was made available to the general public and all who attended the reunion.

CHAPTER 18. NORTHERN ITALY

1. Estimates vary on the number of Italian members of the resistance under arms in northern Italy during the fall of 1944. Ernest Fisher, *United States Army in World War 2: Mediterranean Theater of Operations, Cassino to the Alps* (Washington, D.C.: reissue, U.S. Government Printing Office, 1993), p. 458.

2. "Walla Walla Mission Report," NA: Record Group 226, Entry 99, Box 45.

3. Author interview.

4. Author interview.

5. Roosevelt, *War Report of the OSS,* Volume II, p. 113.

6. Author interview.

7. Author interview with Howard Chappell, one of the toughest and best OG officers. Chappell's Tacoma Mission report was also consulted. "Tacoma Mission Report: Chappell," NA: Record Group 226, Entry 99, Box 45.

8. "Tacoma Mission Report: Buchhardt," NA: Record Group 226, Entry 99, Box 45.

9. Author interview; "Tacoma Mission Report" was consulted. NA: Record Group 226, Entry 99, Box 45.

10. "Tacoma Mission Report: Fabrega," NA: Record Group 226, Entry 99, Box 45.

11. Author interview.

12. Fisher, *Cassino to the Alps*, p. 458.

13. Author interview.

14. Author interview and "Tacoma Mission Report: Chappell," NA: Record Group 226, Entry 99, Box 45.

15. Ibid.

CHAPTER 19. FINAL MISSIONS AND CONCLUSIONS

1. "Sunrise-Crossword Operation Feb 25–May 2, 1945 by Allen Dulles and Gero von Gaevernitz" (May 22, 1945), NA: Record Group 226, Entry 190C, Boxes 25–30.

2. Ibid.

3. Ibid.

4. William Casey, *The Secret War Against Hitler* (Washington, D.C.: Regnery Gateway, 1988), p. 208.

5. "Map Room Files," FDR Library, Box 28.

6. Ibid.

7. "Sunrise-Crossword Operation Feb 25–May 2, 1945 by Allen Dulles and Gero von Gaevernitz" (May 22, 1945), NA: Record Group 226, Entry 190C, Boxes 25–30.

8. "Cross Project," Record Group 226, Entry 210, Box 310. "Cross Project Planning," Record Group 226, Entry 210, Box 310. Additionally, author interview with Tom Polgar, an officer assigned to Cross.

9. Ibid.

10. "Report on Mission Hammer," NA: Record Group 226, Entry 115, Box 43.

11. "Mission Ruppert," NA: Record Group 226, Entry 210, Box 7.

12. Author interview.

13. Author interview.

14. "Simmons Project," NA: Record Group 226, Entry 210, Box 166.

15. Author interview.

16. R. Harris Smith, *OSS*, p. 239.

17. Troy, *Donovan and the CIA*, p. vi.

18. Joseph Persico, *Roosevelt's Secret War* (New York: Random House, 2001), p. 294.

19. Several American Communists who fought during the Spanish Civil War came under suspicion. They were actually never the problem and all had excellent service records.

20. Bradley F. Smith, *The Shadow Warriors*, p. 307.

21. Author interviews.

22. Anthony Cave Brown, *The Last Hero: Wild Bill Donovan* (London: Times Books, 1982), p. 832.

Glossary

AAA Antiaircraft artillery

Abwehr German military foreign intelligence service and sabotage service of the German general staff

AFHQ Allied Force Headquarters

agent provocateur Agent planted to associate with and detect foreign agents

Andartes Greek Communist guerrillas

"Aunt Jemima" A plastic explosive that looks like baking flour

BACH OSS London cover section

BAR Browning Automatic Rifle

BCRA Bureau Centrale de Renseignement et d'Action (Gaullist secret intelligence agency)

Belgian Sûreté Belgian intelligence service

"blind" An agent that is infiltrated or parachuted without a prearranged reception with groups in an occupied country

BSC British Security Coordination (BSC), the North American arm of British Intelligence

caïques Small fishing vessels

CALPO Comité de l'Allemagne Libre pour l'Quest (French Office of Free Germany Committee)

CCS Combined Chiefs of Staff

CD OSS branch responsible for camouflage and documentation

CE Counterespionage

CI Counterintelligence

Circuit Intelligence / sabotage network

CIB Counter Intelligence Branch of SHAEF

CIC Counter Intelligence Corps

"City Teams" OSS units dispatched to enter newly liberated cities

CLN Comitato di Liberazione Nazionale (Italian resistance central committee)

CLNAI Comitato di Liberazione Nazionale per l'Alta Italia (political and resistance group in Italy)

CO Commanding officer

COI Coordinator of Information (predecessor to OSS)

CP Command post

Counter-scorch Measures designed to prevent the destruction of crucial installations by a retreating army. Most OSS counter-scorch activities were preformed by OGs and Jeds.

Cut-out Intermediary between two agent (Most cut-outs are between a primary agent and subagents.)

D/F Direction-finding

DF Section Element of British SOE (and later of the joint SFHQ) that organized safe routes for undercover travel of persons (such as downed fliers) in enemy-occupied Europe

DGER Direction Générale des Etudes et Recherches (successor to the French BCRA)

DIP Division of Intelligence Procurement (the operations section of OSS/ETO as reorganized in late 1944 for the penetration of Germany)

Double agent An agent who appears to be working for one intelligence service but is actually under the control of another

DP Displaced person

EAM Leftist resistance group in Greece

EDES Anti-Communist Greek resistance group

ELAS The military arm of EAM

EOU Enemy Objectives Unit (a section of the Economic Warfare Division responsible for strategic target selection and analysis)

Espinette Code name for joint venture of OSS and the Belgian Sûreté intelligence

ETO European Theater of Operations

ETOUSA European Theater of Operations, U.S. Army

FAAA First Allied Airborne Army

FFI Force Francaise de l'Interieur (a resistance group aligned with Charles de Gaulle)

FTP Tireurs et Partisans (Communist-controlled resistance group in France)

F Section Element of SOE (later joint SOE/SO and SFHQ) responsible for organizing and exploiting resistance movements in enemy-occupied Europe

Feldwebel German equivalent of staff sergeant

Funkspiel Literally, "radio game" in German—the term used for playing back a captured enemy agent

G-2 Military intelligence, U.S. Army

Gauleiter Highest-ranking Nazi party official in a given region, provisional governor

Gestapo German secret state police (Geheime Staatspolizei)

IAMM Independent American Military Mission to Marshal Tito (OSS-staffed delegation to Yugoslav Partisans)

JCS Joint Chiefs of Staff

J/E Joan-Eleanor (OSS-developed ground-to-plane radio communication device)

Jedburgh team (Jeds) Special team consisting of two officers and one radio operator. Staffed along multinational lines, 83 were American, 90 British, and 103 French. Most teams parachuted into France.

"K" tablet Knockout pill designed to render the recipient unconscious for a specified number of hours

Klaxton Plane-to-ground communication device similar to the J/E

Kripo German criminal investigation police

Lambertsen Amphibious Respiratory Unit (LARU) Underwater breathing apparatus that enabled a swimmer to approach a target underwater without leaving breathing bubbles

"L" tablets Lethal pill

Maquis The general name given to the French Resistance. The term is derived from a thorny bush that thrives in Corsica.

M1 M1 Garand rifle (standard infantry rifle for U.S. forces beginning in 1942)

MedTO Mediterranean Theater of Operations

MI5 British military intelligence unit for domestic counterintelligence

MI6 British foreign military intelligence unit

MO Morale Operations branch (OSS)

MAS boat Fast Italian motor gunboat

MU Maritime Unit of OSS

National Redoubt Proposed Nazi fortress area in Austria that later turned out to be largely a propaganda myth

NKVD Soviet secret police

OG Operational Groups (OSS)

OKW Oberkommando der Wehrmacht (maintained operational control over the German armed forces)

ONI Office of Naval Intelligence

OP Observation post

Order of battle Military units in a given area

POW Prisoner of war

Réseau French word for "network," and OSS/SOE term for intelligence network

R&A OSS Research and Analysis branch

R&D OSS Research and Development branch

Rebecca A radio beacon homing device

S-2 U.S. Army intelligence units below divisional level

SA Sturmabteilung (storm-troopers—it became the Nazi party's instrument for training and indoctrination of its members)

San Marco Battalion Italian marines or commandos trained for specialized maritime operations, later utilized by OSS

SAS Special Air Service (British counterpart of OSS Operational Groups)

SCI Special Counter-Intelligence (X-2 teams that accompanied Allied armies)

SD Sicherheitsdienst (Intelligence and counterintelligence arm of the SS. The SD absorbed most of the Abwehr in 1944.)

SFHQ Special Force Headquarters (joint SO/SOE organization in London for the support and exploitation of European resistance movements)

SHAEF Supreme Headquarters Allied Expeditionary Force

SIM Italian military intelligence

SIS British Secret Intelligence Service

"sleeper" agent An agent left in territory overrun by the enemy

Sleeping Beauty A one-man submersible designed by the British

SO OSS Special Operations branch

SOE Special Operations Executive

Special Force detachments OSS SO liaison teams that were attached to army groups beginning with the Normandy invasion

SPOC Special Projects Operations Center (headquartered in Algiers, and subject to SFHQ). Coordinated SO and SOE and Resistance in southern France

S-phone British air-to-ground communications device

SS Schutzstaffel (the protective guard of the Nazi Party)

SSU Strategic Service Unit (successor to OSS that incorporated OSS's postwar X-2 and SI branches)

SSTR-1 OSS agent's suitcase radio

SSS G-2 Strategic Service Section (G-2) (OSS Seventh Army Detachment)

T-Force X-2 counterespionage units designed to locate key individuals, enemy documents, and information

Todt German construction labor organization that worked on Germany's defensive projects

Underwater Demolition Team (UDT) Also known as frogmen

ULTRA Code name for messages and signals decoded from the German Enigma machine

Waffen SS Military units in the SS. As the war progressed the Waffen SS became the Reich's elite troops, plugging holes on both the Eastern and Western Fronts.

W/T Wireless telegraphy

X-2 OSS Counterespionage branch

XX Committee British Double Cross Committee controlling German double agents

Selected Bibliography

Andrew, Christopher. *Secret Service: The Making of the British Intelligence Community*. London: Heinemann, 1985.

Applegate, Rex. *Kill or Get Killed: Riot Control Techniques, Manhandling, and Close Combat for Police and the Military*. Boulder: Paladin, 1976.

Balfour, Michael. *Propaganda in War, 1933–1945*. London: Routledge and Kegan Paul, 1979.

Bancroft, Mary. *Autobiography of a Spy*. New York: William Morrow, 1983.

Bank, Aaron. *From OSS to Green Berets: The Birth of Special Forces*. Novato: Presidio Press, 1986.

Bazna, Elyesa, with Hans Nogly. *I Was Cicero*. New York: Harper & Row, 1962.

Bowen, Russell J. *Scholars' Guide to Intelligence Literature: Bibliography of the Russell J. Bowen Collection in the Joseph Mark Lauigner Memorial Library*. Georgetown University. Frederick, Md.: University Publications, Inc., 1983. Published for the National Intelligence Study Center.

Borghese, Valerio J. *Sea Devils: Italian Navy Commandos in WWII*. Annapolis: Naval Institute Press, 1995.

Breitman, Richard. *Official Secrets: What the Nazis Planned, What the British and Americans Knew*. New York: Hill & Wang, 1998.

Brown, Anthony Cave. *Bodyguard of Lies*. New York: Quill / William Morrow, 1991. Originally published by Harper & Row in 1975.

———. *"C": The Secret Life of Sir Stewart Graham Menzies.* New York: Macmillan, 1987.

———. *The Last Hero: Wild Bill Donovan.* New York: Times Books, 1982.

———. *Treason in the Blood.* New York: Houghton Mifflin, 1994.

Bruce, David K. E. *OSS Against the Reich: The World War II Diaries of Colonel David K. E. Bruce,* ed. Nelson Lankford. Kent, Ohio: Kent State University Press, 1991.

Casey, William. *The Secret War Against Hitler.* Washington, D.C.: Regency, 1986.

Central Intelligence Agency, Counterintelligence Staff. *The Rote Kappelle: The CIA's History of Soviet Intelligence Networks in Western Europe, 1936–1945.* Washington, D.C.: University Publications of America, 1979.

Chalou, George C., ed. *The Secrets War: The Office of Strategic Services in World War II.* Washington, D.C.: National Archives Trust Fund Board (for National Archives and Records Administration), 1992.

Clark, Mark. *Calculated Risk.* New York: Harper & Brothers, 1950.

Clifford, Alexander. *Conquest of North Africa, 1940–1943.* Boston: Little, Brown, 1953.

Constantinides, George C. *Intelligence and Espionage: An Analytical Bibliography.* Boulder: Westview Press, 1983.

Corvo, Max. *The OSS in Italy, 1942–1945: A Memoir.* New York: Praeger, 1990.

Deacon, Richard. *"C": A Biography of Sir Maurice Oldfeld, Head of MI6.* London: Macdonald, 1985.

Deutsch, Harold C. *The Conspiracy Against Hitler in the Twilight War.* Minneapolis: University of Minnesota Press, 1968.

D'Este, Carlo. *Fatal Decision: Anzio and the Battle for Rome.* New York: HarperCollins, 1990.

Downs, Donald. *The Scarlet Thread: Adventures in Wartime Espionage.* New York: British Book Center, 1953.

Dulles, Allen W. *Germany's Underground*. New York: Macmillan, 1947.

———. *The Craft of Intelligence*. New York: Harper & Row, 1963.

———. *The Secret Surrender*. New York: Harper & Row, 1966.

———. ed. *Great True Spy Stories*. New York: Harper & Row, 1968.

Dunlop, Richard. *Donovan: America's Master Spy*. New York: Rand McNally, 1982.

———. *Behind Japanese Lines: With the OSS in Burma*. Chicago: Rand McNally, 1982.

Eisenhower, Dwight D. *Crusade in Europe*. New York: Doubleday, 1948.

Foot, M. R. D. *SOE in France*. London: Her Majesty's Stationery Office, 1966.

Foote, Alexander. *Handbook for Spies*. London: Hart-Davis, 1976.

Ford, Corey. *Donovan of OSS*. Boston: Little, Brown, 1970.

Ford, Kirk. *OSS and the Yugoslav Resistance, 1943–1945*. College Station: Texas A&M University Press, 1992.

Funk, Arthur Layton. *The Politics of Torch: The Allied Landings and the Algiers Putsch, 1942*. Lawrence: The University Press of Kansas, 1974.

———. *Hidden Ally: The Resistance in Southern France*. Westport, CT: Greenwood Press, 1993.

Gehlen, Reinhard. *The Service: The Memoirs of General Reinhard Gehlen*. New York: World Publishing Co., 1972.

Gisevius, Hans Bernd. *To the Bitter End*. Boston: Houghton Mifflin, 1947.

Goebbels, Joseph. *The Goebbels Diaries*, ed. by Louis P. Lochner. Garden City, N.Y.: Doubleday, 1948.

Grose, Peter. *Gentleman Spy*. New York: Houghton Mifflin, 1994.

Halpern, Samuel, and Hayden Peake, eds. *In the Name of Intelligence*. Privately published. Washington, D.C.: National Intelligence Book Center Press, 1994.

Hayes, Carlton J. H. *Wartime Mission in Spain, 1942–1945.* New York: Macmillan, 1946.

Heideking, Jurgen, and Christof Mauch. *The U.S. and the German Resistance: Analysis and Operations of the American Secret Service in World War II.* Tubingen: A. Franke Verlag, 1993. German language.

Hinsley, F.H., and C. A. G. Simkins. *Security and Counter-Intelligence,* Vol. 4 of *British Intelligence in the Second World War.* New York: Cambridge University Press, 1990.

Hinsley, F. H., E. E. Thomas, C. F. G. Ransom, and R. C. Knight. *Its Influence on Strategy and Operations,* 2 vols of *British Intelligence in the Second World War.* Vol. 1, 2d ed.: London: Her Majesty's Stationery Office, 1986. Vol. 2: New York: Cambridge University Press, 1981.

Hoover, Calvin. *Memoirs of Capitalism, Communism, and Nazism.* Durham, N.C.: Duke University Press, 1995.

Howe, George. *Northwest Africa: Seizing the Initiative in the West.* Washington, D.C.: Government Printing Office, 1957.

Hyde, H. Montgomery. *The Quiet Canadian: The Secret Service of Sir William Stephenson.* Foreword by Ambassador David K. E. Bruce. London: Hamish Hamilton, 1962.

———. *Room 3603: The Story of the British Intelligence Center in New York During World War II.* New York: Farrar, Straus, 1963.

———. *Secret Intelligence Agent: British Espionage in America and the Creation of the OSS.* New York: St. Martin's Press, 1982.

———. *Cynthia: The Most Seductive Secret Weapon in the Arsenal of a Man Called Intrepid.* New York: Ballantine Books, 1965.

Hymoff, Edward. *The OSS in WWII.* New York: Richardson and Steirman, 1972.

Irving, David, ed. *Breach of Security: The German Intelligence File on Events Leading to the Second World War.* London: William Kimber, 1968.

Kahn, David. *Hitler's Spies: German Military Intelligence in World War II.* New York: Macmillan, 1978.

———. *The Codebreakers: The Story of Secret Writing.* New York: MacMillan, 1967.

Katz, Barry M. *Foreign Intelligence Research and Analysis in the Office of Strategic Services, 1942–1945.* Cambridge, Mass.: Harvard University Press, 1989.

Kent, Sherman. *Strategic Intelligence for American World Policy.* Princeton, N.J.: Princeton University Press, 1949.

Kersten, Felix. *The Kersten Memoirs, 1940–1945,* trans. Constantine Fitzgibbon and James Oliver. New York: Macmillan, 1954.

Langer, William L. *Our Vichy Gamble.* New York: Knopf, 1947.

———. *In and Out of the Ivory Tower: The Autobiography of William Langer.* New York: Academic, 1977.

Lankford, Nelson, ed. *OSS Against the Reich: The World War II Diaries of Colonel David K. E. Bruce.* Kent, Ohio: Kent State University Press, 1991.

Laurie, Clayton. *The Propaganda Warriors: America's Crusade Against Nazi Germany.* Lawrence: University of Kansas Press, 1996.

Lewin, Ronald. *Hitler's Mistakes.* New York: Quill/William Morrow, 1984.

Liddell Hart, B. H. *The German Generals Talk.* New York: Quill, 1979.

Lindsay, Franklin A. *Beacons in the Night: With the OSS and Tito's Partisans in Wartime Yugoslavia.* Stanford: Stanford University Press, 1995.

Loewenheim, Francis, ed. *Roosevelt and Churchill: Their Secret Wartime Correspondence.* New York: Saturday Review Press, 1975.

Lovell, Mary S. *Cast No Shadow: The Life of the American Spy Who Changed the Course of World War II.* New York: Pantheon, 1992.

Martin, David. *The Web of Disinformation: Churchill's Yugoslav Blunder.* New York: Harcourt Brace Jovanovich, 1990.

Masterman, J. C. *The Double-Cross System in the War of 1939–1945*. New Haven: Yale University Press, 1972.

Naftali, Timothy. "X-2 and the Apprenticeship of America Counter-espionage, 1942–1944" Dissertation, Harvard University, 1993. Ann Arbor: UMI Dissertation Service, 1994.

Persico, Joseph E. *Nuremberg: Infamy on Trial*. New York: Viking Press, 1994.

———. *Piercing the Reich: The Penetration of Nazi Germany by American Secret Agents During World War II*. New York: Viking, 1979.

Philby, Kim (Harold A.R.). *My Silent War*. New York: Grove Press, 1968. London: Granada Publishing, 1969. Introduction by Graham Greene. Reprinted 1983.

Piekalkiewicz, Janusz. *Secret Agents, Spies, and Saboteurs*. New York: William Morrow, 1973.

Pinck, Dan C., Geoffrey M. T. Jones, and Charles T. Pinck. *Stalking the History of the Office of Strategic Services: An OSS Bibliography*. Boston: OSS-Donovan Press, 2000.

Powers, Thomas. *Heisenberg's War: The Secret History of the German Bomb*. New York: Knopf, 1995.

Rogers, James. *The Secret War: Espionage in World War II*. New York: Facts on File, 1991.

Roosevelt, Kermit. *The Overseas Targets: War Report of the OSS*. Vol. I. Washington, D.C.: Carrollton Press; New York: Walker & Co.; 1976.

———. *The Overseas Targets: War Report of the OSS*, Vol. II. Washington, D.C.: Carrollton Press; New York: Walker & Co.; 1976.

Schellenberg, Walter. *The Labyrinth: Memoirs of Walter Schellenberg*. Trans. Louis Hagen. New York: Harper & Brothers, 1956.

Schwab, Gerald. *OSS Agents in Hitler's Heartland: Destination Innsbruck*. Westport: Praeger, 1996.

Singlaub, John. *Hazardous Duty: An American Soldier in the Twentieth Century.* New York: Summit, 1991.

Smith, Bradley F. "Admiral Godfrey's Mission to America, June, July, 1941." *Intelligence and National Security,* Vol. 3 (September 1986).

———. *The Shadow Warriors: OSS and the Origins of the CIA.* New York: Basic Books, 1983.

———. *The Ultra-Magic Deals and the Most Secret Special Relationship, 1940-1946.* Novato: Presidio Press, 1993.

Smith, R. Harris. *OSS: The Secret History of America's First Central Intelligence Agency.* Berkeley: University of California Press, 1972.

Smyth, Howard McGaw. "The Ciano Papers: Rose Garden." *Studies in Intelligence.* U.S. Central Intelligence Agency, Spring 1969.

Speer, Albert. *Inside the Third Reich.* London: Weidenfeld & Nicolson, 1970.

Stead, John Phillip. *Second Bureau.* London: Evans Brothers, 1959.

Stephenson, William. *Intrepid's Last Case.* New York: Villard Books, 1983.

———. *A Man Called Intrepid: The Secret War.* Historical note by Charles H. Ellis. New York: Harcourt Brace Jovanovich, 1976.

Toland, John. *The Last 100 Days.* New York: Random House, 1966.

Tompkins, Peter. *A Spy in Rome.* New York: Simon & Schuster, 1962.

———. *The Murder of Admiral Darlan.* New York: Simon & Schuster, 1965.

Troy, Thomas. "The British Assault on J. Edgar Hoover: The Tricycle Case." *International Journal of Intelligence and Counter-Intelligence,* Vol. 3, No. 2, 1989.

———. *Donovan and the CIA: A History of the Establishment of the Central Intelligence Agency.* Foreign Intelligence Book Series, Thomas F. Troy, gen. ed. Frederick, Md.: University Publications of America, 1981.

Waller, John. *The Devil's Doctor.* New York: Wiley, 2001.

————. *The Unseen War in Europe: Espionage and Conspiracy in the Second World War*. New York: Random House, 1996.

Warlimont, Walter. *Inside Hitler's Headquarters, 1939–1945*. Novato: Presidio Press, 1964.

West, Nigel. *MI5: British Security Service Operations, 1909–1945*. London: Weidenfeld & Nicolson, 1981.

————. *Introduction to British Security Coordination: The Secret History of British Intelligence in the Americas, 1940-1945*. London: St. Ermin's Press, 1998.

————. *MI6*. New York: Random House, 1983.

Winks, Robin. *Cloak and Gown: Scholars in the Secret War, 1939-1961*. New York: William Morrow, 1987.

Woytak, Richard A. *On the Border of War and Peace: Polish Intelligence and Diplomacy in 1937–1939 and the Origins of the Ultra Secret*. New York: Columbia University Press, 1979.

Yu, Maochun. *OSS in China: Prelude to Cold War*. New Haven: Yale University Press, 1996.

Acknowledgments

Hundreds of OSS veterans shared their experiences, time, and research with me; I'm indebted to each of these dynamic individuals. I'd like to thank the OSS Society (www.osssociety.org), especially its president emeritus and true gentlemen spy, Geoffrey Jones. The society's current president, Charles Pinck, and his father, Dan Pinck, also provided important assistance. I'd also like to thank Al Materazzi and Dick Cutler for their willingness to always help me.

I'm indebted to my close friend Brian Fitzpatrick, who provided crucial comments and ideas throughout the process of putting together this book. Major Mike Horn provided important historical insight, and Eric Minkoff offered feedback that improved the text. I thank Troy Sacquety for coming through with critical feedback and suggestions. I'm most indebted to my editor, Bruce Nichols, for his vision and editorial excellence and for allowing me to pursue my passion; in the process we have preserved the history of hundreds of World War II veterans.

Although the heart of this book is its oral histories, nearly a thousand hours were spent reviewing the official documents and other primary source material located at the National Archives. John Taylor, senior archivist and living legend, is a model for any individual who wants to combine his work with his passion. John always had ideas, veteran contacts, and an endless amount of energy for my questions. I'm also indebted to Dr. Larry McDonald, who spent countless hours guiding me through the massive OSS collection at the National Archives. Sid Shapiro furnished several key finding aids. I can't say enough about the men and women at the National Archives and their willingness to go above and beyond the call of duty. Finally, I can't extend enough gratitude to my agent, Andy Zack of The Zack Company, Inc.

Index

Abraham Lincoln Brigade, 8, 40–41
Abwehr, 76–77, 197–98, 199–200,
    220–21, 303
Adrian, Leon, 250–51
African Americans, 41
Afrika Korps, German, 40
Air Crew Rescue Unit, 96–97
Albania, 81, 92–95
Alexander, Sidney, 24
"Alfred" (aka E. F. Floege), 167, 168
Algeria/Algerians: courier service
    through, 71; and French operations,
    146, 147, 148, 149, 154, 158, 159,
    160, 189; and North Africa
    operations, 31, 36, 37, 39, 43, 44, 45,
    47; and X-2, 201, 202
Allied Forces Headquarters, 49, 51,
    75–76, 182, 186, 189
Alum (OSS team), 83–84, 87–92
Amazon (OSS team), 83
Ammonia (Jed team), 175–76
Amt IV, 222–23
Amt VI, 271–72
Andartes, 108, 109, 113–14
Andersen, Odd, 276
Angaur/Anguar Island, 134, 136–37
Angelos, Mike, 107, 108, 109
"Anick" (aka Helene Deschamps),
    184–86
Anzio, 61–64, 65, 86, 311

Applegate, Rex, 5
Area B, 3, 4–5, 8–9
Area F, 3, 9
Army Group B, U.S., 176
Athens, John, 108–9, 116, 117, 122–23
Athens-Salonika railway, 117–19, 120
atomic bomb/research, 64, 65, 71–72,
    204, 308–9
Audrey, Operation, 124–25
"Aunt Jemima," 7–8, 16
Austria, 87, 100, 191, 253–54, 256–58,
    292, 304–7
Aztec (OG team), 282–83, 290–91

Badoglio, Pietro, 53, 55, 56
Bahamas, 128
Baker, Kenneth, 1
Balkans: potential German surrender in,
    98, 99–100. See also Albania;
    Yugoslavia
Ball, John, 135
ball bearings, 264, 266
Ballists, 93–94
"Baltic Fishing Fleet," 273
Banana operations, 43–44, 45, 47–48
Barrault, Louis, 165
Battalion de Choc (France), 57
Battle of the Bulge, 169, 227, 240–43,
    246, 307, 312
Bazna, Elyesa (aka "Cicero"), 69

BBC, 36–37, 177, 215

Beck, Ludwig, 237

"Beetroot" mission, 44

Belgium/Belgians, 193, 211, 212, 216, 242, 254, 255

Benson, Melvin, 80

Benucci (OG leader), 283, 287, 291

Berg, Moe, 64–65, 71–72

Berger, Heinrich, 252, 253

Berlin, Jacob, 175–76

Berlin, Germany: Allied bombing of, 249, 274; and approaching the Reich, 210; OSS agents in, 208–9, 210, 212, 273–74, 301–4; and overthrow of Hitler, 272; and penetrating the Reich, 246–49; Russians in, 249, 274, 300, 301–3, 308

Bertani, Maura, 253

Betty, Operation, 129–30

Bickford, Jim, 59

Biological Warfare Committee, 21–22

"Birch" (aka Hennings Jessen- Schmidt), 273–74

Black, Robert, 135

"black bag" operations, 26–30

Blathwayt, C. G., 177

Bletchley Park, England, 194, 240

Blonttrock, Alphonse, 254

Blum, Paul, 297

Blumenson, Martin, 63

"Bobby" (aka Anton Schrader), 214–16

"Bobby" (Allied turncoat), 214

Bodine, Les, 138

Bonal (double agent), 157–58

Bonnier de la Chapelle, Fernand, 38–39

Booth, John, 128–29, 139–40

Booth, Waller, 45

"Boston Series" reports, 68

Bouchardon, André "Narcisse," 167–68

Bourgoin, André, 44–45, 54

Brac Island, 91

Bradley, Omar, 204

"Breakers," 76–78

Brenner Pass, 258–62

Britain/British: American Embassy in, 23; and approaching the Reich, 212; in Balkans, 82, 90, 91, 96, 99; in Corsica, 57–58; in Czechoslovakia, 226; EOU in, 23; estimates of German tank production by, 24; in France, 143, 149; German agents in, 195; German Communists in exile in, 246–47; and German secret weapons program, 309; Germans counterfeit money of, 204; in Greece, 108, 120, 122, 276; Italian navy surrender to, 55; in Italy, 53; on Jedburgh teams, 174; and Maritime Units, 129, 139–40; and *Olterra* freighter, 131; OSS candidate training by, 1, 13; and Overlord, 161; Poles in exile in, 250–51; and psych ops, 236; sinking of ships belonging to, 131; in Turkey, 69; in Yugoslavia, 83, 85–86. *See also* British intelligence; *specific person or organization*

British Air Force, 249

British intelligence: code-breaking efforts of, 28, 194, 240; codes of, 269; counterespionage of, 69; in Czechoslovakia, 221, 224; and direct penetration of Germany, 227; "Dogwood" as agent for, 75; and Finnish intelligence, 269; and German resistance, 77; Kolbe as agent for, 68; limits on U.S. activities of, 27; in North Africa, 32, 39; Pack as agent for, 28; and penetrating the Reich, 246, 256; Philby as mole in, 273; SIS branch of, 1, 166, 220; and Swedish operations, 264; and Switzerland, 68, 69; U.S. dispute

with, 32; in Yugoslavia, 83; and X-2, 194, 195, 197, 198, 201, 203. *See also* British Security Coordination (BSC); joint operations; Special Operations Executive (SOE)
British Red Devils, 122
British Security Coordination (BSC), 2, 27, 28. *See also* joint operations
Brittany, 176–77, 179–80
Brittenham, Ray, 216, 254
Brousse, Charles, 26, 27, 28–30
Brown, Frederick "Tommy," 144, 146–49, 159
Browne, Gordon, 34–35, 36–38
Browne, William, 242–43
Bruce, David, 160
Brucker, Herb, 171–73
Bruno, A., 56, 57
BSC. *See* British Security Coordination
Buchenwald concentration camp, 250
Buchhardt, Eric, 284–87, 288, 293, 295
Buckingham, Winthrop, 34
Bulgaria/Bulgarians, 80, 80*n*, 90, 91, 100, 109, 169, 310
Burfish, 134–35
Burma, 129, 139–41
Buta, Serafin, 51, 52

Camouflage Division, 16, 19
Camp X, 2, 4
Camp David, 3, 4–5, 8–9
Camp Patrick Henry, 110–11
Camp Pendleton, 126
"The Campus," 22–25
Canada: Camp X in, 2, 4
Canaris, Wilhelm, 76–77
Cantgelosi, Nick, 290–91
Cappony, Spiro (Spyriolon), 107, 108, 116–17, 122–23
"Carlos" (aka Karl Frick), 44–45
Carlson, William, 268
Carpenter, Emmet, 135

Casey, William J., 246, 262
Cassino (Italy), 61
Catalina Island, 126, 149
Catlos, Steve, 221, 225, 226
Central Intelligence Agency (CIA), 164*n*, 310
Cereus (OSS network), 74–75
Channel Islands, 58
Chapin, Howard, 256
Chappell, Howard, 283–85, 286–89, 290, 293–96
Chauffeur team, 254–55
Chetniks, 79, 80, 82–83, 84–85, 96, 97, 101
"Chicago Mission," 107–9, 116–17, 122–23
Chicago Tribune, 310
Choate, Arthur, 134
Churchill, Winston, 39, 53, 61, 83, 85–86, 99
"Cicero" (aka Elyesa Bazna), 69
circuits, 167, 173, 174, 175. *See also specific circuit*
Clark, Mark, 35–36, 43, 44, 63
CLNAI (Comitato di Liberazione Nazionale per l'Alta Italia), 278–79, 296
codes/ciphers: and Balkan operations, 86; and Battle of the Bulge, 240; and "black bag" jobs, 26–30; British, 86, 269; British efforts at breaking German, 28, 194, 240; Enigma, 28, 63, 268; and Finnish intelligence, 267–69; German, 28, 63, 69, 194, 240, 268; Germans break U.S., 68, 77; importance of, 31; and infiltration of France, 144, 146; Italian naval, 28; Japanese naval, 48; Lussier's work with, 201; Magic (Japanese), 48; Russian, 267–70; and Russians in Berlin, 302–3; of State Department, 77, 267; Ultra, 47, 63,

[codes/ciphers, *cont.*]
(Ultra) 69, 194, 195, 200, 201, 240;
Vatican, 269; and Venona, 269–70;
of Vichy government, 26, 27, 29–30
COI (Coordinator of Information). *See*
OSS; *specific department/division*
Colby, William, 275–77
Cold War, 266, 269–70, 301, 308, 313
Cole, R. Taylor, 267
Collette, Hank, 190, 192–93
commandos: in Balkans, 91; British,
57–58, 91; in Corsica, 57–58;
execution of, 58–60, 282; German,
53; Hitler's orders about, 58–59,
282; in Italy, 53, 59–60. *See also*
specific person or group
Communists: Abraham Lincoln Brigade
members as, 40–41; and
approaching the Reich, 209, 215; in
Balkans, 79, 97, 99, 100, 101; in exile,
246–47; in France, 143, 182*n*, 185,
186–87, 209; in Germany, 246–47,
301; in Greece, 105, 106, 106*n*, 108,
116–17, 122, 276; and interrogation
of prisoners, 215; in Italy, 53–54,
278–79; as OSS personnel, 311; and
penetrating the Reich, 246–47; as
prisoners of war, 182*n*
concentration camps, 204, 273, 306. *See*
also specific camp
Congressional Country Club: as
training Area F, 3, 9
Coon, Carleton, 32, 34, 38–40, 41, 43,
44, 57
Coordinator of Information (COI). *See*
OSS
Cornflakes, Operation, 237–38
Correale, Roberto, 54
Corsica, 50, 56, 57–58, 71, 144, 311
Costello, Frank, 21
Counter-Intelligence Corps (CIC), U.S.
Army, 251

counterespionage: British, 69; German,
220–21, 222–23; and infiltration of
France, 144; and overthrow of
Hitler, 272; purpose of, 195; special,
197–98; and Venona, 270. *See also*
double agents; X-2; *specific agent or*
organization
Cox, Al, 192
Crete, 131, 234
Croatia, 99–100
Cross, Operation, 300–301
Cuckold (OSS team), 86–87
"Cue Ball" (Greek resistance fighter), 123
Curie, Marie, 204, 205
Cutler, Dick, 308
"Cynthia" (aka Elizabeth "Betty" Pack),
26, 27–30, 31
Cyprus, 102
Czechoslovakia, 216, 217–27

Dachau concentration camp, 182*n*, 245,
307–8
Dallas, Augie (experimental subject),
20–21
Dandingé, Count, 147
Dania team, 256–58
Darby's Rangers, 53–54
Davies, Bill, 221
Dawes mission/team, 217–27
de Francesco, Joseph "Jed," 13
de Gaulle, Charles, 143, 161, 167, 184
Dehandschutter, Michel, 254–55
Denmark, 273, 274
dental work, 161
Deschamps, Helene "Anick," 184–86
deserters, 225, 235, 236, 251, 254, 258
Devlin, Frank, 2, 4
Devyak, Mike, 98
Dewart, William, 231
DF Section, 167
"Dick" (aka Ignacio Lopez Dominguez),
45

Dick, Vincent, 146, 147
Doctor team, 254
documents, 10, 16, 19, 161
Doering, O. C., 45
"Dogwood" (double agent), 75
Dominguez, Ignacio Lopez "Dick," 45
Donald (OG team), 179–80
Donovan, William: and Balkans
    operations, 80, 83, 85–86, 96; Berg's
    reports to, 71–72; and "black bag"
    job, 27; death of, 314; and Finnish
    intelligence, 268, 269; initiation of
    training schools by, 1; and Lincoln
    Brigade, 41; mantra of, 313; and
    Maritime Unit, 124, 133; and
    Overlord, 160; and penetrating the
    Reich, 246; and plans to assassinate
    Hitler and Himmler, 271, 301;
    proposal for permanent "central
    intelligence service" by, 310; and
    psych ops, 228–29; R&D initiated
    by, 16; recruitment for OSS by, 8, 41,
    313; and Sardinia operations, 56; in
    Sicily, 49; and X-2, 194
Donovan-Hambro accords, 32, 80, 80n
"Dora" (OSS agent), 247
double agents, 195, 197–200, 242
Downs, Donald, 27, 40, 41, 43, 44, 45,
    47, 53–54
"Dragoman" (Juan Frutos), 197–98
Dragoon, Operation, 181–93, 312
Ducasse, Georges, 163
Duff, William, 187–88
Duke, Florimond, 73–74
Dulles, Allen, 67–70, 72, 76, 77–78, 100,
    297–99, 306, 309, 312–13
Dunlevy, Kenneth, 221, 225

Eagle, Operation, 250–51
EAM group, 105, 106, 106n, 108, 116–17,
    122, 236
Early, Steve, 310

economists, OSS, 23–24
Eddy, William, 31–32, 34, 35–36, 41
Edelweiss unit, 220–21
EDES group, 105, 106, 122
Edward (Jed team), 212–13
Eighth Air Force, U.S., 163
Eighth Army, British, 39, 53, 53n, 276,
    292
Eighth Army, U.S., 132
80th Division, U.S., 242
82nd Airborne Division, U.S., 212, 213,
    243
87th Infantry Division, U.S., 243
88th Division, U.S., 111
801st Bombardment Group, U.S.,
    163
"Eiken" (aka Juan Frutos), 197–98
Eisenhower, Dwight D., 56, 69, 166, 174,
    180, 261, 298, 312–13, 314
ELAS group, 105, 106n, 117
Eleftherios (child), 116
embassies: in Washington, D.C., 26–30,
    48
Enemy Objectives Unit (EOU), 23–24,
    24n, 311
England. See Britain/British; specific
    person or organization
Enigma, 28, 63, 268
Erickson, Eric Siegfried "Red," 263–64
Espinette, 216, 254–55
Eubanks, James, 126, 128

F Section, 167, 173, 175
Fabrega, Salvadore, 284, 286, 287,
    289–90, 294, 295
Fairbairn, William Ewart "Dan," 4–5, 8,
    9, 11
Fairfax, Virginia, 3, 13
Famos, Gastone, 54
Farish, Linn, 90, 96
"The Farm" (RTU-11), 3, 9
fascists, 220, 230–31, 282–83

"Faust" plan, 246, 262
Federal Bureau of Investigation (FBI), 10, 12, 30
Felsen, Milton, 8, 41–42, 43
Fifteenth Air Force, 238
Fifteenth Panzer Regiment, German, 52
Fifth Army, U.S., 43, 44, 53–55, 53n, 61, 62, 66, 276, 292
Finland, 265, 266–70
First Allied Airborne Army (FAAA), 212–13
First Army, British, 39, 212
First Army Group, U.S. (FUSAG), 195
First Army, U.S., 168–69, 241–42, 243
First Division, British, 61
First Infantry Division, U.S., 49
Fischel, Fritz "Red," 244–45
"five-mile run" area, 117–19, 120
504th Panzer Battalion, 294, 295
509th Parachute Infantry Battalion, U.S., 36–38
Fleming, Ian, 2
fliers, Allied, 79, 84–85, 96–97, 173 217, 218, 220, 257, 282, 294
Floege, E. F. "Alfred," 167, 168
Forat, Jean, 151–52
Forces Francaises de L'Interieur (FFI), 143
Ford, John, 59
Foreign Information Service (FIS), 229
42nd Division, U.S., 245
45th Division, U.S., 111
Fourteenth Army, German, 63
404 Maritime Unit of Detachment, 139
492nd Bombardment Group, U.S., 163
France / French: bombing in, 163, 164, 165; Communists in, 143, 182n, 185, 186–87, 209, 301; in Corsica, 57; courier service through, 71; German occupation of, 173; importance of, 143; infiltration of, 143–59; intelligence, 203, 269; on

Jedburgh teams, 174; Maritime Units in, 129–30; in North Africa, 39, 40; OSS operations in, 145, 160–80, 211, 312; and paving way to Overlord, 161; as prisoners of war, 304; recruiting of, 144; scientists, 71, 204, 205; SOE training of operatives from, 38. See also Brittany; Dragoon, Operation; Free French Forces; Normandy; Overlord, Operation; Paris, France; Vichy government; specific person or unit
Francs Tireurs et Partisans (FTP), 143, 185, 186–87
Frankenstein, Maria, 303
Free French forces, 38, 143–44, 166, 168, 169, 171, 174, 178, 185–86
"Free Germany Committee," 246–47
Frick, Karl "Carlos," 44–45
Frutos, Juan "Dragoman," 197–98
Fuchs, Klaus, 270

G-2: and Dragoon, 182, 186, 189; and First Army–OSS relations, 241; and French operations, 165–66, 169; and German secret weapons program, 308; and Innsbruck's surrender, 307; and North Africa operations, 35; OSS turf battles with, 194, 241; and X-2, 194, 197, 198
Gaevernitz, Gero von, 77, 297, 298, 300
Gale, Paul, 49
Gastaud, Pierre, 165
Gehlen, Reinhard, 309–10, 312–13
Geneva Convention, 206
"Georges" (aka Friedrich Kaulen, German case officer), 199–200
"Georgia Cracker," 29–30
Georgiades, A., 107
Gerbner, George, 255–58
German intelligence, 31, 69, 75, 84, 195,

199, 203–4, 212, 312–13. *See also* Abwehr; SD

German scientists, 71–72, 307–9

German troops: desertions from, 235, 236, 251, 254; morale of, 231–33; in Russia, 235; surrender of, in northern Italy, 297–99, 312. *See also specific person or branch of military*

Germany: Allied bombing in, 24n, 249, 274; and approaching the Reich, 206–16; atomic research in, 308–9; direct penetration of, 227; fuel for, 24, 24n, 264, 311; mail system in, 237–38; OSS operations in southern, 254–55; penetrating of, 240–62; precision bombing in, 23–24; railroads in, 24n; resistance in, 76–78; secret weapons program of, 69, 70, 307–9; southern part of, 253–54; surrender of, 307; tank production in, 24; transportation system in, 24n. *See also* Abwehr; Berlin, Germany; German intelligence; German troops; Gestapo; SD; SS; Wehrmacht; *specific person*

Gestapo: and approaching the Reich, 214, 215–16; in Balkans, 82, 89, 95, 100; in Czechoslovakia, 221, 224; in Denmark, 273; in France, 147, 149, 150, 153, 154, 155–56, 157, 158, 164, 167–68, 173, 181, 182n, 196, 205; in Germany, 210; and Gisevius, 78; in Hungary, 73–74; identity disk of, 19, 78; near Innsbruck, 304–7; in Italy, 63, 281; and Kolbe, 69, 70; in North Africa, 42; and penetrating the Reich, 246, 250, 251, 253, 258, 262; and psych ops, 235, 237

Giannaris, John, 110, 114–16, 118–19, 120

Gibboney, Doc, 138

Gibraltar, 131

Giglio, Maurizio, 61, 63

"Gilbert" (Jed team), 177

"Giles" (Jed team), 177, 178

Gilly, Frank, 84–85

Ginny team, 59–60

Girard family, 164, 164n, 165

Giraud, General, 143, 149, 184

Girosi, Marcello, 55

Gisevius, Hans Bernd, 76–78

Gleason, Frank, 6–8

Goebbels, Joseph, 239, 271

Goff, Irv, 41–42

Goiran, Roger, 202

Göring, Hermann, 68, 76, 303

Gothic Line, 132, 276

Greece, 102–23, 234–36, 276, 312

Green, Holt, 217, 218, 220, 221, 223–25

Greenup Team, 258–62, 304–7

Gromyko, Andrey, 269

GRU, 270

Grupo Mezzini d'Asalto, 131, 133

Guam, 138

Guantanamo Bay, 128–29

Guiet, Jean Claude, 169–71

Gulovich, Maria, 218, 220, 221, 225–26

Guntner, Hans, 105

Gurfein, Murray, 49–50

Hahn, Otto, 308

Hall, Virginia, 173–74

Hallamaa, Reino Henrik, 267–68

Halyard Mission, 96

Hamilton, James, 21–22

Hammer Mission/team, 246–49, 301–3

Harriman, Averell, 299

Hayden, J. R., 1

Heckler Mission, 173–74

Heisenberg, Werner, 71–72

Hemlock, Operation, 235–36

Henry-Haye, Gaston, 28

"Hermit" circuit, 171–73
Hewitt, Abram, 271, 272–73
Highball team, 250
Himmler, Heinrich, 68, 78, 264, 270–72,
    273, 300–301
Hirtz, Rafael, 179–80
Hiss, Alger, 270
Hitler, Adolf: assassination plots against,
    22, 76–78, 231, 236–37, 270–72,
    300–301; and Battle of the Bulge,
    240; commando order of, 58–59,
    282; discussion about overthrow of,
    270–72; dissidents who disagreed
    with, 232; and Italy, 53; and Kolbe's
    reports, 68; and North Africa
    operations, 39; order to kill Jews by,
    273; and peace with Germany, 271;
    and potential surrender of Germans
    in Balkans, 100; and Wacht am Rhein,
    227
Hofer, Franz, 305, 306
Holland, 193, 211, 212, 213, 214–16, 270
Hoover, J. Edgar, 310
Horstenau, Glaise von, 99–100
Hostler, Charles, 196, 204–5
Huber, Dick, 268
Hungary/Hungarians, 72–76, 80n, 225,
    230, 237–38, 310, 312
Husky, Operation, 49
Hyde, Henry, 149, 206

Independent American Military Mission
    (IAMM), 100, 101
Innsbruck, Austria, 304–7
Istanbul, Turkey, 75, 80, 107
Italy/Italians: and Balkan operations,
    79, 88, 96, 99; and Greek operations,
    113; and Maritime Units, 125,
    131–33; navy of, 28, 55–56; New
    York Italian underground in, 20–21;
    in North Africa, 39, 40, 42;
    northern, 276–96, 297–99, 312; OSS

operations in, 20–21, 50, 52–66,
    276–96, 312; and OSS
    reorganizations, 53n; and psych ops,
    230–32, 238; scientists in, 55–56, 64,
    65, 71; surrender of German troops
    in, 297–99, 312; surrender of, 131,
    296

"Jacques" (aka Jean de Roquefort), 149,
    150–51, 154
Jadwin Mission, 80
Japan/Japanese, 18, 48, 264, 266, 268,
    299, 308
Jedburgh teams, 13, 174–75, 176–77,
    179, 189, 212–13, 312. See also specific
    team
Jeremy team (Jed team), 174
Jessen-Schmidt, Hennings "Birch,"
    273–74
Jews, 206, 215, 255–56, 273
Jibilian, Arthur, 90, 96–97
"Joan/Eleanor" transmitter, 213–16,
    247, 248, 249, 254
Jodl, Alfred, 307
Johansen, Kai, 276
joint operations, British/OSS: and BSC,
    26, 28–30; and preparation for
    Overlord, 163–64; and SOE, 32, 38,
    39, 44, 79–80, 80n, 106, 166, 169,
    174, 189; and X-2, 194
Joint/Combined Chiefs of Staff, U.S., 27,
    74, 106, 194, 228, 229, 299–300
Joker, Operation, 237
Jones, Geoffrey, 10
Joyeuse, René, 163–64

Kasserine Pass, 40, 42
Kaulen, Friedrich "George," 199–200
Kedia, Michel, 208–9, 210
Kellis, James, 107–8, 109, 123
Kelly, Robert, 132
Kenworthy, Robert, 136–37

Kersten, Felix, 270–73
Kesselring, Albert, 62, 298
Kiellner, Johann, 105
Kindleberger, Charles, 23–24
Knapp, Robert, 235–36
Knatchbull-Hugessen, Hughe, 69
Knight, Ridgeway, 36, 37
Knight's Cross, 236
Knox, Bernie, 177, 178, 292–93
Kolbe, Fritz, 68, 69–70, 78, 309, 312
Kouyoumdjisky, Angel, 80
Kramer, Ellsworth, 97
Krech, Franz, 235–36
Kreipe, Karl, 235
Kröck, Paul, 256–58

L-Unit, 129, 130
Lambertsen Amphibious Respiratory
    Unit (LARU), 126, 128, 129, 130,
    136, 139
Land, Paul, 246–49, 301–3
Langer, William, 23
Lansky, Meyer, 21
Lanz, Walter, 181, 182n
Lauwers, Barbara, 231–32, 233
"League" (double agent), 242
"The League of Lonely German
    Women," 232–33
Lebel, Paul, 177
Lee, Duncan, 310–11
Lescanne, Jean, 150
Leyte, 137–38
"Limping Lady" (aka Virginia Hall),
    173–74
Lindsay, Franklin, 86, 95, 99, 100–101
London, England. See Britain/British
"Lonely Hearts Club," 233
Lotito, Charlie, 279, 281
Lovell, Stanley, 7, 16, 21, 22
Lubienski, Michal, 28
Luciano, "Lucky," 21, 49–50
Lussier, Betty, 200–204

Luzon, 138
Lygizos, Angelo, 112–13, 114

MacArthur, Douglas, 134
McDowell, Robert, 97–99
Macedonia, 119–20
McGregor Project, 53–54, 55, 56, 61,
    276
McKellar Act, 27
MacMahon, John, 135
Mafia, 49–50
Malaga, 47
Malfatti, Franco, 61, 62
Maloubier, Bob, 170–71
Malta, 55
Manhattan Project, 308–9
Mansfield, Walter, 79, 80, 82
Mao Tse-tung, 8
"Maple" (OSS agent), 274
Maquis, 143, 146, 153, 159, 170, 173–74,
    179, 180, 190, 208. See also
    Resistance: in France
Marchese, Fred, 282
"Maria" (aka Madeleine Colotte),
    252–53
Marine Corps, U.S., 11
Maritime Units (MU), 3, 124–42
Market Garden, Operation, 212–13
Marret, Mario "Toto," 149, 150, 151–53
Martini team, 250
Massacre of the Ardeatine Caves (Italy),
    63
Massingham mission, 39
Mast, Charles, 36
Materazzi, Albert, 9, 59–60
Maui, 134
Mauthausen concentration camp,
    221–25
Mayer, Fred, 255–56, 258–62, 304–7, 313
Mediterranean region, 50, 124, 143,
    181–93, 255–56, 312. See also specific
    nation or island

Mesirli, Clio, 105
Mess, Walter, 140–41
MI6. *See* British intelligence
Mihailovic, Draja, 80, 82, 83, 85–86, 95, 96, 98, 99, 100
Milton Bryant, England, 236
Milton Hall (Peterborough, England), 13
Monteleone, Frank, 54–55, 64–66, 132–33
Montgomery, Bernard Law, 39, 176, 212, 243–44
Morale Operations (MO) branch, 228–39
Moretti, Willie, 21
Morocco, 40. *See also* Spanish Morocco
Mousalimas, Andy, 91, 92
Mueller, Carl, 308
Muller, Ernst Georg "George," 244–45
Müller, Werner, 222–23
Murphy, Robert, 31, 35–36, 144
Murphy-Weygand accord, 31, 32
Mussolini, Benito, 53
Musulin, George, 85–86, 96
Mutton Pork network, 154, 159

"Narcisse" (aka André Bouchardon), 167–68
National Guard, 6
National Redoubt, 298–99, 300–301
Navy, U.S., 27, 49–50, 55–56, 124, 126, 142, 194
Neubacher, Hermann, 98
New York Post, 173
Nimitz, Chester W., 134
XIX Corps, French, 36
NKVD, 225, 269–70, 309, 310–11
No. 10, Special Force Detachment, 168–69
Noah's Ark, Operation, 106–7
Normandy, 79, 130, 150, 164, 168, 169,

170, 175, 176, 182, 196, 197, 312. *See also* Overlord, Operation
North, Henry Ringling, 55
North Africa: Allied invasion of (Torch), 31, 32, 36–38, 43, 144, 153, 173, 311; British intelligence in, 32, 39; and Donovan-Hambro accords, 32; and French operations, 143; and German intelligence, 31; as OSS and Allied military proving ground, 42; OSS operations in, 31–42; and paving the way for Overlord, 161; and R&A, 24; resistance movement in, 32, 34–35; Spain's plans to invade French, 32, 45; Spanish refugees in, 40, 41; surrender of Axis forces in, 42, 44; and training candidates, 8; Vichy government in, 26–27, 28–30, 35–39, 311. *See also specific nation*
Norway, 263, 265, 274–77
Nunn, Guy, 74

Obolensky, Serge, 9, 56–57
Office of Naval Intelligence (ONI), U.S., 27, 49–50, 194
Office of Strategic Services (OSS). *See* OSS.
Office of War Information (OWI), 229
OGs. *See* Operational Groups
oil, 24, 24*n*, 43, 44, 264
oil attachés: OSS agents as, 43, 44
OKW Intelligence, 74
101st Airborne Division, U.S., 242, 243, 307
101st Maritime Unit of Detachment, U.S., 139
103rd Division, U.S., 306–7
122nd Infantry Battalion, U.S., 110
Operational Groups (OGs): in Balkans, 91, 92; in Corsica, 57–58; in France, 174, 178–80, 189–93, 312; in Greece,

106, 110–13, 119–20, 122; in Italy, 59–60; and Maritime Units, 139, 141; in northern Italy, 279, 282–83; and penetrating the Reich, 255–56; and preparation for Overlord, 174; and Sardinia operations, 56; training for, 3, 9; typical team of, 58

Oran, 31, 37

Organisation de Résistance de l'Armeé de l'Armistice (ORA), 143

Ornstein, Wilhelm, 224

OSS: achievements of, 311–14; casualties in World War II of, 15; characteristics of personnel in, 15; Communists in, 311; and Coordinator of Information (COI), 228–29; creation of, 1; expansion of, 13, 43, 216; failure to compartmentalize operations by, 75; German penetration of, 310; Germans contact, about potential surrender, 98; growing professionalism of, 160; home-based enemies of, 310; London base for, 144; as pioneer organization, 313; recruitment for, 5–6, 160–61; reduction and disbanding of, 227, 311; reorganization of, 48, 53n; Russian infiltration of, 310–11

Ossining I mission, 131–32

Overlord, Operation, 69, 74, 75, 106, 160–80

Pacific Theater of Operations, 127, 129, 133–41

Pack, Elizabeth "Betty" (aka "Cynthia"), 26, 27–30, 31

Packard, Operation, 132

PAI, 63–64

Pantaleoni, Guido, 51–52

Pappas, Nick, 120–22

Pararescuemen, U.S., 124

Parilli, Luigi, 297

Paris, France, 163, 164, 176, 180, 193, 204–5, 209

Paris Task Force (T-Force), 204

Parkin, Charles, Jr., 6

Parri, Ferrucia, 297–98

partisans: in Czechoslovakia, 216, 217, 218, 220–21; in Italy, 132, 133; and Maritime Units, 124–25, 132, 133; in northern Italy, 282–89, 290, 291–92, 294, 296, 297–98, 300; as prisoners of war, 294; in Yugoslavia, 71, 73, 74, 79, 82–88, 89, 90–91, 93–99, 101

Partito d'Azione party, 278–79

Patch, Alexander, 206

Patton, George, 32, 42, 170, 176, 193, 242, 312

peace talks, 271, 272–73, 299–300

"peach fuzz," 21–22

Peleliu Island, 134–35, 136

Penny, W.R.C., 61

Penny Farthing network, 149–50, 159, 182, 184–86

Perkins, Henry, 44

Peter (king of Yugoslavia), 79, 85–86, 98–99

Peterborough, England, 13

Petit-Jean (OSS agent), 151, 152, 184, 185

Philby, Kim, 273

Philippines, 137–38

Phillips, Alex, 92, 119–20

Photis, Pete, 113

Piday, George, 230, 238

"Pietro" (aka Peter Tompkins), 61–64, 65, 66

Pink Lady team, 250

Pitt Team, 244–45

"Plaka" agreement, 106

plastic explosives, 86–87, 169

Po Valley, 292–93

"poison pen" letters, 235–36, 237–38

"poison pills," 19
Poland/Poles, 28, 217, 250–51, 271
police, 30, 36, 47, 63–64. *See also*
      NKVD
Polson, Al, 17, 18
Portugal, 43, 46, 48
Primbs, Dr., 305, 306
prisoners of war: Allies as, 133, 152–53,
      154–57, 171, 181, 182*n*, 215–16,
      221–25, 226, 245, 250–51, 282, 285,
      286, 289–90; Austrians as, 293; in
      Balkans, 82, 92, 98; Belgian, 255;
      Communists as, 182*n*; in
      Czechoslovakia, 221–25; execution
      of, 224–25, 282; in France, 152–53,
      154–57, 171, 178, 180, 181, 182*n*, 188,
      189–93; French as, 165, 202–3, 304;
      Germans as, 92, 178, 180, 188,
      189–93, 206, 207–8, 231–32, 237, 242,
      244, 292–93, 294–96, 308; in Greece,
      114; interrogation of, 231–32, 233;
      and Maritime Units, 133; in
      northern Italy, 282, 285, 286, 289–90,
      292–93, 294–96, 297–98; OSS agents
      as, 206–8, 231–32, 292–93; partisans
      as, 98, 294, 297–98; and psych ops,
      231–32, 237; release of high-profile,
      297–98; Russian "liberation" of, 226;
      and surrender of German troops in
      northern Italy, 300; in Yugoslavia, 92.
      See also specific person
propaganda: black and white, 229, 236,
      237. *See also* psych ops
prostitutes, 149–50, 255
proximity fuse, 308
psych ops, 228–39
Putzell, Ned, 269

Quebec Conference (1943), 80

radio: German search for Allied, 213–14;
      "ghosting," 239; Joan/Eleanor, 247,
      248, 249, 254; propaganda on,
      236–37
Radio Bionda, 132
Raff, Edson, 36–38
Rah, Tony, 301–3
Rand, H. J., 307–8
Ranger Scout Swimmers, 124
Ranger Team, 97–99
Rathburne, 134, 135, 136
recruitment, OSS, 8, 41, 144, 160–61,
      167, 207–8, 216, 313
Reichenau concentration camp, 306
Renaix, André, 254–55
Research and Analysis Division (R&A),
      OSS, 22–25, 106, 144, 233, 311
Research and Development
      Department, OSS, 1, 7, 16–22
Reserve Unit (RU), 4
Resistance: and approaching the Reich,
      213, 214, 216; in Belgium, 216, 254;
      in France, 143, 164, 166–67, 169, 171,
      173–74, 175–76, 177, 179–80, 185,
      186–87, 312; in Greece, 106, 236; in
      Holland, 214; in northern Italy, 276,
      278–79, 312; in Norway, 274–76;
      religious groups as, 106. *See also*
      Partisans; *specific person or force/group*
RF section, 167, 175
Ribarich, Anthony, 51–52
Rickerson, Roy, 189–93
rockets, German, 70
Roeder, Howard, 135
Romania, 80*n*, 100, 226
Rome, Italy, 53, 61–62, 63, 64, 65, 276
Ronald Team, 177–78
Roosevelt, Franklin D., 27, 83, 85–86,
      99, 227, 229, 232, 268–69, 271, 272,
      299, 310
Roquefort, Jean de "Jacques," 149,
      150–51, 154
Rosenberg, Alfred, 215
Rosenthal, Alfred, 255–58

Rösselsprung, Operation (Knight's
Move), 90
Rosterg, August, 264
Rostow, Walter, 23, 24
Royal Air Force, 163
Royalists, 79, 105, 106, 122
Royse, M. W., 234
RTU-11 ("the Farm"), 9
Ruh, Toni, 246–49
Russell, Ted, 110–11
Russia/Russians: and approaching the
Reich, 216; in Austria, 191; and
Balkans, 79, 98, 100; in Berlin, 274,
300, 301–3, 308; and Czechoslovakia
operations, 217, 218, 225–26; and
Finnish intelligence, 266–70; in
France, 191; German intelligence
about, 312–13; and German secret
weapons program, 307, 308–9;
German troops in, 235; and
Hungary, 72, 76; infiltration of OSS
by, 310–11; and Japan, 299; as OSS
agents, 208; OSS efforts to gather
intelligence on, 308–9, 312–13; and
peace talks, 271, 272; and
penetrating the Reich, 249; and
plans to overthrow Hitler, 270, 272;
in Poland, 217; and R&A Division,
25; SD agents in, 208; and surrender
of German troops in northern Italy,
299, 300; and Swedish operations,
266–70; Wehrmacht intelligence
about, 309–10
Russian embassy (Washington, D.C.),
269
Russo, Vinny, 59
Rype Mission, 275–77

Sacristan circuit, 167–68
safe conduct passes, 230–31
Sage, Jerry, 8, 40–41, 42, 43
Salerno, 53–54, 55, 56, 61, 276

"Salesman" circuit, 169–71
Sampson, Operation, 130
San Marco Battalion, 131–33
Sardinia, 50, 56–57, 311
Sauerkraut, Operation, 231–33
Scerra, Chester, 281–82
Schellenberg, Walter, 271–72
Schoeneseiffen, Manfred, 223, 224
Schrader, Anton "Bobby," 214–16
Schroeder, SS Major, 283, 294–96
Schuyler, Cortland, 226
scientists, 55–56, 64, 65, 71–72, 204, 205,
307–9
Scoles, Bob, 138
SD (Sicherheitsdienst), 208–10, 245, 262,
271–72, 303
SEALs, U.S. Navy, 124, 126, 142
Searchinger, Gene, 13–14, 15
2nd Parachute Division, German, 178
II Corps, U.S., 42
Secret Intelligence (SI): and approaching
the Reich, 206; in Balkans, 93; and
"The Campus," 22; in France, 144,
149, 154, 168, 169, 186–87; in
Greece, 102–3, 105, 122; in Italy,
53n, 279; London base for, 144; and
Maritime Units, 124; and
penetrating the Reich, 256;
reorganization of, 53n; transfer to
SSU of, 311
Secret Intelligence Service (SIS), British,
1, 166, 220
secret weapons program, German, 69,
70, 308–9
Sehmer, John, 224
Serbia, 82, 100
17th Airborne Division, 243, 244
Seventh Army, U.S., 182, 182n, 186,
187–88, 193, 206–7, 208, 209,
244–45, 252, 253, 301
Shaheen, John, 55
Sherwood, Robert, 229

Sherwood, W., 57
"Shingle" (Anzio landing), 61–64
SI. *See* Secret Intelligence (SI)
Sichel, Peter, 206–8, 252, 253
Sicily, 49–53
Sicre, Ricardo, 27, 30, 43, 47, 202–4
Signals Security Agency (SSA), 269, 370
Silsby, Oliver, 283, 284, 285, 286, 287,
    288–89, 290, 294
SIM (Italian intelligence service), 54
Simmons Mission/Project, 102–3, 307
Simpson, Stephen, 214–15
SIS. *See* Secret Intelligence Service (SIS),
    British
69th Division, U.S., 303
Skarzynski, Youri, 208–10, 212, 303–4
Skorzeny, Otto, 53
"Skull" (double agent), 198–200
Slovak Independent Army, 217
SLUs (Special Liaison Units), 200–204
Smashem, Operation, 117–19
Smets, Jan, 254
Smith, Lloyd, 93, 94
Snyder, Jacques, 186–87
Socialists, 206, 207, 278–79
SOE. *See* Special Operations Executive
Soldatensender-Calais, 236–37
Sollenberger, McCord, 212–13
Solomon Islands, 134
Solta Island, 91
Soltau, Gordon, 129–30
Sorrentino, 66
SOs. *See* Special Operations
Sotiriou, Nikolaos, 103, 105
Soviet Union. *See* Russia
Spain: and French operations, 144, 145,
    146, 147, 148, 149, 154, 168; gas and
    oil allocation to, 43, 44; and North
    Africa, 32, 43–45, 47; OSS
    operations in, 40–41, 43–48; OSS
    recruitment of diplomats from, 26;
    police in, 47; and preparation for

Overlord, 161, 168, 173
Spanish Civil War, 8, 40, 301
Spanish embassy, 27, 30
Spanish Morocco, 32, 38, 43, 44
Spanish refugees: OSS recruitment of,
    40, 41
"Sparrow" team, 72–76, 312
Special Air Service (SAS), British, 176
Special Assistants, 16, 19–22
Special Counter-Intelligence units (SCI),
    195–96, 197–98
"Special Force Detachments," 168–69
Special Force Headquarters (SFHQ),
    166, 274–76
Special Forces, 58, 140, 142. *See also*
    specific force
Special Forces Combat Divers, U.S.
    Army, 124
Special Liaison Units (SLUs), 200–204
Special Operations Executive (SOE),
    British: and "Beetroot" mission, 44;
    in Czechoslovakia, 220, 224; and
    Donovan-Hambro accords, 80, 80n;
    in France, 143, 166, 167, 169, 173,
    174, 189; in Greece, 106; Hall
    recruited by, 173; joint OSS
    operations with, 1, 7, 32, 38, 39, 44,
    79–80, 80n, 106, 166, 169, 174, 189;
    jurisdiction of, 32; and North Africa,
    32, 39; and Norwegian operations,
    274–76; OSS turf wars with, 79–80;
    and psych ops, 235; in Spanish
    Morocco, 44; training by, 1, 7, 38;
    and Yugoslavia, 79–80
Special Operations (SOs): first, 40; Fort
    Bragg as home for, 142; in France,
    144, 166, 167, 168, 169, 174, 189,
    312; in Greece, 106–7, 122; London
    base for, 144; and Maritime Units,
    124; in North Africa, 32; in northern
    Italy, 279; and Norwegian
    operations, 274–76; and plans for

assassination of Hitler, 300–301; in
    Sicily, 51–52; SOE operations with,
    166, 169, 174, 189; training for, 3, 13
Special Project Operations Center
    (SPOC), 102, 189
SS: and approaching the Reich, 215–16;
    in Czechoslovakia, 217–18, 220, 221,
    222, 223–24; in France, 150–51, 156,
    157, 165, 169–70, 175–76, 182n, 191,
    193; in Greece, 102, 113; in Holland,
    215–16; in Italy, 63, 283, 286–87, 289,
    294–96, 297, 298; near Innsbruck,
    305; as OSS agents, 251; and
    overthrow of Hitler, 272; and
    penetrating the Reich, 240, 244–45,
    251; and psych ops, 231–32; and
    surrender of German troops in
    northern Italy, 297, 298
Stalin, Josef, 83, 272–73, 299, 300, 309
Stärker, Rudi, 98
State Department, U.S.: and Finnish
    intelligence, 268–69; Germany
    breaks Bern code of, 77; and Greek
    operations, 106; and Hungarian-U.S.
    relations, 74; and intelligence about
    Russians, 267, 268–69; and Mayer's
    operations, 305; and North Africa
    operations, 31; and peace talks,
    272–73; R&A transferred to, 311;
    and Russian relations, 272–73; and
    Spanish operations, 43, 47; and
    Swedish operations, 263
Station S, 3, 13
"stay behinds," 196
Steinitz, Bernd, 255–56, 258
Stella Polaris, 266–70
Stephenson, William, 2, 27, 201
Stettinius, Edward, 268–69
Strategic Services Unit (SSU), 311
"Strings" (North African Muslim), 32, 43
Suarez, Alfred, 74
suicide missions, 41, 120–21, 130

Sumatra, 140
Sunrise, Operation, 298, 299–300, 312
Supreme Headquarters Allied
    Expeditionary Force (SHAEF), 165–66,
    195, 206
Sûreté, Belgian, 216
Sussex mission, 163–64, 165–66
Sweden: OSS operations in, 263–77
Swiss intelligence, 67, 297
Switzerland, 67–78, 99–100, 149, 161,
    209, 212, 312

Tack, Gordon, 177
Tacoma (OG team), 282–90, 293–96
Tangiers, 31, 44
Tarawa, 134
"Tassels" (Rif leader), 32, 34–35, 43
Technical Division, 16–18
Tehran Conference (1943), 83
10th Light Flotilla, U.S., 131
10th Panzer Division, German, 40
testing: of OSS candidates, 13–15
Tetuan school, 44
Thailand, 140–41
Third Army, U.S., 176, 242, 303, 304, 312
30th Corps, U.S., 213
Thomas, Mrs. Bertram, 34–35
Thompson, Robert, 125
Thost, Hans Wilhelm, 223–24
Thun-Hohenstein, *Graf* (Count), 220–21
Tikander, Ty, 264, 268, 269, 273
Tito (aka Josip Broz), 72, 79, 80, 83, 86,
    90, 92, 95, 99, 100, 101, 124–25. *See
    also* Partisans: in Yugoslavia
"Todt Organization," 60, 294
"Tommy" (aka Frederick Brown), 144,
    146–49, 159
Tompkins, Peter "Pietro," 61–64, 65, 66
Torch, 31, 32, 36–38, 43, 144, 153, 173,
    311
"Toto" (aka Mario Marret), 149, 150,
    151–53

"tourist missions," 242

Traficante, Paul, 60

training: of agents to assassinate Hitler and Himmler, 300, 301; and approaching the Reich, 208; British help in, 1, 13; culmination of, 9–10; curriculum in, 2, 4–5, 7–9; Donovan initiates, 1; on East Coast, 3; and expansion of OSS, 13; facilities for basic, 3; first independent schools for, 9; of Jed teams, 175; of Maritime Units, 3, 124, 125–26, 127, 128–29, 134, 136, 138, 139; of OGs, 179; and Operation Eagle, 251; of partisans in northern Italy, 291; and preparation for Overlord, 160, 161; realistic, 9; relaxing party during, 15; of SO teams, 13; of Spanish Republicans, 43–44; and testing of candidates, 13–15; tragic mistakes in, 9; of women, 12–13; for X-2, 10–12

Trieste, Italy, 255

Trohan, Walter, 310

Troy, Thomas, 310

Truman, Harry S, 300, 311

Trump, Ray, 177–78

truth drugs, 19–21

Tsirmulas, Michael, 118

Tunisia/Tunisians, 31, 32, 39, 40, 41, 42, 202

turds: as explosives, 39–40, 41

Turkey, 69, 75, 80, 102, 106, 107

Twelfth Army Group, U.S., 204, 237, 243, 308

"Twelve Apostles," 31–32, 144

Ultra, 47, 63, 69, 194, 195, 200, 201, 240

Ulysses Mission, 235–36

Underwater Demolition Team 10 (UDT), U.S. Navy, 134, 135–36, 137–38, 142

Union Democratica Espanola (UDE), 41

United Nations, 271

U.S. Army Command and General Staff College, 7

Ushminiani, Antonio, 297–98

Ustashe, 82, 85, 257

Utah Beach, 169, 196

Varsity, Operation, 243–44

Vatican, 269

Velky Bok lodge, 220–21

Venona, 269–70

Verghis, George, 111–13

vice-consuls: OSS agents as, 31

Vichy government, 26–30, 31, 35–39, 43–44, 173, 311

Victor Emmanuel (king of Italy), 52–53

Viertel, Peter, 207, 252, 253

Vietinghoff, Heinrich von, 298, 299, 300

Vinciguerra, Stephan, 244

Vis Island, 124–25

Vitrail Team, 166

Wacht am Rhein, 227

Waibel, Max, 297

Walla Walla (OG team), 279, 281–82

war crimes trials, 222, 307

War Refugee Board, 273

Washington, D.C.: foreign embassies in, 26–30, 269

Washington Post, 233

Weber, Franz, 258–62

Wehrmacht, German, 240, 249, 254, 298, 302, 309–10

Weismiller, Edward, 11–12, 197–98

Werewolves, 254

Westfield mission, 274–76

Wheeler, William, 279, 281–82

White, George, 20–21

"Who? Me?" (chemical), 18

Winks, Robin W., 22

"Witch" (double agent), 242–43

Wolff, Karl, 297, 298, 299, 300
women, 12–13, 231–32, 251–52. *See also*
    specific person
Wood, George. *See* Kolbe, Fritz
Wuchinich, George, 83–84, 87–92
Wynberg, Hans, 255–56, 258–62

X-2, 10–12, 22, 149, 194–205, 242, 307,
    310, 311
XVIII Airborne Corps, U.S., 243
XX/"Twenty Committee," 195

Yap Island, 134, 135
Yugoslavia: and Greek operations, 117;
    and Maritime Units (MU), 124–25;
    OSS operations in, 79–87, 98, 99, 100,
    101; and penetrating the Reich, 257;
    and Sparrow mission, 71, 73, 74

Zenopian, Stefan "Steve," 220, 225
Ziereis, Franz, 222–24
Zwillman, Longie, 21

About the Author

PATRICK K. O'DONNELL is the author of *Beyond Valor,* which won the Colby Circle Award for outstanding military history, and *Into the Rising Sun.* He provided historical consultation for Dreamworks' award-winning television miniseries *Band of Brothers* and for documentaries produced by the BBC, The History Channel, and Fox News. O'Donnell is also the founder of The Drop Zone (www.thedropzone.org), an award-winning website dedicated to preserving the oral histories of veterans. His books and his website have been widely acclaimed by newspapers across the country, including *USA Today, The Washington Post, The Wall Street Journal,* and *Los Angeles Times.* He lives in Fairfax Station, Virginia.